Drawing and the Non-Verbal Mind
A Life-Span Perspective

Drawing and its analysis has been an important discipline of Developmental Psychology since the early twentieth century. This unique collection of essays unites leading empirical researchers from Europe, the United States and Canada to provide a valuable introduction to state-of-the-art drawing research. Focusing on the core problems associated with the visual mind, the contributors examine how drawing development relates to changes in cognition. Topics covered include visual (self) recognition, style, media understanding, inhibition, executive attention, priming, memory, meaning, and figural and spatial concepts. The effects of biological constraints such as motor control, grip and handedness, blindness, neuropsychological conditions and old age are also explained. The book provides a fascinating insight into the life-span and productivity of the non-verbal, visual mind.

Chris Lange-Küttner is Senior Lecturer in the Department of Psychology at the London Metropolitan University and Visiting Professor at the University of Bremen

Annie Vinter is Professor of Psychology at the Université de Bourgogne, LEAD-CNRS, Dijon, France.

Drawing and the Non-Verbal Mind
A Life-Span Perspective

Chris Lange-Küttner
London Metropolitan University

Annie Vinter
Université de Bourgogne, Dijon

CAMBRIDGE UNIVERSITY PRESS
Cambridge, New York, Melbourne, Madrid, Cape Town, Singapore,
São Paulo, Delhi, Dubai, Tokyo, Mexico City

Cambridge University Press
The Edinburgh Building, Cambridge CB2 8RU, UK

Published in the United States of America by Cambridge University Press, New York

www.cambridge.org
Information on this title: www.cambridge.org/9780521182881

© Cambridge University Press 2008

This publication is in copyright. Subject to statutory exception
and to the provisions of relevant collective licensing agreements,
no reproduction of any part may take place without the written
permission of Cambridge University Press.

First published 2008
First paperback edition 2010

A catalogue record for this publication is available from the British Library

Library of Congress Cataloguing in Publication data
Drawing and the non-verbal mind / [edited by] Chris Lange-Küttner, Annie Vinter.
    p. cm.
Includes index.
ISBN 978-0-521-87205-8 (hardback)
1. Drawing, Psychology of. 2. Visual perception. 3. Cognition. I. Lange-Küttner, Christiane, 1957– II. Vinter, Annie. III. Title.
BF456.D7D73 2008
153–dc22   2008015933

ISBN 978-0-521-18288-1 Hardback
ISBN 978-0-521-87205-8 Paperback

Cambridge University Press has no responsibility for the persistence or
accuracy of URLs for external or third-party internet websites referred to in
this publication, and does not guarantee that any content on such websites is,
or will remain, accurate or appropriate.

Contents

Contributors *page* vii

1 Contemporary enquiries into a long-standing domain: Drawing research 1
   CHRIS LANGE-KÜTTNER AND ANNIE VINTER

Part I Self, symbols and intention 21

2 Understanding reflections of self and other objects 23
   KIM BARD

3 Drawing production, drawing re-experience and drawing re-cognition 42
   JOSEPHINE ROSS

4 Style and other factors affecting children's recognition of their own drawings 63
   ROBIN N. CAMPBELL, PAULINE A. DUNCAN,
   ANITA L. HARRISON AND LYNNE C. MATHEWSON

5 Children's understanding of the dual nature of pictures 86
   RICHARD JOLLEY

6 Pictorial intention, action and interpretation 104
   NORMAN H. FREEMAN AND ESTHER ADI-JAPHA

Part II Syntax, space systems and projection 121

7 The interaction of biomechanical and cognitive constraints in the production of children's drawing 123
   GREGORY BRASWELL AND KARL ROSENGREN

8 Graphic syntax and representational development ... 139
ANNIE VINTER, DELPHINE PICARD AND VIVIANE FERNANDES

9 Spatial structures in children's drawings: how do they develop? ... 159
SERGIO MORRA

10 Figures in and out of context: absent, simple, complex and halved spatial fields ... 195
CHRIS LANGE-KÜTTNER

11 Spatial and symbolic codes in the development of three-dimensional graphic representation ... 217
MARIA A. TALLANDINI AND LUISA MORASSI

12 On contours seen and contours drawn ... 239
JAN B. DEREGOWSKI

Part III   Aging, blindness and autism ... 259

13 Benefits of graphic design expertise in old age: compensatory effects of a graphical lexicon? ... 261
ULMAN LINDENBERGER, YVONNE BREHMER, REINHOLD KLIEGL AND PAUL B. BALTES

14 Drawing as a 'window' on deteriorating conceptual knowledge in neurodegenerative disease ... 281
KARALYN PATTERSON AND SHARON W. ERZINÇLIOĞLU

15 Drawings by a blind adult: orthogonals, parallels and convergence in two directions without T-junctions ... 305
JOHN M. KENNEDY AND IGOR JURICEVIC

16 Differences between individuals with and without autism in copying tasks: how knowledge interferes when drawing perspective ... 325
ELIZABETH SHEPPARD, PETER MITCHELL AND DANIELLE ROPAR

Index ... 344

Contributors

ESTHER ADI-JAPHA, Bar-Ilan University, Ramat-Gan

PAUL B. BALTES†, Max Planck Institute for Human Development, Berlin, and University of Virginia

KIM BARD, University of Portsmouth

GREGORY BRASWELL, Illinois State University

YVONNE BREHMER, Karolinska Institute, Stockholm

ROBIN N. CAMPBELL, University of Stirling

JAN B. DERĘGOWSKI, University of Aberdeen

PAULINE A. DUNCAN, University of Stirling

SHARON W. ERZINÇLIOĞLU, MRC Cognition and Brain Sciences Unit, Cambridge

VIVIANE FERNANDES, Université de Bourgogne, Dijon

NORMAN H. FREEMAN, University of Bristol

ANITA L. HARRISON, University of Stirling

RICHARD JOLLEY, University of Staffordshire

IGOR JURICEVIC, University of Toronto at Scarborough

JOHN M. KENNEDY, University of Toronto at Scarborough

REINHOLD KLIEGL, Universität Potsdam

CHRIS LANGE-KÜTTNER, London Metropolitan University and University of Bremen

ULMAN LINDENBERGER, Max Planck Institute for Human Development, Berlin

LYNNE C. MATHEWSON, University of Stirling

PETER MITCHELL, University of Nottingham

SERGIO MORRA, Università di Genova

LUISA MORASSI, Università de Trieste

KARALYN PATTERSON, MRC Cognition and Brain Sciences Unit, Cambridge

DELPHINE PICARD, University of Montpellier III

DANIELLE ROPAR, University of Nottingham

KARL ROSENGREN, University of Illinois at Urbana-Champaign

JOSEPHINE ROSS, University of Stirling

ELIZABETH SHEPPARD, University of Nottingham

MARIA A. TALLANDINI, University College London and Università de Trieste

ANNIE VINTER, Université de Bourgogne, Dijon

1 Contemporary enquiries into a long-standing domain: Drawing research

Chris Lange-Küttner and Annie Vinter

DRAWING BEHAVIOUR has occupied European psychologists from the turn of the last century (Kerschensteiner, 1905; Luquet, 1927; Ricci, 1887; Rouma, 1913), maintained their interest ever since, and subsequently also attracted some attention from psychologists in other continents such as the United States. The main contribution of the early work was to describe how this typically human behaviour develops, and in particular which stages it follows (Piaget and Inhelder, 1956). Still, perhaps like many other scientists nowadays, Piaget saw drawing only as a figurative, illustrative instrument of representation, as opposed to rational and operational thought devoted to the genuine understanding of reality. Thus, drawing behaviour was not frequently studied in relation to cognitive development. However, a notable exception was the 'Draw-a-person test' designed by Goodenough (Goodenough, 1926; Goodenough and Harris, 1950) which assesses mental age in children via the human figure drawing, and, because it has a high correlation with intelligence tests until adolescence, it is still in use today.

Since the 1970s and 1980s, a refreshed interest in drawing from developmental and cognitive psychologists from an empirical, experimental, statistically underpinned perspective has flourished, as evident in two books by Freeman (Freeman, 1980, see also his current contribution to this book; Freeman and Cox, 1985). Since then a productive scientific research area has opened and progressed, embedding drawing research into mainstream cognitive and developmental psychology, as shown by the many journal articles and books which followed (e.g. Cox, 1986; Golomb, 1973; Goodnow, 1977; Thomas and Silk, 1990; as well as Lange-Küttner and Thomas, 1995). The current book offers an up-to-date and state-of-the-art overview of the main lines of research currently conducted on drawing from a cognitive perspective.

Producing and understanding artificial and technical reflections of reality needs considerable intelligence. Understanding visual reflections requires an awareness of a second-order reality, perceptual discrimination and memory. Furthermore, already when young children begin to scribble with a pen on paper, motor learning also begins to play a role as they set out to represent an object on paper. A fascinating communication network evolves in children's minds in these years where non-verbal intelligence interacts with social skills to communicate meaning. Meaning is conveyed either in symbolic form, where canonical templates lend the picture some unambiguous quality, or in literal form, where the greatest effort is taken to convey the actual optical impression. While, in the former, the viewer shares the knowledge of the functional properties of objects, in the latter the viewer just needs to have seen a scene. It thus appears that the type of picture production in pictorial space changes considerably, making communication easier and more immediate for the viewer. In this way, non-verbal communication is intrinsically social. But to achieve this facilitation effect for somebody else, the rules and requirements for productivity need to be changed, and many children and adults drop out. There are intricate changes in cognitive, motor and psychological functioning necessary which are described and explained in this book, which unites the most original and active researchers in this field.

Two more general points are worth making before introducing the contribution of each of the chapters in turn. We would first like to emphasize the great role attributed by most researchers in drawing behaviour to executive functions, particularly to working memory. Sutton and Rose (1998) were amongst the first authors to point to the important contribution of attentional processes in drawing production, revealing the importance of parallel, simultaneous processing of model and product in the transition from intellectual to visual realism, which even overruled instructional manipulation by the experimenter. Today, there is a large agreement between authors that factors like working memory and inhibition influence drawing production and drawing understanding. This functionalist view is shared by several authors in this book. The second point is related to the impact of the work published by Peter Van Sommers (Van Sommers, 1984, 1989) and the late John Willats (Willats, 1985, 1995), who both single-handedly introduced important concepts into research on drawing, such as conservatism versus flexibility, or drawing systems versus denotation systems.

The book is divided into three parts, each dealing with specific aspects of drawing that make this behaviour so interesting to study for developmental psychologists. The organization of chapters into three sections follows a developmental progression. Chapters in the first part of the book are concerned with the beginnings and roots of drawing behaviour, understood as a typical symbolic behaviour, and they report mainly from the infancy and preschool period. Chapters in the second part refer essentially to the school period, studying influencing factors and their interactions on drawing behaviour which determine the transition to visual realism. Finally, adulthood and old age are at the centre of the chapters in the third part of the book, tackling the role of expertise, and explaining the impact of diverse conditions such as blindness, dementia or autism on drawing.

The first part (Self, symbols and intention) comprises the first five chapters. This section is quite original in a book on drawing behaviour and deals with the relationships between drawing and the self, which leads to a discussion of children's understanding of drawings as genuine symbols that stand for something else. Indeed, in the same way as infants must understand mirror images as reflections or re-presentations of something else (e.g. the self, others, objects alike), also drawings must be conceived of as independent symbolic representations or reflections of something else. In each case, infants must understand the one-to-one relationship between the image (reflected in a mirror or on a paper) and its referent together with their differentiation or separation. A common difficulty emerges in each case: acknowledging that the image constitutes an object in itself, that refers to something else at the same time. However, while mirror images are reflections strongly constrained in the present time and space, and share the same space at the same time with their referents, drawings act as symbols independently of time and space, and make the evocation of absent referents possible. Within the Piagetian theory, mirror images could be construed as fully differentiated perceptual signifiers whose understanding should emerge at the end of the sensorimotor stage, whereas drawings constitute conceptual signifiers where understanding should expand largely beyond two years of age.

From this perspective, it is most interesting and appropriate to start our journey through drawing development in this book with the chapter by Kim Bard, dedicated to the comparative development of mirror self-recognition in infants and primates, continuing with studies, by Josephine Ross in chapter 3 and Campbell, Duncan, Harrison and Mathewson in chapter 4, on the question of the link between self-recognition and recognition of their own drawing products in young children. To anticipate the result, it turns out that mirror self-recognition behaviour did indeed predict true productivity insofar as a drawing is recognized, as a product of oneself, or as that of somebody else.

In chapter 2, Bard develops a fascinating comparative and developmental approach to the question of mirror self-recognition, and argues that mirror self-recognition is a product of similar epigenetic processes in hominids, including humans and the great apes, following similar developmental paths across these species. A 'great divide' appears between hominids and the rest of the primate species in this regard. In agreement with the traditional literature on mirror self-recognition, she assumes that success in the mark and mirror test devised by Gallup (1970) indicates fully differentiated self-awareness, allowing children to understand reflections of self (in the mirror) as one's representation of oneself. Bard recalls briefly the main developmental milestones shown in self-awareness as revealed by the mirror situation in human infants, and demonstrates that the pattern of responses to the mirror shown in the chimpanzees follows a similar evolution, from social responses through contingency testing, to self-directed behaviour. However, showing self-directed behaviours does not imply passing successfully the mark test. Only at around 24 months in human infants, and between 28 and 30 months in chimpanzees, does mirror self-recognition truly emerge. Bard suggests that mirror self-recognition has to do with secondary intersubjectivity (the capacity to think mentally about the self and the other as differentiated intentional agents), with empathy and with a capacity to use symbols. We share all these abilities with the great apes. Interestingly, Bard considers that the mark test, passed at around 2 years of age, 'provides a behavioural index of an ability to hold simultaneously two views of the self', the self who is acting and the self in the mirror. We will see later, in chapter 5, that Jolley claims that the understanding of the dual nature of pictures, achieved between 4 and 5 years, similarly relies on a capacity to hold two representations of an entity simultaneously in mind. The similarity of these dual-processing assumptions is a nice illustration of the link that can be drawn between understanding reflections (of self, others or objects) in the mirror and understanding reflections (of self, others or objects) in drawing. The gap of two years between both achievements is probably due to the fact that mirror self-recognition is more immediate and requires less memory.

In chapter 3, Ross weaves the links between the mirror test situation and self-drawing production, claiming that self-drawings, or self-portraits, may reveal the content of self-knowledge, through details and levels of differentiation, and could thus be considered as advanced forms of the mirror test of self-recognition. Consistent with a finding from Gellert (1968), Ross shows that the quality of self-figure drawings is higher than the quality of other figure drawings, implying that self-drawings production is inherently linked to the ability to self-differentiate. However, the beam of relationships linking self-drawings and self-awareness as indexed by mirror recognition appears rather more complex. The quality of self-drawing relates to self-aware mirror behaviours, which are themselves related to the ability to recognize one's own drawings. Interestingly, Ross reveals that recognition of drawings made by others can increase when children are asked to trace over these drawings before having to recognize them. This highlights the importance of a 'physical' component of self-engagement in the very act of drawing with respect to drawing recognition. Thus, memory of perceived graphic objects improves when information can be in parallel and congruently encoded by the motor system. A similar result was obtained in a study comparing the effect of either a handwriting training or a typing training on letter recognition in preschool children aged 3–5 years (Longcamp, Zerbato-Poudou and Velay, 2005): letter recognition was better following a motor training in which kinaesthetic or proprioceptive information was congruent with visual information. On the other hand, one could say that tracing another person's drawing is like drawing it yourself, and thus it is by definition not another person's drawing anymore, but a 'shared' drawing. This immediate benefit of repetition of other people's work has been rarely discussed in the literature (Wilson and Wilson, 1982); however, it does not need to be seen in a negative way. On the contrary, it explains that recognition both of one's own drawing and of somebody else's appears to rely on perceptual and kinaesthetic/proprioceptive memory, i.e. early sensory components of self-awareness which exist from very early on (e.g. Bahrick and Watson, 1985; Rochat and Morgan, 1995; Schmuckler, 1996).

Chapter 4 focuses directly on the development of the ability of children to recognize their own drawings. Campbell, Duncan, Harrison and Mathewson list further factors that may support this ability, from the idiosyncratic constituents of the drawing (related to what may be called the child's style) to the memory of the drawing episode itself. They report several experiments which demonstrate that recognition of own drawings develops between 4 and 5 years, and is scarce before 4 years of age, contrary to the conclusions drawn from the original experiment of Gross and Hayne (1999). As a matter of fact, these last experiments suggest that the ability to recognize self-drawings, at least within delays of less than 6 months, emerges somewhere between 3 and 4 years. Van Sommers (1984) showed that children as young as 3 or 4 years of age are able to represent idiosyncratic features that ground distinctive styles. In the chapter, it is documented that although these individual styles do indeed exist – and are documented in the chapter with intriguing illustrations of drawing series of the Snodgrass and Vanderwart objects – children's recognition of their own drawings rarely seems to take advantage of these individually based or biased features. The authors conclude that improvement of episodic memory is probably a key factor in the development of one's drawing recognition. Endorsing the claim made by Ross (chapter 3) that drawing recognition relates to self-awareness, and following Povinelli's theory of self (1995), it could be suggested that the development of one's drawing recognition may rely on the emergence of autobiographical self, i.e. on improvement of episodic autobiographical memory. Povinelli (1995) sustains the view that the self in children around 4 to 5 years can be seen as a genuine representational agent, developing an organized and unified autobiographical self-representation. As noted by Gergely (2006), for an event to be encoded in autobiographical memory, not only the event itself must be represented, but also the fact that memory has been caused by that event, i.e. the event must be encoded as an event one 'personally experienced' among others. Povinelli and Simon (1998) consider that the ability to hold multiple representations of the world in mind simultaneously, and thus the capacity to establish temporal and causal relationships between diverse 'personally experienced' events, would be a key factor in the emergence of autobiographical memory.

Interestingly, the conclusion reached in the following chapter by Jolley is close to the idea of a coherent, autobiographical self as developed by Povinelli and Simon (1998). In chapter 5, Jolley offers an overview of the developmental progression through which children gain conceptual understanding of pictures and their dual nature: pictures are objects in themselves, and simultaneously they stand for some other realities from which they must be conceived of as differentiated. Jolley argues that the conceptual understanding of this dual property of pictures involves being able 'to think about an entity in two ways at the same time' (chapter 5, final page), that is, to hold in mind multiple representations of this entity simultaneously. This would be fully achieved somewhere between 4 and 5 years, an age period similar to the one which sees the emergence of an autobiographical self.

When occur the first signs of an ability to recognize similarity and difference between pictures and the real referents they represent? Whereas newborns have a basic ability to discriminate visually between pictures and their referents, it may take a few months before babies can recognize on some level a similarity between a picture's contents and its referent. Only at about $1\frac{1}{2}$ years is there clear evidence that infants can recognize familiar subject matter in pictures and behave towards pictures in a way that indicates they would understand that pictures are different from their real referents. However, Jolley shows that there is still a long way to go before children capture a complete understanding of the dual nature of pictures. He reports findings of DeLoache and others from two different tasks, a search task for a real item in space, using a picture as a guide, and the 'false picture' task, where children need to point to the photo of an object taken at a particular point in time. Between 2 and 2½ years, children are able to use information from a picture to locate a toy hidden in a room, while it is only between 4 and 5 years that children's responses in 'false picture' tasks show an understanding that a change made to an object does not modify the picture taken of this object shortly before the change was made. Although both tasks were taken as measures of understanding the dual nature of pictures, Jolley accounts for the apparently contradictory developmental findings. He argues that while the search task primarily investigates the child's understanding of the representational property of the pictures, the false picture task would be assessing also the child's understanding of the independent existence of pictures. He claims that the delayed success in the false picture task is due to a more general cognitive limitation experienced by young children in being able to think simultaneously in two ways about an entity. Thus, an increase in attentional resources or in the size of working memory might constitute one major general cognitive factor underlying this development. We wonder, however, whether a space-mapping task is easier than a time-mapping task, just because space offers a visible extent, while a time scale is much more difficult to grasp.

The role of executive functions in drawing development is also highlighted in the following chapter by Freeman and Adi-Japha. They give a comprehensive overview of the several steps involved in the production of a drawing and how they relate one to the other. These authors focus on whether an interpretation is afforded by the final product, i.e. whether children form an intention to draw something a priori, or allocate a convenient interpretation post hoc, which suits the graphic object they happened to create. They show how children come to relate initial intentions and subsequent interpretations via a complex process that involves both activating and inhibiting or suppressing drawing rules. Interestingly, these notions of intention and interpretation throw new light on the above discussed question of the dual nature of drawings as symbols. Drawing with the prior intention to depict, for example, recognizable lion makes it easier to confer representational and referential attributes to the drawing, but also makes failure more likely, if the aim was too ambitious. In absence of intention, it is likely that the drawing can be seen literally as a series of lines or marks or as a scribble, i.e. as an object in itself, possessing some incidental, geometrical attributes. Though some observations suggest that children as young as 2 years can form some connections between intention, action and interpretation, these links really start to operate by 3 years, that is, approximatively at the same age when children resolve the DeLoache tasks, or the picture recognition tasks of Campbell *et al.* Thus, the angle under which Freeman and Adi-Japha tackle the question of the entry of children into representational drawing brings them to delineate the same age period as the previous approaches. This certainly shows that general or domain-general representational capacities underly the different drawing-related behaviours examined so far. However, throughout the chapter, Freeman and Adi-Japha prevent us from adopting a uniquely forward-looking orientation towards each next advance in development, as if only progressive acquisition of new abilities, or new drawing rules, occurred. They repeatedly point to the fact that development is also a story of recursive 'rejections' or suppression of old rules, of inhibition of up-to-now dominant behaviours. Similar to Jolley, also Freeman and Adi-Japha consider that changes in executive processes sustain the development of drawing behaviour. Freeman and Adi-Japha's chapter focuses on the role of inhibition, while Jolley attaches importance to the role of working memory. Note that attention is perhaps a key common function underlying these two functional processes. In chapter 9, in the next part of the book, Morra will in fact discuss an entire array of factors which develop and interact during the development of drawing.

In conclusion, the chapters included in this first section illustrate how progressive cognitive expertise and behavioural mastery is gained by children in drawing from the very beginning until their fourth or fifth year of life. The constitution of a representational and autobiographical self accompanies this development, where a self as producer engages in intentions, graphic actions and interpretations, and exercises or rejects drawing rules, which are progressively assembled or disassembled, partly as a function of the ease with which connections between the produced drawing and the model can be established. The next section examines how drawing develops thereafter.

The second part (Syntax, space systems and projection) has six chapters; chapters 7 and 8 deal essentially with syntax in drawing, while chapters 9 to 12 take an 'internal' perspective on drawing, asking how graphic objects are organized within pictorial space, and what the effects of the transition from 'intellectual' to 'visual' realism are on the early representations.

Syntax in drawing refers to the way the movements are organized and ordered in a sequence. As pointed out by Braswell and Rosengren in their chapter, the study of the motor aspects of drawing has received less consideration than the study of the final outcome of a drawing episode, at least in children. Note that a move from a product-oriented approach to a process-oriented research approach characterizes not only the drawing domain, but more generally the study of graphic activities, particularly the study of handwriting (e.g. Thomassen and Van Galen, 1992). The interest in graphic syntax was elicited by Goodnow and Levine (1973), who described several starting and progression rules. This work was further developed by Goodnow's Australian collegue Van Sommers' (1984) very clever and original investigations on drawing carried out in the years thereafter. He carefully demonstrated how perceptual, geometrical, biomechanical and cognitive forces act together in the production of drawing, and proposed heuristic notions, for instance the notion of 'conservatism' in children's drawings, which is now often used to contrast cognitive 'flexibility'.

In their chapter, Braswell and Rosengren review a series of studies demonstrating that biomechanical and cognitive constraints interact with task and cultural constraints during drawing development. With respect to biomechanical constraints, they examine the development of grip configurations as well as its variability, and the influence of handedness on stroke directionality. They show that cognitive constraints linked to planning ability interfere with the application of some syntactical rules, like starting rules when drawing a line, or threading, i.e. connecting shapes with each other. Braswell and Rosengren refer also to the scarce literature that explores how cultural constraints act on syntactical behaviour, in particular how writing systems impact on drawing. For instance, Arab writing systems bias directionality from right to left, while Hebrew writing systems bias it from left to right. Likewise, Braswell and Rosengren explored laterality effects in drawing, i.e. not only where children and adults start to draw, but also how they coordinate their drawing when using both hands, demonstrating entirely different behaviours in adults, who used the hands in a mirror fashion, while young children had both hands carrying out the same movements. Indeed this poses many unanswered questions, such as whether the amount of specialization and expertise, which occurs in adulthood, is matched by different underlying brain processes, such that drawing becomes a truly right-brain activity. Does drawing involve increasingly less verbal labelling with which objects are denoted, as drawing becomes more focused on irregular, view-specific contour of shapes, and thus becomes increasingly and exclusively part of non-verbal intelligence (Edwards, 1992)? It was shown that drawing becomes an increasingly effortful and pressurized activity (Lange-Küttner, 1998), so much so that it can elicit epilepsy (Kho, Van den Bergh, Spetgens and Leijten, 2006; Miller, 2006) and fits of action-induced myoclonus-dystonia (M-D) (Nitschke, Erdmann, Trillenberg, Sprenger, Kock, Sperner et al., 2006) in young people. In the elderly, impairments in drawing spatial position predicted death in a condition of chronic obstructive pulmonary disease (Antonelli, Corsonello, Pedone, Trojano, Acanfora, Spada et al., 2006) and was more common in schizophrenia (Lowery, Giovanni, Harper Mozley, Arnold, Bilker, Gur et al., 2003). It appears that expert drawers activate more frontal brain activity, related to working memory, while novices activate more the parietal brain area, related to perceptual aspects of spatial position (Solso, 2001). A parieto-frontal network for drawing was indeed also revealed by Ino, Asada, Ito, Kimura and Fukuyama (2003), with a stronger activation on the right side of the brain, but when naming was involved parietal lobes were activated bilaterally (Makuuchi, Kaminaga and Sugishita, 2003; Moritz, Johnson, McMillan, Haughton and Meyerand, 2004). Thus, for expertise, the anterior–posterior brain axis appears to be relevant, while the amount of verbal involvement seems to be reflected in the left–right brain axis. The chapters of Lange-Küttner in the second section and of Lindenberger as well as Patterson in the third section discuss further neuropsychological aspects of drawing.

The central thesis of Vinter, Picard and Fernandes in chapter 8 is that the way reality is parsed into representational units determines the way drawing movements are grouped and ordered in a sequence. More precisely, they argue that changes in drawing behaviour during development result from changes in the *size* of the cognitive units or mental representations used to plan behaviour, and in the capacity to manage *part–whole* relationships. The way an object is conceptualized affects the way it is drawn, not only in its final content, but also in the specific sequencing of the movements used. Therefore, the study of drawing syntax is almost entirely a non-verbal approach to representational development in children. The hypothesis is tested in several experiments carried out by Vinter and her colleagues, from the study of local application of graphic rules to the study of the global strategies followed by children when they copy more or less complex patterns. At a local level, the authors show that the rules are applied segment by segment, then are planned taking into consideration the entire figure, before children become able to take simultaneously into account the constraints imposed by the segments and by the overall figure configuration. A similar three-step model seems to characterize drawing syntax development at a more global level, where authors consider children's graphic strategies or their capacities to introduce innovations in their drawings (representational flexibility) through modifications of their drawing movement sequences (procedural flexibility). Note that such a perspective is not contradictory to a functionalist view asserting the role of working memory in this development, for instance. Indeed, managing part–whole relationships necessitates focusing simultaneously on both the parts and the whole. Finally, in the same way as Pew (1974) has shown that visuo-manual tracking behaviour can become an interesting non-verbal test of implicit learning (see also Wulf and Schmidt, 1997), Vinter, Picard and Fernandes conclude their chapter reporting on a new use of syntactical drawing behaviour as a method for studying implicit learning processes, i.e. how behaviour can be incidentally modified through repeated confrontations in a structured situation. Indeed, syntactical drawing behaviour is structured quasi-naturally by rules or principles which usually are not under a deliberate, conscious control. This allows, unbeknown to the subjects, the introduction of systematic manipulations of these rules in a drawing task, and thus the design of new non-verbal paradigms for the investigation of implicit or incidental learning.

Chapters 9 by Morra and 10 by Lange-Küttner are both concerned with the internal spatial relations in pictorial space. Morra's approach is theoretical. To begin with, he lays out neo-Piagetian theory as conceptualized by Pascual-Leone and Case as a starting point, specifying the many factors which contribute to the final product, such as the Field factor (F-factor), the Inhibition factor (I-factor), etc. The chapter itself capitalizes mainly on the Memory factor (M-factor) and convincingly demonstrates the amount of cognitive steps which need to be taken in order to solve a graphical problem, and the insufficient solutions which are only possible with more limited memory power. Morra conceptualizes apparently diverse phenomena in drawing, such as transparency in partial occlusion drawing, where children do not omit the contours of the overlapped graphic object, as well as drawing a horizontal line into a tilted container in the classical water-level task and the representation of movement in the static medium of graphic representation in terms of figurative and operative schemes. His careful task analyses are not only exercises in specifying task difficulty; they enlighten the reader about the cognitive complexity of the processes involved in implementing a strategy and facilitate the control of the design of experiments so that causative factors can be unambiguously identified. It also makes researchers aware of the limits and possibilities of what we can tap into with a single experiment.

In chapter 10 Lange-Küttner presents a set of studies which investigated the interaction between figures and spatial systems. Also, in cognitive psychology and neuropsychology, the question whether visual cognition functions are object-based, space-based or display-based, and whether an attention window can be narrowed or widened towards an object or a spatial field are long-standing issues. Renaissance artists used a grid in order systematically to capture visual reality segment by segment, cutting across meaningful figures in order to concentrate on psychophysical parameters such as contour and colour. Lange-Küttner shows that young children appear to feel some compulsion to draw a complete figure, and would rather omit a part than draw half a figure. The axis-based half-figures which Driver, Marshall and others could find in adult stroke patients appear to be impossible to draw for young children. Children draw explicit spatial context only relatively late, but the spatial context appears to have a profound impact on the appearance of objects. The only theory so far which is concerned with interactions of objects and the spatial field is Lewin's field theory, albeit this was more focused on social phenomena. Lange-Küttner uses the parameter of size to demonstrate the profound impact that the new explicit orthogonal and diagonal axes systems have on objects. While initially size was found to be based on the competition of objects within pictorial space, i.e. size modification was object-driven (i.e. the more objects, the smaller the size), in older children size modification was axes-driven, based on the level of the explicit axes system. Thus, space appeared to change from being object-based to axes-based. There was also a 'wildlife'-factor in young children, where they would draw a kind of habitual size, which could, for instance, depend on activities in their ecological environment, but this dropped out with age. Yet, even 7-year-olds were shown to be able to react towards a logically ordered increase of complexity in spatial systems. There are some crucial implications of this research for the space concept (Piaget and Inhelder, 1956). Like other researchers in spatial cognition (Hund and Plumert, 2002, 2005; Liben, 1988; Mandler, 1988; Newcombe and Huttenlocher, 2003; Spencer and Hund, 2003), Lange-Küttner finds that also in drawing, even young children are familiar with all kinds of space systems, but they do learn (1) to become more explicit, (2) to recognize spatial constraints and use a spatial scale, and (3) to see through randomness. Not all these abilities are directly linked to spatial cognition, but they nevertheless increase the power of the spatial concepts.

In chapter 11, Tallandini and Morassi describe in detail a Three-Dimensional Representation Scale (Q3DS) which they used in order to ascertain whether there is a trade-off between meaning and spatial sophistication in terms of 3D depiction, i.e. between the spatial and the symbolic code. Piaget had qualified a pre-operational stage where representations are still constructed as symbolic relations, where one object stands for another. However, this is now seen as part of a skill within analogical reasoning (Goswami, 1992). As in research on language and reading (Treiman, Goswami and Bruck, 1990), also in drawing research, the role of meaning is often explored by contrasting normal, meaningful with nonsense objects as drawing models (see also chapter 12 by Deregowski and chapter 16 by Sheppard, Mitchell and Ropar). Tallandini and Morassi could identify a 'meaning effect' where the semantic component in the model (face and clothes-like decoration) was suppressing spatial elaboration. That a sparse model would encourage spatial 3D elaboration, while a detailed, decorated model would encourage a depiction which is more 2D and thus intellectually rather than visually realistic is very interesting, as it suggests that indeed some individual features may be better represented in the early depictions. In future research it might be interesting to analyse whether there are gender differences involved in this experimental effect. Boys notoriously underperform compared to girls in the Draw-A-Person Test because they draw less detail, but they excel in spatial tests such as the Mental Rotation Test.

Chapter 12 gives an overview on Jan Deręgowski's longstanding research on the drawing of non-sense objects which he used in order to investigate the depiction of contour. Children do not always draw the contours they see; on the contrary, they seem to have a template which is canonical for each object (e.g. Davis, 1985) and specifies obligatory defining details. Deręgowski describes the various ways in which our perception can be tricked and our identification of contour can be made difficult by geometrically ambiguous contours as well as by a figure melting perceptually into a background. The first problem causes a conflict about the typical contour; the second problem causes a conflict about the boundary contour. Deręgowski found in his empirical studies that onlookers, whether children or adults, were biased towards the fronto-parallel plane. However, in drawing the problem presented itself not as easily, e.g. as animal models do not always show their 'best side', compared to the situation when a model is sitting for portrait, with the result that parts can be depicted in a 'twisted' perspective, for which Deręgowski found many examples in art history. Deręgowski and Dziurawiec demonstrated also that children apply this strategy when challenged with tripartite models. The spine of animals and humans constitutes indeed an important body axis around which figures can be rotated. The processes involved in the 'false' rotation of twisted perspective, which is built as a compromise in response to difficult models, and the 'real' rotation according to viewpoint, seem to be so different in quality that Deręgowski asks whether canonical shapes are really flat or compressed into some typical, defining template, rather than being a true referent for the real objects as seems to be the case in mental rotation tasks. Also, very recently Hayworth and Biederman (2006) were suggesting that there are intermediate object representations in the occipital cortex that neither result from simple extraction of surface boundaries, nor exist as a complex hierarchy of nested arrangements of local features such as lines and vertices, but would consist of a simple specification of parts and their relations. It may well be that canonical shapes with typical contour belong to a kind of graphic vocabulary through which one can iterate with different levels of graphic fluency. This is discussed by Lindenberger et al. in chapter 13, in the next and final part of the book.

In this third section of the book (Aging, blindness and autism), only adults were investigated: in chapter 13 by Lindenberger et al. young and old graphic experts; in chapter 14 by Patterson and Erzinçlioğlu, the graphic object concepts of older adults with semantic dementia; in chapter 15 by Kennedy and Juricevic blind adults' projective abilities in pictorial space; and in chapter 16 by Sheppard, Mitchell and Ropar autistic adults' hyperrealism in projective drawing. Thus, Part III is relatively homogeneous in terms of adult age studies, and topics such as graphic object concepts, spatial context and projective space do reoccur in the different frameworks.

That graphic designers' expertise may protect them against the cognitive effects of aging was the central hypothesis in chapter 13 by Lindenberger, Brehmer, Kliegl and Baltes. They investigated the expertise of graphic designers and normal controls at the beginning of 20 years, and between 60 and 80 years of age, with a test battery that included the Torrance Creativity Test, the Card Rotation Test and several subtests of the Wechsler Intelligence Test. The visuo-spatial memory test 'Method of Loci', which uses landmark objects as memory cues, was devised as the most obvious indicator to detect aging-related decrease of cognitive power. Lindenberger et al. found that older graphic designers consistently were top of their age cohort in terms of both graphic vocabulary and mental rotation, demonstrating the result of a life-time of specialization, while younger designers' scores were still more intermingled with those of controls. Younger participants recalled more words in the correct serial position, but graphic designers remembered more words than controls independently of age, i.e. in young people, expertise and brain power did not combine to surpass that of older designers. This showed unambiguously that graphic expertise appears to create a graphic vocabulary which is more fluent in graphic designers than in normal controls and which does facilitate visuo-spatial memory tests. Thus, we must assume that like words in sentences, graphic objects are visibly delineated entities which can be stored to build a graphical lexicon, and like verbal fluency, there is graphic fluency.

This is also demonstrated in the research of Patterson and Erzinçlioğlu in chapter 14, albeit in the opposite direction of decline rather than enhancement and expertise. When we assume that the graphical lexicon is a long-term memory store just like vocabulary in language, we could also think of language disorders like dyslexia as occuring in the visual domain. Patterson and Erzinçlioğlu show that elderly patients with semantic dementia not only cannot name objects anymore, as they retrieve just an arbitrary name in the apparent absence of achieving a proper fit between seen object and retrieved verbal label, they also cannot retrieve the drawing template for the object, when it is not visually fixated and is just seconds out of sight. However, patients with semantic dementia are perfectly able to copy the object when in sight. This contrasted starkly with the drawing behaviour of patients with visual agnosia (Servos, Goodale and Humphrey, 1993), who showed just the opposite pattern. Patients with visual agnosia were unable to extract an object shape when the model was in sight, but could draw the object well enough when relying on the long-term stored graphic template. Patterson and Erzinçlioğlu also specify and analyse the amount of intrusions and omissions of features into the graphic templates, i.e. whether features are from the same domain or the same category, or distinctive for an individual exemplar. In the delayed copying tasks, patients with semantic dementia rarely omitted shared-by-domain features, sometimes omitted shared-by-category features, and frequently omitted features distinctive for an individual exemplar. Likewise, intrusions were rare for distinctive features, but increasingly more likely the more generally they were shared by objects. This showed that semantic knowledge for small, relatively unique, distinct detail was the most vulnerable, and the boundaries of the larger semantic fields for more generalizable features had become very porous. Furthermore, in comparison with research of Karmiloff-Smith (1990), they showed that patients with semantic dementia were more likely to make detailed form-related changes to existing shapes of the type young children make, while implementation of novelty, i.e. novel elements, novel position, novel category, rarely happened. This showed that it was not a kind of 'arbitrary' inventiveness that was leading to the altered graphic figures. The chapter by Patterson and Erzinclioğlu thus provides more evidence for the existence of a graphic lexicon equal in importance to verbal vocabulary and conceptual knowledge.

The two chapters which follow take the reader again into the problems of projective space. In chapter 15, Kennedy and Juricevic ask whether projective space is an optical law, or a pictorial rule which could be trained with practice. The overall impression from the drawings is that there is an enormous sparseness in object drawings, but that projective spatial relations such as in a 3D cube are surprisingly well represented. This is definitely not what one would have expected, as one would think that the haptic exploration of objects in near space would have produced more detailed knowledge of individual, distinct object features, while the absence of depth perception in far space would have led to the absence of projective spatial relations in the drawings. Kennedy and Juricevic argue that we indeed might acquire skills during drawing practice, which are independent of vision and touch, and have largely to do with logical priority, i.e. orthogonal and oblique axes are levels of complexity which can be gradually mastered without any visual input. This is very much in agreement with the studies of Lange-Küttner showing that a logical sequence of space systems would lead already 7-year-olds to diminish size in orthogonal and diagonal axes systems. People may sometimes draw what they know, rather than what they see, but others draw not what they see, but what they know they could see. Thus, blind people tackle projective space like sighted people, but the question still remains, why the templates themselves remain so underspecified. One reason could be that blind children only experience object shapes in the graphic medium when reading Braille. However, this occurs only with the onset of school, so that young children receive no early practice with object shapes on paper. There is some progress in this area by a French research group in Dijon and Grenoble lead by Vinter on the haptic perception and graphic construction of object shapes in innately and partially blind young children, which will inform us in the future on how to enrich the early object templates of blind people.

Last but not least, in the final chapter of the book, Sheppard, Mitchell and Ropar take the reader into the hyperrealistic visual world of some autistic people (see also Selfe, 1977, 1983, 1985). Sometimes this high-level ability that is achieved without tuition is also called 'savant skills' because it involved some social isolation causing at least some autistic features. As for Piaget, who argued that concepts are developed within a social structure, the suggestion of Frith (2003) is taken up that autistic individuals would have a less conceptual approach, which allows 'lower-level' perceptual processing to prevail. In a strong version of this assumption, it would be predicted that, in development, people with autism would not have developed intellectually realistic drawing, and thus would not need to reject outdated concepts when they would have to draw in a visually realistic fashion (see also chapter 6 by Freeman and Adi-Japha). In a weaker version of this assumption, people with autism would still develop the same kind of pictorial concepts, yet make fewer mistakes in more artful visually realistic depictions, in which they would be just more interested rather than in meaningful and functional, communicative pictograms. The authors find evidence for the weaker version, as there is no difference in 2D depictions, but a significant, statistically reliable and replicable difference in 3D depictions, whether primed or not. They demonstrate that while children appear to struggle to draw a three-dimensional visual illusion, people with autism seem to thrive on it, especially when a literal copy of a 3D line drawing is involved. Thus, it seems out of the question that 'lower-level' perception would be involved in the elaborate drawings of people with autism; it rather seems that their unsupervised learning style sets them apart.

This introduction was aimed to give readers a context for the chapters which our authors have written for this volume. Authors have had no input into this introduction. Thus, the discussion of their work is entirely within the responsibility of the editors. We hope that you will find the reading interesting, and that the researchers were able to reveal at least as much structure, meaning and logic in the non-verbal, visual mind of people as we know exists in their language. Drawing is a domain which is superbly suited for this purpose, as it involves the productive side of visual intelligence. This may appear as obvious to the viewer as spoken language to someone listening, yet under normal circumstances both need many years of vocabulary and syntax development to change from crude approximations to elaborate descriptions and distinctions.

REFERENCES

Antonelli, I. R., Corsonello, A., Pedone, C., Trojano, L., Acanfora, D., Spada, A., Izzo, O. and Rengo, F. (2006). Drawing impairment predicts mortality in severe COPD. *Chest*, 130, 1687–94.

Bahrick, L. E. and Watson, J. S. (1985). Detection of intermodal proprioceptive-visual contingency as a potential basis of self-perception in infancy. *Developmental Psychology*, 21, 963–73.

Cox, M. V. (1986). *Children's drawings*. London: Penguin.

(2005). *The pictorial world of the child*. Cambridge: Cambridge University Press.

Davis, A. (1985). Conflict between canonicality and array-specificity in young children's drawings. *British Journal of Developmental Psychology*, 3, 363–72.

Edwards, B. (1992). *Drawing on the right side of the brain*. London: Souvenir Press.

Freeman, N. H. (1980). *Strategies of representation in young children*. London: Academic Press.

Freeman, N. H. and Cox, M. V. (eds.) (1985). *Visual order*. Cambridge: Cambridge University Press.

Frith, U. (2003). *Autism: explaining the enigma*. Oxford: Blackwell.

Gallup, G. G., Jr (1970). Chimpanzees: self-recognition. *Science*, 167, 86–7.

Gellert, E. (1968). Comparison of children's self-drawing with their drawings of other persons. *Perceptual and Motor Skills*, 26, 123–38.

Gergely, G. (2006). The development of understanding self and agency. In U. Goswami (ed.), *Childhood cognitive development* (pp. 26–46). Oxford: Blackwell.

Golomb, C. (1973). Children's representation of the human figure: the effects of models, media and instruction. *Genetic Psychology Monographs*, 87, 197–251.

Goodenough, F. L. (1926). *Measurement of intelligence by drawings*. New York: World Book Company.

Goodenough, F. L. and Harris, D. B. (1950). Studies in the psychology of children's drawings. II. *Psychological Bulletin*, 47, 369–433.

Goodnow, J. J. (1977). *Children's drawings*. London: Fontana.

Goodnow, J. J. and Levine, R. A. (1973). The 'grammar of action': sequence and syntax in children's copying behaviour. *Cognitive Psychology*, 4, 82–98.

Goswami, U. (1992). *Analogical reasoning in children*. Hove: Erlbaum.

Gross, J. and Hayne, H. (1999). Young children's recognition and description of their own and others' drawings. *Developmental Science*, 2, 476–89.

Hayworth, K. J. and Biederman, I. (2006). Neural evidence for intermediate representations in object recognition. *Vision Research*, 46, 4024–31.

Hund, A. M. and Plumert, J. M. (2002). Delay-induced bias in children's memory for location. *Child Development*, 73, 829–40.

  (2005). The stability and flexibility of spatial categories. *Cognitive Psychology*, 50, 1–44.

Ino, T., Asada, T., Ito, J., Kimura, T. and Fukuyama, H. (2003). Parieto-frontal networks for clock drawing revealed with fMRI. *Neuroscience Research*, 45, 71–7.

Karmiloff-Smith, A. (1990). Constraints on representational change: evidence from children's drawings. *Cognition*, 34, 57–83.

Kerschensteiner, G. (1905). *Die Entwicklung der zeichnerischen Begabung*. Munich: Gerber.

Kho, K. H., Van den Bergh, W. M., Spetgensx, W. P. J. and Leijten, F. S. S. (2006). Figuring out drawing-induced epilepsy. *Neurology*, 66, 723–6.

Lange-Küttner, C. (1998). Pressure, velocity and time in speeded drawing of basic graphic pattern by young children. *Perceptual and Motor Skills*, 86, 1299–1310.

Lange-Küttner, C. and Thomas, G. V. (eds.) (1995). *Drawing and looking*. London: Pearson/Prentice Hall (distributed by www.amazon.co.uk).

Liben, L. S. (1988). Conceptual issues in the development of spatial cognition. In J. Stiles-Davis, M. Kritchevsky and U. Bellugi (eds.), *Spatial cognition: brain bases and development* (pp. 167–94). Hillsdale, NJ: Erlbaum.

Longcamp, M., Zerbato-Poudou, M.-T. and Velay, J.-L. (2005). The influence of writing practice on letter recognition in preschool children: a comparison between handwriting and typing. *Acta Psychologica*, 119, 67–79.

Lowery, N., Giovanni, L., Harper Mozley, L., Arnold, S. E., Bilker, W. B., Gur, R. E. and Moberg, P. J. (2003). Relationship between clock-drawing and neuropsychological and functional status in elderly institutionalized patients with schizophrenia. *American Journal of Geriatric Psychiatry*, 11, 621–8.

Luquet, G. H. (1927). *Le dessin enfantin [Children's drawing]*. Paris: Alcan.

Makuuchi, M., Kaminaga, T. and Sugishita, M. (2003). Both parietal lobes are involved in drawing: a functional MRI study and implications for constructional apraxia. *Cognitive Brain Research*, 16, 338–47.

Mandler, J. M. (1988). The development of spatial cognition: on topological and euclidian representation. In J. Stiles-Davis, M. Kritchevsky and U. Bellugi (eds.), *Spatial cognition: brain bases and development* (pp. 423–32). Hillsdale, NJ: Erlbaum.

Miller, B. L. (2006). Figuring out drawing-induced epilepsy. Commentary. *Neurology*, 66, 619.

Moritz, C. H., Johnson, S. C., McMillan, K. M., Haughton, V. M. and Meyerand, M. E. (2004). Functional MRI neuroanatomic correlates of the Hooper

Visual Organization Test. *Journal of the International Neuropsychological Society*, 10, 939–47.
Newcombe, N. S. and Huttenlocher, J. (2003). *Making space: the development of spatial representation and reasoning*. Cambridge, MA: MIT Press.
Nitschke, M. F., Erdmann, C., Trillenberg, P., Sprenger, A., Kock, N., Sperner, J. and Klein, C. (2006). Functional MRI reveals activation of a subcortical network in a 5-year-old girl with genetically confirmed myoclonus-dystonia. *Neuropediatrics*, 37, 79–82.
Pew, R. W. (1974). Levels of analysis in motor control. *Brain Research*, 71, 393–400.
Piaget, J. and Inhelder, B. (1956). *The child's conception of space*. London: Routledge and Kegan Paul.
Povinelli, D. J. (1995). The unduplicated self. In P. Rochat (ed.), *The self in infancy: theory and research* (pp. 161–92). Amsterdam: Elsevier.
Povinelli, D. J. and Simon, B. B. (1998). Young children's understanding of briefly versus extremely delayed images of the self: emergence of the autobiographical stance. *Developmental Psychology*, 34, 188–94.
Ricci, C. (1887). *L'arte dei bambini [The art of children]*. Bologna.
Rochat, P. and Morgan, R. (1995). Spatial determinants in the perception of self-produced leg movements in 3- to 5-month-old infants. *Developmental Psychology*, 31, 626–36.
Rouma, G. (1913). *Le langage graphique de l'enfant [The graphic language of children]*. Paris: Alcan.
Schmuckler, M. A. (1996). Visual-proprioceptive intermodal perception in infancy. *Infant Behaviour and Development*, 19, 221–32.
Selfe, L. (1977). *Nadia: a case of extraordinary drawing ability in an autistic child*. London: Academic Press.
  (1983). *Normal and anomalous representational drawing ability in children*. London: Academic Press.
  (1985). Anomalous drawing development. In N. H. Freeman and M. V. Cox (eds.), *Visual order: the nature and development of pictorial representation* (pp. 135–54). Cambridge: Cambridge University Press.
Servos, P., Goodale, M. A. and Humphrey, G. K. (1993). The drawing of objects by a visual form agnosic: contribution of surface properties and memorial representations. *Neuropsychologia*, 31, 251–9.
Solso, R. L. (2001). Brain activities in a skilled versus a novice artist: an fMRI study. *Leonardo*, 34, 31–4.
Spencer, J. P. and Hund, A. M. (2003). Developmental continuity in the processes that underlie spatial recall. *Cognitive Psychology*, 47, 432–80.
Sutton, P. J. and Rose, D. H. (1998). The role of strategic visual attention in children's drawing development. *Journal of Experimental Child Psychology*, 68, 87–107.
Thomas, G. V. and Silk, A. M. J. (1990). *An introduction to the psychology of children's drawings*. New York: New York University Press.
Thomassen, A. J. W. M. and Van Galen, G. P. (1992). Handwriting as a motor task. In J. J. Summers (ed.), *Approaches to the study of motor control and learning* (pp. 113–44). Amsterdam: North-Holland.

Treiman, R., Goswami, U. and Bruck, M. (1990). Not all nonwords are alike: implication for reading development and theory. *Memory and Cognition*, 18, 559–67.

Van Sommers, P. (1984). *Drawing and cognition: descriptive and experimental studies of graphic production processes*. Cambridge: Cambridge University Press.

(1989). A system for drawing and drawing-related neuropsychology. *Cognitive Neuropsychology*, 6, 117–64.

Willats, J. (1985). Drawing systems revisited: the role of denotation systems in children's figure drawings. In N. H. Freeman and M. V. Cox (eds.), *Visual order* (pp. 78–100). Cambridge: Cambridge University Press.

(1995). An information-processing approach to drawing development. In C. Lange-Küttner and G. V. Thomas (eds.), *Drawing and looking* (pp. 27–43). London: Pearson/Prentice Hall (distributed by www.amazon.co.uk).

(2005). *Making sense of children's drawings*. Mahwah, NJ: Erlbaum.

Wilson, M. and Wilson, B. (1982). The case of the disappearing of the two-eyed profile or how little children influence the drawings of little children. *Review of Research in Visual Arts Education*, 15, 19–32.

Wulf, G. and Schmidt, R. A. (1997). Variability of practice and implicit motor learning. *Journal of Experimental Psychology: Learning, Memory and Cognition*, 23, 987–1006.

Part I

Self, symbols and intention

2   Understanding reflections of self and other objects

Kim Bard

Bard explains how understanding reflections of reality via the mirror begins at about 2 years of age. Recognizing reflections of the self appears to follow a different developmental route than recognizing reflections of objects. Research on the development of mirror experience in infants and chimpanzees is reviewed, and some intriguing research using video techniques is described. The chapter provides insight into the general factors and specialized pathways involved in the onset of awareness of reflective reality.

THIS CHAPTER reviews developmental and comparative studies of mirror self-recognition. In children and also in chimpanzees, self-awareness has been studied using the mark-and-mirror test (for overviews see Bard, Todd, Bernier, Love and Leavens, 2006; Courage, Edison and Howe, 2004). In this assessment, the objective target behaviour is the ability to touch a mark on one's own face, as a result of seeing the self-image reflected in the mirror. Mirror self-recognition (MSR) is often considered the point of origin for self-awareness because it appears to be the first time when the self is objectively identified. We take a comparative perspective, reviewing the literature on the development of MSR in human and chimpanzee infants, and in other primate species, and suggest that passing the mark test isn't about understanding the reflective properties of the mirror, isn't about discovery of the mark by looking at the mirror image, but is something special about being self-aware.

Self-awareness in human infants

Amsterdam (1972) devised the mark-and-mirror test for human infants. The testing procedure paralleled 'everyday' experiences. All children were tested while in a playpen, with a tall thin mirror attached to one side. After a 5 minute familiarization period, the mother was asked to remove the child's clothes (leaving on underpants or diapers) and to apply the mark. The mother was instructed to place the infant in front of the mirror, and say 'see' three times while pointing to the mirror image of the child's face. Then, after a short pause, the mother was asked to point to the child's face in the mirror again and ask 'Who's that?' Then the mother sat in a chair without distracting the infant. This constitutes the first trial. After 2.5 minutes, the mother was instructed to repeat her behaviour (saying 'see' while pointing to the mirror image three times, and asking 'Who's that?') for the second trial. The mother was allowed to hold the infant on her lap between trials, if the infant became distressed.

There were two categories of behaviours that indicated 'Recognition of the image'. One category involved the mark ('touches dot') and the nose (turns head and observes nose). The other category involved labelling the self ('saying name') or pointing to the self. The number of infants who exhibited the recognition behaviours was tallied, and percentage of infants within each age range who exhibited recognition behaviours was determined (e.g. 42 per cent of 18–20-month-olds; 63 per cent of 21–24-month-olds).

Amsterdam (1972) was quite explicit that she was assuming that the 20–24-month-olds' ability to locate the mark on their own face indicated that infants of this age associate the face in the mirror with their own face, and that it is an inference 'that this behaviour indicates self-recognition' (p. 304). She noted that younger infants might appear concerned about their face, but that among infants of less than 20 months, only one 18-month-old and one 19-month-old showed 'recognition' of their mirror image. She did not discuss the interpretation of either verbal labelling or the pointing to self as indices of self-recognition.

Developmental context

Amsterdam's research was well received in developmental psychology. The mark test was accepted as providing the desired objective procedure. Many researchers and many laboratories have replicated and extended the study of mirror self-recognition, providing a firm foundation for a description of development in the typical human infant (Lewis and Brooks-Gunn, 1979), for furthering the study of the development of the self from infancy through childhood (Brooks-Gunn and Lewis, 1984) and to develop theories of the self (Lewis, Sullivan, Stanger and Weiss, 1989).

Developmental path to self-awareness

The developmental path leading to mirror self-recognition is well documented for human infants (e.g. Amsterdam, 1972; Bertenthal and Fischer, 1978; Brooks-Gunn and Lewis, 1984; Chapman, 1987; Johnson,

1982). The following describes responses to the mirror (and mirror image) from 5 to 24 months. Social responses, for example, treating the mirror image as a playmate, begin around 6 months and decline by 18 months (Amsterdam, 1972; Schulman and Kaplowitz, 1977). In the first half of year, infants may smile and vocalize in engagement with the mirror image, but do not respond differently to images of the self versus images of others. General rhythmic body behaviour, including affective displays, occurs between 9 and 15 months. Prior to self-recognition, infants can locate objects that are reflected in the mirror (e.g. around 22 months according to Robinson, Connell, McKenzie and Day, 1990 but at a mean age of 16.6 months according to Courage et al., 2004). The understanding of the reflective qualities of the mirror is distinct from understanding the self (contra Courage et al., 2004). Infants typically demonstrate that they understand the reflective quality of the mirror, by preferring the self-reflections over others' reflections, probably due to the contingency detection (e.g. Bigelow, 1981). Self-conscious behaviours, e.g. self-admiration, 'silliness' or 'coyness', occur at 13 to 24 months (but see Reddy, 2000, for emergence of coy expressions in response to the mirror very much earlier in life). It is often suggested that such reactions, either avoidant or admiring, are indicative of the early stages of self-awareness (e.g. Schulman and Kaplowitz, 1977). Self-recognition, indicated by passing the mark test, is present in human infants by 18 to 24 months (see Bard et al., 2006 for review): average age of onset is 17 months (Courage et al., 2004).

An emerging view of the development of self-awareness involves a progression from the 'I' to the 'me', in other words from the existential self to the categorical self (Lewis et al., 1989). Young infants develop an awareness of their own agency, their ability to act as an independent agent on the world (Piaget, 1954). Around 24 months, toddlers display knowledge of the objective self by identifying images of the self, either in photographs, mirrors or videotape, through guided mark touching and/or self-labelling. Pronoun use emerges around 20 months, and amount of personal pronoun use relates to recognizing the self (Courage et al., 2004). Lewis and colleagues (Lewis et al., 1989) suggest that it is at this time that self-conscious emotions arise, e.g. shame, embarrassment and pride, as the toddler is able to compare the behaviour of the self in relation to others. Knowledge of the categorical self develops into social comparisons of self to others (and vice versa).

Newer developmental studies

Recent studies carry on the developmental traditions, and extend investigation into antecedents, correlates and consequences of early self-awareness (Asendorpf and Baudonniere, 1993). For example, if we consider how current developmentalists define mirror self-recognition, we see that Amsterdam's ideas have been extended to more specific cognitive mechanisms. Asendorpf and Baudonniere (1993) state that mirror-guided mark-directed behaviour indicates that infants 'infer from the mirror image that they themselves have the mark' (p. 88). They propose that the development of mirror self-awareness parallels the development of other-awareness, based on the same cognitive substrate, of comparing their self-image with their own and others' standards. Asendorpf (2002) clarifies the developmental perspective: 'mirror self-recognition requires coordinating a mirror-image (primary representation) with one's representation of oneself' (p. 66), therefore mirror self-recognition requires a 'cognitive capacity for secondary representation' (p. 67). Harel, Eshel, Ganor and Scher (2002) present the argument that mirror self-recognition reflects the mental comparison of the infant's mental representation of her face (without the mark) with the image reflected in the mirror (with the mark). That mirror self-recognition is a cognitive ability is supported by its demonstrated links with other representation and metacognitive abilities. Harel et al. linked the development of self-awareness with early emotional responsiveness of infants in interaction with the mother.

Comparative assessment of self-awareness

Chimpanzees

Gallup (1970) concluded that chimpanzees were self-aware based on the following changes in response to the mirror; social responses (initially high but decreased to 0); self-directed responses (initially 0 but increased); viewing in the mirror (decreased but with spiked increase when marked); touches to the mark (none in the absence of the mirror, compared with high levels in the presence of the mirror).

Gallup (1970) equated self-directed and mark-directed behaviours, and stated that these 'require the ability to project, as it were, proprioceptive information and kinesthetic feedback onto the reflected visual image so as to coordinate the appropriate visually guided movements via the mirror'. Gallup (1970) states that 'self-recognition of one's mirror image implies a concept of self' (p. 87), asserting that apes and humans have a sense of self: 'The capacity to correctly infer the identity of the reflection presupposes an identity on the part of the organism making that inference' (Gallup, 1982, p. 240). Moreover, Gallup defines self-awareness in chimpanzees as 'the ability to become the object of your own attention' (p. 243).

Comparative context

At the time, Gallup was advocating the idea that MSR tests constituted objective proof that chimpanzees have a self-concept. Moreover, he argued that the self-concept emerged spontaneously in chimpanzees and humans, and was not based on simple associative learning. 'My technique . . . is free from contamination due to manipulative intervention. I simply create the opportunity for organisms to decipher the significance of mirrored information about themselves. Chimpanzees do not have to be taught to recognize themselves in mirrors' (Gallup, 1982, p. 241). These arguments were defences against the behavioural attacks by Skinner and colleagues on the 'mentalistic' conceptualization of MSR. Operant conditioning techniques had been used to elicit self-directed pecking in pigeons while in front of mirrors (Epstein, Lansa and Skinner, 1981). Gallup argued that because the pigeon's behaviour was operantly trained, it did not constitute proof that pigeons have a self-concept (Gallup, 1982).

Most subsequent comparative studies have adopted similar procedures for assessing self-awareness in non-human primates which involved (1) using mirror-naïve subjects; (2) isolating individuals and documenting their responses to the mirror over days or weeks; (3) covertly applying dye to the face (typically under anaesthesia); and (4) documenting mirror-guided touches to the marked face. The focus of comparative research has been to identify those species that possess self-awareness (note the contrast with the focus of developmental research to identify the age at which self-awareness emerges).

The evolution of self-awareness

Over the past thirty years, comparative research on self-awareness has documented a 'great divide', but not between humans and other primates, as might be expected, but rather between hominids (humans, orangutans, chimpanzees, bonobos and gorillas) and the rest of the primate species (e.g. Russon and Bard, 1996). Hominids have the capacity to recognize their own image in a mirror, provided that they have had prior experience with mirrors and prior social experience (Gallup, 1977; Hyatt and Hopkins, 1994; Lin, Bard and Anderson, 1992; Miles, 1994; Patterson and Cohn, 1994; Povinelli, Rulf, Landau and Bierschwale, 1993; Suarez and Gallup, 1981; Swartz, 1997; Westergaard and Hyatt, 1994). The non-hominids do not recognize their mirror image: none of the Old World monkeys, such as macaques or colobus, passes the mirror and mark test (see Anderson and Gallup, 1999, for an overview); nor do New World monkeys such as capuchins, tamarins (Hauser, Miller, Liu and

Gupta, 2001) and talapoins (Posada and Colell, 2005). Self-awareness does not appear to be a cognitive capacity present in monkeys. This difference across primate species appears to demarcate an evolutionary timeline for the emergence of self-awareness, and allows for many interesting comparative analyses.

Humans and African apes shared a common ancestor approximately 7 million years ago, and humans and Asian orangutans shared a common ancestor approximately 15 million years ago. Monkeys and apes shared a common ancestor approximately 30 million years ago (see Leavens, Hopkins and Bard, in press for further review). Therefore a characteristic, such as self-awareness, that appears in humans and all the great apes, but not in any species of monkey, most probably evolved sometime between 30 and 15 million years ago.

The 'great divide' between apes and monkeys is typically characterized in terms of particular cognitive skills; tool-use and manufacture, perspective taking (including gaze following), theory of mind and symbolic communication are the most often cited capacities of apes not shared by monkeys (e.g. Russon and Bard, 1996). The sociality basis for 'higher-level' cognition has been cited as well (e.g. Dunbar, 2003; Humphrey, 1976; Jolly, 1966). Convincing evolutionary arguments have been made for the existence of each particular skill, but it seems what set humans and apes so far apart also includes cognitive problem-solving abilities that include generativity and creativity, which are based arguably in symbolic capacities (e.g. Russon, 2004). The search for the evolutionary origins of human cognition must be informed by the emerging list of shared capacities, as well as those that are unique to the human lineage.

The other aspect of evolution that is important to consider in discussions of mirror self-recognition is that mirrors are a very recent technology (see Pendergrast, 2003). Mirrors were not in the Environment of Evolutionary Adaptedness (EEA); thus, it is reasonable to argue that mirror self-recognition, per se, was not selected. So, researchers have proposed that in the natural environment there are visually reflective surfaces: standing pools of water, for example. However, few propose a scenario in which detecting the self in pools of water was the characteristic favoured by natural selection (Barth, Povinelli and Cant, 2004; Bekoff, 2002; de Waal, Dindo, Freeman and Hall, 2005). Rather there is something special about self-awareness that allows an individual who possesses it to pass the mark-and-mirror test (Gallup, 1977).

Some argue that it is likely that there are cognitive correlates of mirror self-recognition, and many cognitive criteria have been proposed (e.g. secondary representation, theory of mind, imitation: Gallup, 1970; Parker, 1998; Suddendorf and Whiten, 2001). Others argue that it is social complexity (Humphrey, 1976), empathy (Bischof-Kohler, 1991) or a representation of the body (Barth et al., 2004) that underpins mirror self-recognition and was the product of natural selection. We will revisit some of these ideas after reviewing another perspective on this issue, namely that mirror self-recognition is a product of epigenetic processes.

The developmental comparative approach

Developmental researchers are interested in changes with age, and in exploring the effects of social-cultural environments on performance (among other variables). Comparative researchers are interested in species-unique characteristics, or in identifying those characteristics shared across species in order to propose evolutionary paths. Shared characteristics are important as they provide some information as to what our ancestors were like. In the 30 million years since humans and monkeys shared a common ancestor, humans and chimpanzees have 23 million years of shared evolutionary history, that is 7 million years of independent evolution. One value of conducting comparative studies includes gaining a better understanding of the evolutionary process. By comparing early development across species, we can learn more about the evolutionary commonalities in the process of development, and increase our understanding of plasticity and flexibility in human behaviour.

This approach places value with the idea of extending developmental comparisons to cross-species comparisons. Many researchers who advocate and practise a 'comparative developmental' approach (e.g. Parker, 1998; Povinelli et al., 1993; Tomasello, Savage-Rumbaugh and Kruger, 1993) use developmental data from human infants to compare with non-human primate species. Thus, typically the skills of 18–24-month humans are compared with the skills of adult primates. It is rare to find a study in which the ages in the non-human primates are matched with those of human infants (see Bard et al., 2006; Inoue Nakamura, 2001; Lin et al., 1992; Robert, 1986 for exceptions).

This approach of comparing adult primates to human infants may find similiarities, which inform us about common characteristic outcomes across species, and also finds differences, which are more difficult to interpret. Often these differences between the adult primates and human infants are interpreted as definite species differences, when in fact species and development are confounded in this two-group comparison. Additional comparisons are needed to tease apart the variables. Leavens, Hopkins and Bard (2005) use this logic to explain the emergence of pointing in some groups of humans and some groups of chimpanzees (but not in other groups of same species). How then do we apply this framework to the study of mirror self-recognition?

Comparative developmental study

With the growing appreciation of epigenesis (Gibson, 2007; Gottlieb, 2007; Jablonka and Lamb, 2007), there is an increased need to attend to developmental trajectories in comparative psychology. Karmiloff-Smith (2007) argues this eloquently when comparing typical and atypically developing children: 'it is clear that phenotypical differences in outcome must be traced back to their origins in infancy' (pp. 86–7). Matsuzawa (2007) applies similar reasoning in advocating the importance of affectionate bonds during development to cognitive outcomes in chimpanzees, highlighting very similar postnatal growth rates of human and chimpanzee brains (see DeSilva and Lesnik, 2006, for more detailed comparative data on chimpanzee (40 per cent) and human (30 per cent) brain growth *in utero*) and suggesting that environmental variables have comparable strength to change behavioural development of chimpanzees and humans.

Lin, Bard and Anderson (1992) conducted a study on the development of MSR in chimpanzees from the Yerkes Centre, Emory University, using the mark test. We tested nine chimpanzees ranging in age from 19 to 61 months (four 2-year-olds, two 2.5-year-olds, four 4-year-olds and two 5-year-old chimpanzees), giving them three sessions with the mirror: baseline, and two sessions when the chimpanzee was marked with children's make-up. We let the chimpanzees remain in their familiar social groups, and we applied the make-up covertly (pretending to wipe their faces: we did not use anaesthesia). We found that a pattern of responses to the mirror emerged in the chimpanzees, from social responses, through contingency testing, to self-directed behaviour, following a similar development as found in human infants. Self-recognition was found in both 5-year-olds, in three of the four 4-year-olds, and in both 2.5-year-olds, but not in either of the 2-year-olds. Thus, we concluded that chimpanzees pass the mark test at a slightly older age than do humans, at 28 months compared with humans at 24 months (Lin *et al.*, 1992).

From 1992 to 1995, we conducted follow-ups to this initial study, in order to specify more closely the age at which chimpanzee infants pass MSR tests. We documented an important behaviour involving exploration of self-generated movement, called contingent behaviours. Contingent behaviours are important because they demonstrate the growing appreciation that the movement reflected in the mirror corresponds to the movement of the self. The chimpanzee would move while intently watching the movement in the mirror image. Occasionally, the chimpanzees would move in a strange way, either abbreviated or distorted, sometimes looking back and forth from their own moving limb to the mirror image of their moving limb, providing behavioural evidence that there was explicit notice of and testing of the contingency. Contingent behaviours occurred in all the chimpanzees that we tested, as young as 18 months. In human infants, contingent behaviours occur between 9 and 18 months.

Contingent behaviors occurred in chimpanzees from the youngest ages. In contrast, the next most complex behaviour, using the mirror image to direct behaviour to the self, mirror-guided, self-directed behaviour, occurred at 24 months. Some argue that this ability is evidence that the subjects already *know* that it is the self in the mirror, since the mirror image is used to direct behaviour to the self (e.g. looking in the mirror and picking food out of the teeth – not trying to pick food out from the mirror image). Most of the chimpanzees also exhibited self-directed behaviours. But chimpanzees at 24 months who exhibited mirror-guided, self-directed behaviour did not pass the mark test. So, it appears that this is a separate stage in the development of MSR.

Finally, the definitive sign of mirror self-recognition is touching the mark while guided by the mirror. Here we found indices of self-recognition in individuals of 28 months and older. The 24-month-olds did not show the expected pattern of social responses to the mirror image, which decreased over sessions, but did show self-directed responses that increased over sessions, albeit only at a low level in the final session. Based on the reasoning used by Gallup (1970), we concluded that chimpanzees 'passed' the mark test between the ages of 28 and 30 months (Bard et al., 2006; Lin et al., 1992), and that this is slightly later than 18 to 24 months, when human infants pass the rouge test (Amsterdam, 1972, but see caveats in Bard et al., 2006).

Initial critiques of our comparative development studies concerned how the chimpanzee 'discovers' the mark (see Mitchell, 1993 for extended discussion of inductive and deductive reasoning concerning mirror self-recognition). One argument is that, regardless of how the mark is discovered, if the chimpanzee uses the reflection in the mirror to guide its movements to the mark on its own face, it is properly considered mirror-guided mark-directed behaviour, the behavioural index of mirror self-recognition. This might be considered similar to the following type of everyday event: someone tells you that you have something on your face, you wipe it, and then look in the mirror, and while looking at your reflection, you wipe the remainder of the mark off. Is this an invalid test of your ability to 'know' that it is your self reflected in the mirror because you have both been told that you have a mark and have already touched the mark? A second argument is that these procedures cannot *cause* chimpanzees to exhibit mirror self-recognition since all subjects were exposed to the same set of procedures but only some subjects exhibited mirror self-recognition. This raises the question of whether one can teach a chimpanzee infant to be self-aware, much like Skinner's pigeons were taught to peck at the blue dot (Epstein, Lanza and Skinner, 1981).

In our opinion, the reviews highlighted the growing rift between developmental and comparative studies, with ever increasing controls in the latter and more reasonable and naturalistic procedures allowed for testing children in the former. The good news is that these reviews were the impetus for a follow-up study with human infants, in particular on the intriguing idea of 'false positives': Can MSR be enhanced? What is being assessed in the mirror-and-mark test? How important is maternal scaffolding for the development of self-awareness? These questions are considered at length by Bard *et al.* (2006).

So, to review our assessment of what is important across MSR methods – how the mark is discovered is not important, whereas the target behaviour, consisting of mirror-guided and mark-directed behaviours, is important. If we use the same criteria and similar procedures to study mirror self-recognition in human and chimpanzee infants, we find similar developmental patterns in behaviours leading to MSR (Bard *et al.*, 2006). In fact, we find very similar ages at which they 'pass' the mark-and-mirror test. It is important to use similar methods, based on solid rationale, when making comparisons across species, because we want to assess species difference without the confound of methodological differences. By studying MSR in different groups and different species, we can learn something about the flexibility in cognition, in humans and other animals. By adding a developmental perspective to our comparative studies, we can learn about necessary and sufficient conditions for the emergence of self-awareness.

The comparative developmental approach has great value in furthering our knowledge of evolution, of developmental processes and of comparative psychology. By making multiple comparisons across primate species, one can delineate likely evolutionary origins for self-awareness. By studying the development of self-awareness across multiple primate groups, we can delineate necessary and sufficient conditions for the emergence of self-awareness. One value of conducting comparative studies includes gaining a better understanding of the evolutionary process, of shared characteristics such as self-awareness as well as those that are unique to each species. Shared characteristics are important as they provide some information as to what our ancestors were like. By taking a truly developmental comparative perspective while studying non-human species, we increase our understanding of the evolutionary foundations for plasticity and flexibility in development.

A link between experimenting with contingency and MSR?

The role of contingency detection and contingency experimentation is intriguing as an aspect of developing self-awareness. Evidence exists that experimenting or testing contingency is found across self-recognizing species and across human cultures. Keller, Kartner, Borke, Yvosi and Kleis (2005) have linked early socialization in contingency responsiveness with early development of self-awareness. Keller suggests that cultural values supporting the experience of contingency in early face-to-face interactions may relate to the early onset of mirror self-recognition in German compared to Nso infants (Keller *et al.*, 2005).

The Papouseks first remarked on the detection of contingency responses when 5–7-month-old infants were placed in front of mirrors (Papousek and Papousek, 1974). Recently, rhesus macaques have been shown to recognize 'being imitated', as they preferred to view exact imitation of their actions on objects over actions that were merely contingent but not matching (Paukner *et al.*, 2005). It appears that contingency detection is a required element for emergence of self-awareness, but it is not sufficient. All the great apes and human infants from different cultures engage in contingency testing (see also Custance, Whiten and Bard, 1995). They experiment with the contingency, not only looking back and forth between their own action and the actions reflected in the mirror, but moving in strange ways that appear to be testing the one-to-one correspondence between their own movements and the visualized movements of the mirror image.

A link between intersubjectivity and MSR?

Primary intersubjectivity, or mutual engagement, develops through social and emotional communicative exchanges (Trevarthen, 1979; Trevarthen and Hubley, 1978). Primary intersubjectivity has been demonstrated in young chimpanzees (newborns, Bard, 2007, and 3-month-olds, Bard *et al.*, 2005). Chimpanzees, 7–15 days of age, imitated tongue protrusion, mouth opening, and a series of three mouth actions including tongue clicks, with a suggestion of better performance in an interactive paradigm compared with a structured one. Neonatal imitation, in chimpanzees, as in humans, may be the foundation for communication.

When chimpanzees were slightly older, at 3 months of age, I was struck with their ability to engage with human partners in emotionally meaningful and face-to-face interactions, that is, to engage in social games (the importance of social-emotional engagement is further explored in Bard, 2005).

Primary intersubjectivity, moreover, is the foundation for secondary intersubjectivity, evident in two behavioural forms, intentional communication and social referencing. Leavens, Hopkins and Bard (2005) investigated the occurrence of intentional communication in chimpanzees as indicated by their production of pointing. Russell, Adamson and Bard (1997) provide evidence that young chimpanzees, between 1 and 3 years of age, engage in social referencing. Using the classic social referencing paradigm, we found that young chimpanzees seek information about novel objects from their caregivers through referential glances. Moreover their behaviour was influenced by the emotional message that they received. Negative messages, distress or fear displayed by the caretaker increased the chimpanzee's avoidance of the object. In contrast, positive messages from the caregiver about the object, such as a chimpanzee play-face or a human smile, positively influenced their visual attention towards the object. Chimpanzees looked longer at toys when given a positive emotional message. So, I suggested that intersubjectivity is common to the great ape–human lineage, and propose that it is the basis for communication – not language per se (e.g. Bard, 1998, 2007). Intersubjectivity appears to be independent of language, as it occurs from birth and becomes elaborated in secondary intersubjectivity in contexts that typically do not involve language (often occurring in human infants prior to language). In human infants, these abilities in secondary intersubjectivity develop at about the same time that human infants begin to explore their own reflection in the mirror, that is, around 12 months of age.

Something special about social cognition?

The link between social cognition and higher intelligence has been explored by primatologists for decades. Parker (1998) extends discussions of the evolutionary basis of mirror self-recognition into the evolutionary basis of self-awareness, by pursuing a link with self-conscious emotions. She suggests that the cognitive foundations for self-awareness were an adaptation for assessing self-characteristics relative to those of conspecifics, linked to ritualized food sharing that serves to motivate and to enforce social reciprocity. Many researchers have proposed a link between MSR and empathy (e.g. Bischoff-Kohler, 1991; de Waal, Dindo, Freeman and Hall, 2005; Gallup, 1970; Parker, 1998; Parker and

Milbraith, 1994). Self-awareness is linked with being able to take the perspective of others (Parker and Milbraith, 1994) and, of course, to theory of mind (see for example Gergely, 1994).

Something special about self-awareness?

There appears to be something special about understanding that the mirror reflects the self. Younger infants and monkeys come easily to the understanding that the mirror reflects objects in the world, yet when the mirror reflects the self, young infants and monkeys do not understand the self. Monkeys may prefer the contingency inherent in mirror images (a possible explanation for why cebus monkeys do not react the same to a mirror image as they do to a complete stranger: deWaal et al., 2005), and prefer to look at someone who is not only contingent but also copying their own actions (Paukner et al., 2005). Human infants, from 9 months, also prefer to look at someone who imitates contingently their actions on objects (Agnetta and Rochat, 2004). Chimpanzees also recognize when they are being imitated (Nielsen, Collier-Baker, Davis and Suddendorf, 2005).

But the species divide appears to occur in the capacity to ascertain whether the contingency is real, by testing or experimenting with contingency, which apes (e.g. Boysen, Bryan and Shreyer, 1994; Gallup, 1970; Menzel, Savage-Rumbaugh and Lawson, 1985) and humans do (e.g. Agnetta and Rochat, 2004; Gergely, 1994), but monkeys do not (Paukner et al., 2005). Old World and New World monkeys are able to understand the reflected nature of objects, and are able to recognize 'being imitated', but monkeys do not understand the reflected nature of the self and do not test contingencies of self-movement. The aspect of noticing contingency appears to underpin the understanding of 'the refection of self as other' and understanding 'the reflection of objects as real objects'. Human and chimpanzee infants engage in contingency testing: humans in attempting to localize the mark, and chimpanzees in monitoring the one-to-one correspondence between their actions and the actions of the mirror image. This aspect of contingency knowledge may underpin the development of understanding 'the reflection of the self as self'. The comparative perspective, thus, suggests that self-awareness evolved between 12 and 20 million years ago when humans and the great apes diverged from the Old World monkey lineage (e.g. Itakura, 2001; Parker, Mitchell and Boccia, 1994).

An additional link appears to exist between MSR and symbolization. It may not be a coincidence that human infants pass the mark test at the same time that they use pronouns to refer to the self. Apes and humans share the capacity to use symbols and share the capacity for self-awareness. The mark-and-mirror test provides a behavioural index of an ability to hold simultaneously two views of the self: when the self who is acting can become represented in the mirror, then mirror-guided touching of the self can occur (see Bard *et al.*, 2006 and Suddendorf and Whiten, 2001 for further discussions).

Summary

By considering the development of self-recognition in humans and chimpanzees, we've elaborated on how understanding the reflective properties of a mirror is not sufficient to explain understanding when the mirror reflects the self. We suggest that understanding of the reflected self emerges with understanding of contingency, which develops into contingency testing or experimentation with contingency. This process, the height of sensorimotor intelligence, allows humans and apes to discover that the mirror reflects the self. However, the evolutionary roots of self-awareness probably had little to do with mirrors or other reflective surfaces, but instead had to do with special qualities such as secondary intersubjectivity needed in social interactions. The developmental comparative perspective highlights the two-stage difference between understanding reflections of self as other (or as object) and understanding reflections of self as self.

REFERENCES

Agnetta, B. and Rochat, P. (2004). Imitative games by 9-, 14-, and 18-month-old infants. *Infancy*, 6, 1–36.

Amsterdam, B. (1972). Mirror self-image reactions before age two. *Developmental Psychobiology*, 5, 297–305.

Anderson, J. R. and Gallup, G. G., Jr (1999). Self-recognition in nonhuman primates: past and future challenges. In M. Haug and R. E. Whalen (eds.), *Animal models of human emotion and cognition* (pp. 175–94). Washington, DC: American Psychological Association.

Asendorpf, J. B. (2002). Self-awareness, other-awareness, and secondary representation. In A. N. Meltzoff and W. Prinz (eds.), *The imitative mind: development, evolution, and brain bases* (pp. 63–73). Cambridge: Cambridge University Press.

Asendorpf, J. B. and Baudonniere, P. M. (1993). Self-awareness and other-awareness: mirror self-recognition and synchronic imitation among unfamiliar peers. *Developmental Psychology*, 29, 88–95.

Bard, K. A. (1998). Social-experiential contributions to imitation and emotion in chimpanzees. In S. Braten (ed.), *Intersubjective communication and emotion in*

early ontogeny: a source book (pp. 208–27). Cambridge: Cambridge University Press.
  (2005). Emotions in chimpanzee infants: the value of a comparative developmental approach to understand the evolutionary bases of emotion. In J. Nadel and D. Muir (eds.), *Emotional development* (pp. 31–60). Oxford: Oxford University Press.
  (2007). Neonatal imitation in chimpanzees (*Pan troglodytes*) tested with two paradigms. *Animal Cognition*, 10, 233–42.
Bard, K. A., Myowa-Yamakoshi, M., Tomonaga, M., Tanaka, M., Costall, A. and Matsuzawa, T. (2005). Group differences in the mutual gaze of chimpanzees (*Pan troglodytes*). *Developmental Psychology*, 41, 616–24.
Bard, K. A., Todd, B. K., Bernier, C., Love, J. and Leavens, D. A. (2006). Self-awareness in human and chimpanzee infants: what is measured and what is meant by the mirror-and-mark test? *Infancy*, 9, 191–219.
Barth, J., Povinelli, D. J. and Cant, J. G. H. (2004). Bodily origins of SELF. In D. R. Beike, J. M. Lampinen and D. A. Behrend (eds.), *The self and memory* (pp. 11–43). New York: Psychology Press.
Bekoff, M. (2002). Animal reflections. *Nature*, 419, 255.
Bertenthal, B. I. and Fischer, K. W. (1978). Development of self-recognition in the infant. *Developmental Psychology*, 14, 44–50.
Bigelow, A. E. (1981). The correspondence between self- and image movement as a cue to self-recognition for young children. *Journal of Genetic Psycholology*, 139, 11–26.
Bischof-Köhler, D. (1991).The development of empathy in infants. In M. E. Lamb and H. Keller (eds.), *Infant development: perspectives from German-speaking countries* (pp. 245–73). Hillsdale, NJ: Erlbaum.
Boysen, S. T., Bryan, K. M. and Shreyer, T. A. (1994). Shadows and mirrors: alternative avenues to the development of self-recognition in chimpanzees. In S. T. Parker, R. W. Mitchell and M. L. Boccia (eds.), *Self-awareness in animals and humans: developmental perspectives* (pp. 227–40). New York: Cambridge University Press.
Brooks-Gunn, J. and Lewis, M. (1984). The development of early visual self-recognition. *Developmental Review*, 4, 215–39.
Chapman, M. (1987). A longitudinal study of cognitive representation in symbolic play, self-recognition, and object permanence during the second year. *International Journal of Behavioral Development*, 10, 151–70.
Courage, M. L., Edison, S. C. and Howe, M. L. (2004). Variability in the early development of visual self-recognition. *Infant Behaviour and Development*, 27, 509–32.
Custance, D., Whiten, A. and Bard, K. A. (1995). Can young chimpanzees (*Pan troglodytes*) imitate arbitrary actions? Hayes and Hayes (1952) revisited. *Behaviour*, 132, 837–59.
DeSilva, J. and Lesnik, J. (2006). Chimpanzee neonatal brain size: implications for brain growth in *Homo erectus*. *Journal of Human Evolution*, 51, 207–12.
de Waal, F. B. M., Dindo, M., Freeman, C. A. and Hall, M. J. (2005). The monkey in the mirror: hardly a stranger. *Proceedings of the National Academy of Science*, 102, 11,140–7.

Dunbar, R. (2003). The social brain: mind, language, and society in evolutionary perspective. *Annual Review of Anthropology*, 33, 163–81.
Epstein, R., Lansa, R. P. and Skinner, B. F. (1981). 'Self-awareness' in the pigeon. *Science*, 212, 695–6.
Gallup, G. G., Jr (1970). Chimpanzees: self-recognition. *Science*, 167, 86–7.
   (1977). Self-recognition in primates: a comparative approach to the bidirectional properties of consciousness. *American Psychologist*, 32, 329–38.
   (1982). Self-awareness and the emergence of mind in primates. *American Journal of Primatology*, 2, 237–48.
Gergely, G. (1994). From self-recognition to theory of mind. In S. T. Parker, R. W. Mitchell and M. L. Boccia (eds.), *Self-awareness in animals and humans: developmental perspectives* (pp. 51–60). New York: Cambridge University Press.
Gibson, K. R. (2007). Epigenesis, mental construction, and the emergence of language and toolmaking. In D. A. Washburn (ed.), *Primate perspectives on behaviour and cognition* (pp. 269–78). Washington, DC: American Psychological Association.
Gottlieb, G. (2007). Probabilistic epigenesis. *Developmental Science*, 10, 1–11.
Harel, J., Eshel, Y., Ganor, O. and Scher, A. (2002). Antecedents of mirror self-recognition of toddlers: emotional availability, birth order and gender. *Infant Mental Health Journal*, 23, 293–309.
Hauser, M. D., Miller, C. T., Liu, K. and Gupta, R. (2001). Cotton-top tamarins (*Saguinus oedipus*) fail to show mirror-guided self-exploration. *American Journal of Primatology*, 53, 131–7.
Humphrey, N. K. (1976). The social function of intellect. In P. P. Bates and R. A. Hinde (eds.), *Growing points in ethology*. Cambridge: Cambridge University Press.
Hyatt, C. W. and Hopkins, W. D. (1994). Self-awareness in bonobos and chimpanzees: a comparative perspective. In S. Parker, R. W. Mitchell and M. Boccia (eds.), *Self-awareness in animals and humans: developmental perspectives* (pp. 248–53). New York: Cambridge University Press.
Inoue-Nakamura, N. (2001). Mirror self-recognition in primates: an ontogenetic and a phylogenetic approach. In T. Matsuzawa (ed.), *Primate origins of human cognition and behaviour* (pp. 297–312). New York: Springer.
Itakura, S. (2001). The level of self-knowledge in nonhuman primates: from the perspective of comparative cognitive science. In T. Matsuzawa (ed.), *Primate origins of human cognition and behaviour* (pp. 313–29). New York: Springer.
Jablonka, E. and Lamb, M. (2007). Evolution in four dimensions. *Behavioral and Brain Sciences*, 30, 353–65.
Johnson, D. B. (1982). Self-recognition in infants. *Infant Behaviour and Development*, 6, 211–22.
Jolly, A. (1966). Lemur social behaviour and primate intelligence. *Science*, 153, 501–6.
Karmiloff-Smith, A. (2007). Atypical epigenesis. *Developmental Science*, 10, 84–8.
Keller, H., Kartner, J., Borke, J., Yovsi, R. and Kleis, A. (2005). Parenting styles and the development of the categorical self: a longitudinal study on

mirror self-recognition in Cameroonian Nso and German families. *International Journal of Behavioral Development*, 29, 496–504.
Leavens, D. A., Hopkins, W. D. and Bard, K. A. (2005). Understanding the point of chimpanzee pointing: epigenesis and ecological validity. *Current Directions in Psychological Science*, 14, 185–9.
  (in press). The heterochronic origins of explicit reference. In J. Zlatev, T. P. Racine, C. Sinha and E. Itkonen (eds.), *The shared mind: perspectives on intersubjectivity*. Amsterdam: John Benjamins.
Lewis, M. and Brooks-Gunn, J. (1979). *Social cognition and the acquisition of self*. New York: Plenum Press.
Lewis, M., Brooks Gunn, J. and Jaskir, J. (1985). Individual differences in visual self-recognition as a function of mother–infant attachment relationship. *Developmental Psychology*, 21, 1181–7.
Lewis, M., Sullivan, M. W., Stanger, C. and Weiss, M. (1989). Self development and self-conscious emotions. *Child Development*, 60, 146–56.
Lin, A. C., Bard, K. A. and Anderson, J. R. (1992). Development of self-recognition in chimpanzees (*Pan troglodytes*). *Journal of Comparative Psychology*, 106, 120–7.
Matsuzawa, T. (2007). Comparative cognitive development. *Developmental Science*, 10, 97–103.
Menzel, E., Savage-Rumbaugh, E. S. and Lawson, J. (1985). Chimpanzee (*Pan troglodytes*) spatial problem solving with the use of mirrors and televised equivalents of mirrors. *Journal of Comparative Psychology*, 99, 211–17.
Miles, H. L. W. (1994). Me Chantek: the development of self-awareness in a signing orangutan. In S. T. Parker, R. W. Mitchell and M. Boccia (eds.), *Self-awareness in animals and humans: developmental perspectives* (pp. 254–72). New York: Cambridge University Press.
Mitchell, R. (1993). Mental models of mirror-self-recognition: two theories. *New Ideas in Psychology*, 11, 295–325.
Nielsen, M., Collier-Baker, E., Davis, J. and Suddendorf, T. (2005). Imitation recognition in a captive chimpanzee (*Pan troglodytes*). *Animal Cognition*, 8, 31–6.
Papousek, H. and Papousek, M. (1974). Mirror image and self-recognition in young human infants: I. A new method of experimental analysis. *Developmental Psychobiology*, 7, 149–57.
Parker, S. T. (1998). A social selection model for the evolution and adapative significance of self-conscious emotions. In M. D. Ferrari and R. J. Sternberg (eds.), *Self-awareness: its nature and development* (pp. 108–34). New York: Guilford Press.
Parker, S. T. and Milbraith, C. (1994). Contributions of imitation and role-playing games to the construction of self in primates. In S. T. Parker, R. W. Mitchell and M. Boccia (eds.), *Self-awareness in animals and humans: developmental perspectives* (pp. 108–28). New York: Cambridge University Press.
Parker, S. T., Mitchell, R. W. and Boccia, M. (eds.) (1994). *Self-awareness in animals and humans: developmental perspectives*. New York: Cambridge University Press.

Patterson, P. and Cohn, R. H. (1994). Self-recognition and self-awareness in lowland gorillas. In S. T. Parker, R. Mitchell and M. Boccia (eds.), *Self-awareness in animals and humans: developmental perspectives* (pp. 273–90). New York: Cambridge University Press.

Paukner, A., Anderson, J. R., Borelli, E., Visalberghi, E. and Ferrari, P. F. (2005). Macaques (*Macaca nemestrina*) recognize when they are being imitated. *Biological Letters*, 1, 219–22.

Pendergrast, M. (2003). *Mirror, mirror: a history of the human love affair with reflection.* New York: Basic Books.

Piaget, J. (1954). *The construction of reality in the child.* New York: Basic Books.

Posada, S. and Colell, M. (2005). Mirror responses in a group of *Miopithecus talapoin*. *Primates*, 46, 165–72.

Povinelli, D. J., Rulf, A. B., Landau, K. R. and Bierschwale, D. T. (1993). Self-recognition in chimpanzees (*Pan troglodytes*): distribution, ontogeny, and patterns of emergence. *Journal of Comparative Psychology*, 107, 347–72.

Reddy, V. (2000). Coyness in early infancy. *Developmental Science*, 3, 186–92.

Robert, S. (1986). Ontogeny of mirror behaviour in two species of great apes. *American Journal of Primatology*, 10, 109–17.

Robinson, J. A., Connell, S., McKenzie, B. E. and Day, R. H. (1990). Do infants use their own images to locate objects reflected in a mirror? *Child Devopment*, 61, 1558–68.

Russell, C. L., Bard, K.A. and Adamson, L. B. (1997). Social referencing by young chimpanzees (*Pan troglodytes*). *Journal of Comparative Psychology*, 111, 185–93.

Russon, A. (2004). Evolutionary reconstructions of great ape intelligence. In A. Russon and D. Begun (eds.), *The evolution of thought: evolutionary origins of great ape intelligence* (pp. 1–14). Cambridge: Cambridge University Press.

Russon, A. and Bard, K. A. (1996). Exploring the minds of the great apes: issues and controversies. In A. Russon, K. Bard and S. T. Parker (eds.), *Reaching into thought: the minds of the great apes* (pp. 1–20). New York: Cambridge University Press.

Schulman, A. H. and Kaplowitz, C. (1977). Mirror-image response during the first two years of life. *Developmental Psychobiology*, 10, 133–42.

Suarez, S. D. and Gallup, G. G., Jr (1981). Self-recognition in chimpanzees and orangutans, but not gorillas. *Journal of Human Evolution*, 10, 175–88.

Suddendorf, T. and Whiten, A. (2001). Mental evolution and development: evidence for secondary representation in children, great apes, and other animals. *Psychological Bulletin*, 127, 629–50.

Swartz, K. B. (1997). What is mirror self-recognition in nonhuman primates, and what is it not? In J. G. Snodgrass and R. L. Thompson (eds.), *The self across psychology: self-recognition, self awareness, and the self concept* (pp. 65–71). New York: New York Academy of Sciences.

Tomasello, M., Savage-Rumbaugh, E. S. and Kruger, A. C. (1993). Imitative learning of actions on objects by children, chimpanzees, and enculturated chimpanzees. *Child Development*, 64, 1688–1705.

Trevarthen, C. (1979). Communication and cooperation in early infancy. In M. Bullowa (ed.), *Before speech: the beginning of interpersonal communication* (pp. 121–347). New York: Cambridge University Press.

Trevarthen, C. and Hubley, P. (1978). Secondary intersubjectivity: confidence, confiding, and acts of meaning in the first year of life. In A. Lock (ed.), *Action, gesture, symbol: the emergence of language* (pp. 183–229). New York: Academic Press.

Westergaard, G. C. and Hyatt, C. W. (1994). The responses of bonobos (*Pan paniscus*) to their mirror images: evidence of self-recognition. *Human Evolution*, 9, 273–9.

3 Drawing production, drawing re-experience and drawing re-cognition

Josephine Ross

Referring to the literature concerned with recognition of drawings, Ross suggests that self-drawings may be seen as advanced forms of the mirror test of self-recognition, and, as such, are likely to reveal the content of self-knowledge. She explores this proposition through two instructive experiments carried out with children aged 3 to 9 years. The first study establishes that the quality of self-drawings as well as the ability to recognize one's own drawings are related to self-awareness as measured by mirror recognition. The second experiment offers a deeper understanding of these relationships and shows that drawing recognition constitutes an act of self-recognition in itself. In this experiment, besides producing drawings, children were asked either to trace over their peers' drawings with a pencil (a drawing task involving a certain level of self-engagement) or to examine them visually while also hearing a verbal description. Whereas traced drawings were recognized as such after sizeable delays, those only visually examined were not. Ross concludes that 'children's retrospective analysis of their own drawings has the potential to reveal their self-awareness'.

THE MAXIM 'Children draw what they know, rather than what they see' is a formative and recurring topic in the study of children's art. This characteristic, implying a communicative or expressive function for children's drawings, has led many to reason that early artwork can be used to study cognitive development. Study of the psychology of children's drawings is now in its second century (key works include: Cox, 1992; Eng, 1931; Freeman, 1980; Goodnow, 1977; Harris, 1963; Kellogg, 1970; Kerschensteiner, 1905; Lange-Küttner and Thomas, 1995; Luquet, 1913; Ricci, 1894). A substantial body of work has concerned the expression – or 'projection' – of emotions in children's art (for a summary, see Burkitt, Barrett and Davis, 2003). The intellectual correlates of drawing ability have also been repeatedly examined (Bensur, Eliot and Hedge,

1997; Harris, 1963). However, the bulk of literature regarding children's drawings has focused on the ontogenetic development of drawings as graphic representations.

Common to the developmental accounts of drawing advanced by modern theorists (Cox, 1992; Freeman, 1980; Goodnow, 1977; Kellogg, 1970) and their predecessors (Eng, 1931; Kerschensteiner, 1905; Luquet, 1913) is the proposal that children's drawings develop in a conventional way, building towards the representation of perceptual reality. Kerschensteiner (1905) offered the first detailed stage theory of drawing based on a massive sample of almost 300,000 drawings produced by school children. The schematic development of drawing was further qualified by Luquet (1913) and Eng (1931) following the longitudinal study of individual children. Each of these theorists emphasized the child's path to attainment of conventional drawing skills, advancing graphic expression from an exercise in motor skill to a representative product. Later, Kellogg (1970) proposed that young children's drawings begin with pre-representational graphic elements, reflecting a common perceptual experience of reality (i.e. geometric shapes), which are gradually modified until representational drawings are produced (e.g. circles for heads). Freeman (1980) focuses on children's acquisition of specific techniques used to plan drawing performance and overcome misleading perceptual cues (e.g. the representation of occluded objects). Similarly, Goodnow (1977) and Cox (1992) give comprehensive descriptions of the sequence of veridical errors (e.g. missing or wrongly assembled features) and achievements (e.g. the grasp of proportion and perspective) which typify children's drawings at each developmental stage.

As noted, the developmental psychologist's focus on perceptual reality may be motivated by the view that representations of reality express knowledge, i.e. what the child knows about the world. However, although considerable consensus has been reached regarding the ontogenetic development of objective reality (the outside world) in terms of its appearance on paper, qualification of what this appearance means in terms of the child's subjective reality (the inside world) has been less explicit. Drawing topics (e.g. family drawings) and devices (e.g. relative size, colour) have historically been considered expressive of emotional state (Burkitt, Barrett and Davis, 2003). However, less attention has been given to the idea that drawing schemes may be expressive of children's cognition regarding the drawing topic. Perhaps the most striking evidence in support of this statement is the observation that only a handful of experiments in the history of children's drawings research have employed children, as opposed to adults, in the evaluation of their own and/or other children's drawings.

An early study consulting children about their drawings was carried out by White and Johnson (1930). They reported that children under the age of 5 were more successful in naming the subject matter of drawings produced by their peers than interpreting the paintings of masters such as Monet and Picasso. Stacey and Ross (1975) later extended this result, demonstrating that young children are capable of making cognitive evaluations of drawing ownership. In this study, 5- to 7-year-old children were asked to recognize their own drawing from a set of twenty similar drawings produced by their peers. Of the sample, 73 per cent were able to recognize a drawing that they had produced one week earlier, and 60 per cent were able to recognize a drawing produced five weeks before. This rate of success is notably high given the high number of matched topic distracter drawings present at the recognition stage.

Nolan, Kagan and colleagues (1980a, 1980b, 1981) ran a series of studies which confirm that children are capable of recognizing their own products under challenging conditions. In their studies, young children were asked to identify four drawings that they had made a week earlier of a bird, a flower, a man and a tree. During the test phase, each drawing was presented to the child together with three foils produced from the original and altered to vary from it in small aspects of size, detail and perspective. Despite high levels of similarity between distracter drawings and their original product, children as young as $4\frac{1}{2}$ years of age were typically able to identify over a third of their own drawings (Nolan, Adams and Kagan, 1980a). Nolan and Kagan (1980b, 1981) reported equivalent success rates for children aged between $2\frac{1}{2}$ and $3\frac{1}{2}$ years. These success rates are marginally higher than the quarter of correct identifications predicted by chance.

Interestingly, Nolan and Kagan (1981) found children's memories for others' drawings to be similarly impressive. When children were asked to recognize peers' drawings which they had been shown, encouraged to label and memorize one week earlier, they were again successful on over a third of occasions. However, Nolan and Kagan (1981) found no correlation between the recognition tasks for own versus others' drawings. Further, the correlations between recognition success and age, and recognition success and cognitive ability (as measured by the 1975 Winett Preschool Inventory) that were present for own drawings, were not apparent for performance regarding others' drawings. The authors took this to suggest that recognition of own and others' products may rely on cognitively different processes.

Gross and Hayne (1999) have provided the most recent evidence concerning children's memory for drawings, reporting that children are capable of recalling drawing episodes following substantial delays. They asked 3- to 6-year-old children to draw and describe three pictures depicting what happens during a birthday party, a trip to the park and a visit to the supermarket. Later, the children were asked to recognize their birthday party drawing when placed alongside two similar drawings produced by their peers. Using this paradigm, Gross and Hayne (1999, Experiment 1A) found that 60 per cent of 3- to 4-year-olds were able to recognize and correctly interpret aspects of their drawings up to three months after drawing production; 5- to 6-year-old children performed at ceiling in recognizing their birthday party drawings up to six months following production. Moreover, Gross and Hayne (1999, Experiment 1B) subsequently demonstrated that the vast majority (90 per cent) of 5- to 6-year-old children were capable of correctly identifying a drawing of a class-outing when presented with two similar distracters made one year before.

In an effort to determine the importance of drawing production for later recognition, Gross and Hayne (1999, Experiment 2) ran a further experiment comparing children's memory for their own versus a peer's drawing of an emotional event (a time when they were happy, sad or scared). After making their own drawing, children were shown and asked to listen to a description of another child's drawing. To test for recognition, these drawings were presented separately after a delay of three months alongside two similar 'distracter' drawings. Interestingly, although the majority (70 per cent) of 3- to 6-year-old children were capable of identifying and qualifying their peers' drawing, children were significantly more accurate in identifying their own drawings (90 per cent recognition rate).

As implied by the motivation of Gross and Hayne's (1999) second experiment, the finding that recognition of others' drawings differs from recognition of own drawings is intuitively viable. When asking children to recognize their own drawings one is asking them to recognize a self-production. Freeman (1972) notes that when producing representative drawings children are required to hold in mind conceptual and perceptual components of the chosen topic, and physically to translate perceptual parts into coordinated graphic schema. By this account drawing production requires cognitive reasoning (in terms of drawing topic, and in terms of the placement of constituent parts relative to other drawing features on the page) in addition to visual input and motor coordination. Freeman's (1972) analysis makes clear that drawing production implies a level of self-engagement – both physical and cognitive – unparalleled by relatively passive engagement with another's finished product.

In addition to the high level of self-involvement inherent in producing a drawing, it is possible that the finished product is self-reflective in terms of style. Van Sommers (1984) offers extensive documentation of idiosyncrasy and conservatism (or originality and consistency) in the artwork of young children. The presence of style in children's artwork has also been demonstrated empirically; adult judges are apparently able to sort sets of drawings provided by children between the ages of 3 and 5 years according to artist (Hartley et al., 1982). Nolan, Adams and Kagan (1980a) note that appreciation of style would suggest a well-articulated conception of subtle aspects of an artist's products. When applied to one's own products, this would entail holding a relatively high-order conceptualization of the self. In support of this mechanism of recognition, the data of Nolan and colleagues (1980a, 1980b, 1981) suggest that young children are sensitive to small changes in the way particular topics are represented.

What recognition studies make clear is that drawings are open to claims of ownership. Whether claims of ownership are based on recognition of style or on memory of the drawing's creation, they are ultimately based on a link between the drawing and the self. For this reason, drawing recognition studies have the potential to reveal recursive self-awareness. Moreover, it seems reasonable that certain drawing episodes are in themselves capable of revealing aspects of self-awareness. For example, the link between drawing production and the self is particularly clear on occasions where the child is both the producer and the topic of the drawing. Self-portraits may be regarded as advanced forms of the mirror test of self-recognition, involving both the recognition of one's external self and the internal maintenance of that image. Although successful graphic representation of the self-image may vary depending on motor ability, a necessary requirement for embarking on such a task is a concept of the self. This reasoning suggests that certain features of self-drawings – for example, levels of differentiation and detail – are likely to reveal the content and/or extent of self-knowledge. In support of this argument, there is evidence for a self-referent bias in figure drawing. Research suggests that between 5 and 7 years of age children consistently include more body features in self-drawings than in drawings of other, presumably less familiar, people (Gellert, 1968).

Empirical substantiation of a link between self-drawings, drawing recognition and self-awareness may add weight to the historical assumption that drawings offer a route to the child's conceptual (as opposed to perceptual) reality. Following this reasoning, I carried out two studies designed to investigate the impact of the self in the production and recognition of drawings. The methodology and results of each study are described below.

The impact of the self in the production and recognition of drawings

Study One: Exploring the relationship between self-drawings and self-awareness

The first study aimed to test the hypothesized link between children's self-drawings and their developing self-awareness. Children ranging in age from 3 to 9 years produced a self-drawing, and, to allow comparison between representations of self and other, a drawing of a same-sex peer. Drawings were scored for quality according to established guidelines provided by the Goodenough-Harris Drawing Test manual (Harris, 1963). This manual describes how drawings accumulate credit based on levels of feature inclusion, realism and motor skill. To provide empirical support for a relationship between the quality of self-representation and self-awareness, two additional measures of 'self-recognition' were included. Firstly, children were required to discriminate their own figure drawings from four distracter figure drawings after a delay of two weeks. Secondly, children's reactions to the introduction of a mirror following completion of a verbal task were observed. Mirror self-recognition is currently the only implicit developmental measure of self-awareness routinely employed (see Bard, chapter 2 in this volume). By the age of 2, children are able to recognize their image, as evidenced by their reaching towards a surreptitiously introduced head-mark on the introduction of a mirror (Amsterdam, 1972). However, behavioural reactions to the self-reflective properties of the mirror also have the potential to elucidate self-awareness later in development.

An intriguing tool for formalizing the antecedents and consequents of self-reflection is provided by Duval and Wicklund's (1972) theory of self-awareness. Duval and Wicklund (1972) dichotomize self-awareness according to attentional focus. Attentiveness to feedback from the environment is regarded as 'subjective' self-awareness, whilst attentiveness to one's self as an object in that environment is categorized as 'objective' self-awareness (OSA). Objective focus upon the self can be induced by stimuli highlighting the self, such as a salient audience or mirror image. The major consequence (and evolutionary advantage) of objective self-reflection is thought to be self-evaluation, which leads to appropriate behavioural regulation. Dependent on situational factors, Duval and Wicklund (1972) predict that self-evaluation will usually result in (a) behavioural adjustment to become consistent with internalized or externalized standards, and/or (b) withdrawal from the evaluation-inducing situation. In this way, cognitive and affective equilibrium regarding the self is maintained. Crucially, Duval and Wicklund's (1972) behavioural predictions can be used to develop implicit measurement of self-awareness beyond that indexed by early mirror self-recognition.

Originally it was assumed that OSA would be a negative state, to be avoided. However later work showed that where evaluation of the self meets one's standards, OSA can result in positive affect and may be actively sought (Greenberg and Musham, 1981). In the first study, this positive aspect of OSA was used to create a situation allowing implicit observation of self-aware behaviour. Children were given the opportunity to view themselves in a mirror following a verbal description task with an undefined outcome. Immediately before the introduction of the mirror, half of the children were given high levels of praise, and half offered no feedback. All children were then asked to look in the mirror 'to see how well they had done'. It was expected that children given praise would evaluate their performance relatively positively, and therefore spend longer looking in the mirror (remaining comfortable in a mirror-induced state of OSA) than children who received no positive feedback.

Although Duval and Wicklund's (1972) theory has received continued interest and empirical support in the adult literature (see Silvia and Duval, 2001, for a review), their methods have rarely been applied in early developmental research. For this reason, a supplementary aim of the first study was to elucidate the age at which children behave as though actively self-evaluative. Where mirror behaviour is not systematically affected by feedback, it seems reasonable to assume that OSA is absent.

The results of the first study supported a link between self-representation and self-knowledge. Consistent with Gellert's (1968) finding that children are more adept at representing themselves graphically than representing others, there was a small, but consistent, self-referent bias in figure drawing quality for all age-groups (see Figure 3.1). Although the quality of self and other figure drawings were positively correlated at 0.90, self-drawings consistently scored more highly than drawings of others on the Goodenough-Harris (1963) drawing scale. The observation that young children employ qualitatively different drawing schemes to represent themselves versus similar others implies that self-drawings are inherently linked to the ability to self-differentiate.

Moreover, the quality scores for self-drawings, but not other-drawings, were related to self-aware behaviour as indexed by mirror recognition. Even the youngest age-group systematically altered their mirror behaviour as a function of feedback, suggesting they held the sophisticated level

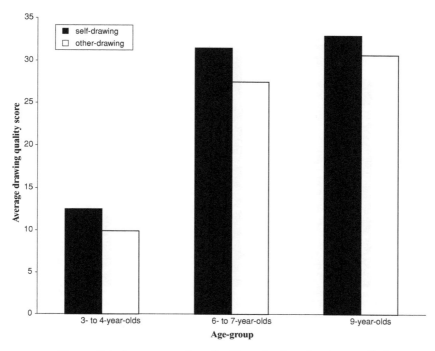

Figure 3.1 Average quality of self- and other-drawings, split by age-group.

of self-awareness described in Duval and Wicklund's (1972) model. Figure 3.2 shows that children of all ages spent significantly longer in front of the mirror when given praise. However, the more advanced children are developmentally, the less their mirror reactions appear to depend on external feedback. As shown in Figure 3.2, the magnitude of the effect of the experimenter's praise decreases with age. These findings suggest that evaluation of the self may first rely on external input before becoming internalized. For this reason, the observation of a child's dependence on external versus internal sources of self-evaluation may provide a relatively fine measure of developing self-awareness.

Interestingly, the time spent in front of the mirror following praise was significantly *negatively* correlated with self-drawing quality at −0.4. A possible interpretation of this negative relationship is to assume that the waiting times of those with a higher level of self-awareness (as reflected by higher-quality self-drawings) were tempered by their own opinion. One's own performance evaluation was likely to be less positive than the

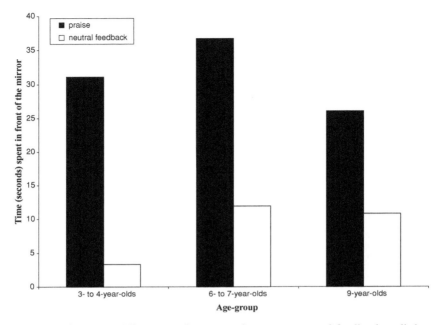

Figure 3.2 Mirror reactions to praise versus neutral feedback, split by age-group.

experimenter's randomly distributed, over-inflated, praise. As a result, spontaneous self-evaluation would probably encourage relatively early withdrawal from the OSA inducing situation.

In addition to being related to self-drawing quality and ontogenetic development, self-aware mirror behaviours can also be linked to the ability to recognize one's own drawing products. Two-thirds of the sample – with representatives from all age-groups – successfully identified both of their own drawings when viewed with distracters after a delay. When considered as a group, these children showed the expected effect of feedback: waiting significantly longer in self-reflective conditions following praise. By contrast, the remaining third of the sample – those who did not recognize their own products – showed no significant evidence of self-evaluation as measured by systematic responses to experimenter feedback. The finding that those who fail to show self-evaluative behaviour in classic OSA inducing conditions also fail to evaluate their own products successfully in terms of ownership suggests that the two capabilities may be related.

Study Two: Exploring the relationship between drawing ownership and self-awareness

The first study offered some empirical support for the proposal that own drawing recognition is likely to be related to self-awareness. The aim of the second study was further to elucidate this association by investigating whether drawing recognition not only relates to but *relies* on self-awareness, i.e. constitutes an act of self-recognition. By increasing sample size and the number of recognition episodes we hoped to provide a more thorough assessment of the development of successful drawing recognition.

Children aged 3 to 7 years were asked to discriminate their own drawings (including a cup, a crocodile and a self-portrait) from five matched-topic distracter drawings after delays of up to four weeks. To further assess the impact of self-involvement on drawing recognition, around a third of the children were also asked to identify a peer's cup, crocodile and self-drawing with which they had previous contact. Peers' drawings cannot be considered equivalent to own drawings in terms of planning (choosing how to represent the topic) or implementation (demonstrating one's own drawing style). However, the extent to which one physically engages with others' drawings is easily alterable. To vary this factor children either traced their peer's drawing with a pencil (active visual and motor input), or viewed the drawing while it was described to them (no motor input or visual mark-making). By separating the physical and cognitive components of drawing production in this way we hoped to compare recognition rates for drawings which had required ascending levels of self-involvement, and thus involved ascending levels of self-recognition.

We also observed the impact of variations in drawing skill on drawing recognition. To provide a global measure of each child's drawing skill we classified self-drawings in reference to Luquet's (1913) popular account of drawing development. Luquet (1913) suggested that children's drawing development proceeds sequentially from non-representational scribbles, to failed or 'pre-conventional' attempts at realism in which a poorly coordinated selection of the constituent parts of the topic is represented, to a schematic and more accurate 'conventional' representation of the topic. These developmental stages imply cognitive and motor advances in representation in terms of the level of realism aimed for and achieved, and can be easily distinguished when viewing human figure drawings provided by children ranging in age from 3 to 7 years (see Figure 3.3).

To provide a finer measure of the impact of drawing quality, drawings of all topics were also scored according to a scale inspired by the

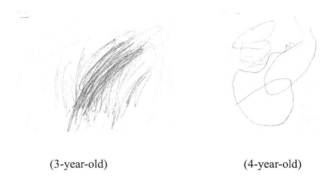

(3-year-old)   (4-year-old)

NON-REPRESENTATIVE (SCRIBBLED)

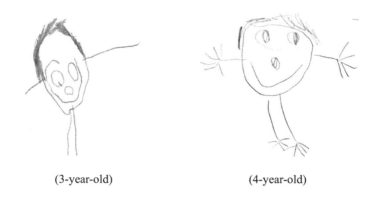

(3-year-old)   (4-year-old)

PRE-CONVENTIONAL

(5-year-old)   (6-year-old)   (7-year-old)

CONVENTIONAL

Figure 3.3 Examples of self-portraits classified according to drawing type.

Goodenough-Harris (1963) draw-a-man test manual. Firstly, drawings attracted credit for the number of features included, for depicting all basic features of the drawing model, and for placing features in the correct place relative to the other features included. Drawings were also credited for motor skill in reference to a component included in the Goodenough-Harris (1963) manual specifying firm and well-controlled pencil lines (Harris, 1963, p. 262). Finally, a global judgement of whether or not the finished drawing was clearly representative of the drawing model was made. As the model was no longer present for the case of self-drawings, this post hoc judgement referred to the drawings which clearly depicted a human figure with 'characteristic' features of hairstyle, dress or other physical appearance. Figure 3.4 gives examples of high-, intermediate- and low-scoring drawings of each topic. Measurement of the level of drawing skill exhibited in individual products, and by the artist globally, allowed thorough investigation of the proposal that successful representation of a topic may be related to its subsequent recognition.

The results of the second study allow further qualification of the development of successful drawing recognition. Given the number of distracter drawings present, children had a one in six chance of correctly selecting their own drawing in each recognition episode. Averaged over three episodes, this gives a chance hit rate of 1.5 drawings per individual. Figure 3.5 shows that although the majority of children performed above chance, recognizing two or more of the three drawings they had provided, only a minority of 3- and 4-year-olds achieved this level of success. This effect is in keeping with the age-related improvement in drawing recognition observed by Gross and Hayne (1999).

Figure 3.6 shows that traced drawings were also likely to be recognized after sizeable delays, with the majority of children over the age of 5 years recognizing two or more of the three drawings they had previously traced. By contrast, recognition performance for drawings previously only viewed (shown in Figure 3.7) was very poor. The majority of children recognized one or less of the drawings that they had simply seen, and even by the age of 7 only half of the children achieved recognition success.

Direct comparison of recognition rates for drawings encountered in different conditions confirms that the drawing recognition is affected by the level of self-involvement at the production stage (see Figure 3.8). Children who simply had visual contact with others' drawings were less able to recognize them as successfully as their own productions. However, on average, when children traced others' drawings they later recognized them just as successfully as they recognized their own. Further, those who traced others' drawings appeared to have depressed own drawing recognition rates relative to those who viewed others' drawings. This result

| SELF-PORTRAIT | CROCODILE | CUP |

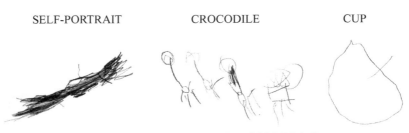

DRAWINGS GAINING LOW SCORES (<5)

DRAWINGS GAINING INTERMEDIATE SCORES (<10)

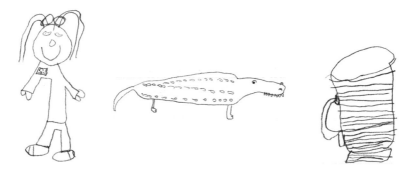

DRAWINGS GAINING HIGH SCORES (>15)

Figure 3.4 Examples of low-, intermediate- and high-scoring drawings of each drawing topic.

can be interpreted as resulting from interference due to an increase in the number of competing *production* episodes.

The finding that recognition rates for tracings and original productions were statistically equivalent implies that at this age the conceptual aspects of drawing production are less important for recognition than physical

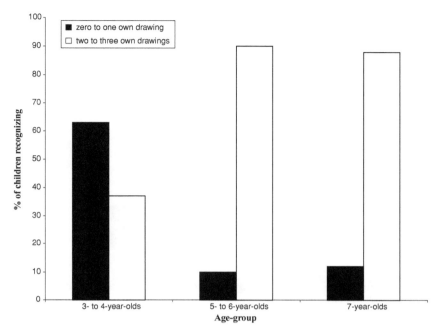

Figure 3.5 Profile of recognition performance for own drawings, split by age-group.

aspects. The observed effect of personal physical input is reminiscent of a self-referent bias found in verbal recall; there is an established mnemonic advantage for action statements that one has performed relative to those one has described verbally, imagined, or witnessed being performed by another person (Engelkamp and Zimmer, 1997). The implication is that the depth of processing involved in physically producing a drawing is enough to secure its subsequent recall, or to interfere with recall of other drawings.

The results discussed so far challenge the hypothesis that drawing recognition relies on recognition of cognitive input, emphasizing instead the physical trace of the drawing episode. However, close observation of individual recognition profiles revealed that proportionately more children performed at ceiling when recognizing their own drawings (38 per cent) than when identifying previous tracings (17 per cent). This implies that the 'full' drawing experience provides optimal conditions for recognition.

Further, analysis of the relationship between drawing quality and recognition confirms that representative aspects of the drawing process do

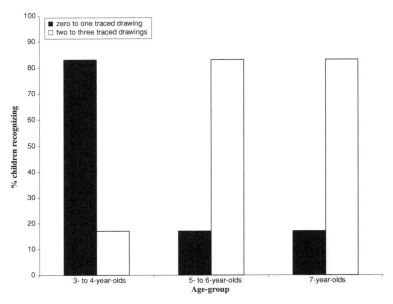

Figure 3.6 Profile of recognition performance for **traced** drawings, split by age-group.

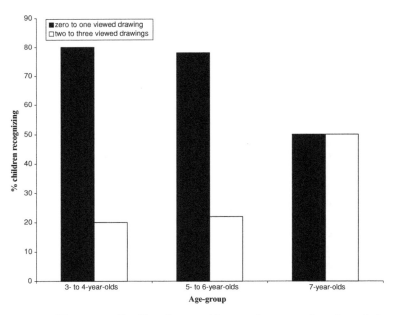

Figure 3.7 Profile of recognition performance for **viewed** drawings, split by age-group.

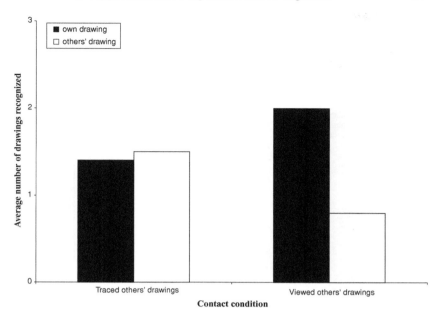

Figure 3.8 Recognition rates for **own versus others'** drawings, split by contact condition.

impact on recognition, showing a correlation of 0.6. There was a significant difference in the number of drawings recognized by scribblers, pre-conventional drawers and conventional drawers, even when controlling for age. Figure 3.9 shows that children who drew themselves non-representatively – whose mark-making appeared to be purely an exercise in motor skill – were never successful in recognizing their own products above the level expected by chance. Around half of children who drew pre-conventionally were successful, while an impressive majority of conventional drawers recognized two or more of their own drawings. This result confirmed that the *content* of motor input – which is dictated by cognitive engagement during the drawing process – is crucial for subsequent recognition (for further discussion see Campbell, this volume).

The quality scores of individual drawings also had a significant effect on drawing recognition, again, even when controlling for age. Those recognizing one or less drawings had significantly lower-quality scores (mean 4.3) than those recognizing two or three drawings (mean 8.9). Moreover, each individual component of the quality scale was strong enough to predict drawing recognition independently of overall scores. This result confirms that the more articulated and successfully representative the

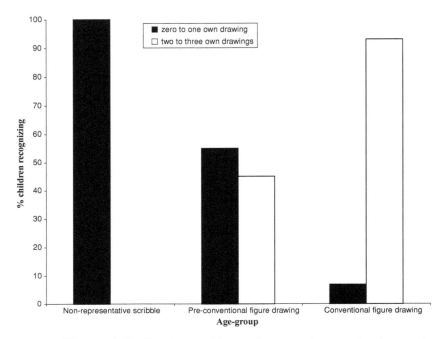

Figure 3.9 Profile of recognition performance for own drawings, split by drawing type classification.

drawing product – as dictated by cognitive-behavioural input – the more likely it is to be recognized.

As may be anticipated, self-drawings were again found to be of consistently higher quality than drawings of other topics. The superior quality of self-drawings is likely to be in part due to children's familiarity with the subject matter. Figure drawings are a popular topic choice relative to crocodile and cup drawings, meaning that a suitable drawing scheme is likely to be readily available. Besides, Study 1 demonstrated that self-drawings are likely to be advanced even relative to other figure drawings. As predicted by the observed relationship between drawing quality and recognition, self-drawings were also recognized more frequently than drawings of other topics. Despite the confound between drawing topic and drawing quality, it is worth noting that in this study self-drawings had an added advantage at the recognition stage. Distracter 'self' drawings were produced by children of the same age and sex; however, they ultimately referred to different models. As a result, children who successfully represented themselves should have had the opportunity to identify their own drawing via recognition of their own likeness.

Figure 3.10 Examples of characteristic features included and recognized by artists in self-drawings.

Figure 3.11 An illustrative example of likeness captured in a drawing by a six-year-old child.

In anecdotal support of self-image recognition, several of the children in both the first and the second studies pointed out their own characteristic features in self-drawings during the recognition process (see Figure 3.10). Figure 3.11 shows an accurate portrait of the author drawn by a 6-year-old child and supports the suggestion that young children are capable of capturing likeness in drawings. In empirical support of this strategy, there was some evidence to suggest that recognition of self-portraits relied on qualitatively different processes. In an interesting reflection of the importance of physical self-involvement, linear regression (stepwise) suggested that the component motor-coordination, lines – indicating confident mark-making – was the single most influential quality factor in drawing recognition for both cup and crocodile drawings. For these topics, this factor was more predictive of recognition than the number and accuracy of drawing features included, and the extent to which the drawing was successfully representative. However, for self-portraits, being credited as successfully representative of the model was the most influential factor for later recognition.

The impact of the self in the production and recognition of drawings

This research offers clear support for the proposal that drawings can be usefully employed to investigate developing self-awareness. In the first study, the quality of self-drawings predicted reactions to self-reflexive media. Those who produced higher-quality graphic self-representations were more likely to index self-recognition via mirror behaviours. This result supports the hypothesis that self-drawings are indicative of self-knowledge. Moreover, drawing recognition could also be independently linked to self-awareness; those who failed to index self-recognition in front of the mirror also failed to recognize their own drawings. This finding supports the proposal that the ability to recognize one's own drawing products may be considered an act of self-recognition.

There was some anecdotal and empirical evidence to suggest that children refer to cognitive self-representation not only to produce but also to identify self-drawings. This suggests that self-drawing recognition may be considered a 'specialized' act of self-recognition. However, the second study, which emphasized the importance of drawing production (a self-referent event), confirmed that the link between drawing recognition and self-awareness is not limited to recognition of self-drawings. The level of physical self-involvement in drawing production was shown to affect subsequent drawing recognition rates. Own drawing recognition improved considerably with age, and it appeared that this relationship was mediated by cognitive-behavioural input at the production stage. Drawings which were better planned and implemented, particularly in terms of topic representation and purposeful mark-making, were recognized more frequently. Most strikingly, children who produced unrepresentative drawings – requiring only minimal levels of cognition – were unsuccessful in claiming ownership of their own products.

Conclusions

This chapter presents and supports the argument that children's drawings have the capacity to reflect conceptual knowledge (what children know) in addition to perceptual knowledge (what they see). In particular, it is suggested that the cognitive and physical demands of drawing production make all drawing episodes self-referent. For this reason, children's retrospective analysis of their own drawings has the potential to reveal their self-awareness. At least in the case of self-drawings, objective analysis of drawing content can also be indicative of self-knowledge. In the past, content-based analysis of children's drawings has allowed valuable comment on the problem-solving processes involved in representing one's 3D reality in 2D. However, by exploring children's drawings in a context-based manner, drawing recognition studies make clear that it should also be possible to make the converse journey: inferring children's 3D reality from their 2D productions. Specifically, by exploring graphic self-representation via both self-drawings and retrospective claims of drawing ownership, it may be possible to track the problem-solving processes involved in representing oneself cognitively.

REFERENCES

Amsterdam, B. (1972). Mirror self-image reactions before the age of two. *Developmental Psychobiology*, 5, 297–305.

Bensur, B., Eliot, J. and Hedge, L. (1997). Cognitive correlates of the complexity of children's drawings. *Perceptual and Motor Skills*, 85, 1079–89.

Burkitt, E., Barrett, M. and Davis, A. (2003). Children's color choices for completing drawings of affectively characterised topics. *Journal of Child Psychology and Psychiatry*, 44, 445–55.

Cox, M. V. (1992). *Children's drawings*. Harmondsworth: Penguin.

Duval, T. S. and Wicklund, R. A. (1972). *A theory of objective self-awareness*. New York: Academic Press.

Eng, H. (1931). *The psychology of children's drawings*. New York: Harcourt, Brace.

Engelkamp, J. and Zimmer, H. D. (1997). Sensory factors in memory for subject-performed tasks. *Acta Psychologica*, 96, 43–60.

Freeman, N. H. (1972). Process and product in children's drawing. *Perception*, 1, 123–40.

(1980). *Strategies of representation*. New York: Academic Press.

Gellert, E. (1968). Comparison of children's self-drawing with their drawings of other persons. *Perceptual and Motor Skills*, 26, 123–38.

Goodnow, J. (1977). *Children drawing*. Cambridge, MA: Harvard University Press.

Greenberg, J. and Musham, C. (1981). Avoiding and seeking self-focused attention. *Journal of Research in Personality*, 15, 191–200.

Gross, J. and Hayne, H. (1999). Young children's recognition and description of their own and others' drawings. *Developmental Science*, 2, 476–89.

Harris, D. B. (1963). *Children's drawings as measures of intellectual maturity*. New York: Harper and Row.

Hartley, J. L., Somerville, S. C., Von Cziesch Jensen, D. and Eliefa, C. C. (1982). Abstraction of individual styles from the drawings of five-year-old children. *Child Development*, 53, 1193–1214.

Kellogg, R. (1970). *Analysing children's art*. Palo Alto, CA: National Press Books.

Kerschensteiner, D. G. (1905). *Die Entwickelung der zeichnerischen Begabung*. Munich: Gerber.

Lange-Küttner, C. and Thomas, G. V. (1995). *Drawing and looking: theoretical approaches to pictorial representation in children*. London: Pearson/Prentice Hall (distributed by www.amazon.co.uk).

Luquet, G. (1913). *Les dessins d'un enfant* [*The drawings of a child*]. Paris: Alcan.

Nolan, E., Adams, S. and Kagan, J. (1980a). Children's recognition memory for their drawings. *Journal of Genetic Psychology*, 137, 11–15.

Nolan, E. and Kagan, J. (1980b). Recognition of self and self's products in preschool children. *Journal of Genetic Psychology*, 137, 285–94.

(1981). Memory for products in pre-school children. *Journal of Genetic Psychology*, 138, 15–25.

Ricci, C. (1894). The art of little children. Translated by L. Maitland. *Pedagogical Seminary*, 3, 302–7. (Original work published 1887.)

Silvia, P. J. and Duval, T. S. (2001). Objective self-awareness theory: recent progress and enduring problems. *Personality and Social Psychology Review*, 5, 230–41.

Stacey, J. T. and Ross, B. M. (1975). Scheme and schema in children's memory of their own drawings. *Developmental Psychology*, 11, 37–41.

Van Sommers, P. (1984). *Drawing and cognition: descriptive and experimental studies of graphic production processes*. Cambridge: Cambridge University Press.

White, R. and Johnson, B. (1930). Children's choices in modern art. *Child Development*, 1, 347–9.

4 Style and other factors affecting children's recognition of their own drawings

Robin N. Campbell, Pauline A. Duncan, Anita L. Harrison and Lynne C. Mathewson

Previous research suggests that 4-year-old children can recognize their own drawings after significant delay. Five possible bases for such recognition are identified by Campbell et al. Two of these, recognition of personal drawing style and recollection of the drawing episode, are perhaps available to most 4-year-olds capable of drawing objects. A preliminary study shows that most children of that age have a distinctive personal drawing style. Three studies explore the developing ability to recognize drawings after a one-month delay, and refine methods for studying this achievement, at individual and group level. These studies show little success at group level until late in the fifth year. However, at the individual level, the proportion of children demonstrating recognition ability increases steadily throughout the fifth year, and even some young 4-year-olds show competence. The contributions of the factors of style and episodic memory in achieving this ability remain elusive. However, it is argued that the task is a promising one for studying these developing aspects of self-knowledge.

THE AGE at which children can reliably recognize their own drawings was investigated around thirty years ago by Stacey and Ross (1975), and a few years later by Nolan, Adams and Kagan (1980), and Nolan and Kagan (1980, 1981). Five-year-old children recognized their own drawings without difficulty after delays of a week or more (five weeks in one of Stacey and Ross's conditions). The position with younger children was less clear. Some success was reported, but it was marginal, and the method used (identification among a set of three experimenter-constructed distracters) is open to criticism. Although the alternative hypothesis of pure guessing may be rejectable, a guess is greatly improved by even one implausible distracter, and so some apparent successes may have been spurious.

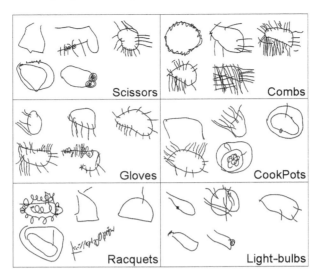

Figure 4.1 Constant depiction strategy: Louise (40 months) draws different objects in the same distinctive way. Accommodation to the object drawn is slight and inconsistent. The five repeated drawings in each cell were made a week apart.

If such recognition is possible, how might it be achieved? The following five factors all deserve consideration:

Content. The drawing might have a particular content that the child could identify as peculiar to his/her experience. For example, if children are asked to draw their own birthday parties (as in Gross and Hayne, 1999), these events have unique content, and some aspect of this might be included in the drawing. The same circumstances apply to self-portrait drawings (see the chapter by Josephine Ross, this volume).

Depiction strategy. What we have in mind here is illustrated by the drawings in Figure 4.1. The distinctive quality of Louise's drawings is not a matter of style, since almost every object is drawn in the same way. Her drawings are what Kellogg (1969) called *combines*, mostly consisting of a closed figure with radiating lines. Because of this consistent approach to depiction, we might expect Louise to be able to recognize her drawings, and certainly they are easily picked out by adult judges. The same would apply to the efforts of a solitary scribbler placed along with other children who draw. On occasion, Louise accommodates her drawing strategy to the object to some degree, and such drawings might be regarded as a form of 'fortuitous realism', following Luquet (1927).

Facture. The drawing might have particular formal characteristics that the child recognizes as marking his own work. The term 'facture' is used by John Willats (1997) in discussions of adult art to refer to distinctive ways of using the brush or applying paint, but it is readily applicable to the drawings of young children, which show considerable variation in weight and length of line, and overall drawing size.

Style. The drawing methods used to represent the object and its parts (representational strategies) may be sufficiently idiosyncratic and consistent in the child's work to allow recognition. A brief report of a study confirming the existence of this sort of 4-year-old style is given below.

Memory. Memory of the drawing episode may persist sufficiently to allow recognition, and the drawing itself may contain enough information to cue recollection of the episode. Notice that both elements are necessary here. We would not recognize our signature on a cheque as our signature – despite complete similarity – unless we remembered writing the cheque. And if we were presented with a small piece of paper bearing only our signature, we would be unable to recognize it with confidence, since it reminds us of no particular episode. Put another way, explicit memory – or some other solid 'chain of evidence' – is necessary for secure recognition of *particular* objects or events such as personal items like signatures or drawings, although implicit memory may be sufficient to recognize items as the same *kind* as an item encountered previously – see Hayes and Hennessy (1996) for discussion of these sorts of memory in the context of picture recognition.

In general, the last two factors are likely to be more important than the first three, which will be of use only in particular circumstances, and with particular children. It should also be noted that while in general explicit memory is crucial – since you can't be absolutely sure that it's your drawing unless you remember making it – in the context of experiments where you know that one of the presented drawings is yours, and that the others are not yours, then style (and the other factors mentioned above) can be a decisive cue to recognition.

Study 1: Is distinctive style a feature of 4-year-old drawings?

Van Sommers (1984) argued that young children's drawings show strong idiosyncrasy and conservatism. These claims are based on a range of ingenious studies and demonstrations carried out with children around 6 years old. So far as idiosyncrasy is concerned, his basic demonstration was to ask a class of schoolchildren to draw a tree or a nose. Under these circumstances a very diverse range of drawings results, with different children adopting radically different strategies of representation. Figure 4.2 shows the attempts of a Scottish P1 class (one year younger

66 R. Campbell, P. Duncan, A. Harrison and L. Mathewson

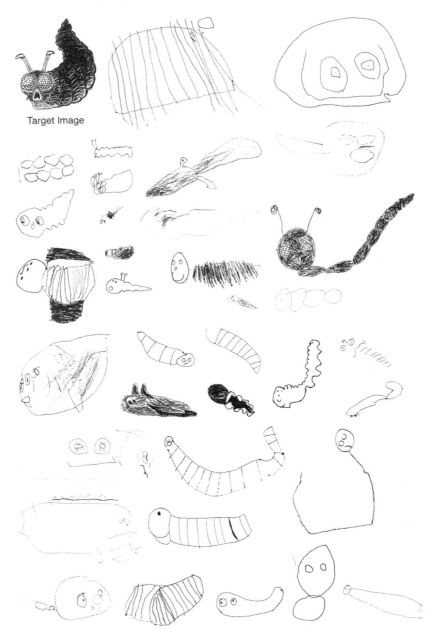

Figure 4.2 Idiosyncrasy: these young 5-year-olds each find a different way of drawing the creature in the top-left corner.

than Van Sommers' children) to copy the drawing shown in the top left corner. The idiosyncrasy is evident. Van Sommers' claim is amply supported by many other examples in his monograph (bicycles, light-bulbs, tennis shoes, tape-dispensers, etc.).

The claim about conservatism is supported by studies of repeated drawings of the same object. When children draw the same object on successive occasions, there is strong resemblance between the repeated drawings. Van Sommers argues that this resemblance lies in the finished products, rather than in the details of execution, suggesting that children have a particular graphic goal in mind when constructing a drawing and are not simply repeating a stored sequence of drawing movements. In order to reduce this or other effects of memory, Van Sommers' technique was to allow some considerable time, as much as a week, to elapse between drawings. Although he does not acknowledge Kellogg's work, nor refer to it, Van Sommers' claims regarding conservatism are strongly consistent with Kellogg's (1969) view that children's drawings have a strong evolutionary character. Kellogg and Van Sommers may be thought of as offering an account of the development of drawing which differs from the standard stage theory reaching back to Luquet (1927) and ultimately to Kerschensteiner (1905): that a stage of intellectual realism (in which drawings record what children know about the object) precedes a stage of visual realism (in which drawings show the visual appearance of the object from the artist's viewpoint). Instead, they claim or imply that at any stage in development the way in which a child will draw an object depends more on the way they have drawn that kind of object before than on other factors.

If these findings can be replicated with younger drawers, this provides a method for deciding whether the often unrecognizable drawings of younger children should be ascribed a content. For if children make unrecognizable but similar drawings of some object over several repetitions, but different unrecognizable drawings of different objects, then it seems reasonable to say that they have produced a drawing of that object, despite our inability to penetrate the artistic conventions used. This point about conventions or 'iconography' is a standard one in art-historical discussions. There is no doubt, however, that there is an iconography of child drawing, albeit a spontaneous one that varies from child to child, and perhaps from object to object. It is inevitable that drawers whose repertoire of graphic elements is restricted to lines, simple closed figures and dots will adopt a less iconic style of representation than the adult norm. The literature of child drawing is replete with examples. Two well-known cases are Arnheim's (1954, p. 141) famous drawing of a Man with a Saw, in which the teeth of the saw and all parts of the man are represented by closed figures, and Willat's (1985) drawing of a tennis ball in which the closed figure represents not the visible surface of the ball but the whole interior volume of the ball. So we have good reasons for thinking that what may be quite unrecognizable to us might nevertheless constitute an attempt to produce a picture with definite content.

The study reported here investigates the repeated drawings of 3- and 4-year-old children using a judging method which establishes whether content can be reasonably ascribed to their drawings. The method uses evidence of conservatism across the repeated drawings. For those drawings that can be so characterized, a second judging method establishes whether the work of one child can be reliably distinguished from the work of others, and this method uses evidence of idiosyncrasy of drawing method. These judges were not told which objects were being drawn by the children.

Twenty-four 3- and 4-year-old children took part in the study, twelve girls and twelve boys, with mean age 44 months, and range 37 to 55 months. The objects used for drawing were a plastic comb, a pair of metal scissors, a tennis racket, a light-bulb, a woolly glove and a small metal cooking pot. These were presented in a standard orientation on all drawing trials, namely: comb – teeth pointing to child; scissors – open, blades to left; racket – handle to right; bulb – fitting pointing to child; glove – fingers pointing left; pot – handle on right. The objects were chosen in the expectation that no child would have drawn any of these objects before, but that children would be familiar with them and would find them reasonably straightforward to draw. Drawings were made on A4 paper with large-diameter graphite pencils.

The children were interviewed five times at weekly intervals. In each session they made one drawing of each of the six objects. A different random ordering of the six drawing tasks was used in each session. Each object was handed to the child for examination, then removed and laid on the table in the specified orientation. The child was supplied with paper and pencil and asked to draw the object.

The 720 drawings (24 children × 6 objects × 5 drawings) were hand-copied onto 9 × 7 cm cards to eliminate gross differences in facture. The drawings were sorted by two sets of judges. In Stage 1, twelve judges were used. Each judge carried out four sorting tasks – sorting the full set of thirty drawings from each of four children. Children were assigned to judges so that each child's drawings were sorted twice, by different judges. The judges were not told what objects had been drawn, but were told that there were five drawings of six different objects, and that their task was to try to sort the drawings *according to the object drawn*. A relatively strict criterion was adopted to decide (for a given object and child) whether the child had drawn the object distinctively (when compared with other objects). Both judges had to include at least four of the five drawings in a sorted group. Using calculations following David and Barton (1962), the probability that two judges could achieve such groupings by chance is less than 0.01. Drawings which were not distinctive in this sense were eliminated at the conclusion of this judging stage.

Drawing sets which survived Stage 1 were combined according to object, so that all the scissors-drawings, all the comb-drawings, etc. were brought together. These six new sets of drawings varied in size, depending on the outcome of the judging process in Stage 1, and these were then sorted by a second group of twelve judges. Each judge sorted one such set, assigned so that each set was sorted by two different judges. Once again, the judges were told nothing about the object depicted, but only that each drawer had made five drawings of the object and that their task was to sort the drawings *according to artist*. Clearly the judges will succeed in their task only if (for a given object and child) the object is drawn in a consistent and distinctive style. The criterion used in this stage was more liberal: both judges had to include three of the five drawings of the object in a sorted group. Again using calculations following David and Barton (1962), the probability that two judges could achieve these groupings by chance is less than 0.05, provided that at least five children's drawings are sorted.

The judges greatly enjoyed these sorting tasks and would not relinquish the material until they were fully satisfied that they had done the best possible job. They were sometimes quite sceptical when informed about the nature of the objects drawn at the conclusion of the judging process, and were always eager to see the correct solutions to the task. Judges varied greatly in time taken, but the zeal with which they tackled this aesthetic task was evident, since times exceeded two hours on two occasions.

Stage 1: Only 220 drawings, comprising forty-four drawing-sets from thirteen children, survived this stage of judging. The typical output of a child whose drawings were all eliminated at this stage is shown in Figure 4.1 above. Louise (40 months) sometimes achieved a tolerable resemblance, but her habit of including the kind of all-purpose sun-figure drawing discussed by Kellogg made sorting by object impossible.

The number of surviving sets is strongly correlated with age, $r = .627$ [$n = 24$, $p < .01$]. There were substantial differences between objects in number of surviving sets: comb – 11; glove – 10; scissors – 9; pot – 6; light-bulb – 4; racket – 4; and this is perhaps due to differences in distinctiveness of the objects.

Stage 2: Twenty-five drawing sets from ten children survived. Clearly distinctiveness within a child's output does not guarantee distinctiveness between children. Nevertheless most children drew at least one object in a distinctive fashion.

When assessing the relationship between age of drawer and survival of drawings in this stage, two measures seemed worth examining: the number of surviving drawing sets, and the proportion of surviving drawing sets. The latter measure is perhaps more appropriate, since it is independent of the number surviving Stage 1. However, proportions are bound to be very unreliable with low-denominator values ranging between 1 and 6. But both correlations are low and non-significant.

Figure 4.3 shows the nine scissors and glove drawing sets that survived Stage 2. Inspection of these drawings sets reveals the sources of style very plainly. Some comments are offered:

Gloves: Jamie's sawtooth fingers are distinctive, as are William's linear representations for both fingers and hand. Only Shonagh draws a pure threaded outline. Laura draws a square hand and invariably three fingers.

Scissors: Only John succeeds in crossing the blades, a feat which lies beyond the reach of most scissor-drawers younger than 6 years old. Kara, Jamie and Laura, though they do not achieve a satisfactory crossing, make different sorts of failed attempts.

The judging method adopted seemed to work well in Stage 1, since the size of set to be sorted was constant, and was sufficiently large to meet criteria of arbitrary severity. Application of the method shows that many drawings which are inadequate (in the sense that they do not resemble the object to any great degree and do not permit identification of the object drawn) are nevertheless drawings of the object. Survival of drawings in Stage 1 is related to age of drawer at a satisfactory level. Considering the ages of the sample studied here, it looks as if most children begin to make drawings which vary in a stable way with the object drawn between 42 and 48 months.

The judging method worked less well in Stage 2, because of the considerable variation in the sizes of set to be sorted. However, there are indications that the combinations of idiosyncrasy and conservatism that constitute distinctive style are not particularly age-dependent, and are present in the efforts of most children who pass Stage 1, although they are not constant either within drawers across objects or within objects across drawers.

The technique of repeated drawing of a presented object, when combined with the judging methods used here, therefore provides the drawing researcher with a tool to answer the important question of whether the child is attempting to draw the object, and whether their drawings are sufficiently distinctive to be recognized as theirs, by judges or perhaps by the children themselves.

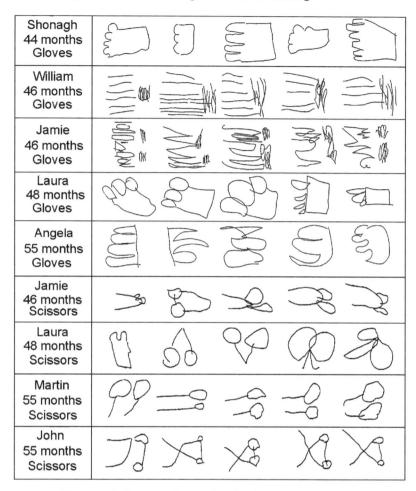

Figure 4.3 Conservatism and style: these 3- and 4-year-olds have distinct ways of drawing gloves and scissors, and they repeat their method of drawing consistently. The five repeated drawings in each row were made a week apart.

We return now to the question of when children are able to recognize their own drawings, and the means employed to achieve such recognition. Gross and Hayne (1999) reported confirmation that 3- to 4-year-old children are able to recognize their own drawings after delay. In their Experiment 1a, fifty children drew three complex events: a visit to the park, a visit to the supermarket and a birthday party. They also described each drawing. In a second interview, following a delay of a day, a week, a month, three months or six months, subgroups of ten children attempted to pick out their own drawing of the birthday party in the presence of two distracter drawings, selected by the experimenters on the basis of similarity to the target drawing. Recognition was almost perfect after a day, and remained around 60 per cent correct – above chance – in all other groups except the six-month group. In their Experiment 2, similar results were obtained using a different complex topic – 'something that made you (happy/sad/scared)'.

These experiments have limitations that suggest further research is needed. Only two experimenter-selected distracters were used, so guessing would succeed on 33 per cent of occasions. And if one drawing could be ruled out – as might well be possible, guessing would come close to the reported degree of success. Moreover, children were given only one recognition trial, so diagnosis of success at the level of the individual is impossible. A second weakness is that the drawing topic used – a birthday party – is an episode likely to be well remembered. This is helpful in two ways: it provides elements of unique detail (content) that may be recorded in the drawing, and it supplies a strong context for the recall of the drawing episode and comments made about it. In the three experiments we report here, we have increased the number of distracters (to reduce the guessing factor) and the number of recognition trials (to allow individual diagnosis of recognition ability), and the drawing topics used are common objects drawn from life. The last modification ensures that there are no particular extra-experimental episodic associations, and that there are no content differences between drawing trials for a given topic.

In our first experiment a younger sample was used, three distracters were provided in recognition trials to reduce the guessing probability, and five trials were given to each child, to permit diagnosis of success at the individual level.

Study 2: Recognition of object drawings after one-month delay

Twenty-eight children participated, 3 and 4 years old, with mean age 43 months, and range 36–56 months. Five objects were presented for drawing: a shoe, a light-bulb, a toy sheep, a mug and miniature kitchen scales. Drawings were made on A4 paper with large diameter graphite pencils.

Recognition was tested after four weeks' delay, using three distracter drawings of the same object chosen for similarity to the child's own drawing (as in Gross and Hayne, 1999). The four drawings were laid out on the table-top in a randomized square formation and the object drawn was identified verbally: 'Do you remember last time you drew [a shoe] for me? Well, I've got your drawing of [the shoe] here. And I've got three drawings of it that other children made. So three of these drawings of [the shoe] were drawn by other children and one was drawn by you. Which picture did you draw? Which one is your drawing of the shoe?' If the choice was incorrect it was removed, and children were told, 'No, someone else drew that one. Yours is one of these ones [point]. Can you remember which is your one?', until they picked their own drawing. A score of 3 for correct on Trial 1, 2 for correct on Trial 2, etc. was recorded.

Figure 4.4 shows frequencies of first trial success in recognizing drawings of the five objects. Plainly there is no evidence of recognition in these group data. Figure 4.5 shows overall recognition success. With a guessing probability of .25, expected mean score for a guesser is 1.25, and t $[\mu = 1.25, \text{df} = 27] = 1.8$, $p = .08$, so again there is little evidence of ability to recognize. However, at the individual level, four of the twenty-eight children (44, 50, 51 and 56 months old) recognized four of their five drawings (the criterion required for a successful binomial test at $p < .05$). Mean recognition scores per object were close to the guessing value of 1.5.

Although the aggregate data showed no evidence of ability to recognize, examination of individual performance suggested that one 3-year-old and three 4-year-olds (14 per cent of sample) were recognizing successfully. Several examples of constant depiction strategy or unusual facture were noticed in the data (see Figure 4.6). However, none of the four children who successfully recognized fell into these categories, and so they were presumably utilizing style or memory. Some examples of successfully recognized drawings are shown in Figure 4.7. One child identified a sheep drawing as her own, saying, 'It's mine 'cause I drew that little bell.' But it wasn't her drawing, and she hadn't drawn a bell on her sheep!

In our second study, a sample was chosen to match the sample used by Gross and Hayne (1999) more closely, and a larger number of distracters – fourteen, all available drawings – was used. This modification was introduced because of worries that the guessing probability was still too high at 0.25, and that the device of using experimenter-chosen distracters was difficult to use, and open to bias. In addition a matching task was included as a check that children could identify the content of their drawings.

Study 3: Recognition of object drawings and object–drawing matching

Fifteen children participated, 3 and 4 years old, with mean age 51 months, and range 44–58 months. Two sets of four objects were used for drawing.

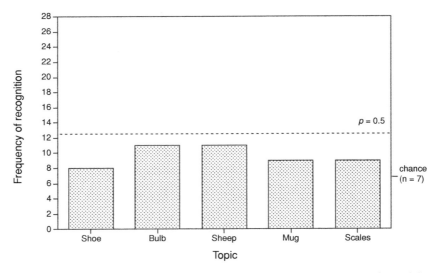

Figure 4.4 Study Two: frequency of successful recognition (first trial) by object drawn.

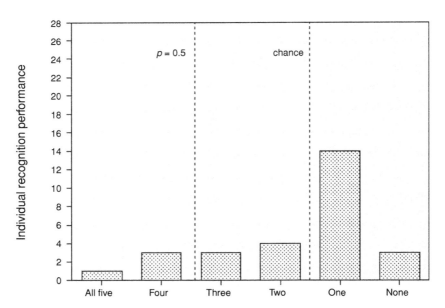

Figure 4.5 Study Two: distribution of individual recognition successes (first trial).

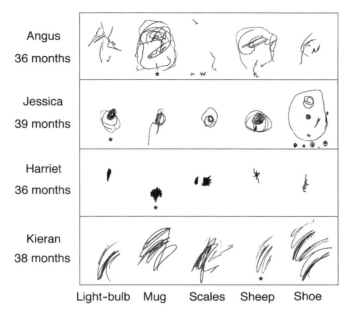

Figure 4.6 Study Two: constant depiction strategies and distinctive facture: Angus uses a distinctive uneven wavering line. Jessica combines the strategy of an outer and inner circular figure with 'ball of wool' facture. Harriet uses many short heavy lines. Kieran uses diagonal continuous scribble. Successful recognition (first trial) is marked with an asterisk.

Drawings were made on A5 paper with large diameter graphite pencils. The Matching Task Set consisted of a shoe, a cow, a mug and a doll. The Recognition Task Set was a toy sheep, a toy crocodile, a toy car and a spoon. The order of presentation of the objects for drawing was randomized.

The Matching and Recognition Tasks occurred four weeks after drawing the objects, and the task order was counter-balanced. In Matching Tasks the four objects were placed in a line in randomized order, and child's four drawings laid out similarly in front of them. Each object was pointed at in turn, and children were asked to pick out their drawing of it. Possible scores were 0 to 3, since if three are correctly matched, the fourth object is necessarily correct. In Recognition Tasks, all fifteen available drawings were laid out in random order on the table-top. To make the task of searching the set manageable, all drawings were photocopied to half size, and laminated. Instructions were as in Study 2. If the first choice was incorrect, children were asked to try again. Only five trials

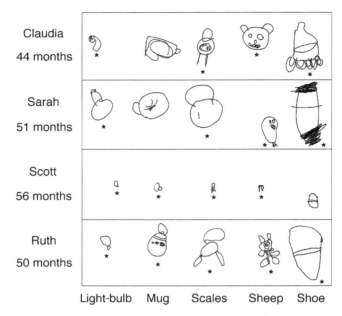

Figure 4.7 Study Two: successful recognition: Scott has the assistance of distinctive facture (tiny drawings). Claudia – though very young – draws distinctively and with good detail. Successful recognition (first trial) is marked with an asterisk.

were allowed. A score of 5 for correct on Trial 1, 4 for correct on Trial 2, etc. was recorded. The order of presentation of the four recognition trials was randomized. A summary of the score data from both tasks is shown in Figure 4.8.

Matching Task. The mean matching score was 2.33. The expected matching score for a guesser in this kind of matching task is always 1, regardless of the number of objects to be matched (see Erikson, 1996, p. 73). This is a welcome proof of an old conjecture in the theory of matching, known as 'the Monkey Secretary Problem', in which a monkey randomly encloses N letters in N addressed envelopes. So matching success is much better than chance, $t\ [\mu = 1,\ df = 14] = 6.33$, $p < .01$.

Recognition Task. The overall first trial recognition success rate was low (13 per cent), which is consistent with guessing ($p > .25$) and again varied little from object to object (range 7 per cent to 20 per cent). At the individual level, however, four of the fifteen children (27 per cent) recognized two of their four drawings on the first trial (the criterion needed

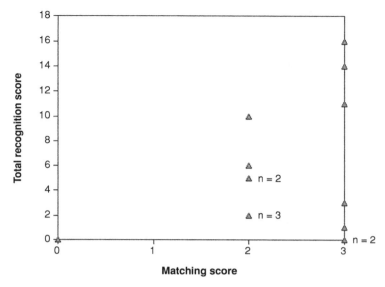

Figure 4.8 Study Three: individual matching and recognition scores.

for a successful binomial test with guessing probability 0.07 at $p < .05$). The remaining eleven recognized none of their drawings on the first trial. Examination of recognition score does not alter these findings. Mean total recognition score over the four trials was 5.6 ($p > .20$). Recognition score was better than chance for only one of the four drawings – the car (mean 2.27, $t\,[\mu = 1,\,df = 14] = 2.35$, $p < .05$), and the object with the lowest mean was the crocodile (0.47 – which means that most children could not find their crocodile drawing in five attempts). Crocodile and car drawings are shown in Figure 4.9 for comparison. Matching and Recognition Task performance were positively correlated ($r = .45$, $p < .05$, one-tailed).

As in Study 2, the group data show no evidence of recognition ability. However, individual performance assessed by binomial tests suggests that a fair proportion of children in the age range sampled are able to recognize their drawings on some occasions. Matching performance was very good (apart from one child), confirming the fact (obvious from the drawings) that enough content is included in them to identify the topic approximately. However, inspection of the drawing sets of successful and unsuccessful children (see Figure 4.10) gives little clue to the basis of either successful matching or successful recognition. The drawings of Participant 11, who successfully matched, have no apparent distinctive content. The drawings of Participant 15, who scored 16/20 for recognition,

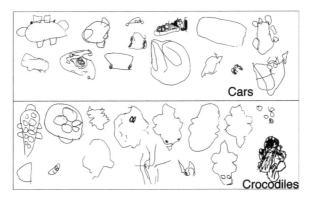

Figure 4.9 Study Three: car and crocodile drawings.

have little distinctive content but perhaps show some helpfully distinctive facture.

Gross and Hayne (1999) found close to uniform success in identifying their own drawings with a 5-year-old sample. One of our experiments not reported here confirmed this finding with a sample of mean age 66 months, drawing objects from life as in the present series of experiments. Together with Studies 2 and 3, this suggests that the ability develops rather sharply around 5 years old. The next experiment therefore used a sample of presumed transitional age. Four distracters were used in recognition trials, giving a guessing probability of 0.20, but these were randomly chosen from all available drawings of the given topic. This approach to the selection of distracters is perhaps the soundest, since it combines a low guessing probability with random selection – to prevent experimenter bias. A simple picture memory task was added as a preliminary attempt to assess the importance of the factor of episodic memory.

Study 4: Recognition of object drawings and picture recognition memory

Fifteen children participated, 4 and 5 years old, with mean age 55 months, and range 48–63 months. The Drawing Recognition Task Set consisted of a toy sheep, a toy crocodile, a toy car, a spoon. The Picture Recognition Task Set used sixteen drawings of familiar objects from the Snodgrass and Vanderwart (1980) set (baby carriage, camel, fence, helicopter, lightbulb, roller-skate, telephone, watch; barrel, bee, bicycle, guitar, glasses, kite, monkey, scissors). The first eight were presented for study and the additional eight were used as new items at the testing stage four weeks

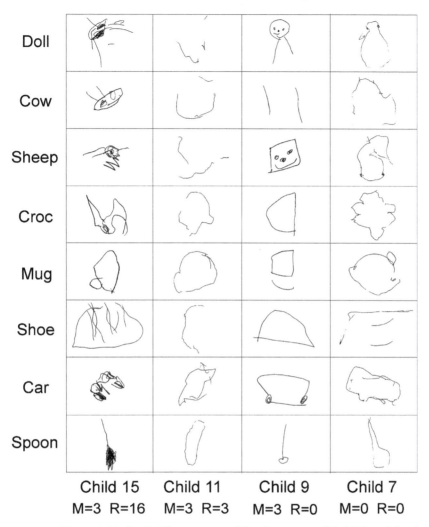

Figure 4.10 Study Three: successful and unsuccessful children. Matching (M) and Recognition Scores (R) are shown below. Drawings are centred and (when necessary) reduced to fit cells.

later. Drawings were made on A5 paper with large diameter graphite pencils.

Objects were presented for drawing in random order. The drawing task was followed by a picture task. The order of presentation of the eight pictures was randomized. For each picture the child was handed the card and asked what it was. If they failed to name the object shown they were provided with the usual name (note: 'pram' for baby carriage) and asked to say it. After a delay of four weeks the drawing recognition tasks were presented. These were carried out as in the previous experiments, with children asked to choose again if they picked out an incorrect drawing, yielding recognition scores of 5 (first choice correct) to 1 (correct by default on the last trial). These tasks were followed by a picture recognition task. All sixteen pictures were used, presented in a fixed random order. For each picture the child was told, 'Do you remember I showed you some pictures last time and asked you what they were? I've got them all here and I've got some other new cards that I didn't show you.' The picture cards were shown in sequence, and the child asked, 'OK, what's this one? [name supplied if necessary]. Do you remember this card? Did you see this one last time, or is it a new one?' The child's response was recorded.

Drawing recognition. The mean number of drawings recognized on the first trial was 2.13, and this is substantially better than the chance expectation, $t\ [\mu = 0.8, \text{df} = 14] = 5.21, p < .01$. Mean Recognition Score was 4.07, again comfortably better than chance, $t\ [\mu = 3, \text{df} = 14] = 6.96$, $p < .01$. However, examining first trial performance at the individual level, only one child recognized all four of their drawings, four children recognized three of their drawings, seven recognized two drawings, and the remaining three children recognized one or none. With a guessing probability of 0.20, three or four correct is required for a successful binomial test at $p < .05$, so only five children (33 per cent) convincingly demonstrated ability to recognize their drawings. Performance at the individual level was also examined using recognition score. All but one of the children scored better than chance, and eight were significantly better (see Figure 4.11). Age is significantly correlated with first trial recognition ($r = .75$), but not with recognition score ($r = .28$). Considering the four objects drawn, recognition was better than chance for each object except the spoon, whether first trial recognition is used or recognition score. The complete set of drawings is shown in Figure 4.12.

Inspection of the drawings suggests that neither distinctive *style* nor *facture* is facilitating recognition in this age-group. Zara's drawing style is perfectly distinctive, yet she performed worst in the group. Jamie recognizes his routine spoon, but fails to recognize his very distinctive crocodile. On the other hand, Holly's drawings have minimal content and are not distinctive, yet she recognized three of them. As for facture, Blain is the only child to use shading, but his recognition is unconvincing – his drawing style is very distinctive too, especially his aerial view of a fold-out sheep! Stanley's facture is also unusual – short lines and tiny circles, but his recognition is unconvincing too.

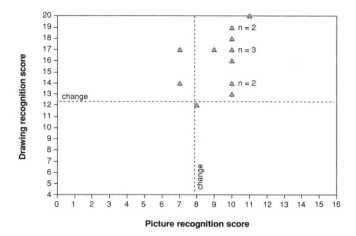

Figure 4.11 Study Four: individual drawing and picture recognition scores. Drawing: eight children had significant recognition scores, one-tailed *t*-tests, $\mu = 3$, df = 3, $p < .05$. Picture Task: no children had significant recognition scores, binomial tests, $p < .05$.

Picture memory. Individual picture memory scores are also plotted in Figure 4.12. Mean picture memory score was 9.5, which is reliably better than chance, $t\,[\mu = 8, \mathrm{df} = 14] = 4.78$, $p < .01$, but no child achieved the score of 12 or better needed for a successful binomial test with $p < .05$. And closer examination of performance calls the group mean in question too. Figure 4.13 plots Hits (Old items called Old) against False Positives (New items called Old). Correct judgements are Hits and True Negatives. But children who adopted the strategy of calling almost everything Old (n = 2) or almost everything New (n = 2) fall close to the chance line for Number correct, and therefore boost the group performance spuriously. Mean Hits Score is only 3.27, which is worse than chance. It is doubtful whether Signal Detection analysis is appropriate here, but Sensitivities (d') are less than 1, apart from the group of six children who made no False Positive errors, and these scored only 2 or 3 Hits. Age correlates positively with Number of correct judgements ($r = .58$), but negatively with Hits ($r = -.43$). Examination of Figure 4.13 shows that the older children eliminated False Positives, but scored few Hits. In other words they called most pictures New.

There was a significant positive correlation between first-trial recognition and number of correct judgements in the picture memory task ($r = .55$), and a significant negative correlation with number of Hits, but correlations between recognition score and picture memory measures were non-significant.

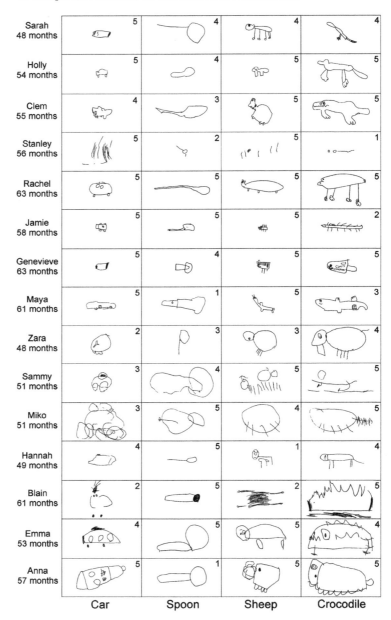

Figure 4.12 Study Four: car, spoon, sheep and crocodile drawings. Blain's sheep is rotated 90° to fit. Recognition scores are shown in cell corners (5 – First trial success, 4 – Second trial, etc.).

Style and children's recognition of own drawings

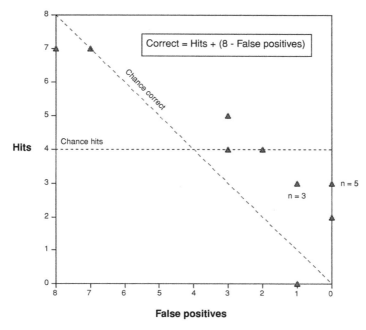

Figure 4.13 Study Four: individual picture recognition performance.

Drawing recognition at group level is now significantly better than chance. However, when individual performance is examined, we see no jump in performance compared with previous samples, but only a modest increase in the proportion reaching criterion. Age is correlated with recognition performance for the first time in these experiments, which is perhaps a sign that around 5 years is indeed the transitional age for this ability. Explanation of the emergence of this ability remains obscure. The case of Blain is particularly daunting, since his drawings show impressively distinctive style and facture, and his use of shading meant that he spent much more time on them than did other children – strengthening memory of the drawing – yet he recognized only two drawings, which is consistent with chance.

The Picture Memory Task provided confusing data which seemed to show a mixture of perseverative response strategies with some indication of recognition. The simplest explanation of the data shown in Figure 4.13 is that younger children are biased to call everything Old, producing False Positives, whereas older children favour responding with New, and miss several Old items as a result. It seems doubtful whether such tasks, adapted from adult models, are well suited to examining children's episodic memory. It may also be the case that the long delay of a month eliminates so much explicit memory that instances of confident recognition are rare. The more subtle methods adopted by Josephine Ross (this volume) are more promising.

General discussion

The present series of experiments, together with previous work, supports the following conclusions. When group data are considered, 3-year-olds do not recognize their own object drawings, whereas 5-year-olds do so with little difficulty. The ability to recognize efficiently emerges late in the fifth year. When individual performance is examined, however, success rates climbed from 14 per cent to 33 per cent in the samples studied, and so we may suppose that individual age-of-attainment of the ability to recognize varies widely in the population. We should perhaps expect this in children not yet forced into the homogenizing mould of school. If we are to avoid results which are unduly sensitive to small changes in experimental presentation and design, it may be necessary to choose research methods which allow individual diagnosis. Smedslund (1969) provides an old but useful discussion of this problem, which is brought up to date in the closing chapter of Flavell, Miller and Miller (2002).

Although it is plain that distinctive style and facture are available to older 4-year-olds as a basis for recognition in these tasks, there is little to support the idea that they make use of them. It may be, then, that improvement of episodic memory is the key factor, but this in turn may depend on subtle developments of a sense of responsibility or ownership (see Josephine Ross, this volume, for some discussion of these difficult notions). It is sometimes said that the study of children's drawings is neglected because it fails to make strong connections with more general aspects of child development. It seems to us that the achievement studied here – children's recognition of their own drawings – makes such strong connections, and offers the prospect of revealing features not just of cognitive development in general, but of important individual differences in such development between the ages of 4 and 5.

REFERENCES

Arnheim, R. (1954). *Art and visual perception*. Berkeley: University of California Press.
David, F. N. and Barton, D. E. (1962). *Combinatorial chance*. London: Charles Griffin.
Erickson, M. J. (1996). *Introduction to combinatorics*. New York: Wiley.

Flavell, J., Miller, P. and Miller, S. (2002). *Cognitive development*. Hillsdale, NJ: Prentice Hall.
Gross, J. and Hayne, H. (1999). Young children's recognition and description of their own and others' drawings. *Developmental Science*, 2, 476–89.
Hayes, B. K. and Hennessy, R. (1996). The nature and development of nonverbal implicit memory. *Journal of Experimental Child Psychology*, 63, 22–43.
Kellogg, R. (1969). *Analyzing children's art*. Palo Alto, CA: National Press Books.
Kerschensteiner, G. (1905). *Die Entwickelung der zeichnerischen Begabung*. Munich: Carl Gerber.
Luquet, G.-H. (1927). *Le dessin enfantin* [*Children's drawing*]. Paris: Alcan.
Nolan, E., Adams, S. and Kagan, J. (1980). Children's recognition memory for their drawings. *Journal of Genetic Psychology*, 137, 11–15.
Nolan, E. and Kagan, J. (1980). Recognition of self and self's products in preschool children. *Journal of Genetic Psychology*, 137, 285–94.
  (1981). Memory for products in pre-school children. *Journal of Genetic Psychology*, 138, 15–25.
Smedslund, J. (1969). Psychological diagnostics. *Psychological Bulletin*, 71, 237–48.
Snodgrass, J. G. and Vanderwart, M. (1980). A standardized set of 260 pictures: norms for name agreement, image agreement, familiarity, and visual complexity. *Journal of Experimental Psychology: Human Learning and Memory*, 6, 174–215.
Stacey, J. T. and Ross, B. M. (1975). Scheme and schema in children's memory of their own drawings. *Developmental Psychology*, 11, 37–41.
Van Sommers, P. (1984). *Drawing and cognition: descriptive and experimental studies of graphic production processes*. Cambridge: Cambridge University Press.
Willats, J. (1985). Drawing systems revisited: the role of denotation systems in children's figure drawings. In N. H. Freeman and M. V. Cox (eds.), *Visual order* (pp. 78–100). Cambridge: Cambridge University Press.
  (1997). *Art and representation*. Princeton, NJ: Princeton University Press.

5 Children's understanding of the dual nature of pictures

Richard Jolley

Jolley explains that humans have invented symbols to extend the means by which we can communicate with each other, and pictures are a symbol system that plays an important role in that communication. In order to participate in our society, therefore, it is crucial to understand the conceptual nature of symbols, including pictures. In essence, this means to understand their dual nature: that they are objects in themselves and representations of some other reality. This chapter introduces four facets that contribute to a fully mature understanding of the dual nature of pictures, and discusses the literature on babies, infants and children that relates to their understandings of each of these facets. The chapter concludes by collating this evidence to describe a developmental path by which children come to understand the conceptual basis of pictures.

Our symbolic world

HUMANS' invention of symbols is one of our most important achievements. It allows a degree of communication and understanding not present in animals. The range and pervasiveness of symbols in the world are so endemic to our species that it is easy to forget how much we depend upon them, or that they are symbols at all. We are so experienced with symbols that, on most occasions, we read the meaning of the symbol directly without first having to decode it from the arbitrary and meaningless properties of the symbol (e.g. the squiggly marks that form written language). It is worthwhile, therefore, to spend a moment's reflection appreciating how important symbols are to each of us to communicate, understand and fully participate in our society.

Language is perhaps the most important symbol system we have invented. Without it our ability to understand and communicate information, thoughts and feelings would be severely limited. But language is only one of many symbol systems that we use. The concept of quantity appears in many aspects of our everyday lives and in our work, and is communicated through the numeric and scientific symbols systems. Our spatial understanding of our environment is facilitated by traditional maps, signs and compasses in our travel across land, sea and air, and more recently aided by satellite navigation systems. Even our own bodies can be used symbolically to express how we feel by our facial expressions, gestures and postures.

Pictures are yet another important symbol system, and are the focus of this chapter and book. There are a number of different forms pictures take, such as drawings, paintings, photographs, television and cinema film to name but a few. Pictures can complement our understanding of accompanying text, but they also communicate feelings and ideas, have an aesthetic value, and at times make us laugh. The creation of 'moving' film as presented through television and cinema screens has enabled us to see the finite incremental movements in real-life and imaginary events. Such is the level of realism in these pictures that when watching certain genres of film, such as thriller and horror movies, even adults can react as if they are actually in the event or scene rather than watching projections on a flat screen. This begs the question of what represents a fully mature understanding of the pictorial symbol system, that the picture we are watching both is a thing in itself (e.g. marks on a page or pixels on a screen) and refers to some other reality (e.g. an event from life).

In this chapter I shall first consider some of the different facets of understanding that constitute an appreciation of this dual nature of pictures. I will then discuss in depth the literature that has informed us about the developmental path by which children come to understand these facets, and in so doing present how children come to understand the dual nature of pictures.

Understanding the dual nature of pictures

Pictures are things in themselves (e.g. marks and colours on a page) and refer to something else (e.g. a person or scene from our world). Hence, they have been described in the literature, like all symbols, as having a dual nature (e.g. Beilin and Pearlman, 1991; Callaghan, 2000; DeLoache, 1987, 2004; Schwartz, 1995; Thomas, Jolley, Robinson and Champion, 1999). What constitutes a fully mature understanding of this dual nature? The literature has suggested at least four components. First, an ability to perceive the referent from our world represented in the picture. Second, that pictures are not limited to representing generic or prototype exemplars of subject matter from our world, as often portrayed in books for very young children, but can represent an actual example or instance in reality (e.g. a real scene from our environment) and the spatial relationships therein. Third, that pictures are different from the subject matter they depict. For example, pictures are physically different and serve a different purpose from what they refer to, and subsequent changes to either the picture or the referent do not affect the other. Fourth, that the above three characteristics of pictures' dual nature are comprehended simultaneously. That is, an individual is not constrained to thinking about the picture either as a thing in itself *or* as a representation of another reality (the referent), but is aware of both components at the same time.

I shall now discuss how children come to understand these four facets of the dual nature of pictures.

Recognizing referents from pictures

A straightforward approach to testing whether a child can recognize what a picture is referring to is to ask him or her to name the subject matter referred to in some pictures. In the classic Hochberg and Brooks (1962) study a 19-month-old boy was presented with line drawings and photographs of objects and toys that the boy already knew the names of. What is particularly interesting about this study is that the boy could name the content of many of the pictures despite having been brought up with very minimal exposure to pictures. Although only a single case study, it does suggest that children can recognize familiar referents in pictures without requiring learning through prior exposure to those pictures or to pictures generally.

But can younger infants or even babies recognize that pictures refer to some other reality? Of course the difficulty with testing such a young sample is that their language competence is such that they cannot yet verbalize, or even know, the names of the pictures' contents. What we need is another procedure that does not rely on linguistic ability. Using an adaptation of the habituation procedure, DeLoache, Strauss and Maynard (1979) reported findings indicating that babies as young as 5 months could recognize a picture's depiction of a doll they had just seen. The doll was repeatedly presented over a number of trials and, as is typically found in the standard habituation phase of such experiments, the babies spent less time looking at the doll with each presentation. The doll was then removed and the babies were presented with two pictures, one of the doll they had just seen and one of a novel doll. The babies preferred to look at the picture of the novel doll. DeLoache *et al.* interpreted this finding as the babies recognizing the picture of the familiar doll, and, because they had already become uninterested in it, choosing instead to look at the picture of the novel doll. But does this behaviour of the babies conclusively show that they recognized the picture of the familiar doll?

DeLoache et al.'s interpretation should be treated with caution. Even if the babies did recognize some similarity in the picture of the familiar doll, how do we know the extent of this recognition? Perhaps it was merely a single feature rather than the whole doll? Furthermore, their preference for looking at the picture of the novel doll indicates only a detection of relative difference between this picture and the familiar doll. Seen in this light the preferential looking may signify a perception of difference more than noticing similarity. My reading of Bovet and Vauclair's (2000) review of studies on babies' perception of pictures is that experiments twenty years on from DeLoache et al.'s study have still not been designed that show unambiguously when babies can recognize a picture's contents. There are studies showing early cross-modal ability, such as matching the touch of a 3D object to viewing its 2D picture. But although such studies show a level of recognition of the picture's contents they do not directly test recognition of the picture–referent similarity within the visual domain. Those that do have shown that babies as young as 3 months old prefer to look at a picture of their mother than that of a stranger. But we need to be cautious in extending this finding to pictures showing other content, as newborns appear to have a special interest in faces (Johnson and Morton, 1991). In conclusion, studies on babies' picture perception suggest at least some level of ability in recognizing a picture's content a long time prior to the 19-month-old boy reported by Hochberg and Brooks (1962). But the ambiguous nature of interpreting babies' responses, and the need to design studies that more clearly test for their picture–referent recognition, prevent a clear message of what exactly babies can recognize from a picture and when they are able to do it.

Recognizing real exemplars of referents from pictures

Pictures can depict generic or prototype exemplars of referents, or represent a particular example of a referent from reality. In order fully to comprehend the representational relationship between a picture's contents and a real referent one needs not only to recognize the depiction but to perceive the one-to-one correspondence of the picture to the referent.

In a long-established series of studies reported by Judy DeLoache and her colleagues (for a review, see DeLoache, 2002) young children around 2 and 3 years of age have been presented with a symbol (a picture, miniature model, map or video) representing a room. An actual room which the symbol refers to is also present. In experiments where a picture is shown of the room (e.g. DeLoache, 1987) the experimenter informs the infant that a toy is hiding in the room in the same place as the experimenter points to in the picture. The infant is then asked to search for the toy in the room. The task is therefore testing more than children's recognition of the contents of the symbol but their comprehension of its correspondence to a particular reality so that the toy can be retrieved.

In an early study DeLoache (1987) reported that approximately 70 per cent of 30- to 33-month-olds successfully searched after being shown where a toy was hiding in the picture. As we know that infants and potentially babies can recognize the contents of pictures we might also expect infants younger than the $2\frac{1}{2}$-year-olds tested by DeLoache to perform these search tasks successfully. Findings reported by DeLoache and Burns (1994) suggest, however, that most 2-year-olds cannot, as only 13 per cent of the 24-month-olds they tested succeeded. Their difficulty seemed to relate to an inability in conceiving the one-to-one relationship of the picture to the room, as a number of alternative explanations could be ruled out. First, their poor performance could not have been due to misrecognizing the contents of the picture as the infants could name them. Second, they did not have any difficulty recalling where in the picture they had been shown the toy was hiding. And third, they went into the room to search for the toy, so they understood the task requirement was to locate the toy in the room.

The developmental shift in performance on this search task between the 2-year-olds and the $2\frac{1}{2}$-year-olds is explained by DeLoache and Burns (1994) as understanding pictures of a particular reality taking longer than recognizing pictures of generic exemplars. They argued that the 2-year-olds treated the picture as a generic example of a room rather than a specific representation of the particular room they were asked to search in. One potential reason the authors suggest for this is that children's early experience of picture books is that of seeing generic examples (e.g. a prototype of an animal) rather than a real animal from life captured in a picture. This is a contentious explanation and needs testing for. Although young infants in particular do experience picture books of generic subject matter they also see pictures taken of reality, such as photographs. Elsewhere (Jolley, in press) I have commented that it would be useful to test DeLoache and Burns' (1994) interpretation by taking those infants who fail the search task and teaching them the relationship of the contents of pictures to their referents. If the training resulted in improved performance on the search tasks then this would provide supporting evidence for DeLoache and Burns' (1994) position. There is, however, another question mark over their study. More recently, Suddendorf (2003) reported that 2-year-olds *can* successfully search using a picture under certain conditions. As it currently stands, it is unclear at what point infants gain an understanding of the one-to-one correspondence between a picture's contents and the specific reality they refer to. But it is likely to be a developmental step from merely recognizing its content.

So far I have dealt with children's developing understanding of pictures as representations of something else. But what about their appreciation of pictures as objects in themselves? It is their understanding of pictures as independent objects that I turn to in the next section.

Understanding the independence of pictures from their referents

Work has been carried out on newborns' ability visually to discriminate pictures from the objects they represent. For instance, Slater, Rose and Morison (1984) found that when shown a 3D object side by side with its 2D representation (such as a photograph), newborns preferred to look at one or the other. It seems, therefore, that babies can perceive a difference at birth between objects and their depictions in pictures. But this ability visually to discriminate pictures from their three-dimensional referents gives a false notion of understanding the independence of pictures. Over many years now, there have been anecdotal reports in the literature of young infants' manual interaction with pictures which suggest they may think that the depiction actually *is* the referent (e.g. Ninio and Bruner, 1978; Perner, 1991; Piaget, 1929; Werner and Kaplan, 1963). For instance, they have been seen to try and scratch and 'pick up' the depiction from the page or photographic paper. Indeed, some of my own students have confirmed they have witnessed such behaviour in young infants they know.

Such observations have also been found in experimental conditions. DeLoache, Pierroutsakos, Uttal, Rosengren and Gottlieb (1998) presented picture books displaying highly realistic colour photographs of common toys to American 9-, 15- and 19-month-olds. The authors noticed a developmental pattern in the way these babies and infants interacted with the pictures. Whereas the 9-month-olds felt, rubbed, patted and grasped the depicted toys as if they were exploring whether they were real, such behaviour was rare among the 19-month-old infants. Instead, these older infants pointed to the depicted objects: a behaviour that is more 'adult-like' and indicative of a conventional approach to pictures. Evidence of a developmental shift from manual exploration to pointing was further supported by the intermediate levels of exploring and pointing behaviour of the 15-month-olds.

How can we collate newborns' ability visually to discriminate pictures from their referents with older babies' and infants' apparent confusion over depicted objects being the objects themselves? DeLoache et al.'s (1998) observations of the video evidence led them to conclude that the young participants they studied were merely unsure whether the depictions were not the real objects rather than firmly believing that the depictions were real objects. In another experiment they reported 9-month-olds preferring to touch toys rather than pictures of the toys. This behaviour depends upon the same visual discrimination ability found in studies on newborns' data (e.g. Slater et al., 1984). It appears, therefore, that while newborns can perceive that pictures are visually different from the three-dimensional objects they depict, for a few months they will be unsure about the extent to which they are not the same. The degree of confusion and the age at which it evaporates will depend upon the degree of realism in the picture (Pierroutsakos and DeLoache, 2003) and the prevalence of pictures in the baby's environment (DeLoache et al., 1998). In respect of the latter DeLoache et al. (1998) found that infants aged between 8 and 18 months from the Ivory Coast Beng community, where pictures are uncommon, behaved towards pictures in similar ways to the American 9-month-olds they reported.

Although it is interesting to note that some babies' early manual interaction with pictures can reveal a lack of certainty that the depictions are not the real entities, it would be wrong to attribute too much significance to this behaviour. The experimental evidence from DeLoache et al.'s (1998) study, and the very transitory nature of this phenomenon in observations of babies' and young infants' natural interaction with pictures, indicates any initial uncertainty is likely soon to disappear with continued exposure to pictures. What are surprising, however, are findings from what have become known as false picture (or false photo) tasks that seem to suggest that even 3- to 4-year-olds have not yet understood that pictures are independent of the objects they refer to. The tasks test children's understanding that a change made to a referent does not effect any change on the contents of a picture representing the referent prior to the change. Beilin and Pearlman (1991) called this the existence principle. Although it is highly improbable that children as old as 3 and 4 years of age could believe that pictures update when changes occur to their referents, the research literature nevertheless has consistently reported such errors on false picture tasks in this age-group (e.g. see Leekam and Perner, 1991; Leslie and Thais, 1992; Robinson, Nye and Thomas, 1994; Thomas, Jolley, Robinson and Champion, 1999; Zaitchik, 1990).

In an influential paper on children's understanding of 'false' pictures[1] Zaitchik (1990) introduced an instant Polaroid camera to 3-, 4- and

5-year-olds. In one version the children observed a picture being taken of a puppet in one position (A) and then saw the puppet being moved to a different position (B). In the test question the children were shown the back of the picture only and were asked where the puppet was in the picture. Zaitchik reported a number of studies using this procedure and variations thereof, and found that the 3-year-olds performed worse than would be expected by chance alone, 4-year-olds performed at no better than chance, and only the 5-year-olds consistently reported the correct contents of the picture. The data from the 3- and 4-year-olds indicated, therefore, a surprising if not indeed an implausible finding, that children up to and including 4 years of age do not understand the independent existence of pictures from their referents.

Implausible findings are particularly in need of replication, and subsequent research sought to check whether alternative explanations for children's 'updating' errors could be ruled out. For this purpose Robinson et al. (1994) sought to replicate Zaitchik's findings but with a number of amendments. Instead of a photograph, a drawing was made by the experimenter of its referent, a doll wearing a sticker (e.g. a sheep) that had just been introduced to the child. Although Zaitchik's samples of children were pre-trained on the processes of photography and saw the picture develop, Robinson et al. argued that children are much more familiar with drawings and the process by which they are made. After the drawing had been completed by the experimenter in front of the child it was placed face down, and then the sticker on the doll was exchanged for a different one (e.g. a monkey). Robinson et al. commented that because Zaitchik's children could see the current reality of the puppet (e.g. at its new location) during the test question phase the greater saliency of this reality compared to the (hidden) picture might have seduced children into thinking about the current reality of the puppet when asked about the contents of the picture. To counteract this the doll in Robinson et al.'s procedure was also placed face down like the drawing in the question phase of the experiment. Furthermore, the question directed to the doll ('Remember Anne, what sticker is on Anne's tee shirt?') and to the picture ('Remember this picture, what sticker is drawn on the tee shirt?') was accompanied by appropriate pointing to ensure each child understood whether it was the doll's or the picture's contents they were being asked about.

The amendments introduced by Robinson et al. appeared to account for the fewer updating errors they reported compared to those found in the samples of children studied by Zaitchik. Nevertheless, Robinson et al. still found a number of lines of evidence of a misunderstanding about the picture–referent relationship among their 3- to 4-year-olds. First, there were significantly more updating errors than in control conditions where a change was made in one item within a pair but neither item within the pair was a representation of the other (either two dolls or two pictures). Picture updating errors were therefore not due to a misunderstanding of change per se; they occurred where the picture was a representation of a referent that subsequently changed. In addition, 'backdating' errors were also found where a change was made in the picture instead of the referent (e.g. rubbing out the sheep and drawing a monkey on the picture of the doll), indicating a belief that pictures which have changed regain their original features in match with those of their referents. These updating and backdating errors were significantly more frequent than children's errors to questions directed towards the referent, confirming that the children perceived that pictures change to keep in line with their referents not vice versa. Interestingly, Robinson et al. also reported that when presenting children with an object (e.g. a teddy wearing a scarf), and then making a drawing of the object but with an item missing (teddy without the scarf), many children erroneously reported that the picture actually depicted the missing item.

Taking all the lines of evidence from Zaitchik's (1990) and Robinson et al.'s (1994) studies it appears that young children do have difficulty with understanding the independence of pictures from their referents. But how are we to explain this implausible discovery? I shall begin to answer this question in the next section, which deals with the fourth facet of understanding the dual nature of pictures, that of holding in mind at the same time that pictures are representations and objects in themselves.

Simultaneously understanding pictures as symbols and objects

Robinson et al.'s explanation for the picture errors they reported was that children were confusing pictorial features with referent features in their mind, rather than holding a belief that pictures magically update to match their referents: 'they cannot hold in mind and recover the picture's features distinctly from those of the real referent, yet know perfectly well that pictures do not *change* magically without intervention' (p. 189, their italics). I agree with Robinson et al.'s view that 3- to 4-year-olds do not imbue pictures with magical updating qualities. I know of no anecdotal reports in the literature of children's natural interaction with pictures where they behave towards pictures in any way indicative of such a belief. For instance, children of any age do not comment or show confusion in respect of why the depictions in family photographs have not updated to match how their family currently appear in life! There are two possibilities to Robinson et al.'s suggestion that young children cannot hold in mind the picture's features distinctly from those of the referent. One is that the problem is merely a result of young children's memory difficulties. The other is a more fundamental problem grounded in their understanding of the dual nature of pictures in that they cannot conceive pictures as representations of referents *and at the same time* consider the independence of pictures from their referents.

In order to establish which of these two explanations was the more likely, Thomas, Jolley, Robinson and Champion (1999) adopted the same false picture task as described in Robinson et al. (1994) but with an important addition to the procedure. We asked children about what operations had been performed on the picture in the form of 'change' questions. We reasoned that if children's errors are merely the result of being confused in memory between the features of the picture and the referent, then being asked whether a change had been made to the picture should give assistance in disentangling the pictorial features from those in the referent. Furthermore, we expected that once children acknowledge that no change had been made to the picture they should answer correctly the following (identity) question regarding the contents of the sticker drawn in the picture. In our first experiment the change picture question was, 'Remember this picture; has the sticker drawn in the picture changed?' We also asked a change doll (referent) question to the doll, 'Remember Anne; has the sticker she's wearing changed?' We were surprised to find that the 3- to 4-year-olds we tested performed poorly on both change and identity questions directed to the picture.

In the second experiment we modified both the picture and doll change questions to direct the child's attention explicitly to the experimenter's actions they had just observed. We asked, 'Remember this picture; did we change the sticker drawn in the picture?' and 'Remember Anne, did we change the sticker Anne's wearing?' We expected that these modified change questions would be particularly helpful in alerting the child to recalling that the doll's sticker had been changed but not the sticker on the drawing. As in Experiment 1, however, we were surprised by the number of errors children were making in the picture questions (modified change and identity). Furthermore, the level of picture question errors reported in the first experiment was replicated on a different sample of children in the second experiment who were given the original change question. These errors we found on the picture questions from both experiments were not shown in (change and identity) questions directed at the doll.

As errors persisted in these two experiments, despite the child's attention being explicitly directed to whether a change had been made to the picture, it is very unlikely that any confusion in memory could account for the errors. The children's difficulty appears to be a more fundamental problem of not conceiving the picture as an independent object at the same time as considering it as a representation of a referent (Thomas *et al.*, 1999). In essence, 3- to 4-year-olds cannot simultaneously hold in mind the dual nature of pictures. In Thomas *et al.* (1999) we commented that the literature on false picture tasks indicates that this difficulty with the dual nature of pictures may be prevalent in up to at least half of 3- to 4-year-olds in the population, but by 5 years of age the errors disappear (see also Robinson *et al.*, 1994).

There is an apparent conundrum, however, with the findings from false picture tasks and those reported by DeLoache's search tasks. While errors are found on false picture tasks among 3- to 4-year-olds, children as young as $2\frac{1}{2}$ years pass DeLoache's search task using a picture (or even at 2 years according to Suddendorf, 2003). Indeed, in the wider context of the variety of symbols used in DeLoache's search tasks (e.g. scale model, picture or video) DeLoache and her colleagues have consistently interpreted the search tasks as a measure of children's understanding of the dual nature of the symbol presented (DeLoache, 1987, 1991, 2000, 2002, 2004; DeLoache and Burns, 1994; DeLoache, Miller and Rosenberg, 1997; DeLoache, Peralta de Mendoza and Anderson, 1999; Troseth and DeLoache, 1998; Uttal, Schreiber and DeLoache, 1995).

Considering the well-established literatures of the false picture and search tasks it is surprising that this apparent conundrum has not been addressed. Recently (Jolley, in press), however, I have presented an explanation for the apparent developmental disparity and argue that the findings from both tasks are actually complementary. The essence of my argument is that each task has a different bias towards one property of dual nature. The search task is primarily a test of children's understanding of the one-to-one relationship of a symbol to its referent, whereas the false picture task is essentially measuring children's understanding of the independence of pictures from their referents.

I have expanded upon this further (Jolley, in press). While DeLoache's search task focuses on the child's ability to conceive the one-to-one correspondence between the symbol (e.g. picture) and the referent, it is only a basic measure of the child's knowledge of the picture as a thing in itself. The child is asked to point out where in the picture the miniature version of the toy is hiding. Even children who fail the search tasks (such as the 2-year-olds tested by DeLoache and Burns, 1994) can do this. DeLoache (DeLoache, 1987; DeLoache and Burns, 1994) argues that as the children point to the correct place in the picture it shows that they understand the picture as an object in itself. This is because they respond to a question about the picture with an action directed to the picture, rather than a response to the room (e.g. pointing to an item in the room). But the young child's response to being asked where the miniature toy is hiding in the picture can only be treated as a limited measure of the child's understanding of the picture as an object in itself. It measures the same understanding as discovered by DeLoache *et al.*'s (1998) 19-month-old infants who pointed to pictures presented to them, rather than the 9-month-olds' touching of the pictures in ways suggesting a lack of complete awareness that the depicted objects were not the real items. Using Beilin and Pearlman's (1991) terms, the pointing behaviour indicates an understanding of the functional and physical differences pictures have from their referents. However, the children sampled on the search task are not required to appreciate the third of Beilin and Pearlman's principles of pictorial independence, that of existence. That is, they are not asked whether they know the contents of the picture remain stable if a change is made to the room, as there is never a mismatch between picture and room. Accordingly, the search task is an incomplete test of children's understanding of the independence of pictures, because it does not test for the existence principle (Jolley, in press).

It is precisely this knowledge that the false pictures tasks are testing for. This is engineered by making a change to the referent subsequent to a picture being created of the referent, and then asking test questions concerning the contents of the picture and the referent. In contrast, although the procedure of initially drawing the referent sets up the notion in the child's mind that the picture represents the referent, something they are happy to acknowledge, it does not require the child to consider the one-to-one correspondence of the picture–referent relationship as the search task does.

I am not suggesting that the search task using a picture as the symbol and the false picture task are not tapping into children's understanding of the dual nature of pictures. They are. But each task is testing for a deep understanding of one property of dual nature while testing for a more basic level of understanding of the other property. I argue (Jolley, in press) that seen in this light the apparent contradictions in the findings reported by search and false picture tasks are in fact complementary. They show that young children first acquire a mature understanding that pictures can represent the spatial one-to-one correspondence to their referents, but only later show a complete understanding of the independence of a picture while at the same time considering it as a representation of a referent. The fact that children first acquire an understanding of pictures' representational qualities is unsurprising, as the principal purpose of representational pictures is to refer to some other reality.

In the false picture task, children's natural inclination to think about pictures as representations rather than objects in themselves is tapped into by a picture being made of the referent in the procedure. Thomas et al. (1999) argue that while considering the picture as a representation, 'they tend not (or are unable) to simultaneously attend to the physical properties of the picture as a thing in itself' (p. 17). It is important to emphasize that children (whether they answer correctly or incorrectly the picture questions) do still report that the picture is of the referent even after the referent is altered in some way (see Thomas et al., 1999). The proposition that 3- to 4-year-olds only have a difficulty with the independent existence of pictures when at the same time they are thinking about the picture as a representation is borne out by findings reported by Beilin and Pearlman (1991). They asked 3- to 4-year-olds directly about what would happen to a picture if something was changed to its referent, and most recalled that nothing happens. For example, one of the questions Beilin and Pearlman (1991) asked was, 'What would happen to this picture of a flower if we cut off the petals of this [real] flower?' Very few 3- to 4-year-olds said that the picture would change. I comment (Jolley, in press) that Beilin and Pearlman's questions and the procedure in false picture tasks have two important distinctions. First, whereas the false picture task procedure leads the child to consider the picture as a representation of the referent, the existence question used by Beilin and Pearlman does not. Second, the picture questions (including the change questions used by Thomas et al., 1999) only implicitly refer the child to think about the independence of pictures, whereas the existence question explicitly brings this to the child's attention. So the difficulty in false picture tasks compared to the Beilin and Pearlman questions is that children have to think about the picture in two ways, with the accompanying problem that the test question only implicitly refers to the picture as an object in itself.

As 3- to 4-year-olds know very well that pictures do not update to match changes in their referents, it begs the question of whether the errors on false picture tasks are rooted in a misunderstanding of pictures per se. In the next section I will argue that they actually lie in a more generic and cognitive deficit of young children's difficulty in holding in mind two alternative representations about a given entity.

Children's flexibility of thought

It is now clear from my discussions above that children's errors on false picture tasks are not due to any intrinsic misunderstanding of pictures. Long before the age at which children are tested on false picture tasks, they have understood that pictures are objects in themselves as well as referring to something else. Despite giving an appearance of a misunderstanding of the existence principle, their errors are actually due to a more generic cognitive ability in simultaneously thinking about an entity in two ways. This difficulty in flexibility of thought is shown in a number of tasks tested on 3- to 4-year-olds. In the appearance–reality task, children are shown objects that are made to look like something else, such as a sponge painted to look like a rock (e.g. see Flavell, Flavell and Green, 1983; Gopnik and Astington, 1988). Typically in appearance–reality tasks, children are asked a reality question (e.g. 'What is this really? Is it really a rock or is it really a sponge?') and an appearance question (e.g. 'What does this look like? Does it look like a rock or does it look like a sponge?'). Three-year-olds tend to respond to both questions with what the object really is ('sponge'), and hence such errors are similar to the 'realist' errors found on false picture tasks by similarly aged children.[2]

Other lines of evidence that underline further young children's difficulty in multiple representations are their responses to ambiguous figures that have two pictorial representations, and 'inhibitory control' tasks that require switching between two pieces of information. In the ambiguous figure task a single line drawing figure is shown in which two representations can be perceived (e.g. a duck or a rabbit) depending upon which features of the figure are being attended to. The child is asked what they see and then encouraged to report anything else they might see. If only one representation is reported by the child (e.g. duck) the experimenter points at certain features to encourage the child to perceive the alternative representation (e.g. rabbit). In the test session the child is asked to look again at the ambiguous figure and say whether they can see the picture 'changing' between the two representations. Typically, children aged 3 to 4 years report they cannot (e.g. see Gopnik and Rosati, 2001). So although children of this age know (and have perceived) the two representations of ambiguous figures they cannot switch/reverse between the two representations. A similar difficulty has been observed in tests of inhibitory control, such as card sorting tasks. Initially, they are asked to sort the cards by one rule (e.g. 'sort by colour') and then by another rule (e.g. 'sort by shape'). In these post-switch trials children below 4 years tend to continue sorting by the first rule even though they report both rules when asked (e.g. see Zelazo, Frye and Rapus, 1996). In the appearance–reality, ambiguous figure and card-sorting tasks, therefore, young children have a difficulty switching between two representations.

It is this inability to switch between two meanings of an entity that lies at the heart of false picture task errors. The task sets up their conception of the picture as a representation of the referent but the test question implicitly requires them to switch to thinking about the picture as an object in itself. Switching to this (less salient) property of pictures is exactly what many 3- to 4-year-olds fail to do.

Summary

Symbols and their meanings are endemic in our world to such an extent that understanding of, and participation in, our society depends upon a conceptual understanding of symbols. In the case of pictures, the symbol system which is the focus of this chapter, there are at least four conceptual facets that must be acquired to achieve a mature understanding of the pictorial symbol system. First, that pictures can represent a referent from our world. Second, that they can represent not only generic exemplars of referents but also specific instances of referents from reality. Third, that pictures are distinct from their referents in crucial ways, most notably in their physical, functional and existence independence. Finally, that a mature conceptual understanding of pictures requires the ability simultaneously to hold in mind that pictures are representations (of their referents) and objects in themselves. That is, that pictures have a dual nature.

By collating the developmental findings relating to each of the above four facets of understanding from studies on babies, infants and children it is possible to map the developmental path to how we come to understand the dual nature of pictures. Newborn babies have a basic ability visually to discriminate between pictures and the referents they represent. Within the first few months of life they may begin to show early signs of being able to recognize familiar referents from the contents of pictures. This ability to recognize referents from pictures can be overextended, so that babies around 9 months of age behave as if they are unclear that pictures are different from the reality they refer to, a realization that may take longer if the picture has a high iconic similarity to the referent or in cultures where babies have limited exposure to pictures. Such confusion shows signs of waning by 15 months and evaporates by 19 months in a culture where pictures are commonly found. Between 24 and 30 months, infants understand the one-to-one correspondence of a picture to its specific referent from reality. Although by $2\frac{1}{2}$ years children understand that pictures are both representations and distinct from their referents, they cannot yet hold in mind simultaneously these two aspects of dual nature. Their difficulty lies in a general cognitive limitation of being unable to think about an entity in two ways at the same time, a limitation that is still evident in many 3- to 4-year-olds. It is not until this general cognitive limitation is lifted (typically between 4 and 5 years of age) that children can consider simultaneously their previously acquired understanding that pictures are representations and objects.

NOTES

1. Strictly speaking, pictures that no longer reflect the current reality of their referent are not 'false' but out-of-date (see Leekam and Perner, 1991; Perner, Aichhorn, Kronbichler, Staffen and Ladurner, 2006).
2. One exception to these 'realist' errors on appearance/reality tasks is where a colour filter is placed around an object, with children tending to respond that the object looks like and really is the colour of the filter (e.g. see Flavell, Green and Flavell, 1986).

REFERENCES

Beilin, H. and Pearlman, E. G. (1991). Children's iconic realism: object versus property realism. In H. W. Reese (ed.), *Advances in child development and behaviour* (Vol. 23, pp. 73–111). New York: Academic Press.
Bovet, D. and Vauclair, J. (2000). Picture recognition in animals and in humans: a review. *Behavioral Brain Research*, 109, 143–65.
Callaghan, T. C. (2000). Factors affecting children's graphic symbol use in the third year. Language, similarity, and iconicity. *Cognitive Development*, 15, 185–214.
DeLoache, J. S. (1987). Rapid change in the symbolic functioning of very young children. *Science*, 238, 1556–7.
  (1991). Symbolic functioning in very young children: understanding of pictures and models. *Child Development*, 62, 736–52.
  (2000). Dual representation and young children's use of scale models. *Child Development*, 71, 329–38.
  (2002). Symbolic development. In U. Goswami (ed.), *Blackwell handbook of childhood cognitive development* (pp. 206–26). Oxford: Blackwell.
  (2004). Becoming symbol-minded. *Trends in Cognitive Sciences*, 8, 66–70.
DeLoache, J. S. and Burns, N. M. (1994). Early understanding of the representational function of pictures. *Cognition*, 52, 83–110.
DeLoache, J. S., Miller, K. F. and Rosengren, K. S. (1997). The credible shrinking room: very young children's performance with symbolic and non-symbolic relations. *Psychological Science*, 8, 308–13.
DeLoache, J. S., Peralta de Mendoza, O. A. and Anderson, K. (1999). Multiple factors in early symbol use: instructions, similarity and age in understanding a symbol–referent relation. *Cognitive Development*, 14, 299–312.
DeLoache, J. S., Pierroutsakos, S. L., Uttal, D. H., Rosengren, K. S. and Gottlieb, A. (1998). Grasping the nature of pictures. *Psychological Science*, 9, 205–10.
DeLoache, J. S., Strauss, M. S. and Maynard, J. (1979). Picture perception in infancy. *Infant Behaviour and Development*, 2, 77–89.
Flavell, J. H., Flavell, E. R. and Green, F. L. (1983). Development of the appearance–reality distinction. *Cognitive Psychology*, 15, 95–120.

Flavell, J. H., Green, F. L. and Flavell, E. R. (1986). Development of knowledge about the appearance–reality distinction. *Monographs of the Society for Research in Child Development*, 51, 1–87.

Gopnik, A. and Astington, J. W. (1988). Children's understanding of representational change and its relation to the understanding of false belief and the appearance reality distinction. *Child Development*, 59, 26–37.

Gopnik, A. and Rosati, A. (2001). Duck or rabbit? Reversing ambiguous figures and understanding ambiguous representations. *Developmental Science*, 4, 175–83.

Hochberg, J. and Brooks, V. (1962). Pictorial recognition as an unlearned ability. *American Journal of Psychology*, 75, 624–8.

Johnson, M. H. and Morton, J. (1991). *Biology and cognitive development: the case of face recognition*. Oxford: Blackwell.

Jolley, R. P. (in press). *Children and pictures: drawing and understanding*. Oxford: Blackwell.

Leekam, S. R. and Perner, J. (1991). Does the autistic child have a metarepresentational deficit? *Cognition*, 40, 203–18.

Leslie, A. M. and Thaiss, L. (1992). Domain specificity in conceptual development: neuropsychological evidence from autism. *Cognition*, 43, 225–51.

Ninio, A. and Bruner, J. S. (1978). The achievement and antecedents of labelling. *Journal of Child Language*, 5, 5–15.

Perner, J. (1991). *Understanding the representational mind*. Cambridge, MA: MIT Press.

Perner, J., Aichhorn, M., Kronbichler, M., Staffen, W. and Ladurner, G. (2006). Thinking of mental and other representations: the roles of left and right temporo-parietal junction. *Social Neuroscience*, 1, 245–58.

Piaget, J. (1929). *The child's conception of the world*. New York: Harcourt, Brace Jovanovich.

Pierroutsakos, S. L. and DeLoache, J. S. (2003). Infants' manual investigation of pictured objects varying in realism. *Infancy*, 4, 141–56.

Robinson, E. J., Nye, R. and Thomas, G. V. (1994). Children's conceptions of the relationship between pictures and their referents. *Cognitive Development*, 9, 165–91.

Schwartz, D. L. (1995). Reasoning about the referent of a picture versus reasoning about the picture as the referent: an effect of visual realism. *Memory and Cognition*, 23, 709–22.

Slater, A. M., Rose, D. and Morison, V. (1984). Newborn infants' perception of similarities and differences between two and three dimensional stimuli. *British Journal of Developmental Psychology*, 2, 287–94.

Suddendorf, T. (2003). Early representational insight: twenty-four-month-olds can use a photo to find an object in the world. *Child Development*, 74, 896–904.

Thomas, G. V., Jolley, R. P., Robinson, E. J. and Champion, H. (1999). Realist errors in children's responses to pictures and words as representations. *Journal of Experimental Child Psychology*, 74, 1–20.

Troseth, G. L. and DeLoache, J. S. (1998). The medium can obscure the message: young children's understanding of video. *Child Development*, 69, 950–65.

Uttal, D. H., Schreiber, J. C. and DeLoache, J. S. (1995). Waiting to use a symbol: the effects of delay on children's use of models. *Child Development*, 66, 1875–89.

Werner, H. and Kaplan, B. (1963). *Symbol formation: an organismic developmental approach to language and the expression of thought.* New York: Wiley.

Zaitchik, D. (1990). When representations conflict with reality: the preschooler's problem with false beliefs and false photographs. *Cognition*, 35, 41–68.

Zelazo, P. D., Frye, D. and Rapus, T. (1996). An age-related dissociation between knowing rules and using them. *Cognitive Development*, 11, 37–63.

6 Pictorial intention, action and interpretation

Norman H. Freeman and Esther Adi-Japha

Freeman and Adi-Japha show that drawing production necessarily involves several steps that are specifically analysed in this chapter. Forming an intention precedes and accompanies the action sequences making up the process of production. The emerging product, the trace left on the graphic surface, stimulates an interpretation that normally should conform to the intention. The authors argue evidence is needed that bears on the child's emerging grasp of intention–action–interpretation links. Some evidence shows that the links in the production system start operating separately by approximately age 3 years, though even earlier indications of drawing-related symbolic actions can be observed in scribblers. In that light, a special case is made for reviving research on human figure drawing. Throughout the chapter, Freeman and Adi-Japha develop an original point of view arguing that researchers should take both a backwards look at drawing rules that children have to suppress and a forwards look at the rules they newly engage with, in order to generate a process model of drawing development. Evidence coming from the literature on the so-called canonical bias in drawing is particularly enlightening in this respect. Note that this perspective shares some features with the one suggested by Jolley, in the sense that Freeman and Adi-Japha give much attention to the changes occurring in executive processes, in particular to inhibition, when they address drawing behaviour.

WHENEVER child development is orderly enough for typical progressions to be identified, researchers often devote much effort to specifying advances that children learn to make. We shall call that a 'forward-looking' orientation, because it is devoted to explaining (a) each next step that a child may be expected to take, (b) what might be easy or difficult about that step, and (c) what powerful new tool thereby acquired may lay the groundwork for the next advance. Research into children's drawing often takes a forward orientation towards analysing how children progressively discover increasingly complex and productive rules for organizing lines on the page: 'children do this by seeking appropriate solutions to specific drawing problems' (Willats, 1997, p. 319). We agree. Indeed, devising specific drawing problems to challenge children was the focus of foundational experiments in children's drawing in the 1970s (Freeman, 1980). One feature of this chapter is that, after analysing relations between intention, action and interpretation in development, we found ourselves having to return to those founding studies and ask what fresh questions may be asked in the light of an updated perspective on children's problem-solving. We enquire below into what conditions might help children find solutions to specific problems.

But current cognitive accounts often embody radical doubt about the extent to which a forward orientation of looking at each next advance can be sustained on its own. Much research in this millennium is taking a fresh look at learning processes in all domains. In a target article, Kuhn and Pease (2006) envisage development being impelled both by (largely facilitatory) metacognitive processes and by executive inhibitory processes: 'Cognitive development can be conceived of, not only as the progressive *acquisition* of knowledge, but also as the enhanced *inhibition* of reactions that get in the way of demonstrating knowledge that is already present' (Diamond, 1991, p. 67, italics original); and 'Inhibitory processes are ubiquitous in psychological functioning' (Leslie and Polizzi, 1998, p. 247). For functions serving inhibition, we here settle for the term 'executive function', as is most frequently invoked in mainstream cognitive development literature. The modern backwards-and-forwards approach is certainly applicable to the study of drawing. Willats (2005, as early as page 17) reached the point that: 'It is only by adopting new rules, *and abandoning the old ones*, that children can produce drawings that provide vivid pictorial images' (italics added). It is hard to consolidate gains whilst dragging baggage from the recent past. Not all analysis should fixate on the developmental next step. In sum, a complementary analysis has to take a backwards glance at the child's *disengagement* from her current position. Our proposal is that wherever a large innovation in analysis is required, it makes sense to re-evaluate earlier research and to see how aspects of the designs and of the writing-up might provide ready-made evidence in the light of the new analysis. We shall show how a reassessment of a tradition of work is worthwhile in the drawing domain, and we shall present some ongoing new studies designed to build on the earlier work. Note: schooling begins at different ages in different countries; from here on, we use the term 'preschooler' to indicate children of 3 and 4 years of age.

Approaches to human figure drawing

Successful human figure drawing involves the child in finding a way of fulfilling an intention to use an appropriate drawing rule, a rule appropriate to avoiding misinterpretations in a particular situation. A complementary process involves the child in finding a way to suppress a temptation to use an executively easier rule that could result in a misinterpretation. The emphasis on both intention and interpretation is needed for a functional analysis (Schier, 1986) when characterizing a successful picture as one which triggers in a viewer the appropriate recognition of what the artist intends the picture to represent (Freeman, 1993, 1995). A consideration of interpretation and intention involves crosstalk from the theory of mind domain into the pictorial domain (Freeman, 2000, 2004). An intention precedes the process of production; an interpretation is what is afforded by the product at the end of the process. When does the child come to connect the initial intention and the subsequent interpretation via an often lengthy and complex production process involving both activation and suppression of drawing rules?

Luquet (1927) summed up the prevailing position around the start of the twentieth century: young children's pictorial intentions are connected to graphic action in such a fragile way that the intention can easily change in mid-action (see Freeman's 1972 critique of the Piagetian incorporation of the approach). Figure 6.1 shows a scribbler of nearly 3 years of age engaging with pictorial intention, production and interpretation. But a scribble of a snail falls short of depicting her: the scribble 'simply does not represent her as having any visual properties – properties she may be seen to have' (Lopes, 1997, p. 98). Later on in the century, researchers vacillated between optimistic views of scribblers' nascent connections between intention and interpretation (Matthews, 2004; Smith, 1979; Stephan, 1990) and the pessimistic conclusion that preschoolers 'show the utter lack of any apparent connection between a mental picture in consciousness and the movements made by the hands and fingers in trying to draw it' (Lukens, 1896, pp. 79–80). It is fair to say that the largely descriptive approach engendered pessimism about finding evidence for preschoolers' grasp of how to follow through an initial pictorial intention or, by the same token, preschoolers' ability to maintain subsequent pictorial interpretation.

Rather than engage in debating circumstantial evidence, one needs reliable experimental evidence on connections between (a) pictorial intention and graphic action, (b) graphic action and pictorial interpretation, (c) pictorial intention and pictorial interpretation. We shall have to move back and forth between these three pairs of connections in

Pictorial intention, action and interpretation

Miriam

Figure 6.1 Miriam (2:10) said that she would draw a flower. While drawing she said that she was drawing a flower. But following the drawing she said that it came out as a snail.

the sections below. The next section opens with the problem of pictorial interpretation. One reason for starting with interpretation instead of with intention is that children look at pictures long before developing the capability of wielding a pen. Analyses of pictorial interpretation have been slowly accruing in both psychological and philosophical literature (Freeman, 2004).

A focus on pictorial interpretation

It is perennially intriguing that a picture can be seen to represent something else, thereby having dual reality merely by virtue of a few lines on a flat page. Two-year-olds treat pictures differently from the objects that the pictures depict (Pierroutsakos *et al.*, 2005). There is universal psychological agreement that well before 3 years of age scribblers are already aware of the dual reality of a drawing both as a graphic signifier and as an object existing in separate reality. There is philosophical agreement that pictures 'must provoke contrary recognitional abilities' (Schier, 1986, p. 195). It is easy to forget that there is a complexity to the innocuous phrase 'dual reality': the two realities bear the following asymmetrical relation. The lines on the page that can be described in geometrical terms as curves, angles, dots, dashes and so forth are the *vehicle* of the representation. No lines, no image of, say, a balloon. In terms borrowed from Searle (1983), the *direction of fit* is from lines to referent: if the drawing is not recognizable as a balloon, the job of the artist is to change the lines fittingly. Yet the lines are not dedicated 'balloon-lines reserved for balloons': they are just plurifunctional lines, potentially available for depicting lollipops, road signs or trees. The two realities are entwined one with another, demanding differential attention or allowing differential salience as required. What determines scribblers' balance of attention to one or other aspect of picture-plane reality?

Control of selective attention is the process by which attention is selectively directed to specific aspects of a representation (as in a visual search task, Huang-Pollock, Carr and Nigg, 2004). Control of attention is studied particularly in situations in which there are potentially competing claims on attention which the person has to disentangle. Accordingly, let us briefly consider a dual-reality test of executive function taken from theory of mind research, concentrating on developmental changes in the 'appearance reality test' (Flavell, Green and Flavell, 1986). The test is germane to our concerns because the dual reality involved in the procedure is comparable with the asymmetrical dual reality involved in disentangling a representational aspect of a drawing from its geometrical vehicle.

In an appearance–reality test, children are shown an object that looks like one thing but is really something else (e.g. a toy that looks edible, a bath sponge that looks like a rock). Children are asked, 'What does it look like?' (the appearance question) and 'What is it really?' (the reality question). Children under 4 years of age are prone to unite reality and appearance. Once they discover by touch that the object really is a sponge, children say that it not only is a sponge but that it also looks like a sponge. However, there is another approach to the test that will later be shown to be most useful in new drawing research. Rice, Koinis, Sullivan, Tager-Flusberg and Winner (1997) made salient the *interpretative possibilities* of the situation. One version involved a trick task in which the appearance question was placed in the context of a deceptive game which may prime children to think about mental states. Another version involved a contrasting-interpretation context, in which a dual object (e.g. a sponge-rock) was presented along with an object that matched only the dual object's identity (a sponge) and another object that matched only the dual object's appearance (a rock). Preschoolers were more likely to pass the new tasks and fail the standard task than the reverse. Three-year-olds often grasped the distinction between appearance and reality (a) when their goal was to trick someone, and (b) when they were supported in identifying conflicting object identities. That is, children often perform best, moving between alternative representations, when some factor is present in the situation that enables the children to focus their attention. That consideration applies directly to scribblings that the child herself produces, where the earliest attention-focusing factor has been identified as follows. When invited to interpret her scribble to an inquisitive adult, the child may (a) *describe* a non-representational geometrical attribute (e.g. *a circle, a scribble, just marks*), or (b) *identify* a representational-referential attribute (e.g. *a kite, an apple*). Children use both options, but tend to allocate attention to geometrical description when asked either about their scribble in general or about smooth curves within it, and tend towards representational interpretation when asked about local angular or discontinuous lines in their scribble. Thus, while referring to the whole pattern on the page as 'a scribble' the child may refer to its parts by representational interpretations (e.g. 'rain'). Moreover, when children are asked to reinterpret the same angular curves two weeks later, they tend to fall back on geometrical attributes, such as by calling the shapes 'lines' (Adi-Japha, Levin and Solomon, 1998). The mere existence of the within-subject alternation suggests that children are engaged with representing the two possibilities of interpretation of the same curve: as a geometrical entity or as a referential sign. The older the child, the more she tends to interpret the curve to be a referential sign. The child's disengagement from the picture plane broadens out to encompass more and more shapes as potential signifiers. The suggestion is that the process of making an angular curve demands an attentional effort from the child. That investment helps the child notice what she is doing, and recruits a tendency to name the resulting mark. The effort–effect of Adi-Japha *et al.* (1998) was disrupted by moderate delay, ruling out the possibility that the angular advantage was solely a product of any bias in associative visual memory towards storing a greater number of inflected forms than smooth forms. The effect also disappeared when the child was asked about another child's scribble, or about the experimenter's copy of the child's own scribble. It had to be the child's own investment in the drawing process that facilitated subsequent interpretation. Long before children's own graphic activity can result in a recognizable picture, a basis is laid for some connection being made between own graphic activity and subsequent pictorial interpretation. It cannot be maintained that there was any role for prior intention in accounting for the above data: there was no evidence that any of the 2-year-olds' interpretations were other than post-hoc.

There is evidence for components of the intention–action–interpretation links being set up in 2-year-olds, and starting to operate in 3-year-olds. The ages 3 and 4 years are marked by often intense interest in the links as children come to ponder their solutions to specific drawing problems. The literature contains many examples documenting children's intense absorption in intention, action and interpretation. Researchers have commented at length on preschoolers spontaneously 'reading off' a representation for their scribble based on a bit of visual similarity between lines and referent (Golomb, 1974). 'Reading off' can best be described as an effort to read a hidden meaning off the scribble-picture. It is an interpretation offered after the fact of scribbling. But there seem to be as many cases where preschoolers name a scribble whilst no observer can see any visual resemblance at all between the drawing and the signified instances (the 'romancing' of Gardner, 1980; Golomb, 1974). Such fanciful naming has been observed at all points in the production process, prior to drawing, concomitantly with drawing or after completion. In 'reading off' her drawings the child is actively looking for a representational interpretation aided by perceptual clues. In 'romancing', the child resorts to fantasy and nonchalance instead of a matter-of-fact response such as 'this is just a scribble'; or 'doesn't look like anything'. 'Romancing' is considered to be a transitional phase en route to more adequate perceptually based representation. However, by that very token, transitional romancing offers researchers a clue to the act of representation, whereby the child has to suppress a matter-of-fact geometrical attribute in favour of a representational response. A switch between two views of the same object (e.g. 'a line' and 'a lion'), more specifically disengagement from the first interpretation and reassigning the perceived features with their new meanings, may be related to executive processes of selective attention and inhibitory control (see Doherty and Wimmer, 2005). We suggest that changes in executive process, whether impelled by increment in capacity or by complexity of processing, may launch the liberation of drawing skills to serve representational intentions. Let us now examine experimental evidence on the strengthening of intention–action–interpretation connections in 3-year-olds.

From pictorial intention to interpretation

It is straightforward to examine the connection between intention and interpretation when the children have had no part in the process of production of those particular pictures. Gelman and Ebeling (1998) used

Pictorial intention, action and interpretation

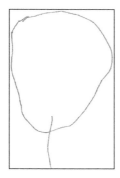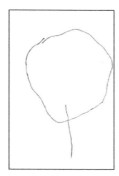

Figure 6.2 A balloon and a lollipop drawn by a 4-year-old, collected by Katie Sheehan and Norman Freeman, where the child was certain about which interpretation was which, to the extent of resisting gentle countersuggestion.

pictures that could be seen as representational (e.g. a teddy). Some children were told that the product had come from someone accidentally knocking over a paint pot. Other children were told that the product had been intentionally produced by someone. The children were later asked to describe each picture. The intentional group named an interpretation of the contents (e.g. 'a teddy') twice as often as did the accidental group. The role of pictorial intention in forming interpretation of other people's pictures is reliably established in the minds of older 3-year-olds.

Now we turn to a case in which the child herself produces the graphic action. Bloom and Markson (1998) asked preschoolers to draw different people, or a lollipop and a balloon on a string. Such drawings often come out similar (see Figure 6.2); but if the intention had been to draw a balloon then in the eyes of the children the eventual product had to be called a balloon, regardless of whether the picture equally looked like a lollipop. That admirable firmness of purpose is presumably the first developmental step in a viable theory of pictorial meaning (for the philosophical aesthetics of adult pictorial intention, see Baxendall, 1985). The child comes to see how to implement an intention so that the picture sustains an intended interpretation. The child uses her memory of her particular intention to (a) transform one of a pair of possible interpretations into a correct interpretation, and (b) transform the other interpretation into a misinterpretation. It would be nice to have a third-person version run, one in which the child is told the other person's intentions and then is asked about the products.

Preschoolers' decision to stand by their original intentions may tell us something more. Consider the fact that an initial intention is part of the causal history of a picture. You yourself have unwittingly been photographed many times by security cameras. You had no intention of being photographed; nevertheless you played a crucial role in the causal history of those particular pictures. Accordingly, a picture of you represents you and not your identical twin who, let us suppose, had successfully avoided ever causing a self-photograph in any way, as recorded in the history books. Freeman (2004) suggested that the situation is a representational analogue of a marriage contract: someone who marries you does not thereby marry your twin, not even if your parents had absentmindedly given both of you the same name. Let us take another look at the close relation between intention and interpretation so as to identify three analytically distinct possibilities that fortunately turn straightforwardly into empirical alternatives.

An initial intention is a mental state which an agent uses to mobilize a set of processes that the agent hopes will realize the intention. If the processes go wrong, the end product will be misinterpretable or even uninterpretable. A picture can be used as *evidence for* an intention. If an artist is asked to prove that she had meant to depict something, she might reasonably call the picture in evidence to support her claim about what she had been trying to achieve that afternoon. If the picture looks like a picture of, say, a shoe, the artist can reasonably claim to have had the intention of depicting a shoe, rather than, say, an aardvark. So we now have three analytically distinct reasons why young children might lay great store on making a connection between initial intention and final interpretation. First, the mental state has a *prospective role* in inaugurating the process of production: no intention, no guaranteed interpretation (see Freeman, 2004). Secondly, during the production, the intention is part of the *ongoing* causal chain of the picture production: if the intention ceases prematurely to guide selection of drawing rules, no appropriate picture will result. Thirdly, the intention can be proved by citing the picture as *retrospective* evidence: 'Children might call a picture that looks like a bird "a bird" not merely because it looks like a bird, but because its appearance makes it likely that it was created with the intent to represent a bird. In general, appearance – and shape in particular – is seen as an excellent cue to intention' (Bloom and Markson, 1998, p. 20). It follows that one would like to know exactly when and how preschoolers start to connect intention and interpretation in their own drawing practices, as follows.

First, an intention is not the only mental state that plays a prospective trigger role in inaugurating production. A desire to depict something may inaugurate production. Yet desire and intention are not at all the same thing. Someone may desire something without intending to do anything at all to fulfil the desire; and conversely, someone might intend to do something most unwillingly. When do children understand such distinctions as they apply to the initial state in production? When do children allow the considerations to inform their own practice? Such questions self-evidently would take a perspective on considerations from theory of mind research in order to inform drawing research (Freeman, 2000, 2004).

Secondly, intention has two particular roles in the ongoing process of production, facilitating appropriate rules and suppressing inappropriate rules. Rather than asking whether the child understands those roles, we can more usefully ask under what conditions the child can do each effectively in practice. Let us contrast this research question with the Bloom-Markson situation in which the child cannot foresee whilst she is drawing that her finished balloon drawing might *become* confusable with a lollipop drawing (and vice versa). In contrast, we now need a technique whereby the child is alerted to potential confusability between products before she even starts to draw. The question is whether such a prospective cue about problems of interpretation and misinterpretation will help the child towards a balance between (a) mobilizing the rules that will lead to a correct interpretation, and (b) suppressing rules that will lead to a misinterpretation. We note evidence on these topics below.

Finally, there is the question of whether the child grasps that a drawing is evidence about what led up to the product. There has been some work on children's retrospective inferences from product to production (Freeman, 2004). However, the research lies just outside the scope of this chapter. We accordingly set it aside for work in the near future to relate retrospective inference to prospective judgement and to ongoing process control via developing concepts of evidence.

General perspective on pre-representational intention and graphic action

We previously noted evidence for pictorial *interpretation and production* in scribblers. We next survey pre-representational drawing with a view to diagnosing the earliest evidence for *intention and production* in scribbling, the earliest phase inaugurating the whole representational drawing enterprise. We shall suggest that even young scribblers form a connection between interpreting a picture, forming a representational graphic intention and following it through with what they regard as an appropriate drawing rule. Even if to an observer the children merely seem to be scribbling: children's first representational attempts remain invisible because they are buried in the visual noise of the scribbling (Freeman, 1980).

Researchers agree that drawing evolves from the scribbling which typically appears at 18–24 months (Freeman, 1993). Two salient aspects of the scribbling phase are that children (a) often readily continue the ongoing *process of production* by moving from one scribble to the next, yet (b) show only transient interest in their own scribbles as *products* to be interpreted (Gardner, 1980; Thomas and Silk, 1989). It might even be best to talk of 'scribblings' rather than 'scribbles' so as to preserve the sense of the scribbler immersed in exploring immediate feedback of the actions rather than aiming at a pre-specified visual goal. Scribbling in its initial phases can be viewed as a motor activity determined mainly by on-the-spot motor functioning of arm, wrist and hand, unguided by prospective intentions serving advance visual planning. However, when Matthews (2004) summed up spirited opposition to such a mechanical account, he was undeniably on to something, for preliminary indications of drawing-related symbolic actions can be traced as early even as the second year of life, even if unambiguously achieved representational drawing, preplanned by the child and recognizable to a viewer, first tends to appear by 3 or 4 years (Freeman, 1993; Golomb, 1992). Let us consider some evidence and draw out its implications.

Freeman (1980) briefly introduced a technique of examining the role of prior intentions in directing production. The reason for doing that is because one cannot necessarily take a scribbler's word for her intention. The then-new technique was initially to train the child to announce intentions that had nothing to do with drawing, such as pushing a pencil off the desk. The action and its effect thereby formed evidence corroborating the announced intention. The procedure then moved on to handing the child a pencil and presenting the child with a saliently incomplete drawing of something, e.g. a face lacking one eye or one ear. It was important that the experimenter remained silent now, so that any announced intention genuinely had to come from the child. It was equally important that the drawing was incomplete, so that the child's intention could be identified as an attempt to fulfil a specifiable graphic goal inspired by an initial interpretation of the drawing on the table. Under such circumstances, it was easy to get a preschool scribbler to announce an intention, e.g. 'eye', and one could record the placement of the pen in the appropriate place on the drawing. Even if thereafter the child utterly failed to recruit appropriate rules for drawing an eye, and failed to suppress letting the pencil wander over the face and beyond it, the first-hit placement gave the requisite evidence on the role of the intention in inaugurating the graphic process. Yet there was an unconsidered limitation on the power of the evidence. How can one distinguish the child's placement of the pen as being (a) the start of making a drawing, from (b) merely pointing with the pen to the place of the missing eye? Two experiments indicate that the latter possibility can be dismissed.

The logic behind setting the next two experiments in the context of the present account is that a simple indicative pen hit need only mark the precise place where the indicator *currently* wants to point at; the mark is confined to being a *retrospective* sign of what the person meant. In contrast, a point that starts a drawing process has *prospectively* to serve the next step in drawing. Freeman (1980) reported a method which empirically serves to distinguish between the two actions. Children were presented with pages each of which contained a face in a different orientation with respect to the child, set within a square or a diamond frame. The child was asked to complete each human figure drawing. A series of experiments established that both the orientation variables determined the point of first hit of the pen. Children were monitoring orientation cues internal and external to the face that would serve subsequent direction of the pen in completing the drawing. That involves inordinately more complex mental computation than is required merely to make a mark at the bottom of the face to show that a trunk needs to go beneath the face. The conservative conclusion is that even scribblers consciously use a graphic intention to facilitate selection of an appropriate drawing rule, even if the final product eventually comes out looking completely uninterpretable.

The next study bears on whether the child can use her intention to *suppress* a tempting graphic option. The starting point was a study by Freeman (1975), who had proposed that human figure drawing involved the child inhibiting premature end-anchoring in executing a serial action plan. That is, Freeman canvassed an early conception of executive suppression as a mechanism for advance in human figure drawing between (a) the tadpole form that has only one circle as a body-plan and (b) a segmented head-trunk which, for lack of a term in the literature, Freeman called the 'conventional form'. Preschoolers were given pre-drawn heads and bodies of different relative sizes for arms and legs to be drawn on. The result was 'the body-proportion effect' whereby the child attached arms to whichever was the larger, head or trunk. Freeman and Hargreaves (1977) modified the procedure by getting the child to place her pen in the centre of either the head or the trunk to draw either nose or navel, thereby identifying which was head and which was trunk for graphic purposes. (We shall return later to the problem of interpretation of the pre-drawn figures.) Only when the pen was securely in place was the child then asked for arms to be drawn. The results were that the body-proportion effect appeared in full strength. Strikingly, on trials in which the head had been pre-drawn larger than the trunk, and the children identified the trunk by putting their pen on the trunk to draw a navel, the children avoided the easy option of just drawing arms on the trunk near to the navel where their pen was at the time of asking them to form the intention; but instead the children paused and shifted the pen to the head to draw arms, thereby laboriously inaugurating whatever drawing rule they would normally inaugurate on interpreting the whole pre-drawn figure. We suggest that that particular part of the data goes beyond showing inauguration of a drawing rule in that it shows suppression of an easy (and correct) option in favour of a more demanding (and incorrect) graphic option. Consideration given to relative difficulties of different graphic options facing the child was in fact the trigger for the very first modern paper on children's drawings (Freeman and Janikoun, 1972).

Deeper into intention, action and interpretation: new work on human figure drawing

By using the foregoing to return to the main question of specifying relations between intention, action and interpretation, we can identify new techniques for investigating human figure drawing.

First, some incomplete pre-drawn figures that generate the body-proportion effect may look a little odd. Whilst a small-headed figure may be interpreted as a fat person, a big-headed figure may look rather monstrous. The method so far has been cavalier about possible problems in interpretation. That can easily be rectified by presenting the child with a plastic big-headed doll to make it clear that the incomplete drawing is indeed meant to have the proportions that it does. In sum, by manipulating projection rules between page and referent, one can investigate 'variant doll interpretations' in the *initial* direction of preschoolers' actions.

Secondly, there is the converse of the above: consider the interpretative *consequences* of alternative graphic actions. Such an approach is already established in the drawing literature, awaiting application to human figure drawing as follows. Freeman and Janikoun (1972) presented children with a cup oriented so that a motif on its exterior surface was in direct view, while its handle was out of view. The request was for the children to draw exactly what they could see. Children under 8 years mostly included a side-view handle in their drawing of the cup, which they couldn't see, and were disinclined to draw the motif which they could see. Older children were not inclined to portray a handle, and drew the motif instead. The handle of a cup enables one to interpret the cup as a cup rather than as a glass or a tube, whereas a motif is not category-relevant. Many variables can moderately influence the age effect one way or another (Lewis, Russell and Berridge, 1993; Picard and Durand, 2005). The most powerful variable we know of comes from Davis' (1985) demonstration that the introduction of a second cup in a canonical orientation (handle at the side) beside the target cup with its handle turned helped children avoid the error of drawing a handle on the target cup. The paired cups created a visual contrast between the two objects to which children were sensitive (for other instances of the power of contrast in drawing see Bremner, 1985; Cox, 1985; Light, 1985). Such a facilitation effect looks like the success of Rice *et al.* (1997), as noted in an earlier section, in displaying both a sponge and a rock in the appearance–reality sponge–rock task. Making physical alternatives clear often aids children in focusing attention on the representational alternatives they are faced with, and thereby helps them choose one alternative and suppress the other. In Davis' case, drawing a handle in side view would generate a misinterpretation because the drawing looks like the second cup which has the handle in full view and not like the target cup which has its handle hidden. Precisely that logic can be applied to preschoolers' human figure drawing.

Recall that the body-proportion effect was the tendency to attach arms to whatever was the larger body segment. Imagine modifying the procedure so as to provide contrasting models for the child to draw. One model would have its arms on the trunk as all people do, and the other model would have its arms on the head, as monsters indeed do. Merely by having the models on the table and asking the child to complete the pre-drawn head and trunk of one of the models would determine what was a correct interpretation and what was a misinterpretation. On some trials it would be correct for the child not to suppress the body-proportion temptation whilst on other trials attaching the arms to the larger segment would be misinterpretable as drawing the wrong model. A 'contrasting dolls and monsters' technique should prime the child as to the interpretative consequences of her action.

A small team with M. Chen, L. Davies, C. Jones, E. Pegrum, R. Smyth and C. Young was formed to advance the techniques in various ways. Provisional results are as follows. Providing variant plastic dolls to validate the pre-drawn figures has not, so far, helped children to avoid the body-proportion effect at all. Children will agree which pre-drawn picture shows a big-headed doll, and yet still draw arms on the head. The suggestion thus is that adding arms to the pre-drawn head does not occur because of any interpretative problem over picture–referent interpretation. In that case, the finding might direct our attention to the intention–action link more than the interpretation–action link. That is, we can usefully consider the action–interpretation link via the contrast technique of priming the child with the consequences of her action. Arms on the trunk make a person; arms on the head make a monster. The contrast seems only moderately to dampen the body-proportion effect even in some 4-year-olds. That does suggest that there is strong suppression needed in order to choose a correct drawing rule. Accordingly, whilst pursuing the above, we open a third line of work directly on suppression, as follows.

It may be recalled that near the outset of this chapter we noted the trend towards testing for suppression processes in various domains. There is again a useful precedent in a follow-up to Freeman and Janikoun (1972) where the sole alteration was that the cup was made of clear glass. Thus, when the glass cup was turned so that the handle was opposite the child, the handle seen through the body of the glass looked like a straight rod instead of a canonically side-view graspable curve. Many older children who avoided drawing the handle in the original cup situation now 'regressed' to a side-view handle in the glass situation (Freeman, 1980). Freeman suggested that the atypical view of the glass handle acted to remind the children that the object indeed did have a handle to be drawn, and the children failed to inhibit drawing that handle in canonical form. In contrast to the above two techniques on studying children who are in the throes of the body-proportion effect, this third approach focuses on whether some earlier error can be reactivated in children who have progressed to a more advanced phase. The experimental logic is general in that it applies to other domains too (Freeman, Hood and Meehan, 2004). Entirely tentatively, we note that a few older 4-year-olds who have passed the phase of the body-proportion effect have reliably had the effect reactivated. Whether these children are typical or atypical remains to be seen.

We reaffirm that it is worthwhile taking a backwards look at drawing rules that children have to disengage from, alongside taking a forwards look at the rules they newly engage with. The optimism of the 1980s over explanatory models being already then within grasp was a bit overoptimistic. It is taking somewhat longer than anyone would have wished to model how children master human figure drawing.

REFERENCES

Adi-Japha, E., Levin, I. and Solomon, S. (1998). Emergence of representation in drawing: the relation between kinematic and referential aspects. *Cognitive Development*, 13, 23–49.
Baxendall, M. (1985). *Patterns of intention*. London: Yale University Press.
Bloom, P. and Markson, L. (1998). Intention and analogy in children's naming of pictorial representations. *Psychological Science*, 9, 200–4.
Bremner, J. G. (1985). Provoked use of height in pictures as a depth cue in young children's drawings. *British Journal of Developmental Psychology*, 2, 95–8.

Cox, M. V. (1985). One object behind another: young children's use of array-specific or view-specific representations. In N. H. Freeman and M. V. Cox (eds.), *Visual order: the nature and development of pictorial representation* (pp. 188–281). Cambridge: Cambridge University Press.

Davis, A. M. (1985). The canonical bias: young children's drawings of familiar objects. In N. H. Freeman and M. V. Cox (eds.), *Visual order: the nature and development of pictorial representation* (pp. 202–13). Cambridge: Cambridge University Press.

Diamond, A. (1991). Neuropsychological insight into the meaning of object concept development. In S. Carey and R. Gelman (eds.), *The epigenesis of mind* (pp. 67–110). Hillsdale, NJ: Erlbaum.

Doherty, M. J. and Wimmer, M. (2005). Children's understanding of ambiguous figures: which cognitive developments are necessary to experience reversal? *Cognitive Development*, 20, 407–21.

Flavell, J. H., Green, F. L. and Flavell, E. R. (1986). Development of knowledge about the appearance–reality distinction. *Monographs of the Society for Research on Child Development*, 51 (1, serial no. 212).

Freeman, N. H. (1972). Process and product in children's drawing. *Perception*, 1, 123–40.

(1975). Do children draw men with arms coming out of the head? *Nature*, 254, 416–17.

(1980). *Strategies of representation in young children*. London: Academic Press.

(1993). Drawing: public instrument of representation. In C. Pratt and A. F. Garton (eds.), *Systems of representation in children* (pp. 113–32). Chichester: Wiley.

(1995). The emergence of a framework theory of pictorial reasoning. In C. Lange-Küttner and G. V. Thomas (eds.), *Drawing and looking: theoretical approaches to pictorial representation in children* (pp. 135–46). London: Pearson/Prentice Hall (distributed by www.amazon.co.uk).

(2000). Communication and representation: why mentalistic reasoning is a lifelong endeavour. In P. Mitchell and K. J. Riggs (eds.), *Children's reasoning and the mind* (pp. 349–67). Hove: Psychology Press.

(2004). Aesthetic judgement and reasoning. In E. W. Eisner and M. D. Day (eds.), *Handbook of research and policy in art education* (pp. 359–78). Mahwah, NJ: Erlbaum/National Art Education Association (USA).

Freeman, N. H. and Hargreaves, S. (1977). Directed movements and the body-proportion effect in preschool children's human figure drawings. *Quarterly Journal of Experimental Psychology*, 28, 227–35.

Freeman, N. H., Hood, B. M. and Meehan, C. (2004). Young children who abandon error behaviourally still have to free themselves mentally: a retrospective test for change in intuitive physics. *Developmental Science*, 7, 277–82.

Freeman, N. H. and Janikoun, R. (1972). Intellectual realism in children's drawings of a familiar object with distinctive features. *Child Development*, 43, 1116–21.

Gardner, H. (1980). *Artful scribbles*. New York: Basic Books.

Gelman, S. A. and Ebeling, K. S. (1998). Shape and representational status in children's early naming. *Cognition*, 66, B35–B47.

Golomb, C. (1974). *Young children's sculpture and drawing.* Cambridge, MA: Harvard University Press.
  (1992). *The child's creation of a pictorial world.* Berkeley: University of California Press.
Huang-Pollock, C. L., Carr, T. H. and Nigg, J. T. (2004). Perceptual load influences early versus late attentional selection in children and adults. *Developmental Psychology*, 40, 545–58.
Kuhn, D. and Pease, M. (2006). Do children and adults learn differently? *Journal of Cognition and Development*, 7, 279–94.
Leslie, A. M. and Polizzi, P. (1998). Inhibitory processing in the false belief task: two conjectures. *Developmental Science*, 1, 247–58.
Lewis, C., Russell, C. and Berridge, D. (1993). When is a mug not a mug? Effects of content, naming, and instructions on children's drawings. *Journal of Experimental Child Psychology*, 56, 291–302.
Light, P. (1985). The development of view-specific representation when considered from a socio-cognitive standpoint. In N. H. Freeman and M. V. Cox (eds.), *Visual order: the nature and development of pictorial representation* (pp. 214–30). Cambridge: Cambridge University Press.
Lopes, D. (1997). *Understanding pictures.* Oxford: Clarendon Press.
Lukens, H. T. (1986). A study of children's drawings in the early years. *Pedagogical Seminary*, 4, 79–110.
Luquet, G. H. (1927). *Le dessin enfantin [Children's drawing].* Paris: Alcan.
Matthews, J. (2004). The art of infancy. In E. W. Eisner and M. D. Day (eds.), *Handbook of research and policy in art education* (pp. 253–98). Mahwah, NJ: Erlbaum.
Pierroutsakos, S. L., DeLoache, J. S., Ground, M. and Bernard, E. N. (2005). Very young children are insensitive to picture- but not object-orientation. *Developmental Science*, 8, 326–32.
Picard, D. and Durand, K. (2005). Are young children's drawings canonically biased? *Journal of Experimental Child Psychology*, 90, 48–64.
Rice, C., Koinis, D., Sullivan, K., Tager-Flusberg, H. and Winner, E. (1997). When 3-year-olds pass the appearance–reality test. *Developmental Psychology*, 33, 54–61.
Schier, F. (1986). *Deeper into pictures.* Cambridge: Cambridge University Press.
Searle, J. R. (1983). *Intentionality.* Cambridge: Cambridge University Press.
Smith, N. R. (1979). How a picture means. *New Directions for Child Development*, 3, 59–72.
Stephan, M. (1990). *A transformational theory of aesthetics.* London: Routledge.
Thomas G. V. and Silk, A. M. J. (1989). *An introduction to the psychology of children's drawings.* New York: Harvester Wheatsheaf.
Willats, J. (1997). *Art and representation.* Princeton, NJ: Princeton University Press.
  (2005). *Making sense of children's drawings.* Mahwah, NJ: Erlbaum.

Part II

Syntax, space systems and projection

7 The interaction of biomechanical and cognitive constraints in the production of children's drawing

Gregory Braswell and Karl Rosengren

Research investigating the process of drawing has often been overshadowed by a focus on the end product of this process. However, it is important to acknowledge that various factors that shape the process also impact on the final drawing outcome. In this chapter, Braswell and Rosengren examine how biomechanical, cognitive and contextual factors shape how children and adults draw. For example, the physiology and structure of the fingers, hands and arms often influences the direction in which strokes are produced on a page. Numerous studies demonstrate the effect of handedness on drawing horizontal lines, for instance. Other research has demonstrated that cognitive factors shape where drawers begin figures and the direction in which strokes are produced. In some cases, drawers rely on relatively stable, procedural representations to guide the sequencing and placement of strokes for entire images. Contextual factors, such as writing systems, also play important roles in determining how individuals construct a drawing. They discuss these factors and how they interact using the TASC-based approach, which views development as driven by constraints internal and external to the individual.

DRAWING is a complex skill that emerges during the second year of life, changes significantly over the course of childhood, and involves both higher-order symbolic processes and a motor system capable of producing a desired representation in the real world. Much of the research on children's drawings has focused on the cognitive aspects of children's drawing, often with an emphasis on the final product of a drawing episode. This body of research has provided a relatively detailed account of what children draw, how these drawings relate to underlying mental representations, and how these drawings vary as a function of age and experiences (e.g. Cox, 1992; Goodnow, 1977; Kellogg, 1969; Willats, 1977).

Much less consideration has been given to the motor aspects of drawing. In part, this may be due to the fact that, at least in the United States, motor components and their development are viewed as less important and perhaps less interesting aspects of behaviour than cognitive processes (Rosenbaum, 2005). There has been some research, however, looking at certain motor components involved in drawing and writing that we will discuss shortly. Although it is generally acknowledged that cognitive and motor components interact in the production of a child's drawing, it is often difficult to tease apart the relative contribution of these different factors. It is also commonly assumed that even though biomechanical constraints clearly influence the quality of children's drawing the representational desire of the children is not occluded by these biomechanical constraints. The overall goal of this chapter is to explore more closely the role of biomechanical, cognitive and contextual constraints on drawing development.

One way to understand how certain constraints might influence the drawing process and its outcome is to examine them through the TASC-based approach proposed by Rosengren and his colleagues (Rosengren and Savelsbergh, 2000; Rosengren, Savelsbergh and Van der Kamp, 2003), which envisions development in terms of '*task*-related *adaptation* and *selection*, influenced by *constraints* both within and external to the child' (Rosengren and Braswell, 2003, p. 60).

Constraints involve environmental properties (e.g. gravity, friction), properties of the organism (e.g. handedness, size of hand) and task properties (e.g. the drawing goal, particular instructions for a drawing activity) (Newell, 1986; Rosengren *et al.*, 2003). While some researchers have proposed that culturally specified expectations and artefacts serve as additional forms of constraint (Van Roon, Van der Kamp and Steenbergen, 2003), these can be perhaps best thought of as additional forms of either environmental or task constraints depending upon how they influence the child's behaviour in a particular situation. For example, differences in the preferred direction of writing that are found across cultures may be viewed as an environmental constraint that impacts on drawing and writing in a global manner across individuals, sessions and particular tasks. The presentation of a particular drawing implement that is more common in one culture than another, as calligraphy brushes are to certain Asian cultures, may be best viewed as a task constraint that has more local and specific influences on how a drawing is produced. In this situation, the drawing is potentially more influenced by the implement itself, a task constraint, than by the larger cultural influences, although the larger culture determines in part the implement to be used.

Constraints on behaviour do not work independently but interact in complex ways to produce specific behaviours. For example, the size of a child's hand and his or her grip strength influence the particular grip configuration that he or she might use when given a specific drawing implement by a parent or teacher. The child's grip configuration and the size and type of drawing implement (e.g. crayon, pen or marker) also interact to influence the frictional forces between the implement and the drawing surface (e.g. paper, chalk board or sidewalk). Certain combinations of grips, implements and surfaces may facilitate the drawing of highly detailed, complex figures that fit within a small confined space. Other combinations of grips, implements and surfaces may facilitate the drawing of less refined and less detailed figures that require a larger spatial area. Cognitive and cultural influences also interact in this process, influencing the choice of implements, surfaces and representations to be produced. In this chapter, we will examine various biomechanical and cognitive properties that serve as organismic constraints on the drawing process. We will also explore how these organismic constraints interact with task constraints and cultural constraints (particularly writing systems) during drawing development.

The impact of biomechanical constraints

Numerous studies have demonstrated the impact of biomechanical factors on the process of drawing. The underlying physiology, structure and movement of arms, hands and fingers all constrain how children and adults create images from individual strokes. Researchers examining these factors have examined the development of grip configurations, the influence of handedness, and how biomechanical factors influence stroke directionality. An assumption that appears to underlie much of this work is that various biomechanical factors are at different points in development relatively stable influences on the drawing process. We have argued, however, that much of the research on children's drawing and on children's cognitive development more broadly has ignored important aspects of *variability* (Rosengren and Braswell, 2001, 2003). Siegler (1996) has also argued that the failure to consider variability in children's behaviour has made it difficult to understand the process of developmental change. Likewise, Thelen and Smith (1994) have suggested that variability is inherent in any complex system and that variability may be a driving force underlying developmental change. In our own research (Braswell and Rosengren, 2000, 2002; Braswell, Rosengren and Pierroutsakos, 2007) we have shown that high levels of variability are characteristic of early aspects of children's drawing, and that the relative contribution of biomechanical and cognitive constraints varies as a function of a variety of factors, including drawing experience and different task constraints (Braswell and Rosengren, 2000, 2002).

The development of grip configurations

The manner in which children hold a drawing implement and how this changes with age has received considerable attention (Rosenbloom and Horton, 1971; Saida and Miyashita, 1979; Sasson, Nimmo-Smith and Wing, 1986; Thomassen and Teulings, 1983; Ziviani, 1982, 1983). Traditionally it has been suggested that the form of grasp used for an object or tool is determined primarily by maturational factors (Connolly and Elliott, 1972; Halverson, 1931). Researchers examining children's drawing and writing have described a developmental progression from less mature grasps involving the palm and fingers (palmar or power grips) to more mature grip configurations where the object is held between the thumb and first two fingers (tripod grasp; Rosenbloom and Horton, 1971; Saida and Miyashita, 1979). At the most advanced stage, children use a dynamic tripod, a grasp differentiated from the tripod by relatively small movements of the fingers and thumb. These small movements are thought to enable the drawer to produce fine details in drawing or writing. Traditionally, children were thought to acquire the final grip, the dynamic tripod, by about 5 years of age (Rosenbloom and Horton, 1971).

Even though researchers have generally emphasized the stability of grip configurations in children of the same age, a number of researchers have reported some degree of variability in the grip configurations used by different children (Blöte and Heijden, 1988; Blöte, Zielstra and Zoetewey, 1987). In these studies approximately 40 per cent of 5- to 7-year-old children were found to use a grip other than the dynamic tripod. This is not all that surprising if one conducts an informal survey of grip configurations commonly used by adults. A quick survey of pen grips used in any undergraduate class will demonstrate that many adults do not employ the standard dynamic tripod. Blöte *et al.* (1987) also report variability *within* individual children in the grip configurations they use in a particular drawing session. They found that while many 6-year-old children begin drawing with a tripod grip they sometimes shift to use a power grip over the course of the drawing session.

One reason for looking at grip configurations is that it has often been assumed that a child's grip configuration influences various aspects of drawing or writing. The results of these studies have been somewhat mixed. For example, Ziviani and Elkins (1986) found no relation between pen grips and writing speed or legibility in a sample of 8- to 14-year-olds. One possible explanation of this result is that children of this age have had extensive experience drawing and writing and that these participants primarily used variations of a single grip, the dynamic tripod. In another study of younger children, Martlew (1992) reported that

4- and 5-year-old children using a tripod grip produced higher-quality letters than children using other grip configurations. We have suggested that one reason for these disparate findings is that the actual grip configuration may be less important than whether the child has adopted a stable grip.

We explored this hypothesis in a series of studies where we varied the types of implements that 3- to 4-year-olds could use and the particular tasks that they were required to perform (Braswell, Rosengren and Pierroutsakos, 2007; Rosengren, DeGuzman and Pierroutsakos, 1995). The tasks included simple shape copying, rapid line drawing and free drawing. The results of these studies showed that there is considerable variability in the manner in which 3- to 4-year-old children hold a drawing implement. We found that on average children switched between three different grip configurations over the course of the drawing sessions. We also found considerable individual differences in the stability of children's grips. The majority of the children exhibited no or only one overall grip change. Other children changed their grips almost constantly over the drawing session. These latter children may be in a transitional state, and it is likely that, if they were followed over time, we would find that they would settle into a particular grip configuration (see Greer and Lockman, 1998).

Although many of the children in our studies exhibited stable grip configurations, *all* of the children frequently changed their finger and/or thumb contact over the drawing sessions without varying their overall grip configuration. This type of variability in grip varied as a function of the task performed. Children were most likely to change their grip in some manner during free drawing than during any of the other tasks. Most studies examining the development of grip configurations have used a shape copying task that may lead to an overestimation of stability. For example, participants in Greer and Lockman's (1998) study drew horizontal and vertical lines. We suggest that free drawing places a variety of task demands on the child, increasing the likelihood that the child might need to adjust her grip in order to produce fine detail or large shapes.

We also found that more grip changes occurred while children were engaged in particular drawing tasks than when children switched between different drawing tasks. This result suggests that the majority of young children may have a preferred grip that is used to begin different drawing tasks, but that the demands of specific tasks lead children to vary their grip configuration.

Young children who varied their grip often were also found to produce less accurate copies of simple shapes than children who rarely changed their grip. One implication of these results is that it is not a particular grip, but the stability of the grip that enables children to copy shapes accurately. Another implication of these results is that the quality of children's drawings may not improve substantially until children have settled into relatively stable grip configurations.

Although we focused on task constraints in these studies and how these influence a drawer's grip configuration, additional studies are necessary for investigating other types of constraints. Likely candidates for important organismic constraints include hand size, hand strength and finger coordination. For example, hand size or strength may serve as an important constraint that interacts with the diameter or length of an implement. Young children are often provided with relatively large drawing implements based on the assumption that these implements will be easier for children to use given their relatively small hands and poorly developed fine motor skills. Large diameter implements, such as large, thick crayons, have a larger area of contact with the drawing surface than implements with a smaller diameter. The larger contact surface creates relatively large frictional forces between the implement and drawing surface. In order to overcome these frictional forces, a child using a relatively large implement, such as a large crayon, may need to alter his grip to a power grip in order to apply adequate force to the implement to produce a drawing. A child with relatively weak grip strength using a large crayon and perhaps using a power grip may produce relatively poor copies of shapes and draw relatively large objects lacking in details because of the interaction of these constraints and not because he lacks some representational capacity.

Providing a young child with a marker that produces much less friction on a surface may enable the child to use a non-power grip and potentially create a drawing with more precision. Thus, an implication of our work is that one must consider how the characteristics of the child interact with the characteristics of the implement and the drawing surface.

Stroke direction

Biomechanical factors seem to have a particularly important influence on stroke directionality (Van Sommers, 1984). Finger and hand flexion, which guide drawing implements inward or downward towards the body, allow for more efficient stroke production than finger and hand extension. Thus, adults and children typically draw vertical lines from top to bottom (although there are exceptions to this general rule to be discussed below). The production of horizontal lines is also strongly shaped by the biomechanics of the human body in that individuals tend to draw moving their hands and fingers away from the midline of the body. Thus right-handed drawers tend to draw horizontal strokes from left to right, and left-handed drawers tend to draw these lines in the opposite direction (Van Sommers, 1984). This phenomenon occurs in both children (Gesell and Ames, 1946; Scheirs, 1990) and adults (Van Sommers, 1984).

Directionality preferences have been noted in other types of strokes beyond the straight horizontal or vertical strokes discussed so far. Van Sommers (1984) found that most adults in Western societies draw circles in a counterclockwise fashion, although this tendency is slightly weaker among left-handed individuals. Other patterns may emerge during the production of other circular forms. Right-handed adults often produce upward spirals in a *clockwise* fashion (Thomassen and Tuelings, 1979; Van Sommers, 1984).

Directionality preferences based on handedness appear not only in the production of single lines but also in the construction of entire figures. For example, directionality differences were demonstrated in the order in which 3- to 11-year-old children completed unfinished pictures of human figures (Glenn, Bradshaw and Sharp, 1995). Thus it appears that directionality differences based on handedness apply to isolated horizontal strokes as well as to more complex figures.

There has been mixed evidence regarding age-related differences in the impact of biomechanical constraints on stroke directionality. Van Sommers (1984) and others (e.g. Braswell and Rosengren, 2000; Gesell and Ames, 1946) have demonstrated that children typically draw circles (proceeding clockwise) differently than adults (proceeding counterclockwise), for example. Van Sommers (1984) found few differences in directionality preferences based on age for drawing horizontal or vertical strokes, yet other studies (e.g. Braswell and Rosengren, 2000; Goodnow and Levine, 1973) have noted increases across age-groups in directionality preferences when drawing isolated, straight lines. Glenn, Bradshaw and Sharp (1995) found that their youngest right-handed participants typically finished figures from right to left. These preferences were unstable among 4- to 7-year-olds (suggesting that these children were in a state of transition), and were reversed among 9- to 11-year-old right-handed participants. Left-handed participants typically drew components in the opposite direction from right-handed participants, although this preference was not as strong. In one study, we found that older children and adults were more likely to copy pictures of a human face and a house with a sun from left to right than younger participants (Braswell and Rosengren, 2000).

There is no established explanation for this age-related change in directionality preference, although certain cognitive constraints may inhibit biomechanical factors in early childhood but not in adulthood (Braswell and Rosengren, 2002). It may be that the biomechanics of the arm, hand and fingers have a greater impact as individuals become more efficient and practised in their drawing efforts. It also may be the case that certain tasks requiring speed or repetition are more greatly influenced by biomechanical rather than cognitive factors.

The impact of cognitive constraints

Biomechanical constraints alone do not drive drawing production. There are various cognitive factors that also shape the manner in which children and adults draw. For example, a large body of research has examined the extent to which adults and children rely on mental, procedural representations to guide the sequencing and placement of strokes. Some researchers have suggested that drawers tend to follow set sequences when drawing common images like cubes and human forms (Phillips, Hobbs and Pratt, 1978; Phillips, Inall and Lauder, 1985; Stiles, 1995). Others have questioned the rigidity or uniformity of set procedures and have demonstrated that children and adults often vary how they draw a variety of images, including well-practised ones (Braswell and Rosengren, 2000; Van Sommers, 1983, 1984).

Karmiloff-Smith's (1990, 1992) theory of 'representational redescription' has served as the foundation for many researchers who have studied the use of stable drawing procedures. According to this view, a child is only able to alter a procedural representation for drawing once that procedure is mastered and the child is able to reflect upon the representation. Thus young children often have trouble interrupting how they draw well-practised figures (e.g. human forms and houses) in order to add novel features (Karmiloff-Smith, 1990; Zhi, Thomas and Robinson, 1997). However, this rigidity can be alleviated by the presentation of graphic models (Picard and Vinter, 2005; Zhi et al., 1997), by giving explicit instruction (Barlow, Jolley, White and Galbraith, 2003) or by training children to break down procedural representations into smaller parts (Picard and Vinter, 2006).

The process of drawing may be driven in part by more general cognitive constraints that apply to any figure, whether simple or complex, well-practised or novel. Goodnow and Levine (1973) identified four principles that drive where simple figures are started and the direction in which strokes are produced. Drawers may start at the leftmost point of a figure, at the topmost point, with the top of a vertical line, or with the top of a left oblique line (if one is part of the shape). The first of these principles (starting at the topmost point) overrides the second (starting at the leftmost) point when there is a conflict within a particular figure. Certain start position principles also guide the production of circles, ellipses and other curved figures. Adults typically start at the top of circular forms (Braswell and Rosengren, 2000; Goodnow and Levine, 1973; Meulenbroek, Vinter and Mounoud, 1993; Van Sommers, 1984). Van Sommers (1984) and others have argued that start positions are guided by cognitive constraints, rather than biomechanical ones, because handedness has little effect on where one starts to draw.

Goodnow and Levine (1973) also identified three principles which guide stroke directionality: drawing horizontally from left to right, drawing vertically from top to bottom, and using threading. The third principle involves drawing components of a figuring without lifting the drawing implement. As discussed above, biomechanical forces largely determine how isolated horizontal and vertical lines are drawn. However, threading involves overriding these tendencies and may be guided by cognitive constraints, such as planning considerations.

Developmental patterns have been identified in the use of these cognitive constraints. Following the start principles described above appears to increase with age (Braswell and Rosengren, 2000; Goodnow and Levine, 1973), although there is some variability prior to adulthood in terms of where children choose to start basic figures (Braswell and Rosengren, 2000). Start principles for circles also change, with children typically starting at the bottom and adults typically starting at the top (Braswell and Rosengren, 2000; Meulenbroek et al., 1993; Van Sommers, 1984). In addition, the use of threading follows an inverted U-shaped trajectory, increasing then decreasing with age (Braswell and Rosengren, 2000; Goodnow and Levine, 1973). These developmental patterns may arise owing to a variety of factors, including increased planning ability, becoming literate, and changes in the biomechanical factors described earlier in this chapter. For example, Van Sommers (1984) suggested, 'It is natural to assume that [start position changes are] associated with learning to read and write, but it is possible that there is also an independent discovery being made by each child that graphic work is more straightforward if starting position is consistent with preferred direction of stroke making' (p. 20).

The impact of task constraints

Instructions given to participants and other facets of drawing tasks may complement or override the biomechanical and cognitive constraints discussed above. Van Sommers (1984) conducted several studies that demonstrated the impact of task constraints. In one study, he found that stroke directionality preferences can be manipulated when drawing arrows. Many right-handed adults drew from right to left when drawing arrows that point to the left, thereby overcoming the usual bias towards drawing horizontal lines in the opposite direction. In another study, Van

Sommers noted that the order in which adults drew two letters depended on whether the instructions were 'draw A in front of B' versus 'draw A behind B'. Thus task instructions can also shape the order in which larger graphic units are produced.

The manner in which children and adults produce individual strokes is also shaped by the larger image. That is, a particular drawing task may require a drawer to override general biomechanical or cognitive constraints that govern the production of simple lines. When connecting strokes to already drawn lines, individuals often 'anchor' the new strokes to the old ones. Anchoring involves starting new strokes (e.g. radials) at a previously drawn line (e.g. a circle) and drawing away from that previously drawn line. The evidence for developmental shifts in anchoring is mixed. Van Sommers (1984) found that anchoring was common among children and adult drawers when drawing radials at the bottom of a circle (e.g. when drawing rays on a sun), although the same participants tended to draw radials towards a circle near its top. This approach coincides with biomechanical factors that drive the preference for drawing vertical strokes from top to bottom. Four- and five-year-olds in one of our studies, however, typically anchored radials at the tops *and* bottoms of circles, completely overriding biomechanical considerations (Braswell and Rosengren, 2000). It may be that younger children anchor more because they lack the fine motor control of older individuals and because anchoring helps ensure accuracy (see Thomassen, 1992; Van Sommers, 1984). This demonstrates yet another way in which task parameters affect the drawing process.

Instructions for tasks that involve copying *ambiguous* figures appear to have a particularly strong impact on the drawing process. Van Sommers (1984) asked adult participants to copy a series of images that could be described in different ways. For example, one image was described as either a man holding a telescope or as a cocktail glass with a cherry. Participants tended to follow a certain sequence of strokes when interpreting the image as a man (starting at the top with the head) and tended to follow a different sequence when interpreting the image as a cocktail glass (starting in the middle with the sides of the glass). Meanings attributed to images impact the drawing process even with children as young as 6 years, although this effect seems to be stronger among older drawers (Vinter, 1999). In sum, the work of Van Sommers and others demonstrates the significance of particular task constraints on graphic production.

The impact of cultural constraints

Cultural contexts play an important role in constraining the drawing process. In particular, writing systems constitute an important context that shapes how children and adults draw. The direction in which written characters and strings of text are produced may affect start position, threading preferences and stroke directionality. For example, Wong and Kao (1991) found that children of various ages in Hong Kong adhered to many of Goodnow and Levine's (1973) start position principles, especially starting at the topmost and leftmost points, to a greater extent and at earlier ages than children in English-speaking, Western samples.

Likewise, several differences in start position and threading preferences were found in a comparison of US and Hebrew-speaking Israeli 4- to 7-year-olds and adults (Goodnow et al., 1973). Israeli participants were less likely than US participants to start with vertical components of shapes but more likely to start with horizontal components. Also, Israeli participants were less likely to thread figures than US participants. Goodnow and her colleagues (1973) suggest that these differences reflect variations in the properties of letters and how writing instruction varies across these cultural communities.

Stroke directionality preferences are shaped in part by writing systems, as well. Hebrew-writing Israeli children (between kindergarten and 8th grade) tend to draw horizontal strokes from left to right, whereas Arab-writing Israeli children were more likely to draw from *right to left* across grades (Lieblich, Ninio and Kugelmas, 1975). Interestingly, Goodnow et al. (1973) did not find horizontal stroke directionality preferences between Hebrew and English writers. The manner in which individual letters are produced seems to have a greater impact than the overall direction in which text is produced (Lieblich, Ninio and Kugelmas, 1975). Hebrew and Arabic are both written from right to left, yet individual Hebrew letters are constructed from left to right as are Roman letters. Arabic letters are written from left to right, however. Thus writing systems can overlap with or override biomechanical constraints on the drawing process, depending on the particular system.

The interaction of biomechanical and cognitive constraints

Although we have described biomechanical and cognitive factors separately as organismic constraints, these factors do not operate independently from each other. Sometimes biomechanical factors impact one aspect of drawing (e.g. line directionality) and cognitive factors impact another aspect (e.g. start position). In many cases, start position determines line directionality. The direction in which one draws a circle is driven by where one starts the circle (Meulenbroek, Vinter and Mounoud, 1993). Other parameters, such as the speed of drawing, appear to impact line directionality. Adults typically produce circles in a counterclockwise fashion when drawing slowly and deliberately, but they will draw circles *clockwise* when drawing rapidly (Thomassen and Teulings, 1979). It may be that counterclockwise circle production is driven by cognitive constraints that are more powerful when one is drawing more carefully (Goodnow et al., 1973; Thomassen and Teulings, 1979).

Planning considerations often appear to override biomechanical preferences, as can be seen with anchoring. Anchoring involves drawing new strokes outward from previously drawn lines. This technique is primarily used to ensure accuracy (Thomassen, 1992; Van Sommers, 1984), although there are many potential instances when it may conflict with biomechanical constraints. We explored this issue (Braswell and Rosengren, 2000) in a study of 4- to 7-year-olds and adults who were asked to copy a picture of a house with a sun and a picture of a smiling face with hair. We examined the use of anchoring to produce hairs at the top of the face picture and the rays around the sun in the other picture. Interestingly, the degree to which both hairs and rays were anchored declined across age. In fact, many older participants anchored the rays around the bottom of the sun and drew rays inward around the top of the sun. These participants demonstrated a preference for top-down stroke production. One possible explanation for this pattern is that younger children rely upon anchoring because it is likely to improve accuracy. Older individuals produce these lines more automatically, relying to a larger degree on biomechanical constraints to produce the lines.

The relative impact of biomechanical and cognitive factors may shift over developmental time, as well. We (Braswell and Rosengren, 2002) asked 4- to 6-year-old children and adults to copy a series of shapes with both hands. Adults produced shapes in a mirror fashion across hands. For instance, horizontal components were drawn left to right with the right hand and right to left with the left hand. Children tended to use similar production strategies across hands. Therefore these cognitive constraints appear to be more salient in early childhood. Certain cognitive factors may have a greater impact as children start learning to draw shapes and they need to plan carefully where a particular line or segment must go. Certain biomechanical factors may have a greater impact later in life as drawers become more efficient and practised. Still the interplay between biomechanical and cognitive factors is evident at any age.

Summary and conclusion

Both biomechanical and cognitive factors constrain the drawing process. The biomechanics of the arm, hand and fingers play a significant role in the directionality of strokes. Hand size and finger strength interact with implement size and friction. Cognitive constraints, such as start position principles and planning considerations (e.g. threading), also guide how children and adults draw pictures. Individuals may also be influenced by procedural representations which dictate how well-practised figures are produced. Although both biomechanical and cognitive constraints clearly shape how we draw, it is important to keep in mind that these two types of constraints do not work in isolation.

Multiple sources of evidence demonstrate that biomechanical and cognitive constraints interact in various, complex, ways. Some planning considerations, such as anchoring, may sometimes conflict with (if the previous stroke is below or to the right of the new stroke) and sometimes match (if the previous stroke is above or to the left of the new stroke) biomechanical constraints. Also, the meaning assigned to an image may override or match directionality preferences based on anatomical structure (e.g. drawing arrows that face right or left). The parameters of the drawing task (e.g. pitting speed against accuracy) and the cultural milieu (especially in terms of writing systems) in which one becomes an experienced drawer provide other contexts in which these various constraints interact. Together these and other factors help shape the interplay between constraints on drawing behaviour.

We argue that in order effectively to understand the development of children's drawings and in particular if we are to consider using children's and adults' drawings for diagnostic purposes, we must examine drawing and its development in terms of the interaction of multiple constraints. Children's and adults' drawings do not exactly mirror mental representations, but are filtered through a production process where biomechanical and cognitive constraints interact (Braswell and Rosengren, 2000; Kosslyn, Heldmeyer and Locklear, 1977; Van Sommers, 1984). One may not be able to draw exactly what one sees (or visualizes mentally) because of the challenges of holding drawing implements, planning considerations for placing strokes, the effects of well-practised routines for drawing (e.g. for people, houses, etc.), task parameters and cultural biases (e.g. writing systems, artistic styles, stock imagery). Drawings are best viewed as products of a complex process involving the interaction of motor, cognitive and task components.

REFERENCES

Barlow, C. M., Jolley, R. P., White, D. G. and Galbraith, D. (2003). Rigidity in children's drawings and its relation with representational change. *Journal of Experimental Child Psychology*, 86, 124–52.

Blöte, A. W. and Heijden, P. G. M. Van der (1988). A follow-up study on writing posture and writing movement in young children. *Journal of Human Movement Studies*, 14, 57–74.

Blöte, A. W., Zielstra, E. M. and Zoetewey, M. W. (1987). Writing posture and writing movement in kindergarten. *Journal of Human Movement Studies*, 13, 323–41.

Braswell, G. S. and Rosengren, K. S. (2000). Decreasing variability in the development of graphic production. *International Journal of Behavioral Development*, 24, 153–66.

(2002). Interactions between cognitive and biomechanical factors in drawing development: a glimpse into the role of handedness. *British Journal of Developmental Psychology*, 20, 581–99.

Braswell, G. S., Rosengren, K. S. and Pierroutsakos, S. L. (2007). Task constraints on preschool children's grip configurations during drawing. *Developmental Psychobiology*, 49, 216–25.

Connolly, K. and Elliott, J. (1972). The evolution and ontogeny of hand function. In N. Blurton Jones (ed.), *Ethological studies of child behaviour* (pp. 329–84). Cambridge: Cambridge University Press.

Cox, M. (1992). *Children's drawings*. New York: Penguin.

Gesell, A. and Ames, L. B. (1946). The development of directionality in drawing. *Journal of Genetic Psychology*, 68, 45–61.

Glenn, S. M., Bradshaw, K. and Sharp, M. (1995). Handedness and the direction and sequencing in children's drawings of people. *Educational Psychology*, 15, 11–21.

Goodnow, J. (1977). *Children's drawing*. London: Fontana/Open Books.

Goodnow, J. J., Friedman, S. L., Bernbaum, M. and Lehman, E. B. (1973). Direction and sequence in copying: the effect of learning to write in English and Hebrew. *Journal of Cross-Cultural Psychology*, 4, 263–82.

Goodnow, J. J. and Levine, R. A. (1973). 'The grammar of action': sequence and syntax in children's copying. *Cognitive Psychology*, 4, 82–98.

Greer, T. and Lockman, J. J. (1998). Using writing instruments: invariances in young children and adults. *Child Development*, 69, 888–902.

Halverson, H. M. (1931). An experimental study of prehension in infants by means of systematic cinema records. *Genetic Psychology Monographs*, 10, 107–286.

Karmiloff-Smith, A. (1990). Constraints on representational change: evidence from children's drawing. *Cognition*, 34, 57–83.

(1992). *Beyond modularity: a developmental perspective on cognitive science*. Cambridge, MA: MIT Press.

Kellogg, R. (1969). *Analyzing children's art*. Palo Alto, CA: Mayfield.

Kosslyn, S. M., Heldmeyer, K. H. and Locklear, E. P. (1977). Children's drawings as data about internal representations. *Journal of Experimental Child Psychology*, 23, 191–211.

Lieblich, A., Ninio, A. and Kugelmass, S. (1975). Developmental trends in directionality of drawing in Jewish and Arab Israeli children. *Journal of Cross-Cultural Psychology*, 6, 504–11.

Martlew, M. (1992). Pen grips: their relationship to letter/word formation and literacy knowledge in children starting school. *Journal of Human Movement Studies*, 23, 165–85.

Meulenbroek, R. G. J., Vinter, A. and Mounoud, P. (1993). Development of start rotation principle in circle production. *British Journal of Developmental Psychology*, 11, 307–20.

Newell, K. M. (1986). Constraints on the development of coordination. In W. Wade and H. T. A. Whiting (eds.), *Motor development in children: aspects of coordination and control* (pp. 341–60). Dordrecht: Martinus Nijhof.

Phillips, W. A., Hobbs, S. B. and Pratt, F. R. (1978). Intellectual realism in children's drawings of cubes. *Cognition*, 6, 15–33.

Phillips, W. A., Inall, M. and Lauder, E. (1985). On the discovery, storage and use of graphic descriptions. In N. H. Freeman and M. V. Cox (eds.), *Visual order: the nature and development of pictorial representation* (pp. 122–34). Cambridge: Cambridge University Press.

Picard, D. and Vinter, A. (2005). Development of graphic formulas for the depiction of familiar objects. *International Journal of Behavioral Development*, 29, 418–32.

(2006). Decomposing and connecting object representations in 5- to 9-year-old children's drawing behaviour. *British Journal of Developmental Psychology*, 24, 529–45.

Rosenbaum, D. A. (2005). The Cinderella of psychology: the neglect of motor control in the science of mental life and behaviour. *American Psychologist*, 60, 308–17.

Rosenbloom, L. and Horton, M. E. (1971). The maturation of fine prehension in young children. *Developmental Medicine and Child Neurology*, 13, 3–8.

Rosengren, K. S. and Braswell, G. S. (2001). Variability in children's reasoning. In H. W. Reese and R. Kail (eds.), *Advances in child development and behaviour* (pp. 1–40). San Diego, CA: Academic Press.

(2003). Constraints and the development of children's drawing and writing skills. In G. J. P. Savelsbergh, K. Davids, J. Van der Kamp and S. Bennett (eds.), *Development of movement coordination in children: applications in the fields of ergonomics, health sciences, and sport* (pp. 56–74). New York: Routledge.

Rosengren, K. S., DeGuzman, D. and Pierroutsakos, S. L. (1995). Why can't Johnny draw a square square? Task constraints on children's grip configurations during drawing. Paper presented at the biennial meeting of the Society for Research in Child Development, Indianapolis, Indiana.

Rosengren, K. S. and Savelsbergh, G. J. P. (2000). A TASC based approach to perceptual motor development. Paper presented at the Motor Development Research Consortium, Bowling Green, Ohio.

Rosengren, K. S., Savelsbergh, G. J. P. and Van der Kamp, J. (2003). Development and learning: a TASC-based perspective on the acquisition of perceptual-motor behaviors. *Infant Behaviour and Development*, 26, 473–94.

Saida, Y. and Miyashita, M. (1979). Development of fine motor skill in children: manipulation of a pencil in young children ages 2 to 6 years old. *Journal of Human Movement Studies*, 5, 104–13.

Sasson, R., Nimmo-Smith, I. and Wing, A. M. (1986). An analysis of children's penholds. In H. S. R. Kao, G. P. Van Galen and R. Hoosian (eds.), *Graphonomics: contemporary research in handwriting* (pp. 93–106). Amsterdam: North-Holland.

Scheirs, J. G. M. (1990). Relationships between the direction of movements and handedness in children. *Neuropsychologia*, 28, 742–8.

Siegler, R. S. (1996). *Emerging minds: the process of change in children's thinking*. Oxford: Oxford University Press.

Stiles, J. (1995). The early use and development of graphic formulas: two case study reports of graphic formula production by 2- to 3-year-old children. *International Journal of Behavioral Development*, 18, 127–49.

Thelen, E. and Smith, L. B. (1994). *A dynamic systems approach to the development of cognition and action*. Cambridge, MA: MIT Press.

Thomassen, A. J. W. M. (1992). Interaction of cognitive and biomechanical factors in the organization of graphic movements. In G. E. Stelmach and J. Requin (eds.), *Tutorials in motor behaviour* (Vol. 2, pp. 249–61). Amsterdam: North-Holland/Elsevier.

Thomassen, A. J. W. M., Meulenbroek, R. G. J. and Hoofs, M. P. E. (1992). Economy and anticipation in graphic stroke sequences. *Human Movement Science*, 11, 71–82.

Thomassen, A. J. W. M. and Teulings, H. H. M. (1979). The development of directional preference in writing movements. *Visible Language*, 13, 299–313.

(1983). The development of handwriting. In M. Martlew (ed.), *The psychology of written language* (pp. 179–213). New York: Wiley.

Thomassen, A. J. W. M., Tibosch, H. J. C. M. and Maarse, F. J. (1989). The effect of context on stroke direction and stroke order in handwriting. In R. Plamondon, C. Y. Suen and M. L. Simner (eds.), *Computer recognition and human production of handwriting* (pp. 213–30). Singapore: World Scientific.

Van Roon, D., Van der Kamp, J. and Steenbergen, B. (2003). Constraints in children's learning to use spoons. In G. Savelsbergh, K. Davids, J. Van der Kamp and S. J. Bennett (eds.), *Development of movement co-ordination in children: applications in the fields of ergonomics, health sciences and sport* (pp. 75–93). London: Routledge.

Van Sommers, P. (1983). The conservatism of children's drawing strategies: at what level does stability persist? In D. Rogers and J. A. Sloboda (eds.), *The acquisition of symbolic skills* (pp. 65–70). New York: Plenum Press.

(1984). *Drawings and cognition: descriptive and experimental studies of graphic production processes*. Cambridge: Cambridge University Press.

Vinter, A. (1999). How meaning modifies drawing behaviour in children. *Child Development*, 70, 33–49.

Willats, J. (1977). How children learn to draw realistic pictures. *Quarterly Journal of Experimental Psychology*, 29, 367–82.

Wong, T. H. and Kao, H. S. R. (1991). The development of drawing principles in Chinese. In J. Wann, A. M. Wing and N. Søvik (eds.), *Development of graphic skills* (pp. 93–112). New York: Harcourt Brace Jovanovich.

Zhi, Z., Thomas, G. V. and Robinson, E. J. (1997). Constraints on representational change: drawing a man with two heads. *British Journal of Developmental Psychology*, 15, 275–90.

Ziviani, J. (1982). Children's prehension while writing – a pilot investigation. *British Journal of Occupational Therapy*, 45, 306–7.

(1983). Qualitative changes in dynamic tripod grip between seven and 14 years of age. *Developmental Medicine and Child Neurology*, 25, 535–9.

Ziviani, J. and Elkins, J. (1986). Effect of pencil grip on handwriting speed and legibility. *Educational Review*, 38, 247–57.

8 Graphic syntax and representational development

Annie Vinter, Delphine Picard and Viviane Fernandes

This chapter focuses specifically on the relationships between syntax and cognitive development, particularly representational development. Vinter, Picard and Fernandes promote the take-home message that changes in drawing behaviour during development result from changes in the size of the cognitive units or mental representations used to plan behaviour, and in the capacity to manage part–whole relationships. This hypothesis is first illustrated by reviewing studies in which children's adherence to the graphic rules when they copy elementary or complex figures is assessed. The authors also examine children's syntactical behaviour at a more global level, characterizing the entire drawing sequences built by children when they produce a drawing. Children's graphic strategies appear to reflect how they conceive of the patterns they reproduce. Task constraints (meaning given to the pattern, type of primes used to enhance specific strategies) contribute to modify their syntactical behaviour, but not uniformly throughout development. A three-step developmental model outlined in the first section of the chapter finds further support in studies dealing with procedural and representational flexibility. Finally, the authors report an original perspective on studying syntactical drawing behaviour, where it is shown that this behaviour can be incidentally modified through directed practice in children as well as in adults. By the way, the results reported by Vinter, Picard and Fernandes reveal the extent to which syntax constitutes a flexible component of drawing behaviour.

DRAWING BEHAVIOUR has been studied from many different points of view and used to assess many different aspects of psychological functioning (i.e. perceptual, motor, cognitive, emotional). Among these approaches, one distinguished between the 'syntax' and the 'semantics' of drawing (Van Sommers, 1984). Syntax in drawing refers to the way the movements are executed and ordered in a sequence (the 'how' of drawing), while semantics deals with what is depicted in terms of symbolic content (the 'what' of drawing). The present chapter will focus on drawing syntax, attempting to demonstrate that the way children organize their drawing activity locally (applying graphic rules) and globally (using graphic strategies and routines) provides relevant indicators of the nature of their mental representations, and particularly of the size and degree of flexibility of their cognitive units. It shows that drawing behaviour provides a rich and sensitive non-verbal indicator of mental representations, and particularly of conceptual knowledge. Nice empirical demonstrations of the relationships between drawing and conceptual knowledge can also be found in studies of drawings produced by patients with semantic dementia (e.g. Bozeat, Lambon Ralph, Graham, Patterson, Wilkin, Rowland, Rogers and Hodges, 2003).

The chapter is composed of four sections. A first short section deals with the *local* level of syntactical organization of drawing, studying how children at different ages apply graphic rules in the drawing of simple or complex models, and how contextual factors may modify these processes. The second section deals with the *global* level of syntactical organization of drawing, and encompasses equally a developmental approach together with the study of contextual effects. Then, in a third section, the way both levels coordinate and interact will be studied focusing on the relationships between procedural and representational flexibility in drawing. A sketch for a developmental representational model that can account for syntactical drawing behaviour will be briefly outlined. Finally, in a fourth section, a different viewpoint on syntactical graphic behaviour will be adopted, showing how it can be modelled by experience.

This chapter aims at promoting the idea that most developmental changes in drawing behaviour result from changes in the size of the cognitive units or mental representations used to plan behaviour (reduced to elements first, extended to chunks of elements, then enabling a capacity to process whole entities), and in the capacity to manage part–whole relationships (whole mental representations are first not decomposable, then become progressively decomposable; see Vinter and Marot, 2007). This position is different but complementary to the one expounded in another chapter (see Morra, this volume), which sustains that the main determinants of drawing performances relate to executive functions. Empirical evidence will be progressively accumulated through the next three sections to provide support to a three-steps developmental model that will be introduced later on.

The local level of syntactical organization of children's drawing movements

Goodnow and Levine (1973) defined a 'grammar of action' to account for the executive constraints acting on drawing (see also Simner, 1981;

Van Sommers, 1984). The production of the segments in a drawing is governed by a set of graphic rules which specify where to start (top, left) and how to progress in the drawing (top-to-bottom, left-to-right, threading, i.e. drawing continuously without pen lifts). How children adhere to these rules in the course of development has been examined in different studies (see Goodnow and Levine, 1973; Nihei, 1983; Ninio and Lieblich, 1976), but none of them has included a large range of ages and investigated systematically the sensitivity of rules to geometrical factors. Our own work was guided by the idea that the observance of the rules by children should reveal whether graphomotor activity was planned mainly at the segment or figure level.

In a first study, we asked children aged 4 to 9 years and adults to copy simple models made of two connected segments (L-shapes) of different lengths and presented in different orientations (Vinter, 1994). Between 4 and 5 years, children had a clear preference to start at left and to progress left-to-right, whereas they oscillated between starting at top or at bottom, and progressing top-to-bottom or bottom-to-top, especially at segment level. A transition appeared between 5 and 6 years, with the establishment of a strong dominance of a top start and of threading. Planning the copy occurred at the figure level from this moment, leading to recurrent violations of the left-start rule, or of the left-to-right progression rule. A second transition took place between 8 and 9 years, the 9-year-olds showing syntactical behaviour similar to that of adults in the present task: dominance of threading diminished while the top-to-bottom and left-to-right progression rules gained in importance. A better equilibrium appeared between an economical copy of the figure (minimizing the pen lifts) and a comfortable tracing (observance of the progression rules for the vertical and horizontal segments). We have suggested that this behaviour revealed a capacity to coordinate and integrate planning at figure and segment levels. A similar development was reported in a study where children and adults had to copy multisegmental patterns made of horizontals and verticals (Marot and Vinter, 2003).

To what extent would this local syntactical behaviour be modified when familiar objects instead of geometrical patterns were required to be depicted in different drawing tasks? Effects of context are plentiful in the drawing research domain. A large body of research has shown that modifying the familiarity or complexity of the model to be depicted, the verbal instructions or the episodic information provided to children before they draw elicits a high level of variability (e.g. Barrett, Beaumont and Jennett, 1985; Cox, 1992; Davies, 1983; Nicholls and Kennedy, 1992; Picard and Durand, 2005; Sutton and Rose, 1998). In a second study, children aged 5, 7 or 9 years had to copy, or draw from memory, a familiar object like a house or a television (Picard and Vinter, 2005).

Several points are worth mentioning from this study. Application of the graphic rules was modulated by geometrical factors, especially the size of the drawn segments (*younger* children had a tendency to start drawing the longest segment) and the size of the drawn component of the figure (*older* children used threading only for the smallest components of the depicted figure, like the windows of the house). We again found here a distinction between planning at the segment level (typical from young children) or at the figure level (characteristic from older children). Furthermore, the observance of the starting rules was determined by a syntactical rule of higher order, in the sense that it structured the sequence of drawing movements, more precisely the linkages of components. In the house drawing, the *accretion principle* (starting a new segment by anchoring it in an already drawn segment, see Van Sommers, 1984, p. 41) organized the linkage between the drawing of the body and of the roof of the house, implying a violation of the top-start rule for the drawing of the roof. The same sequence occurred with the drawing of the door. In consequence, the observance of the top-start rule was much less stable than that of the left-start rule, showing that the hierarchy described in our first experiment may be partially a function of the figures depicted. Finally, there was, at an individual level, a rather strong conservatism between the copy and the drawing from memory task in the application of the graphic rules when components of the figures (e.g. the door, the roof, etc.) were considered. This conservatism is at the origin of the graphic routines established for the drawing of familiar objects. However, the copying task tended to cause a slightly less organized behaviour than the drawing from memory task, except children at 5 years who applied threading quite rigidly in both tasks.

The above reported set of studies showed that as soon as the depicted models attain a certain degree of complexity, a compromise must be found between the application of the local graphic rules and the more global strategies of drawing. This higher level of syntactical planning has also been the object of numerous studies and constitutes another entry into the development of mental representations in children.

The global level of syntactical organization of children's drawing movements

How do children proceed in building a drawing? To what extent do they proceed following codified and stable sequences of movements (or 'formulas', or 'strategies') that may give rise to graphic routines in the case of drawing familiar objects (Picard and Vinter, 2005; Stiles, 1995; Van Sommers, 1984)? Van Sommers demonstrated that both geometrical (spatial) and semantic forces act on the way children or adults organize their global sequences of drawing movements, and he subsumed these constraints under three main principles: the *accretion principle* (defined as the tendency to anchor new units on already-drawn ones), the *core-to-periphery progression principle* (which dictates to draw the core or essential units prior to the peripheral or contingent ones) and the *subsystem elaboration principle* (which stipulates that geometrically or semantically linked units are drawn in sequence). Picard and Vinter (2005) have shown that the more semantically based principle, i.e. the core-to-periphery progression principle, predominated when children drew in a drawing from memory task, while the subsystem elaboration principle prevails in a copying task. This suggests that the nature of the drawing task, drawing from memory or copying, contributes to determine whether syntax is driven more by semantics or by geometry, at least in the drawing of familiar objects.

Could semantics directly drive syntax or does it necessarily compete with geometrical constraints (see also Tallandini and Morassi, this volume)? Ingram (1985) revealed that the semantic content of objects affects the way they are drawn by children. In a first experiment, children had to reproduce two plain-faced but different-sized blocks joined by a bridging pin under different spatial arrangements; in a second experiment, doll-like features were added to the smaller of the two blocks. The doll-like object induced the 3-year-old children to draw their tadpole stereotypes, whereas the more abstract object led them to rely on spatial information and to draw more advanced features. However, how much semantics intrudes in syntax cannot be assessed adequately in the experiment because the display to be drawn actually changed from one condition to the other (due to the doll-like features' adjunction), introducing modification at the syntactic level independently of meaning. This question has been elegantly tackled by Van Sommers (1984), who asked adults to reproduce models that were given one of two different labels (for instance, the same display was presented as a pyramid and its reflection in water or as a diamond crossed by a line). He found that, for most designs, adults modified their drawing movement sequencing as a function of the model's meaning. Note that this sensitivity of lower levels of behavioural organization to higher-level semantic influences has also been described with regard to actions other than drawing. Marteniuk, McKenzie, Jeannerod, Athenes and Dugas (1987), for instance, analysed the kinematics of an identical reaching movement when this movement was followed by one of two different actions, either fitting or throwing. They reported that the final goal of the overall sequence of action, its 'meaning', influenced the kinematics of the initial reaching movement.

We investigated the sensitivity of syntax to meaning in children using Van Sommer's procedure (Vinter, 1999), in which different displays were each attributed two different meanings, suggesting different parsings of the model, e.g. a single object could be either one representational unit (e.g. a diamond), or two representational units (a pyramid and its reflection), or different segmentations of two representational units (e.g. a glass with a cherry versus a man with a telescope), or still more subtle, a change of point of view (the letter N versus the letter Z rotated). Children aged between 6 and 10 years and adults participated in the study. An impact of meaning on syntax was reported from 6 years of age on for some displays, and it increased with age. The results suggested that as long as geometry and executive constraints on the one hand, semantic forces on the other, were acting in the same direction, the drawing behaviour of the youngest children was open to semantic influences. However, if a conflict arose (for instance, between the threading constraint, so strong at 6 years, and the necessity to lift the pen for marking a segmentation between two representational units), geometry and executive constraints took priority on semantic affordances in the youngest children. It was only when children were able to introduce flexibility at the lower syntactical level (9–10 years) that their drawing behaviour reflected more or less systematically the parsing dictated by semantics.

In this experiment, meaning was proposed by the experimenter in order to elicit different parsings of the model. We now wonder how graphic syntax would evolve with age when children have to copy models that present both a global and local structure, thus potentially eliciting different meanings (for instance, a square divided into four small squares, or a square and a sign '+' inside, or four small squares joined together). Stiles and her colleagues (e.g. Akshoomoff and Stiles, 1995a, 1995b; Dukette and Stiles, 1996) showed that, when asked to copy such spatial patterns, young children were capable of attending to both local and global information, but they tended to parse out simpler and more independent parts, and to use simpler relations than older children. Using a Navon Figure copying task (Navon, 1977), Lange-Küttner (2000) revealed that global processing largely dominated at 5 years, while an integration of local and global information was apparent at 11 years. We found again in Van Sommers' work a source of inspiration to tackle this question. Indeed, in one of his experiments, he asked adults to copy a pattern made of rectangles arranged in the form of ascending or descending stairs (see Figure 8.1A), and reported the main graphic strategies they employed in this task. Some of these strategies involved building the drawing region by region, starting with the largest rectangle and attaching smaller three-sided rectangles, or with the smallest and embedding one side of each into a larger rectangle

Graphic syntax and representational development

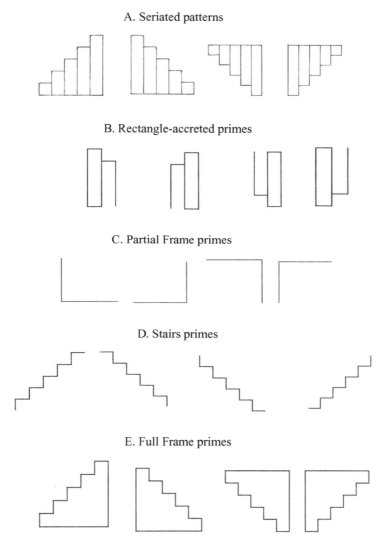

Figure 8.1 Illustration of the seriated models and the primes used in the experiments.

(see Vinter and Marot, 2007, for illustrations). In two other strategies, the pattern was processed partly or wholly as a single unit enclosed in a frame, with the shared boundaries represented as added internal segments. We thought that the first type of strategy could reflect an understanding of the pattern as composed of N rectangles (local structure) that were assembled and seriated, while the second type of strategy could involve a conscious focus on the entire configuration (global structure), which was then decomposed into parts. If this analysis were correct, asking children to copy these seriated patterns would be most interesting because systematic modifications of strategies as a function of age could be expected in relation to their increasing capacity to parse information integrating both local and global dimensions (Carey and Diamond, 1977; Kemler Nelson, 1984, 1989; Tada and Stiles, 1996).

Children aged 5 to 10 years and adults participated in the study (Vinter and Marot, 2007). They were requested to copy the seriated patterns, with an increasing or decreasing structure, and in different orientations. We made a complete inventory of the strategies used by the participants in the task, and noted that some of them were typical for young children. Indeed, 5-year-old children copied the figures as a series of individual, independent rectangles, in a more or less loose length seriation, with sometimes some attempts to juxtapose the rectangles. We construed these strategies as *element-based*, involving a conceptualization of the pattern as a series of rectangles, due to a strong dominance of local information processing, and resulting in a conceptualization of the pictorial space as an *aggregate space* (Lange-Küttner, 1997, 2004). This step was very similar to the one described previously, where young children plan their activity at a *segment level*. Between 6 and 10 years, children correctly depicted the patterns as unique or whole figures made up of a series of rectangles sharing one side, and the drawing was constructed by taking the rectangle located at the extremity of the series as a unit block, accreting the next to it, or embedding the next in it. We construed these strategies as *unit-based*, where the pattern was conceived of as a whole pattern resulting from an assembly of connected rectangles. This step showed that children were capable of planning at the *figure level*. Finally, a third step emerged at 10 years and was characteristic of adults, who used *part–whole-based* strategies, where the frame of the pattern was drawn first, totally or partially, and then complementary segments were added so that the rectangles emerged. These strategies requested the management of part–whole relationships so that the global representation of the pattern could be decomposed into a frame and parts combined in a coordinated structure. We consider that such capacity to process part–whole relationships sustains the ability to plan activity at an integrated figure and segment level.

Would this developmental sequence resist contextual effects such as those involved by a manipulation of the individual's prior experience (see, for instance, Bremner and Moore, 1984; Lewis, Russell and Berridge, 1993; Phillips, Inall and Lauder, 1985)? Outside of the drawing research domain, Schyns and Rodet (1997) have demonstrated that the immediate appearance of patterns, that is, the way a pattern is parsed, can be modified by prior experience. Thus, in four priming experiments, we tested whether children and adults who were exposed to specific parses of the seriated patterns would be subsequently inclined to resort to graphic strategies directly suggested by the primes, when they are asked to copy the entire patterns. Children aged 5, 6, 8 and 10 years and adults participated in four priming conditions (Vinter and Marot, 2007). In the first one, the participants were required to copy a rectangle to which an open rectangle was attached, in several orientations, before the copy of the seriated patterns (see Figure 8.1B). This prime corresponded to the beginning of a *unit-based* strategy and was thus expected to enhance such strategies. In a second condition, the partial frame of the seriated pattern was used as a prime (Figure 8.1C), the stairs part was presented as a prime in a third condition (Figure 8.1D), and the complete frame in a fourth condition (Figure 8.1E). These three last primes should enhance the production of part–whole-based strategies. The priming procedure had a great impact in the 5-year-olds, who tended to abandon the element-based strategies to the benefit of the part–whole-based ones in all experiments but the one where the full frame was used as a prime. They also displayed a typical behaviour, starting the drawing of the seriated pattern by the prime component, some of them continuing with a part–whole-based strategy, others continuing with element-based strategies, thus producing typical prime-induced errors in which the prime component and the individual rectangles co-existed. The 6-year-old children and adults were reluctant to modify their strategies after priming. They produced the same strategies after priming as those in the baseline condition. Finally, the 8- and 10-year-old children were positively influenced by the primes that were expected to increase the production of part–whole-based strategies.

Because the management of part–whole relationships is progressively appearing between 8 and 11 years (e.g. Akshoomoff and Stiles, 1995a, 1995b; Piaget and Inhelder, 1956; Picard and Vinter, 1999), we can easily conceive that the priming phase acted as an external aid that triggered the production of part–whole-based strategies in the 8- and 10-year-olds. The manipulation of the children's personal experience of the patterns helped them to build a new representation of their structure, that, in turn, guided their drawing strategies. That adults constantly produced the part–whole-based strategies, even in a context inducing unit-based strategies, demonstrates that they had stabilized their drawing behaviour around the most powerful and economical solution. Indeed, the part–whole-based strategies are the best adapted to the structural features of the models, allowing for a perfect base alignment of the rectangles, for an optimum use of drawing in preferred directions, and with a minimum number of pen lifts. Accounting for the performance shown by the 5- and 6-year-olds in the priming conditions is less obvious. However, the Karmiloff-Smith (1992) model enables explanations of this performance. In this model, a first phase of development results from accumulated practice in a domain, thanks to highly efficient data-driven processing. This very same efficient data-driven processing would be responsible for the impact of the priming phase at this age. Would this mean that these young children were able to display sophisticated representational abilities (part–whole analysis) upon external triggers? Endorsing the view that apparently identical behaviour can be sustained by qualitatively different representational structures (Karmiloff-Smith, 1999), we suggested that it was not likely (Vinter and Marot, 2007). Recalling that these young children tended to initiate their copy of the seriated patterns by drawing the prime component first, an appropriate use of data-driven processes led some to establish a segment-by-segment correspondence between their drawing and the model. Thus, a part–whole-based strategy emerged, created or assembled anew during the drawing process, independently of any internal reworking of how the patterns were conceived. The exogeneous trigger caused the 5-year-olds not to rely on element-based strategies, but to display apparently more sophisticated drawing behaviour. By contrast, the 6-year-olds did not. This testified to a certain closure of their cognitive system to external inductions, as would be predicted by the Karmiloff-Smith model with its notion of representational redescription (1992), or from a certain degree of conceptual rigidity as postulated by Mounoud (1988, 1996) at this age.

We saw, on several occasions, that the local and global levels of organization in drawing interact in producing the individual's final behaviour. These interactions between a lower executive level, more dependent on biomechanical and geometrical constraints, and a higher planning level, more dependent on representational or conceptual constraints, have been extensively studied in drawing with respect to the relations between the procedural flexibility (the extent to which children can modify or interrupt their ongoing drawing process) and the representational flexibility (the extent to which children can modify their internal representations). The third section focuses on this body of research.

Relationships between procedural and representational flexibility in drawing

The original Karmiloff-Smith study (1990) asked children to draw 'non-existent objects', thus requiring them to introduce innovations into their habitual way of drawing familiar objects (house, man, animal). The 4- to 6-year-old children responded to this requirement by introducing deletions of elements and/or changes in the size and shape of elements (intra-categorical changes). Older children (8–10 years) modified the position and/or orientation of elements, and, more interestingly, introduced new elements in their drawing coming from other conceptual categories, like, for instance, a house with wings (cross-categorical changes). She also reported that young children introduced their innovations at the end of their graphic routine, as if they were subjected to a procedural sequential constraint imposing a fixed ordering of the drawn elements at the executive level. By contrast, the older children interrupted their routine earlier in order to introduce their innovations. She suggested that the ability to introduce cross-categorical innovations, testifying to a high level of representational flexibility, was associated with the relaxation of the procedural sequential constraint, so that innovations could be introduced early in the drawing process, as well as with the relaxation of a constraint of independence occurring between drawing routines, so that they could share common pieces of knowledge. A RR process (representational redescription) was assumed in the Karmiloff-Smith model to account for this developmental transition between a first phase characteristic of the youngest children (implicit level) and a second phase characteristic of older children (explicit level), as well as between successive explicit levels. This theory inspired a lot of subsequent drawing studies, that tested whether young children were able to innovate at a cross-categorical level when explicitly asked to do just that (Berti and Freeman, 1997; Spensley and Taylor, 1999; Zhi, Thomas and Robinson, 1997) and whether they were capable of greater procedural flexibility than originally reported (Barlow, Jolley, White and Galbraith, 2003; Zhi et al., 1997).

Also, for us, the Karmiloff-Smith paradigm was conducive to test further our three-steps developmental model as it emerged from the analysis of the local and global levels of organization of drawing. Vinter and Picard (1996) replicated the Karmiloff-Smith study in children aged 5, 7 and 9 years, aiming at more precision in the specifications of the innovations introduced in the drawings at the different ages. Seven types of innovations were observed and regrouped into three categories. The 5-year-olds mainly deleted, replicated elements and modified their shape or size, i.e. produced *element-based intra-representational* changes. The 7-year-olds also changed the position or orientation of the elements and modified the global shape of the depicted object, i.e. made *figure-based intra-representational* changes. At 9 years, children introduced elements coming from other conceptual categories (for instance, the house has wings) or assimilated the required object to depict another object (for instance, the entire house becomes a flower). These changes demonstrated the capacity to innovate at an *inter-representational* level. To test to what extent such a developmental sequence of changes could be paradigm-dependent, we used a different task (a deletion task) in a second study (Picard and Vinter, 1999), asking children to draw what remained visible from objects after a magician had made them partially invisible. A similar developmental sequence emerged from this last study, which showed that this sequence did not depend on the very act of drawing: using an eraser to produce the requested deletions on pre-drawn models led to similar results. We therefore considered that this sequence revealed internal changes in representational development.

Keeping with our model, it was tempting to try to link the inter-representational changes with the capacity to manage part–whole relations, an analysis that was supposed to sustain the third developmental step. Note that Spensley and Taylor (1999) argued similarly that cross-categorical innovations are related to a comparative analysis of the overall organization of the parts of one category with the overall organization of the parts of the other category. Thus, in order better to capture the nature of these inter-representational innovations, we investigated to what extent the ability to produce inter-representational changes was related to the ability to manage part–whole relations. Picard and Vinter (2006) hypothesized that if both abilities were related, a prior decomposition task devoted to the expression of part–whole analysis should enhance the production of inter-representational changes in a subsequent innovation task. In the priming decomposition task, children aged 5, 7 or 9 years were asked to draw familiar objects (a man, a house) split into two or several parts. A control group was required to draw just two other familiar objects (a bunch of flowers, a car) in the priming task. Then in the innovation task, both groups were requested to produce a 'man-house'. As expected, the children assigned to the priming decomposition task were better at producing inter-representational changes than the controls. The very activation of part–whole analysis processes in the prior decomposition task further benefited the management of inter-representational innovations because inter-representational flexibility is rooted in such segmentation abilities.

In what sense did the flexibility demonstrated at the executive procedural level, i.e. drawing as such, constrain the flexibility emerging at the representational level? Two quite separate aspects were rather confused in the Karmiloff-Smith notion of a sequential constraint in which relaxation should be essential for representational flexibility. This constraint could be expressed in a potentially fixed ordering of the elements within the drawing procedure. The relation of this aspect of sequential constraint with representational flexibility was revealed to be not evident. Zhi *et al.* (1997) reported that whether or not children succeeded at the innovation task (drawing a man with two heads), they tended to maintain a constant order in which the elements of their drawing were produced. Barlow *et al.* (2003) equally observed that the level of rigidity in the usual ordering of elements did *not* predict the capacity to produce subsequently representational changes. However, both studies did only analyse intra-representational changes, and did not deal with inter-representational changes. The second aspect of the sequential constraint refers to the capacity to interrupt early in the drawing process in order to introduce a novelty, rather than only at the end. From age 5, children were shown to be able to interrupt their procedure in the middle to insert a novelty (Berti and Freeman, 1997; Picard and Vinter, 1999; Spensley and Taylor, 1999; Vinter and Picard, 1996; Zhi *et al.*, 1997). However, some authors reported some associations between the production of more or less elaborated representational changes and the capacity to interrupt early the graphic routine.

Picard and Vinter (2007) investigated to what extent these two aspects of a sequential constraint were related to the expression of inter-representational flexibility in a series of four studies conducted with children aged 5, 7 and 9 years. The children were asked to produce inter-representational innovations in four conditions: (1) under verbal instructions ('draw a house with wings', for instance), (2) when 3D clay objects or (3) photographs of the 3D objects or (4) 2D contour line drawings of these objects were given as models to copy to the children. These four drawing conditions differed in terms of cost of the representational and procedural demands. They were the highest in the free task (no model at all), but lowest in the 2D contour line drawing task (because of the availability of ready-made models). The results showed that, in the free task, as the ability to introduce inter-representational changes improved with age, the capacity to interrupt the routine earlier to insert the novelties also improved. By contrast, whatever their age, children maintained relatively constant the sequencing of elements in their drawing procedures. When models were given to copy, inter-representational changes were globally enhanced, as well as the capacity to interrupt the routine, but no great changes occurred with respect to routine sequencing. Procedural rigidity declined as representational flexibility improved, and this decline occurred before the most sophisticated forms of representational flexibility emerged. The results also made clear that only the difficulty in interrupting routine progression could act as a constraint on representational flexibility. As claimed before, however, this constraint is probably only part of the process that leads to the expression of high-level, cross-categorical flexibility. The capacity to manage part–whole decomposition analysis also participates in this process.

In conclusion, whatever the level of analysis on which they focused, our experiments suggested a three-steps development in the capacity to plan and control drawing activity, that is, basically, a movement from processing elements to processing chunks of elements forming global units, and then to processing integrated wholes and parts. We consider that these developmental changes reflect the transformations intervening in the nature and in the size of the cognitive units that children manipulate when they process information and plan their behaviour. These changes would not be domain-specific, and some relations between drawing development and other non-verbal behaviours development are very likely. It is worth noting that the evolution we are pointing to with respect to drawing behaviour shares similarities with the one observed in prehension development for instance. Years ago, Vinter (1990) discussed prehension development in infancy, trying to show that changes in the way information is segmented into units sustain this development. This model can be summarized as follows. In a first step, young children (or infants) would parse information into small units or elements that tend to be isolated or juxtaposed one to the other. Limits in the attentional system are likely to explain this piecemeal parsing. Information parsing being reduced to elements, planning behaviour is locally or step by step organized, without any apprehension of the overall context. Anticipation is consequently strongly limited, and data-driven information processing dominates. Then, in a second step, associations between the previous elementary units are progressively established, and chunks are formed so that the overall organization of incoming information can be conceived of by children. Larger cognitive units are built. Associative learning such as implied in implicit learning surely contributes to this chunking process (see Perruchet and Vinter, 2002). Planning behaviour at a global level becomes possible, and anticipation increases. Mounoud (1988) has suggested that this chunk formation results in a temporary rigid functioning of children, as if their new capacity to represent reality as wholes prevented them from conceiving simultaneously its elements or parts. Finally, in a third step, children analyse progressively the previous global cognitive units in their parts so that relations between whole and parts as well as between parts of different cognitive units are elaborated. The cognitive units become flexible because they can be easily decomposed and recomposed.

In the last section of this chapter, a radically different viewpoint on graphic syntax will be adopted, showing how it can be modelled by experience. We will no longer consider graphic syntax as an indicator of representational development, but will show how it can become the content of incidental manipulations. This body of research concerns implicit learning, that is how, through repeated experiences, the behaviour of individuals becomes sensitive and adapted to a situation without any attempt actually to learn anything about it.

Syntax can be modified incidentally

Van Sommers (1984) discovered that the drawing of closed geometrical figures like circles shows an interesting regularity. If the starting point is set above a virtual axis going from 11 o'clock to 5 o'clock, right-handed subjects predominantly rotate counterclockwise. If it is located under this axis, most subjects' drawings rotate in the clockwise direction. Thus, this Start-Rotation Principle (SRP) (Van Sommers, 1984) implies that the direction of drawing movements is dependent on starting position. This syntactical regularity gains in strength between 4 and 10 years of age and is resistant to different experimental manipulations (Vinter and Meulenbroek, 1993). Between 70 per cent and 90 per cent of adults' production obeys this principle.

We further investigated whether the favoured direction of rotation could be modified by earlier directed practice. In a first experiment, adults were divided into three groups that differed as a function of their training phase (Vinter and Perruchet, 1999). While they thought they participated in a speed–accuracy graphomotor task, adults were required to trace, as accurately and as fast as possible, over a set of forty geometrical closed figures starting either at the top or at the bottom of the figures, and rotating in either a clockwise or a counterclockwise direction. Adults in the control group did not receive any indications with respect to where to start and how to rotate. Without them knowing it, adults in the two experimental groups either violated the SRP in 80 per cent of the cases (incongruent training), or respected the SRP in 80 per cent of the cases (congruent training). Then, following the training phase, the effects of the incidental manipulation were assessed by asking them to trace over the same figures but without any indications in terms of rotation. Only the starting point was imposed. Another test was also used, where only the direction of rotation was indicated, not the starting point. A large impact of training was revealed after the incongruent practice, inducing adults to invert the SRP, while no changes were found between training and test in the congruent training and control groups. A second experiment showed that this effect lasted for at least one hour, supporting the idea that the behavioural syntactical change was due to a genuine, albeit short-term, modification effect (Vinter and Perruchet, 1999). The very same pattern of results was obtained in children aged between 4 and 10 years (Vinter and Perruchet, 2000) as well as in mentally retarded children (Vinter and Detable, 2003).

Interestingly, the impact of training was obtained only in the starting point test, not when the rotation direction was used as a cue in the test. This was certainly due to the fact that the two movement parameters involved in the SRP are asymmetrically related, the driving of the starting position by the movement direction being harder than the reverse (Van Sommers, 1984). Thus, syntax can be changed by experience, but some of the basic procedural constraints inherent in the syntactical behaviour (here, the driving direction between starting point and movement rotation) cannot be modified.

A second interesting point was that young children, aged 4–5 years, followed the SRP less often than controls did, and they also were drawing more often according to the principle after congruent practice than controls. Their spontaneous level for respect of the SRP was not exceeding 50 per cent, compared to on average 70 per cent of the cases in older children and in adults. The high baseline level in older children and adults made a further increase in respect for the principle unlikely but left considerable room for a decrease. In contrast, the baseline in young children was close enough to random level to leave room for both an increase or a decrease. This suggests that syntax can be modified through an implicit learning episode even when developing. It does not need to be a stable behaviour.

Finally, we demonstrated that the very act of drawing, that is the executive motor component, was not necessary for inducing a change in syntactical behaviour (Vinter and Perruchet, 2002). Observing figures being drawn on a monitor screen in a way that either did or did not respect the SRP provoked the same type of incidental learning in children and in adults. The fact of having seen figures traced in a way violating the SRP in 80 per cent of the cases led the participants not to conform to the SRP when they had subsequently to draw the same types of figures. The success of this implicit observational learning procedure testifies to the fact that syntax organizes drawing behaviour at a central planning level, and not only at a peripheral, motor executive level, though it integrates the constraints operating at this executive level.

In conclusion, we would like to point out the richness of the study of graphic syntax in the drawing domain of research. Syntax is at the interface between high planning levels, including semantics and all conscious representational contents of thought, and low executive levels, including biomechanics and spatiotemporal organization of drawing movements. As such, it can provide useful information about how top-down and bottom-up influences interact in behaviour on a very large range of ages, from 2–3 years of age until late adulthood.

REFERENCES

Akshoomoff, N. A. and Stiles, J. (1995a). Developmental trends in visuospatial analysis and planning: I. Copying a complex figure. *Neuropsychology*, 9, 364–77.
  (1995b). Developmental trends in visuospatial analysis and planning: II. Memory for a complex figure. *Neuropsychology*, 9, 378–89.
Barlow, C. M., Jolley, R. P., White, D. G. and Galbraith, D. (2003). Rigidity in children's drawings and its relation with representational change. *Journal of Experimental Child Psychology*, 86, 124–52.
Barrett, M., Beaumont, A. and Jennett, M. (1985). Some children do sometimes what they have been told to do: task demands and verbal instructions on children's drawings. In N. H. Freeman and M. V. Cox (eds.), *Visual order: the nature and development of pictorial representation* (pp. 176–87). Cambridge: Cambridge University Press.
Berti, A. E. and Freeman, N. H. (1997). Representational change in resources for pictorial innovations: a three-component analysis. *Cognitive Development*, 12, 501–22.
Bozeat, S., Lambon Ralph, M. A., Graham, K. S., Patterson, K., Wilkin, H., Rowland, J., Rogers, T. T. and Hodges, J. R. (2003). A duck with four legs: investigating the structure of conceptual knowledge using picture drawing in semantic dementia. *Cognitive Neuropsychology*, 20, 27–47.
Bremner, G. and Moore, S. (1984). Prior visual inspection and object naming: two factors that enhance hidden-feature inclusion in young children's drawings. *British Journal of Developmental Psychology*, 2, 371–6.
Carey, S. and Diamond, R. (1977). From piecemeal to configurational representation of faces. *Science*, 195, 312–14.
Cox, M. V. (1992). *Children's drawings*. Harmondsworth: Penguin.
Davies, A. M. (1983). Contextual sensitivity in young children's drawings. *Journal of Experimental Child Psychology*, 35, 478–86.
Dukette, D. and Stiles, J. (1996). Children's analysis of hierarchical patterns: evidence from a similarity judgment task. *Journal of Experimental Child Psychology*, 63, 103–40.
Goodnow, J. and Levine, R. A. (1973). The grammar of action: sequence and syntax in children's copying behaviour. *Cognitive Psychology*, 4, 82–98.
Ingram, N. (1985). Three into two won't go: symbolic and spatial coding processes in young children's drawings. In N. H. Freeman and M. V. Cox (eds.), *Visual order: the nature and development of pictorial representation* (pp. 231–47). Cambridge: Cambridge University Press.
Karmiloff-Smith, A. (1990). Constraints on representational change: evidence from children's drawing. *Cognition*, 34, 57–83.
  (1992). *Beyond modularity: a developmental perspective on cognitive science*. Cambridge, MA: MIT Press.
  (1999). Taking development seriously. *Human Development*, 42, 325–7.

Kemler Nelson, D. G. (1984). The effect of intention on what concepts are acquired. *Journal of Verbal Learning and Verbal Behaviour*, 23, 734–59.

(1989). The nature and occurrence of holistic processing. In B. E. Shepp and S. Ballesteros (eds.), *Object perception* (pp. 357–86). Hillsdale, NJ: Erlbaum.

Lange-Küttner, C. (1997). Development of size modification of human figure drawings in spatial axes systems of varying complexity. *Journal of Experimental Child Psychology*, 66, 264–78.

(2000). The role of object violations in the development of visual analysis. *Perceptual and Motor Skills*, 90, 3–24.

(2004). More evidence on size modification in spatial axes systems of varying complexity. *Journal of Experimental Child Psychology*, 88, 171–92.

Lewis, C., Russell, C. and Berridge, D. (1993). When is a mug not a mug? Effects of content, naming, and instructions on children's drawings. *Journal of Experimental Child Psychology*, 56, 291–302.

Marot, V. and Vinter, A. (2003). Rôle de la complexité et de l'orientation d'une figure géométrique sur l'application des règles de production graphique chez l'enfant et l'adulte [The role of complexity and orientation of a geometric figure for the application of graphic production rules in the child and adult]. *Archives de Psychologie*, 70, 175–92.

Marteniuk, R. G., McKenzie, C. L., Jeannerod, M., Athenes, S. and Dugas, C. (1987). Constraints on human arm movement trajectories. *Canadian Journal of Psychology*, 41, 365–78.

Mounoud, P. (1988). The ontogenesis of different types of thought: language and motor behaviours as non-specific manifestations. In L. Weiskrantz (ed.), *Thought without language* (pp. 25–45). Oxford: Clarendon Press.

(1996). A recursive transformation of central cognitive mechanisms: the shift from partial to whole representation. In P. Sameroff and M. Haith (eds.), *Reason and responsibility: the passage through childhood* (pp. 85–110). Chicago: University of Chicago Press.

Navon, D. (1977). Forest before trees: the precedence of global features in visual perception. *Cognitive Psychology*, 9, 353–83.

Nicholls, A. and Kennedy, J. M. (1992). Drawing development: from similarity of features to direction. *Child Development*, 63, 227–41.

Nihei, Y. (1983). Developmental changes in covert principles for the organization of strokes in drawing and handwriting. *Acta Psychologica*, 54, 846–9.

Ninio, A. and Lieblich, A. (1976). The grammar of action: phrase structure in children's copying. *Child Development*, 47, 846–9.

Perruchet, P. and Vinter, A. (2002). The self-organizing consciousness. *Behavioral and Brain Sciences*, 25, 297–330.

Piaget, J. and Inhelder, B. (1956). *The child's conception of space*. London: Routledge and Kegan Paul.

Picard, D. and Durand, K. (2005). Are young children's drawings canonically biased? *Journal of Experimental Child Psychology*, 90, 48–64.

Picard, D. and Vinter, A. (1999). Representational flexibility in children's drawing: effects of age and verbal instructions. *British Journal of Developmental Psychology*, 17, 605–22.

(2005). Development of graphic formulas for the depiction of familiar objects. *International Journal of Behavioral Development*, 29, 418–32.

(2006). Decomposing and connecting object representations in 5- to 9-year-old children's drawing behaviour. *British Journal of Developmental Psychology*, 17, 529–45.

(2007). Relationship between procedural rigidity and inter-representational change in children's drawing behaviour. *Child Development*, 74, 521–41.

Phillips, W. A., Inall, M. and Lauder, E. (1985). On the discovery, storage and use of graphic descriptions. In N. H. Freeman and M. V. Cox (eds.), *Visual order: the nature and development of pictorial representation* (pp. 122–34). Cambridge: Cambridge University Press.

Schyns, P. G. and Rodet, L. (1997). Categorization creates functional features. *Journal of Experimental Psychology: Learning, Memory, and Cognition*, 23, 681–96.

Simner, M. L. (1981). The grammar of action and children's printing. *Developmental Psychology*, 20, 136–42.

Spensley, F. and Taylor, J. (1999). The development of cognitive flexibility: evidence from children's drawings. *Human Development*, 42, 300–24.

Stiles, J. (1995). The early use and development of graphic formulas: two case study reports of graphic formula production by 2- to 3-year-old children. *International Journal of Behavioral Development*, 18, 127–49.

Sutton, P. J. and Rose, D. H. (1998). The role of strategic visual attention in children's drawing development. *Journal of Experimental Child Psychology*, 68, 87–107.

Tada, W. L. and Stiles, J. (1996). Developmental change in children's analysis of spatial patterns. *Developmental Psychology*, 3, 951–70.

Van Sommers, P. (1984). *Drawing and cognition: descriptive and experimental studies of graphic production processes*. Cambridge: Cambridge University Press.

Vinter, A. (1990). Manual imitations and reaching behaviors: an illustration of action control in infancy. In C. Bard, M. Fleury and L. Hay (eds.), *Development of eye–hand coordination across the life span* (pp. 157–87). Columbia, SC: University of South Carolina Press.

(1994). Hierarchy among graphic production rules: a developmental approach. In C. Faure, P. Keuss, G. Lorette and A. Vinter (eds.), *Advances in handwriting and drawing: a multidisciplinary approach* (pp. 275–88). Paris: Europia.

(1999). How meaning modifies drawing behaviour in children. *Child Development*, 70, 33–49.

Vinter, A. and Detable, C. (2003). Implicit learning in children and adolescents with mental retardation. *American Journal on Mental Retardation*, 108, 94–107.

Vinter, A. and Marot, V. (2007). The development of context sensitivity in children's graphic copying strategies. *Developmental Psychology*, 43, 94–110.

Vinter, A. and Meulenbroek, R. (1993). The role of manual dominance and visual feedback in circular drawing movements. *Journal of Human Movement Studies*, 25, 11–37.

Vinter, A. and Perruchet, P. (1999). Isolating unconscious influences: the neutral parameter procedure. *Quarterly Journal of Experimental Psychology*, 52a, 857–75.

(2000). Implicit learning in children is not related to age: evidence from drawing behaviour. *Child Development*, 71, 1223–40.

(2002). Implicit motor learning through observational training in adults and children. *Memory and Cognition*, 30, 256–61.

Vinter, A. and Picard, D. (1996). Drawing behaviour in children reflects internal representational changes. In M. Simner, G. Leedham and A. Thomassen (eds.), *Handwriting and drawing research* (pp. 171–85). Amsterdam: IOS Press.

Zhi, Z., Thomas, G. V. and Robinson, E. J. (1997). Constraints on representational changes: drawing a man with two heads. *British Journal of Developmental Psychology*, 15, 275–90.

9 Spatial structures in children's drawings: how do they develop?

Sergio Morra

Morra uses a neo-Piagetian approach to conceptualize the development of spatial organization in children's drawings, which also includes some aspects of transition from intellectual to visual realism. He assumes the existence of graphic figurative schemes, i.e. the child's mental representations of satisfactory graphic denotations of objects, and operative schemes, i.e. procedures to modify or organize the figurative schemes. Furthermore, more general information-processing mechanisms silently affect and control the processing of these basic schemes. In particular, the F-operator (field factor) would aim for the most simple solution with the largest set of activated schemes, i.e. the F-operator is responsible for an economical solution. However, there is no accuracy implied; the F-operator can organize according to a distorting bias as much as according to a Good Gestalt or a composition law. The M-operator (mental energy factor) conceptualizes the more general information-processing capacity, with increases with age by one unit with every second year, while other factors such as the I-operator (inhibit or interrupt factor) and other learning, planning and executive factors contribute to weigh the information. Morra illustrates the neo-Piagetian approach with an analysis of the transparency phenomenon and the task of drawing a partly occluded object. Then, he uses that approach to conceptualize other developmental phenomena, such as drawing flexibility and the acquisition of a spatial axes system, in terms of informational units as well as processes, and explains how the limitation, especially in M-capacity, limits possible solutions.

OBJECTS exist in space and have a spatial structure. Our phenomenological experience tells us that often there is 'space', empty space, between an object and another; thus, young children often leave enough space on paper between one and another object depicted in their drawings. Older children may leave a white section between the representations of the 'ground' and the 'sky' in their drawing, and call that empty space the 'air'. That 'air gap' is not due to a misconception of physical reality, but it is a solution to the problem of arranging on paper the representations of various parts of the phenomenal world (Hargreaves, Jones and Martin, 1981).

It has often been noted that children strive to represent a three-dimensional world on a two-dimensional sheet of paper. I agree, but I would like to add that so many factors interact in constraining or biasing the child's decisions on the spatial organization of a drawing. These include 'drawing systems', that is, systems of rules such as vertical-oblique projection and oblique projection (Willats, 1977, 1985); specific rules, such as separating every figure from each other to avoid overlapping (Goodnow, 1977), or separating the sky region from the ground (Hargreaves *et al.*, 1981); a bias for drawing straight angles rather than oblique ones (Ibbotson and Bryant, 1978; Pascual-Leone and Morra, 1991); various compositional strategies (Golomb, 1992); and also, perhaps, intellectually or visually realistic intentions, that is, the goal of representing what the child knows or what one can see (Luquet, 1927). Sometimes children also face some unexpected problem, such as noting that there is not enough space left on the paper for drawing what they wanted – and thus they may invent on the spot a novel and perhaps not fully satisfactory solution. Some of these factors (such as the perpendicular bias) probably are Gestalt-like field effects, pre-wired in the functioning of the nervous system. Others are rules or systems of rules that children discover and learn through their drawing experience.

Although there are manifold factors that affect the spatial organization of children's drawings, some of which have been studied for a long time, the main point made in this chapter is that *the complexity of the spatial organization rules or strategies that a child can master is constrained by a single factor* – the amount of information that a child can attend to and process simultaneously; that is, what various authors have labelled working memory capacity, attentional capacity or processing capacity (e.g. Cowan, Saults and Elliott, 2002).

Transparency drawing can illustrate the point, before we turn to discussing the matter in a more systematic way. The term 'transparency' refers to drawings in which the child depicts some item that an observer could not actually see, because of some non-transparent interposed obstacle, for instance in a drawing that includes the outline of a house and also some people or furniture inside the house – items that of course an observer could not see through opaque walls. Thus, the house is drawn as though the walls were transparent. Another example would be drawing both legs of a knight on horseback, thus rendering transparent the horse.

Luquet (1927) regarded transparency drawing as a hallmark of children's intellectual realism; they would draw what is inside the house because they know that it is there and they are motivated to represent it, while they are insensitive to the fact that one cannot see both the outside and the inside of the house from a single point of view. Two different points of view are superimposed on each other. The relevant point for the purpose of this chapter is not which intentions drive the child to represent both points of view, or whether older children have acquired more mature views regarding pictures and pictorial representation (e.g. Freeman, 1995), but rather, the spatial aspect of the phenomenon; transparency drawings involve a confusion between two points of view, and overcoming transparency involves an ability to keep to a single point of view and arrange consequently the layout of figures on paper.

The importance of the transparency phenomenon and its incidence may have been exaggerated, however. Russo Pizzo (1974) examined the drawings of a free topic by a large sample of Sicilian schoolchildren, in the age range from 6 to 14, and she found that only 9.4 per cent included some transparency. The age-groups with the highest incidence of transparency (about 12 per cent) were the 7- and 8-year-olds. Russo Pizzo also discussed some other studies that yielded similar conclusions, even in experimental conditions that attempt to prompt transparency; for instance, Parisi and Marini (1974) asked primary school children to draw 'a train, with the passengers clearly visible' and found a maximum of transparency drawings (26.8 per cent) in Grade 2. Hence, Russo Pizzo concluded that transparency is not a major feature in a stage of intellectual realism, but rather a moment of experimentation in children's search for more complex graphic forms. One could ask, however: what is that greater complexity and where does it come from? As will be argued in the following, the increase of working memory capacity is a crucial factor in this regard.

Nevertheless, the phenomenon of transparency exists, and it has been studied with several experimental paradigms, the most important of which is called 'partial occlusion' (e.g. Cox, 1985). In this case, a child is presented with an array of objects, one of which is partly hidden behind another, and required to depict that array. Various strategies are possible; the 'correct' (visually realistic) one is to draw only the visible part of the partly hidden item. Various errors or intellectually realistic types of drawing are possible, of which transparency is only one, and not the most common. In a following section I shall describe in more detail the partial occlusion paradigm. At this point, suffice it to say that, to represent partial occlusion in a visually realistic way, the child has to modify his/her graphic scheme for the partly hidden item in order to represent only that part that is visible from a given point of view, and represent on paper not just an array of objects but the spatial arrangement in which they are seen from that point of view. How can one achieve that? A visually realistic intention is not enough; a child has the difficult task of coordinating and modifying a number of graphic schemes on the basis of the chosen point of view and consequently plan their placement on the sheet of paper.

In this chapter, after a theoretical introduction, I discuss in some detail the partial occlusion paradigm and present our research on this topic. Subsequently, I shall discuss other lines of research that bear on spatial aspects of children's drawings, and come to some general conclusions and suggestions for further research.

Theoretical background

This chapter takes a neo-Piagetian approach to drawing, as proposed in greater detail by Morra (1995; see also Morra, 2005, 2008). To summarize it briefly, the main assumption is that different types of capacities are involved in children's drawing; some are specific schemes, and others are more general resources.

First of all, drawing involves *figurative schemes*. In particular, graphic figurative schemes are analogue mental representations, stored in long-term memory, of satisfactory graphic denotations of objects. A graphic scheme for a certain object is not a representation of the object itself (for instance, a child can know much more about bicycles and their visual appearance than she represents in her graphic scheme for drawing a bicycle). Rather, when the child discovers or learns a satisfactory way to depict a bicycle, she may learn how that successful drawing looks, and reproduce that visual pattern on subsequent occasions when a bicycle has to be drawn (Van Sommers, 1984). Graphic figurative schemes can have a hierarchical structure, that is, they are usually composed of simpler parts, which themselves are endowed with meaning (see also Case, Stephenson, Bleiker and Okamoto, 1996; Van Sommers, 1984; Willats, 1985, 1987).

Besides graphic schemes, other figurative schemes are also important in drawing. They are the visual representations and visual images of real-world objects. A child who has to solve a pictorial problem (e.g. drawing for the first time a shark) may resort to graphic schemes for other animals and for simpler shapes, compare them with visual images or mental representations of the shark itself, and try to use and integrate this information to construct a novel graphic scheme for the shark.

Operative schemes are another important type of resource for drawing. They include all sorts of procedures to modify a graphic scheme; for instance, the 'hidden line elimination' procedure proposed by Freeman, Eiser and Sayers (1977) for partial occlusion drawing, the drawing devices used to represent foreshortening (Willats, 1995), and the various types of modifications of the human figure that can be used to convey particular meanings. Some operative schemes have a major motor component; for instance, the use of wavy contour lines as a metaphorical denotation of fear (Morra, Caloni and D'Amico, 1994) involves not only mental transformation of a graphic scheme, but also fine motor control during execution. Also, the procedures that a child has learned to use to represent spatial relations are regarded as operative schemes. For instance, a child who has acquired a rule to represent distance in the real world by means of the vertical dimension of the drawing sheet, may use that scheme and place on paper item *a* above item *b* to indicate that *a* is farther than *b*. In a later section of this chapter the developmental acquisition of operative schemes for space representation will be discussed in greater detail.

Information-processing mechanisms relevant to drawing include learning processes, perceptual processes, executive functions such as inhibition of misleading information, and working memory. These are sometimes designated by neo-Piagetian authors as 'metasubjective operators' or 'hidden operators' (e.g. Pascual-Leone and Johnson, 2004, 2005) because – contrary to schemes – they do not have a specific content and are not included in the individual's subjective consciousness, but silently affect the activation of existing schemes and the formation of new ones. Learning processes are of different kinds, sometimes slow, context-bound and experience-driven, but sometimes fast, effortful and regulated by mental attention (Pascual-Leone and Goodman, 1979; see Morra, 1995, for a discussion of how such different learning processes are related to acquisition of drawing skills). Perceptual organization according to Gestalt principles is another important general mechanism that affects drawing. Such a field factor (or F-operator in the neo-Piagetian jargon) has a dual role in drawing and art, because it tends to favour a simple solution compatible with the largest set of activated schemes. Sometimes it helps a balanced solution or a good Gestalt to emerge; but sometimes it produces a biased compromise solution or a simple and inappropriate Gestalt. For instance, young children's process of completion of a drawing is likely to involve a compromise between the intended meaning and the available cues that often induce response biases compatible with the current perceptual field (Freeman, 1980).

Pascual-Leone (1989) also suggests that individual differences in cognitive style, such as field-dependence versus independence, are due to differences in the balance between metasubjective operators. High-quality picture composition (e.g. Golomb, 1992; Milbrath, 1998) may demand some features of field dependence, such as a strong F-operator that facilitates production of good Gestalten, and some of field independence, such as the abilities to include several elements in a plan or to disregard obvious solutions. These characteristics are probably found in individuals with an intermediate degree of field independence and a flexible cognitive style.

One information-processing mechanism most extensively studied in neo-Piagetian frameworks, and a very important one for the argument to be presented in the following, is the M-operator. This term refers to an attentional resource that can be used to activate simultaneously a limited number of schemes that are relevant to a current processing goal. It has a limited capacity (called M capacity); an average 3-year-old can only activate one scheme by means of this resource, which grows during the preschool and school years at the pace of approximately two years per each additional scheme, so that an average 5-year-old has an M capacity of two schemes, a 7-year-old three schemes, and so on; the capacity of six schemes would be achieved at about 13 or 14 years of age, and most individuals would reach, later in adolescence, a capacity of seven schemes. Extensive research has provided evidence for this developmental trend (Case, 1995; Foley and Berch, 1997; Morra, 1994; Pascual-Leone, 1970; Pascual-Leone and Baillargeon, 1994; Pascual-Leone, Johnson, Baskind, Dworsky and Severtson, 2000; de Ribaupierre and Bailleux, 1994). According to neo-Piagetian theory, M capacity is an attentional resource; thus, it is a major determinant of working memory, but the two terms are not synonymous (for discussions of the relationship between M capacity and working memory, see Morra, 2000; Pascual-Leone, 2000; Pascual-Leone and Johnson, 2005).

In sum, children's drawing is often a problem-solving activity; the child's current repertoire of graphic schemes and rules to organize a drawing, her sensitivity to the context and organization of the perceptual field, her ability to select the relevant information and to coordinate several schemes, all play a role in shaping the planning and execution of a drawing. According to the approach taken here, drawing would depend on the interaction among a number of specific and general resources, that is, schemes and metasubjective operators. The growth of M capacity with age, in particular, would enable children to find increasingly complex solutions to pictorial problems. For a brief discussion of previous drawing research carried out within a neo-Piagetian approach, see Morra (2005, 2008). In the remainder of this chapter, the spatial aspects of drawing

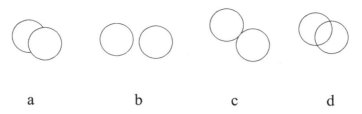

     a   b   c   d

Figure 9.1 Different types of drawing of a pair of balls, one partly occluded by the other.

will be considered, that is, representation of spatial relations, movement and spatial composition.

Partial occlusion drawing

As mentioned above, the 'partial occlusion' experimental paradigm arose as an attempt to clarify the issue of transparency drawing. At the beginning of the cognitive approach to children's drawing, Norman Freeman launched an extensive research programme that aimed to test some of Luquet's claims with more modern theoretical and methodological tools (see Freeman, 1972). In that context, Freeman *et al.* (1977) started a line of experiments where children were required to imagine or to look at arrays of objects, one of which was partly hidden by another, and draw them. Several studies show that it is indeed difficult for children below age 8 to draw a partly occluded object in a visually realistic way, that is, with only part of its shape visible and the contour of that partial shape making contact with the contour of the occluding object (as in Figure 9.1a); however, only seldom do children resort to transparency drawing (as in Figure 9.1d).

Instead, the majority of them tend to depict an object-centred representation of the arrays, in which the partly occluded object is entirely drawn (as in Figure 9.1b), and often placed on paper in a location that shows (more or less accurately) its spatial relationship with the occluding object; e.g. draw it 'above' in order to show that it is 'farther away', or perhaps draw it above and displaced to one side and contiguous to the occluding object (as in Figure 9.1c). It seems that there is a strategy shift for representation of depth, from showing array-specific information such as the spatial relationships between the objects, to using view-specific information on the relationship between the viewer and the objects. Furthermore, the degree of difficulty of partial occlusion drawing varies according to experimental conditions (see Cox, 1991, 2005 for reviews).

One interesting phenomenon, discovered by Cox (1985, 1991), has been called the similarity effect. Children show a stronger tendency to draw the entire shape of the partly occluded object when the occluding and occluded object have similar shape. A weaker similarity effect is sometimes manifest also when the occluding and occluded object have different shape, but similar size.

Morra, Angi and Tomat (1996) have suggested that the similarity effect stems from a field effect. Grouping by similarity is one of Wertheimer's well-known Gestalt laws (e.g. see Kanizsa, 1979). In case the model objects are similar, the child perceptually encodes them as a group, and thus is biased to draw them as a group of similar shapes. Morra et al. (1996, experiment 2) compared the behaviour of first-grade children with two models in different layouts: one composed by two identical shapes (two balls, one partially occluding the other), and the other by two dissimilar shapes (a tall and thin pyramid partially occluded by a cube). Participants were required first to describe and then to draw each of the layouts. A verbal description was required before drawing, to ensure that descriptions were based on how children perceived the layouts – not on how they had just drawn them. We scored children's verbal descriptions in two categories, *singular* or *plural*, according to whether the first noun or pronoun named by the child was singular (e.g. 'a square', 'a yellow ball', 'this') or plural (e.g. 'two little balls', 'they'). Our assumption was that the use of a plural term in the verbal description of the layout can be taken as an indicator of perceptual grouping of the objects referred to.

We have found that the two balls elicit a majority of 'plural' descriptions, while the cube-and-pyramid display elicits almost exclusively 'singular' descriptions. We have also replicated Cox's finding that in the case of the dissimilar objects children tend to draw the partial occlusion in a visually realistic way, but most of them draw two entire round shapes in the case of the two balls. Most important, we have found that the children who described the balls in plural terms overwhelmingly drew them as two distinct, entire shapes, whereas this tendency was significantly weaker among the children who produced 'singular' verbal descriptions. These results lead to two conclusions. First, the similarity effect in partial occlusion drawing is related to a Gestalt field phenomenon, that is, encoding the model objects as a group, rather than individual and distinguishable items. Second, there are individual differences in sensitivity to that field effect; some children are more inclined than others both to describe the balls as a group and to draw the two balls with the same graphic scheme.

Another experiment by Morra *et al.* (1996) addressed the question of when the child decides to draw the entire shape of the partly occluded object; is this decision taken at an initial planning stage, before the drawing is initiated? Or, alternatively, do children observe the model objects during the drawing process and guide their decisions according to such observation? A large sample of 5- to 8-year-olds was divided into four groups, who drew one of the two layouts described above (balls or cube-and-pyramid) in one of two viewing conditions (normal viewing or screened). In the normal viewing condition, the model was visible and children could observe it throughout the drawing task. In the screened condition, the model was shown for 5 seconds and then covered before the child started drawing. We reasoned that, if observation of the model while drawing leads the child to adjust her drawing strategy, one should find more visually realistic partial occlusion drawings, and a larger effect of shape similarity, in the normal viewing condition. Furthermore, drawing strategies could be related to children's looking behaviour, because visually realistic drawings could be an outcome of children's more frequent observation of the model.

Instead, we found no effect of the viewing condition. As usual, more visually realistic drawings were produced with dissimilar model objects than with similar ones; however, screening the model objects before the child started drawing did not affect the drawing outcome, and did not interact with shape similarity. Furthermore, in the normal viewing condition, children looked equally often at either model layout, and there was no difference in the looking behaviour of the two groups of children who drew the model in a visually realistic or in a different way. All these results point to the conclusion that children's decision on how to draw the two model objects takes place at an early planning stage, before they actually start drawing. Having the model in sight does not alter their drawing strategy in this task. The general importance of a planning stage in children's drawings, and the effect of M capacity on the complexity of their drawing plans, has been discussed in previous papers (Morra, 1995; Morra, Moizo and Scopesi, 1988) and here it is not necessary to take the argument further. Rather, the important point here is that the two experiments – together with other findings reported in the literature, including the results of Cox's original studies of the similarity effect – suggest a model of partial occlusion drawing.

When the model layout consists of two similar shapes, children tend to encode it as 'a group of . . .', activate the graphic scheme for the objects with that particular shape, and plan the drawing of a single, repeated graphic scheme. Thus, activation of a single graphic scheme is sufficient to plan a drawing such as Figure 9.1b on page 165. Alternatively, a child could plan a drawing like Figure 9.1c by activating two schemes: a figurative graphic scheme for the shape of the objects, and an operative scheme for the spatial relation between them, depicted not from the observer's point of view but as array-specific information on the position of each object with respect to the other.

Planning a visually realistic drawing, like Figure 9.1a, is possible by activating three schemes:
(a) a graphic figurative scheme for the shape of the object,
(b) a figurative scheme that represents the shape of the part of the object that is occluded,
(c) an operative scheme to perform the operation called 'hidden line elimination' by Freeman et al. (1977), that is, to refrain from drawing that part of the graphic scheme (a) of the occluded object that represents its hidden part (b).

To implement this strategy, a child should be able simultaneously to activate and to coordinate three schemes (that is, have an M capacity of 3 units). In addition, because we have shown that there are individual differences in sensitivity to the Gestalt field factors that bias towards drawing a pair of identical shapes, one should expect that field-independent children (who are less sensitive to field effects) are better able to follow this strategy.

It can also be suggested that *transparency drawings* (such as Figure 9.1d) are a product of *faulty implementation of this strategy*. Suppose that a child with an M capacity of 2 units realizes that one of the objects is only partly visible, understands what part of it is hidden, and wishes to represent that state of affairs. Because of insufficient M capacity, that child will not be able to activate all of the three required schemes. Suppose that the child activates schemes (a) and (b), but not (c). The outcome will be a drawing in which one can recognize the shapes of the visible and the hidden parts of the partially occluded object – but alas, not the fact that a part is not visible, because hidden line elimination has not been carried out while planning. This would be an explanation of the transparency phenomenon, in terms of *insufficient M capacity* to perform a mature, visually realistic strategy.

There is also another strategy that can yield a visually realistic drawing. This only requires two simultaneously activated schemes – but ones that are not granted in the child's repertoire:
(d) a graphic figurative scheme that represents the shape of the visible part of the partially occluded object,
(e) an operative scheme for placing that graphic scheme in the appropriate position, contiguous to the occluding object.

However, a child could lack scheme (d), which often has an unusual shape. It could also be difficult to create such a scheme, by extrapolating the relevant shape from the visual field. For that reason, even though this strategy requires activating only two schemes (and thus in principle could be afforded by children with an M capacity of 2 units), numerous children could not actually use it because the relevant schemes are not available to them. In case the relevant schemes are available to the child, also this strategy would require some degree of field independence, because also this strategy has to be implemented against the Gestalt field factors that bias the child to draw two identical shapes.

Note, however, that faulty implementation of this strategy would not lead to transparency drawings. For instance, if a child only activates scheme (d) and not scheme (e), the outcome would be a curious and rather unusual error, that is, a drawing of the visible part of the partly occluded object that floats freely at a distance from the occluding object.

In short, one can predict that:
> Visually realistic drawing of a partial occlusion is possible to some children with an M capacity of 2 units, in the case that they can follow the latter strategy outlined here.
> Children with an M capacity of 3 units will show a larger proportion of visually realistic drawings of partial occlusions, because they can follow both strategies.
> Visually realistic partial occlusion drawings will correlate with children's field independence.
> Transparency drawing will be related to an M capacity of 2 units.

What would be different in a case where the model layout consists of two dissimilar shapes? The two possible strategies would be the same, that is, the one based on hidden line elimination, or the other one, based on creating a graphic scheme for the visible part. These two strategies would still require activation of 3 or 2 schemes, respectively. However, there would not be a field effect that biases the child to plan the repeated drawing of a single graphic scheme. In some cases, a small visible part with a simple and distinctive shape could even 'pop out from behind' the occluding object, and this salient perceptual relationship could facilitate activation of the relevant schemes. Thus, in the case of dissimilar shapes, the only misleading aspect would be the child's habit to draw the entire shape of the various objects. This habit of course is also present in the case of two model objects with similar shapes. Without the field effect created by shape similarity, implementing either strategy would be easier also for children with a lower degree of field independence.

Morra et al. (1996, experiment 3) tested these predictions in a sample of first-graders, with similar simple shapes (two balls), similar toys with a complex shape (two identical cars), dissimilar simple shapes (a cube and a pyramid), and dissimilar toys with a complex shape (a piggy bank partly occluding a pair of guitar singers). The participants were also administered tests of M capacity and field independence. The results of this experiment provided initial support for the model presented above. Visually realistic drawing of partial occlusions was related to both M capacity and field independence. In particular, the correlations were significant for drawings of pairs of similar shapes (two balls, or two cars). Furthermore, seven transparency drawings were obtained, and all of them had been produced by children with an M capacity of 2 units.

A follow-up study (Morra, 2002) tested the same predictions in a larger sample of 119 5- to 8-year-olds, with a better-controlled set of model layouts, and more measures of M capacity and field independence. Again, the results were in agreement with the predictions. The sample included a small group (n = 8) of children with an M capacity of only 1 unit, who proved unable to draw visually realistic partial occlusions. Children with an M capacity of 2 units made less visually realistic drawings than those with an M capacity of at least 3 units, consistent with the idea that the latter can use either of two strategies, while the former can use only one. M capacity and field independence predicted independent components of variance in partial occlusion drawings. The children who did not make visually realistic drawings of the partial occlusion in layouts of highly dissimilar objects tended to have an M capacity of 1 or 2 units and to be field dependent. Transparency drawings were associated to an M capacity of 2 units.

It seems interesting at this point to pool together the participants of the two experiments in which M capacity has been measured (that is, Morra et al., 1996, experiment 3, and Morra, 2002) in order to test the relationship between M capacity and transparency drawing. Overall, the two experiments involved 197 participants. Only thirteen of those participants made one or more transparency drawings; specifically, in the Morra et al. (1996) experiment there were two children who made two transparency drawings and three children who made one, and all of them had an M capacity of 2 units, while in the Morra (2002) study there were eight children who drew one transparency, and seven of them had an M capacity of 2 units and one an M capacity of 3 units. Table 9.1 shows the relationship between participants' M capacity and whether they drew any partial occlusion.

Our model predicts that only children with an M capacity of 2 units produce transparency drawings in the partial occlusion paradigm, because

Table 9.1 *Relationship between M capacity and transparency drawing*

M capacity	One or more drawings with transparencies		No transparency	Total
1	0	(0.53)	8	8
2	12		86	98
3 or more	1	(6.01)	90	91
Total	13		184	

Note: The table presents the number of children at each level of M capacity who did or did not make transparency drawings. (In parenthesis, the frequencies expected by chance in the cells that our model predicts to be empty.) The row '3 or more' actually comprises eighty-six children with a capacity of 3 units, four of 4, and one of 5; the one child who made a transparency drawing had a capacity of 3.

transparency drawings emerge as the outcome of a faulty implementation of a strategy that requires co-activation of 3 schemes, while the child can only activate two of them. Children with a capacity of 3 or more units should not produce this performance (unless they underperform due to momentary inattention), because they have the capacity to activate all the required schemes at the same time. Also children with a capacity of 1 unit should not draw a transparency, because even the faulty implementation that produces it is too demanding for them. Therefore, in Table 9.1, the frequencies of children who make one or more transparency drawings are expected to be zero in all rows, except the one that corresponds to the M capacity of 2 units.

Actually, one child with a capacity of 3 units made a transparency drawing. Is this a counterfact that falsifies our model, or can it be taken as tolerable error variance? Prediction analysis of cross-classification (Hildebrand, Laing and Rosenthal, 1977) offers an answer to this question. In Hildebrand *et al.*'s method, the index *Del* is used to express the extent to which the prediction that one or more cells are empty can account for discrepancy between observed frequencies and those expected by chance. A positive *Del* value indicates that observed frequencies in the critical cells are lower than expected by chance; its maximum possible value is 1, when all critical cells are empty. A z-value and a confidence interval can be computed for *Del*. For statistical inference, the confidence interval can be used in two ways. First, if the whole confidence interval is in the positive range, this indicates that the model used is better than chance. Second, if the confidence interval not only is positive but also includes $Del = 1$, then one accepts the hypothesis that the crucial cells are empty (that is, the frequencies observed in those cells do not significantly depart from zero). Of course, the first use already involves claims of statistical significance (i.e. that a model is better than chance). However, the second use involves stronger claims, because asserting that the model is better than chance *and* the frequencies in the crucial cells do not differ significantly from zero is a stronger claim than only asserting that the model is better than chance.

The data in Table 9.1 yield $Del = .847$, $z = 5.54$, $p < .001$, and a 95 per cent confidence interval of (.548, 1.146). Thus, not only is the model of transparency proposed here better than chance at a high level of significance, but the single exception of a child with a capacity of 3 units who made a transparency drawing can be considered as negligible error variance, because the confidence interval includes the value of $Del = 1$. The model is fully supported by the data.

To summarize this section, the experiments reported above strongly suggest that children's decision on how to represent a partial occlusion takes place at an early stage of planning, and the choice and successful implementation of a strategy that yields a visually realistic drawing demand a certain amount of M capacity. In particular, the 3 units of M capacity required to implement hidden line elimination exceed the resources available to most preschoolers and many first-graders. In addition, the similarity effect (Cox, 1991) in partial occlusion drawing depends on the fact that similar shapes create a Gestalt field effect, which biases children towards repeating the same graphic scheme. A certain degree of field independence is required to overcome that bias. Dissimilar shapes, instead, do not produce that bias and, in certain cases, may even facilitate the second strategy, based on creating a graphic scheme for the visible part. The construct of M capacity does not account only for children's ability to follow the strategies described above; it also accounts for transparency drawings. These drawings arise as the faulty implementation of a strategy that would require 3 units of M capacity by children who have only 2 units available.

Incidentally, one can note that our data on transparency drawing of partial occlusions also support Russo Pizzo's (1974) intuition that transparency is a relatively infrequent phenomenon, to be characterized not as a hallmark of an intellectual realism stage, but as a temporary form of experimentation by children who are searching for new and complex graphic forms. In the case of partial occlusion, the complex graphic forms that children are searching are those that depict in a realistic way which part of an object is visible and which one is hidden. However, that experimentation could be hindered by the child's insufficient M capacity.

The account of transparency drawing proposed here is valid for the context of the partial occlusion paradigm; it could be extended to other drawing tasks, if one can take into account also the demands for planning the overall drawing. For instance, a child may plan the drawing of a complex scene including several elements among which is a house, and only after having drawn the house decide to draw some elements that are contained in it. In this case, it would be the relationship between the view of the house and its contents that has not been considered at the stage of planning, possibly because the child's M capacity was already occupied with other elements of the scene. Or, in the case of the transparent horse through which one can see the hidden leg of a knight, the child could have planned the depiction of the horse and the knight, but not the appropriate modifications of the horse and the human figure schemes that would represent realistically the spatial relation between them. (The problem of such scheme modifications will be discussed in a later section.) Thus, the present analysis of transparency drawing could be extended from partial occlusion to other drawing tasks; however, for such an extension it would also be necessary to specify carefully all the demands of planning a drawing in such tasks.

Drawing water as horizontal

Another line of research provides converging evidence on the role of M capacity and field independence in children's ability to represent spatial information in a drawing. Piaget and Inhelder (1947/1967) developed a 'water level task', in which children were required to indicate the level of water in a half-filled bottle that was placed in a non-vertical position, for instance sideways or tilted at various angles. Of course, still water is always horizontal, but many children often draw a tilted line, and sometimes also adults do so (e.g. Vasta and Liben, 1996). Pascual-Leone and Morra (1991) review typical error patterns and discuss the factors that are involved in the production of non-horizontal responses. One is everyday experience with upright bottles, where the liquid is parallel to the bottom, which induces participants to imagine and draw water as parallel to the bottom. Another is a field factor, created by the bottom, the sides and the neck of the bottle; people have a response bias for drawing straight angles (see also De Bruyn and Davis, 2005), and tend to generate a response that is compatible with the perceptual field and orthogonal to the sides (or the bottom) of the bottle. Compromise responses can also be produced, which are intermediate between the horizontal line (that is consistent with relevant physical and spatial knowledge) and a line parallel to the bottom, or to the sides.

Pascual-Leone and Morra (1991) also presented a model of the factors that enable children and adults to produce a correct response, i.e. a horizontal line. Basically, these are of three types. One is relevant physical knowledge about the behaviour of liquids, such as understanding that water falls to the lower part of a container, that it spreads evenly in the container, and perhaps even that its surface at rest is horizontal. Another is sufficient M capacity to keep activated all the necessary physical and spatial information, as well as the means to represent it graphically (two strategies were proposed, which involve simultaneous activation of 4 or 5 schemes, respectively). A third factor is some degree of field independence, which is required to resist the misleading effect of the above-mentioned error factors.

A recent article (Morra, in press) presents a study on a large sample of children aged 5 to 13, designed to test the predictions stated by Pascual-Leone and Morra (1991). The results showed that three variables – physical knowledge, M capacity and field independence – separately contributed to children's performance in the water level task. The results were also in agreement with the predictions that children with less than 4 units of M capacity find the task very difficult, and that children with an M capacity of 5 units (who could follow either of the posited strategies) produce more horizontal lines than those with a capacity of 4 units. The model was also supported by other details of the results; for instance, both physical knowledge and field independence affected the performance of children with an M capacity of 4 units (which is a necessary but not sufficient requirement for correct performance) more than those with a smaller capacity (who, according to the model, are likely to fail the task even when they are field independent and have good physical knowledge).

The water level task involves not only the spatial concept of horizontality, but also physical knowledge, and therefore it is not necessary to discuss it here in detail. However, it is relevant for the present line of argument to note that, similarly to the partial occlusion drawing task, also for the water level task one can posit a few successful strategies, each of which requires a minimum M capacity to be implemented. For both tasks, the results support our models.

Movement representation

In this section we turn to children's ability to modify their habitual graphic schemes to convey a particular meaning – sometimes called flexibility (Picard and Vinter, 1999; Spensley and Taylor, 1999; Zhi, Thomas and Robinson, 1997). For instance, the canonical way in which children draw a human figure is standing, in frontal view. However, a number of classical tasks require children to draw the figure in movement, for instance

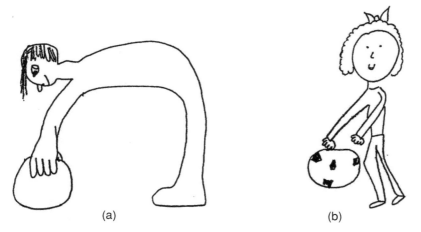

Figure 9.2 Examples of third-graders' drawings of a person who picks up a ball.

running or picking up something from the ground (Goodnow, 1978). As with many other skills, children's flexibility in modifying their habitual drawing schemes also develops with age.

The relevant point for the argument made in this chapter is that representation of human movement can be achieved by rearranging the spatial relationships among the parts of the figure. Some of these rearrangements can be done with little advance planning, as on-the-spot decisions made at the point of drawing a specific part of the figure. For instance, a child who is drawing a running person may decide to draw the hair as windswept without having planned that in advance; when the head has already been drawn and it is time to draw the hair, the child may feel that drawing it in a certain position conveys better the idea of running, and consequently do so. Other rearrangements, however, do need advance planning. This is the case of those major or global changes, in which altering some part of the stereotyped drawing affects the way in which other parts have to be drawn. For instance, a child could not start by drawing a head in the usual way and then decide to draw a bent body axis, because this decision would involve drawing also the head in a different position.

Figure 9.2 presents two examples of drawings of a person who picks up a ball, both made by third-graders. The drawing in Figure 9.2a shows an arrangement of the positions of head, neck, trunk and arms that must have been planned before starting to draw, because the spatial relations among them could not be obtained merely by drawing some parts of the figure and then adjusting the rest of the drawing to the cues provided by the parts already drawn. Furthermore, the continuous line that represents the back and the posterior of the leg is another sign of advance planning. The arm has clearly been attached to the neck and the chest, but it is reasonable to assume that the whole position of the trunk had been planned precisely in a way that would enable the draughtsperson to attach the arm to it in that way. The way of drawing the hair, instead, could either be planned in advance or adjusted on the spot. Overall, Figure 9.2a suggests considerable advance planning and restructuring of the spatial relations among the parts of the human body, as compared with the canonical way of drawing the human figure.

At first sight, Figure 9.2b does not suggest an equally global change or systematic advance planning. For instance, the knees are bent (although the representation is imprecise, because each leg is bent on one side and straight on the other); but the trunk is vertical, and one cannot know whether the bent legs were planned beforehand or just at the moment of drawing them. However, also in Figure 9.2b there is an important detail that indicates planning. The two arms are stretching towards the ball, on the same side of the figure, and the trunk is partially occluded by the left arm. The drawing of the arms and the trunk appears to be well coordinated, and probably planned as a whole.

In a study of flexibility in human figure drawing (Morra, 2005) I have suggested that planning a global change or restructuring involves coordination of *at least three schemes*, that is, a graphic figurative scheme for the human figure, one or more figurative schemes that represent the visual aspect of a person's global feature(s) that will be modified in the drawing, and an operative scheme that mentally transforms the intended feature(s) in the human figure graphic scheme.[1] Instead, a 'local' change of a specific feature, decided at the point of drawing it, requires coordination of only *two schemes*, that is, a figurative scheme for the aspect of that specific body part in a person in movement, and an operative scheme to modify the corresponding feature in the drawing.

Consequently, we can expect M capacity to be a major causal factor in children's ability to restructure a human figure drawing in order to represent a certain movement. Of course, this does not mean that it is the only factor. Other factors are the child's executive schemes that carry her awareness of the task demands, and the availability of perceptual cues that activate figurative schemes regarding how a person who is doing a certain movement looks. As reported elsewhere (Morra, 2005) these factors make distinguishable and independent contributions to children's drawing flexibility. For the sake of the present argument, however, the point to be made is that M capacity affects children's ability to represent human movements by restructuring their habitual graphic scheme of the human figure and the spatial relationships among its parts.

The first two experiments by Morra (2005) presented Goodnow's (1978) tasks of drawing a person who is picking up a ball, one who is walking and one who is running, to children in the age range between 5 and 9 years. For each task, a drawing flexibility score was assigned by counting the number of features in which the drawing of the figure in movement differed from a control condition, the drawing of 'a person who is standing still'.

Both experiments showed that the increase of M capacity with age accounts for a very large proportion of the developmental increase in drawing flexibility scores. In addition, the correlations between M capacity and drawing flexibility with age partialled out showed that M capacity also accounts for a smaller, but still highly significant proportion of individual differences in drawing flexibility scores. Thus, also the line of research on drawing human movements pointed to a major role of M capacity in a drawing task with spatial requirements.

The dimensions of space

Another interesting line of research, designed within a neo-Piagetian theoretical framework, was carried out by Dennis (1987, 1992); in particular, one of her experiments deals directly with the dimensions of space, by means of a cleverly designed series of tasks in which children are explicitly required to represent increasingly complex relations along various spatial dimensions. Groups of children aged 4, 6, 8 and 10 years were presented the following tasks:

1. Draw a picture of a man.
2. Draw a picture of a girl standing in a park next to a tree.
3. Draw a picture of two boys shaking hands in a park with a fence just behind them.
4. Draw a picture of a man and a woman holding hands in a park. Their baby is in front of them and a tree is very far away behind them.
5. Draw a picture of a mother looking out of the window of her house to see where her son is playing in the park across from where they live. She only sees her son's face because he is peeking out from behind a tree.

As evident, the first task merely requires the child to retrieve a single graphic scheme to depict a recognizable human figure. The second task requires placing two graphic schemes according to a simple 'next to' relation in order to create at least the arrangement of a foreground.

The third task involves two dimensions: the boys (usually aligned on the horizontal dimension) are in the foreground and the fence makes a background, but the two dimensions do not need to be finely elaborated and the foreground and background may be uncoordinated, provided that the relation 'behind' is respected. In the fourth task, however, depth must be elaborated in greater detail, as a continuum, because there are a foreground, a middle ground (arranged along a different dimension) and a background, with different distances between each other. Finally, the fifth task requires drawing two scenes (mother-at-window and child-behind-tree) and coordinating them according to the mother's viewpoint, which is clearly a very complex requirement. Dennis (1987) reports that the five tasks make a reliable Guttman scale.

The results show that the first task is passed by almost all children in all age-groups, the second task is passed by a majority of children starting from age 6, and the third task from the age of 8. Almost half of the 10-year-olds and one third of the 8-year-olds passed the fourth task. The fifth task was passed only by a small minority of children (20 per cent in the oldest age-group). As predicted by Dennis, performance on these tasks was also positively correlated with working memory measures and the increase with age of drawing complexity scores was parallel to the increase of working memory.

On the base of this and other research, also including studies with spatial tasks that do not involve drawing, Case *et al.* (1996) propose that children go through stages of spatial competence, which they label *preaxial, uniaxial, biaxial* and *integrated biaxial*. On average, the four age-groups studied by Dennis (1987) would correspond to these stages. In the first stage, the child would have schemes for the objects' shapes and locations, but no conceptual understanding of spatial coordinates. In the second stage, the child could also use a single 'mental reference axis' to understand the location of an object with respect to an edge of a field. In the third stage the child could set up two discrete representations, for instance using two similar mental reference axes for different regions of space. Finally, children would achieve the capability to understand the reference to a whole field of objects according to a pair of orthogonal reference axes, like in a Cartesian plane.

One could note that this analysis stops at the point when the child can coordinate and integrate two dimensions of space, but the third dimension seems to be missing. This is probably due to the fact that Case and colleagues are modelling development up to age 10. In fact (even though the authors did not put it this way) the fifth task of Dennis (1992) requires integrating three dimensions – this point will be developed later in this chapter.

Case et al. (1996) compared the performance of children in this age range on a battery of spatial tasks, only some of which involved drawing. The drawing tasks were the fourth of Dennis' tasks described above, a map drawing task, and the drawing of a still life scene from a model consisting of a coffee cup standing on a table, with an upside-down toothbrush inside it and a tube of toothpaste lying in front of it. All these drawing and other spatial tasks were scored according to criteria based on the four-level sequence that proceeds from preaxial to integrated biaxial. Exploratory factor analysis showed that a single factor loaded the three drawing tasks and four non-drawing spatial tasks, and the progress of children's performance with age was fairly even across the set of these seven tasks.

In short, Case et al. (1996) suggest that working memory increase enables more complex conceptual representation of space along one or more axes, which in turn is the grounds for more complex spatial organization of drawings in tasks like those studied by Dennis (1987, 1992). Of course, there is consistency between this view and the idea, exposed in the previous section, that the developmental increase of M capacity enables more advanced performance in drawing tasks that involve representation of spatial relations. Also the measures used by us for M capacity and by Case's group for working memory are similar, and the respective results broadly compatible.

Other authors have studied the development of spatial dimensions or axes in children's drawing. At least two lines of research are important in this regard. One concerns projection systems or 'drawing systems'; the other concerns the use of spatial axes as a factor that affects the size of figures.

Willats (1977) developed a methodology to classify children's use of projection systems, understood as steps towards drawing in perspective, and Lee and Bremner (1987) followed up that line of research. Different projection systems can be distinguished by how one represents depth, that is, by how those edges of solids that are orthogonal to the picture plane are represented in a drawing. In orthographic projection, they are not represented (or, technically speaking, they are represented as points), and thus depth is ignored. In vertical-oblique projection, the edges that extend only in depth are represented as parallel vertical lines. In oblique projection they are represented as parallel oblique lines. Finally, if these edges are drawn as converging, then some form of perspective is used – often, an approximate one such as 'naive perspective' (Willats, 1977) or 'false perspective' (Lee and Bremner, 1987).

Willats (1977) presented to children of various ages a complex model (a table with several objects on top of it, some of which were partially occluded by others), while Lee and Bremner (1987) required a larger sample of children to draw a simpler model – just a table. Because of differences in their samples, models and other methodological details, one must be cautious in extrapolating from these studies which projection systems are typically used by children at each age. For instance, Willats (who required children to draw a more complex model) reports mean ages that are older than those reported by Lee and Bremner.

However, it is notable that in both studies orthogonal, vertical-oblique and oblique projection seem to follow one another with lags of approximately two years, and the various approximate forms of perspective manifest themselves even later. This is also broadly consistent with the results of Case *et al.* (1996) on still life drawing.

There are important differences in the scoring method used in these studies. Case *et al.* (1996) focus on qualitative characteristics of the items depicted in a scene (e.g. is the cup's opening drawn as an oval or a circle, or not drawn at all?) and on the relations among their positions, while the study of projection systems concerns measurable geometrical properties of the items, or of parts of them (e.g. the side edges of the table plane). Of course, a child's geometry for representing the various edges of a single object could be independent of the way that child represents the relations between different objects in an array. It is also possible that a given child is not consistent in the projection system used to represent different objects; for instance, a child could learn how to draw a cube in oblique projection, but not transfer that particular skill to drawing in oblique projection other shapes (Phillips, Inall and Lauder, 1985). Nevertheless, if the child can discover or learn some rules for representing on paper the dimensions of space, then we should expect at least *some degree of consistency* between the representation of object positions along spatial axes and the representation of object edges according to some sort of projective geometrical rules. From this point of view, it is promising that Case *et al.* (1996), Lee and Bremner (1987) and Willats (1977) all find lags of approximately two years between a set of rules and another for space representation. As Case *et al.* (1996) note, the various systems of axes described in their study follow each other at steps of two years consistently with the development of working memory. This might also apply to projection systems, although we do not have direct evidence on this point because Willats (1977) and Lee and Bremner (1987) did not measure children's working memory or M capacity.

Lange-Küttner (1997, 2004, 2005) studied how children's use of spatial axes influences the size of the figures they draw. In some of her studies (Lange-Küttner, 2004, study 2; 2005) children of different ages (namely, 7, 9 and 11 years old) were required to draw a specified number of children playing a ball game, either on a blank sheet or on a sheet where spatial axes had been pre-drawn – that is, a horizontal line, or a rectangular 'playing field', or one constructed with oblique lines. The dependent measures were the average size of the human figures represented in a drawing and the variability of those figures. The basic idea that motivated Lange-Küttner's research is that, if children have an understanding of spatial axes, then they should also use them to regulate the size of the figures they draw in a certain spatial context. A blank sheet where no spatial organization is defined could invite children to draw large figures with unconstrained variance, but a sheet with pre-drawn orthogonal axes (the rectangular 'playing field') would cue children – or at least, those children who understand a system of orthogonal axes – to draw figures of the same size, while a sheet with oblique axes in perspective could cue older children to adjust figure size according to distance (see Lange-Küttner, this volume).

Relevant to the present argument, it appears that 11-year-olds are much more sensitive than younger children to pre-drawn axes, and can adjust flexibly the size of their figures to the axes system defined by the experimenter. It also appears that 9-year-olds are sensitive to certain properties of the axes; for instance, they can use orthogonal axes to reduce figure size and variability, especially if they are presented with the various axes systems in order of increasing complexity.

Once again, we can note an interesting pattern of developing competence in the use of spatial axes, with signs of new acquisitions at two-year steps – as in Case *et al.* (1996), Dennis (1992), and in the studies of projection systems. Is it possible to tie together the ideas that motivated these different lines of research?

On the acquisition of drawing systems and spatial axes systems

At this point, we can propose some new hypotheses on how the growth of working memory or M capacity could enable children to construct increasingly complex systems of spatial dimensions or axes, which in turn would have a pervasive influence on several drawing tasks, such as those reviewed in the previous section. I am suggesting that each increase in M capacity to 2, 3, 4, 5 and 6 units would have specific consequences on the increasing complexity of the spatial system that a child can understand and use.

For the sake of clarity, Figure 9.3 presents in a diagrammatic fashion the schemes that a child could coordinate when 2, 3 or 5 units of M capacity are available, and the conceptual systems of pictorial space that can

182 *Sergio Morra*

(a)

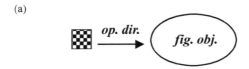

(b)

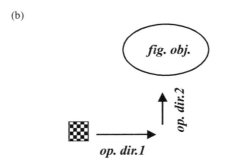

(c)

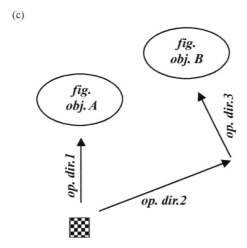

Figure 9.3 Hypothesized process of acquisition of increasingly complex systems of spatial representation.

consequently be abstracted from them. The acquisitions that, according to my hypothesis, are possible with an available M capacity of 4 or 6 units are less dramatic, and will only be presented in the text as corollaries of the conceptual acquisitions that take place with an M capacity of 3 or 5 units, respectively.

Figure 9.3a illustrates a hypothetical mental process carried out by a child with a capacity of 2 units. Suppose that the child has already drawn (or decided to draw; Morra *et al.*, 1988) a certain item, indicated in the figure by a small checkerboard. At that point the child could decide to draw another item beside it; in the figure, the oval 'fig. obj.' indicates the graphic figurative scheme that the child uses to represent that item, and the arrow labelled 'op. dir.' indicates the operative scheme by which the child decides that the item 'obj.' is going to be placed in a certain position – for instance, to the right of the one already present. Thus, by simultaneously activating two schemes – the graphic figurative scheme 'obj.' and the spatial operative scheme 'dir.' – a child can plan the drawing of a certain item in a certain spatial relation with another one.

The process may well be recursive: for instance, after having drawn two items, the child could plan to draw a third one, again to the right of the second; and once again, this step will require activating two schemes, one for the new item to be drawn and one for its position. A few experiences of this sort of mental planning should be sufficient for the child to acquire a new rule for aligning objects according to a single horizontal axis. This experience of mental planning, however, would be unavailable to younger children, with a capacity of a single unit. This could explain the transition from early compositional strategies (such as those described by Golomb, 1987, p. 44, as 'clusters of indeterminate orientation') to compositions based on alignment. Also the spatial organization of 6-year-olds' drawings, described by Dennis (1987, 1992) and by Case *et al.* (1996), could be explained in this way.[2]

Figure 9.3a presents (as an example) the child's decision to draw, as frequently observed, a new item to the right of another one. However, occasionally a child could also decide to depict an item, such as the sun or an airplane, above other ones already placed in the drawing. This could lead the child to discover also the vertical dimension of the drawing sheet as a criterion for composition. The 'air gap phenomenon' (Hargreaves *et al.*, 1981) would arise in this way. Nevertheless, at this point, the horizontal and vertical dimensions would still remain uncoordinated in the spatial organization of a drawing, because the child would not yet have the working memory capacity required to coordinate them.

This further progress would be possible, as illustrated in Figure 9.3b, when the child has reached an M capacity of 3 units. After having drawn or planned the item indicated by a checkerboard (and perhaps having also drawn other items aligned with it), the child could decide to draw also the item indicated as 'fig. obj.', a figurative scheme kept activated by means of M capacity; the other two available units can be used to activate operative schemes, represented by the arrows 'op. dir.1' and 'op. dir.2'. These indicate that the item 'obj.' is going to be placed in a certain position relative to the reference item (the one indicated by a checkerboard) that takes into account both dimensions of the sheet of paper. More generally, two dimensions can be differentiated and used to place, at least in a coarse way, the next item that the child intends to draw. Thus, by simultaneously activating three schemes – the graphic figurative scheme 'obj.' and the spatial operative schemes 'dir.1' and 'dir.2' – a child can organize a drawing with a foreground and a background, each of which could in turn be arranged as an alignment.

Further growth of M capacity to 4 units could enable the child to render such planning more fine-grained, by using a fourth scheme as a sort of scaling unit or measure that regulates placement of items at different distances. Thus, the distinction between foreground, middle-ground and background could emerge, as well as full integration of the two dimensions of the sheet to represent bidimensional space (e.g. in a map). Alternatively, the child could mentally activate a fourth scheme that represents a semantic or pragmatic relation between two or more items in the drawing, and use that non-spatial information to plan spatial placement of an item in a way that conveys such information. For instance a child could represent a football game with one of the players performing a certain action, and thus arrange the placement on paper of that player (and possibly of other ones) in such a fine way that conveys the idea of the action being performed. All these developments can give to observers the impression of better-integrated drawings.

Up to this point, however, the child could not discover how to solve a potential problem. The vertical dimension of the sheet of paper has an ambiguous meaning, inasmuch it can be used to represent both the relation 'behind' and the relation 'above'. That ambiguity is often not a problem, because a tree depicted at a higher point than another tree will suggest to the observer that one tree is farther than the other, while a bird with open wings depicted higher than a tree will suggest that the bird is flying above the tree. However, on some occasions the intentions of depicting A above X and B behind X may conflict. To solve satisfactorily this conflict, the child needs mentally to represent three spatial axes and coordinate them in the drawing. Understanding how to coordinate three spatial axes on a bidimensional sheet of paper requires 5 units of M capacity, as suggested in Figure 9.3c. The reason is that having to plan the placement of a single object elicits no conflict, and therefore generates no solution to it. To have a conflict, two figurative schemes 'fig. obj.A' and 'fig. obj.B' are required. To solve it, three additional operative schemes that represent three spatial axes are needed. This makes five schemes in all – the typical M capacity of an 11- or 12-year-old. At this point, understanding of oblique projection can emerge.[3]

A further progress, not represented graphically in Figure 9.3, is possible when a child reaches the M capacity of 6 units. In addition to the five schemes represented in Figure 9.3c, the child could also activate another operative scheme, for scaling figure size according to the distance of each item. This would enable the child to use drawing systems that are more advanced than oblique projection and can be regarded as rough approximations to perspective – those systems sometimes called naive or false perspective in the literature.

Task demands and working memory load: some possible misunderstandings

In the previous section, I have suggested how the development of M capacity could explain children's acquisition of increasingly complex drawing systems and systems of spatial axes to organize their drawings. This does not entail that M capacity is the *only* factor involved in drawing development (e.g. see Morra, 1995, 2002, 2005). Neither does it entail that spatial concepts (such as drawing systems or spatial axes) are the *only* determinants of the spatial organization of a drawing. On the contrary, neo-Piagetian researchers have always emphasized that psychological modelling requires a careful task analysis, in which the specific demands and constraints of a task are considered, and their interaction with the child's goals, representations and resources is elucidated (see Morra, Gobbo, Marini and Sheese, 2008, for a comprehensive review).

It is important to remind the reader of this broader theoretical framework, to prevent misunderstandings arising from an oversimplified view of what neo-Piagetian theories actually are about. An example of such possible misunderstandings can be found in a paper by Gallo, Golomb and Barroso (2003), who present an experiment with a quite interesting task manipulation – designed, unfortunately, to test a rather caricature-like interpretation of neo-Piagetian theories.

Gallo *et al.* (2003) asked a group of children, aged 5 to 9, to represent various themes in three ways: drawing with a felt-tip marker, arranging pre-cut figures on a board or placing small toys on a Plexiglas board. Because neo-Piagetian theories place great importance on development of spatial concepts and working memory capacity, Gallo *et al.* (2003) assume that (according to neo-Piagetian theories) the same spatial concepts are required by all tasks, and that only the drawing task places a greater load on working memory, because of the additional requirement of creating the forms. Hence, these authors assume that neo-Piagetian theories predict that 'two- and three-dimensional tasks with ready made items should yield similar results and ought to fare better than drawings' (p. 9). In addition, for not fully explicit reasons, they seem to assume that according to Case's theory 9-year-olds should perform as well in the drawing task as in the other two tasks. However, these assumptions about what the neo-Piagetian theories should predict seem to be in part arbitrary, or perhaps based on those possible misunderstandings that I have mentioned above. Actually, the tasks used in their study vary in three different respects:

(a) As Gallo *et al.* recognize, the drawing task places a greater load on working memory than the other two tasks, because the child must think not only of where to place the figures, but also how to draw them. This should make the drawing task harder.

(b) As these authors informally note, the two tasks with ready-made items allow the child to revise and modify her placement of the materials, while such revision is not possible with a marker drawing. Thus, with ready-made items (but not in the drawing task) it is possible for a child to achieve an advanced level of spatial composition without beforehand planning. This distinction is similar to that between the global restructuring of a figure in movement, which requires advance planning, and modifying single parts, which can be done with on-the-spot decisions (Morra, 2005). Thus, ready-made items could enable children to perform well also without taxing too much their working memory for spatial planning; this is another reason, disregarded by Gallo *et al.*, why a neo-Piagetian predicts that the drawing task should be harder than the other ones.

(c) In contrast with Gallo *et al.*'s misinterpretation of neo-Piagetian theories, the three-dimensional task places a smaller load on working memory and is predictably easier than the two-dimensional ones. In two-dimensional tasks children face the problem of representing the world's three dimensions on the two dimensions of paper or the board; thus, they must use bidimensional concepts of space that, as we have seen, evolve in complexity with the growth of working memory or M capacity. In the three-dimensional task, instead, one of the three dimensions of the world is already embodied in the materials, because all the small toys available to participants can stand upright and each has a specific height, so the child only has to place them on a two-dimensional board that represents a two-dimensional ground. Therefore, in the latter task the workload is considerably reduced.

Gallo *et al.* (2003) find that children's compositions are more advanced in the three-dimensional task than in the two-dimensional figure placement task, which in turn proves easier than drawing. This pattern of significant differences between tasks replicates in all age-groups. These authors conclude that their findings are incompatible with (their interpretation of) neo-Piagetian theories. However, as we have seen, the three-dimensional task places a smaller working memory load than the two-dimensional tasks (point (c)) and, between these, the drawing task places a greater load than the figure placement task (points (a) and (b)). Thus, the results of their experiment are precisely as predicted by a neo-Piagetian approach to task analysis.[4]

Summary and prospects

This chapter has focused on theoretical and empirical analysis of development of spatial aspects of children's drawing and its relationship to development of working memory or M capacity. All other aspects of children's drawing and all other sources of developmental progress have been disregarded here, because they are beyond the scope of the chapter. Nevertheless, a fairly wide range of tasks and empirical results has been covered, which support the main point made here, even though (as stated at the beginning of the chapter) many interacting factors affect the child's spatial organization of a drawing.

One can consider, at this point, the hypothesis that growth of M capacity brings about waves of new achievements in drawing. This is not to restate in a new form the old idea (e.g. Luquet, 1927) of drawing stages, defined by different levels of competence. Rather, the suggestion made here is that each increase of 1 unit in M capacity may enable the child to discover or learn a cluster of skills, concepts and solutions to drawing problems. One cannot assume, in a deterministic way, that a child will learn all the abilities that presuppose a given amount of M capacity. In addition, drawing also depends on individual differences in artistic giftedness (Porath and Arlin, 1997), tendency to rely on figurative schemes and visualization (Milbrath, 1998), and field dependence–independence (Morra, 2002). Having acknowledged that several factors limit the amount of variance in drawing skill that can be explained by M capacity growth, it seems appropriate to summarize here the various achievements that such growth makes possible.

Until a child has a capacity of only 1 unit, simple figurative schemes can be invented or learned to symbolize various items, but their flexibility is minimal and the overall spatial organization of the drawing is either quite random or based on field factors (the F-operator).

When a child has a capacity of 2 units, however, alignment emerges as a powerful principle of spatial organization of drawings, and on the vertical dimension of the paper the air gap phenomenon can appear. New graphic schemes can be constructed more easily, owing to the possibility of a deliberate, planned combination of shapes in a new graphic form. This also enables the child to show some flexibility of graphic schemes, that is, an ability to modify at least some part of a scheme in order to convey a given meaning (e.g. movement), and also more global restructuring in case perceptual input from an appropriate model suggests in a clear and simple way how that restructuring can be conceived. Partial occlusion drawing, in such misleading conditions as two similar shapes occluding one another, should be rare but occasionally possible, especially for field-independent children; transparency drawings could also be found, as a consequence of faulty implementation of a strategy that would require one more unit of capacity. In the water level task, horizontal lines could be drawn on sideways and capsized bottles, but not on tilted ones.

A capacity of 3 units enables the child to achieve what Case called a biaxial conceptual structure. Foreground and background can be differentiated in a scene, and (if the particular layout of objects to be represented does not add further difficulty to the task) a vertical-oblique drawing system can be used where appropriate. Flexibility of graphic schemes can extend to overall restructuring, even though drawing remains schematic. Partial occlusion becomes more common and transparency drawings disappear, because the 'hidden line elimination' strategy is now possible (unless the specific task also requires depiction of other spatial relations,[5] which subtract resources from planning the drawing of the partially occluded object). With a capacity of 4 units, mastery of orthogonal axes becomes more fine-grained (Case's integrated biaxial structure); thus, also a middleground can appear between the foreground and the background. In general, depiction of bidimensional arrays becomes more accurate. In the water level task one can find horizontal lines also on tilted items, even though this response is not yet dominant.

A capacity of 5 units enables new major achievements. A system of oblique axes can be learned or discovered for representing the three dimensions of space on the two-dimensional sheet of paper. Thus, oblique projection becomes available. The mapping of three-dimensional space on paper also supersedes the air gap phenomenon (unless children are motivated to complete a drawing quickly). In the water level task horizontal lines become more common (although field dependence and unavailability of domain-specific knowledge still cause errors – but also in case of errors, the deviation from horizontal is not so extreme as in younger children).

Finally, at an average age of about 13 or 14, a capacity of 6 units would open the way to the child's discovery of approximate forms of perspective.

The synthesis proposed in this chapter ties together ideas, theoretical models and experimental results from studies carried out in different labs. I have considered not only studies carried out within neo-Piagetian theoretical frameworks, but also research on aspects of spatial development in drawing that can be related closely to the work of neo-Piagetians. Actually, one weak point of neo-Piagetian research on drawing is that, although most studies yielded convincing results, they were often single-paradigm studies (with the exception of Case *et al.*, 1996), which makes it difficult to grasp how different drawing phenomena are related to one another, and thus capture the 'broad picture' of drawing development. Another potential problem for neo-Piagetian research on drawing is that some studies took Pascual-Leone's theory and some others Case's theory as their general frameworks; the two theories are not mutually contradictory, but emphasize different aspects. This can render less easy the task of a theoretical synthesis of those studies. In this chapter, I have used ideas from both theoretical frameworks, and I have also highlighted the connections with the experimental paradigms used by researchers such as Willats, Bremner, Lange-Küttner and Dennis, in addition to reporting on those used in our lab.

A next step could be trying to relate these drawing tasks, and perhaps other ones as well, in a single research project. If the analyses outlined in this chapter are to some extent accurate in modelling the development of strategies and conceptual structures that underlie children's development in various drawing tasks, then one should find clear relationships among those tasks. Such relationships should be manifest not only as correlations in the appropriate age ranges, but also in the specified relationships of each task with working memory or M capacity measures, in the same sample of participants.

NOTES

1. The drawings presented in Figure 9.2 were actually collected for the Morra (2005) study and both of their authors have an M capacity of 3 units, as measured with the test battery used in that piece of research.
2. I emphasize here that this analysis does not entail that M capacity growth is the *only* factor that affects development of spatial organization in drawings. In previous sections it has already been noted that various factors are involved in drawing flexibility, in partial occlusion drawings and in other tasks. What I am suggesting is that a certain capacity is involved as a *precondition* for new acquisitions in spatial organization.

3. There is no doubt that children can learn how to draw in oblique projection a simple object (a cube, a table) also at an earlier age. However, that learning does not generalize to other shapes (Phillips et al., 1985) and, more important, it is unlikely to help the child to organize the spatial arrangement of items in a complex scene.
4. Actually, our task analysis also entails more specific predictions about Gallo et al.'s tasks. For instance, point (a) entails that at the very least, even in the case that a child plans one item at a time in the drawing task and does not make revisions in the two-dimensional figure placement task, the drawing task requires one more unit of M capacity. Also, some of the scoring categories used by Gallo et al. (2003) afford specific predictions about the capacity required for these solutions. In the drawing task, the pattern they call 'advanced alignment', and all the ones more advanced than this, could not be achieved by children with less than 2 units of M capacity. Their 'thematic unity I' probably requires 3 units, if I interpret properly their mention of interactions or interpositions of items; and 'thematic unity II' definitely requires 4 units, because it involves 'a differentiated space that includes a fore-, middle-, and background' (p. 13). In the figure placement task, each of these amounts should be reduced by one unit (or even more, if children are free to revise their placement of items). These predictions cannot be tested on Gallo et al.'s data because unfortunately these authors have not measured the participants' working memory or M capacity, even though they are interested in evaluating neo-Piagetian theories. However, the more specific predictions offered here could be tested in future, follow-up research.
5. For instance, this seems to occur in Parisi and Marini's (1974) train-and-passengers task, where the train itself has a complex spatial structure that requires some amount of planning before drawing.

REFERENCES

Case, R. (1995). Capacity-based explanations of working memory growth: a brief history and re-evaluation. In F. E. Weinert and W. Schneider (eds.), *Memory performance and competencies: issues in growth and development* (pp. 23–44). Mahwah, NJ: Erlbaum.

Case, R., Stephenson, K. M., Bleiker, C. and Okamoto, Y. (1996). Central spatial structures and their development. In R. Case and Y. Okamoto (eds.), *The role of central conceptual structures in the development of children's thought* (pp. 103–30). Monographs of the Society for Research in Child Development 246. Chicago: University of Chicago Press.

Cowan, N., Saults, J. S. and Elliott, E. M. (2002). The search for what is fundamental in the development of working memory. In R. V. Kail and H. W. Reese (eds.), *Advances in child development and behaviour* (Vol. 29, pp. 1–49). Amsterdam: Elsevier.

Cox, M. V. (1985). One object behind another: young children's use of array-specific or view-specific representations. In N. H. Freeman and M. V. Cox (eds.), *Visual order: the nature and development of pictorial representation* (pp. 188–201). Cambridge: Cambridge University Press.

(1991). *The child's point of view: the development of cognition and language*. Second edition. London: Harvester Press.

(2005). *The pictorial world of the child*. Cambridge: Cambridge University Press.
De Bruyn, B. and Davis, A. (2005). Breakdown of parallel spatial coding in children's drawing. *Developmental Science*, 8, 226–8.
de Ribaupierre, A. and Bailleux, C. (1994). Developmental change in a spatial task of attentional capacity: an essay toward an integration of two working memory models. *International Journal of Behavioral Development*, 17, 5–35.
Dennis, S. (1987). The development of childen's drawing: a neo-structuralist approach. Unpublished PhD dissertation, University of Toronto.
  (1992). Stage and structure in the development of children's spatial representations. In R. Case (ed.), *The mind's staircase* (pp. 229–45). Hillsdale, NJ: Erlbaum.
Foley, E. J. and Berch, D. B. (1997). Capacity limitations of a classic M-power measure: a modified dual-task approach. *Journal of Experimental Child Psychology*, 66, 129–43.
Freeman, N. H. (1972). Process and product in children's drawing. *Perception*, 1, 123–40.
  (1980). *Strategies of representation in young children*. London: Academic Press.
  (1995). The emergence of a framework theory of pictorial reasoning. In C. Lange-Küttner and G. V. Thomas (eds.), *Drawing and looking: theoretical approaches to pictorial representation in children* (pp. 135–46). London: Pearson/Prentice Hall (distributed by www.amazon.co.uk).
Freeman, N. H., Eiser, C. and Sayers, J. (1977). Children's strategies in producing three-dimensional relationships on a two-dimensional surface. *Journal of Experimental Child Psychology*, 23, 305–14.
Gallo, F., Golomb, C. and Barroso, A. (2003). Compositional strategies in drawing: the effects of two- and three-dimensional media. *Visual Arts Research*, 29, 2–23.
Golomb, C. (1987). The development of compositional strategies in children's drawings. *Visual Arts Research*, 13, 42–52.
  (1992). *The child's creation of a pictorial world*. Berkeley: University of California Press.
Goodnow, J. (1977). *Children drawing*. Cambridge, MA: Harvard University Press.
  (1978). Visible thinking: cognitive aspects of change in drawings. *Child Development*, 49, 637–41.
Hargreaves, D. J., Jones, P. M. and Martin, D. (1981). The air gap phenomenon in children's landscape drawings. *Journal of Experimental Child Psychology*, 32, 11–20.
Hildebrand, D. K., Laing, J. D. and Rosenthal, H. (1977). *Prediction analysis of cross classifications*. New York: Wiley.
Ibbotson, A. and Bryant, P. E. (1978). The perpendicular error and the vertical effect. *Perception*, 5, 319–26.
Kanizsa, G. (1979). *Organization in vision: essays on Gestalt perception*. New York: Praeger.
Lange-Küttner, C. (1997). Development of size modification of human figure drawings in spatial axes systems of varying complexity. *Journal of Experimental Child Psychology*, 66, 264–78.

(2004). More evidence on size modification in spatial axes systems of varying complexity. *Journal of Experimental Child Psychology*, 88, 171–92.

(2005). The logic of spatial axes systems. Paper presented at the 12th European Conference on Developmental Psychology. Tenerife, 24–28 August.

Lee, M. and Bremner, J. G. (1987). The representation of depth in children's drawings of a table. *Quarterly Journal of Experimental Psychology*, 39A, 479–96.

Luquet, G. H. (1927). *Le dessin enfantin [Children's drawing]*. Paris: Alcan.

Milbrath, C. (1998). *Patterns of artistic development in children*. Cambridge: Cambridge University Press.

Morra, S. (1994). Issues in working memory measurement: testing for M capacity. *International Journal of Behavioral Development*, 17, 143–59.

(1995). A neo-Piagetian approach to children's drawings. In C. Lange-Küttner and G. V. Thomas (eds.), *Drawing and looking: theoretical approaches to pictorial representation in children* (pp. 93–106). London: Pearson/Prentice Hall (distributed by www.amazon.co.uk).

(2000). A new model of verbal short-term memory. *Journal of Experimental Child Psychology*, 75, 191–227.

(2002). On the relationship between partial occlusion drawing, M capacity, and field independence. *British Journal of Developmental Psychology*, 20, 421–38.

(2005). Cognitive aspects of change in drawings: a neo-Piagetian theoretical account. *British Journal of Developmental Psychology*, 23, 317–41.

(2008). Memory components and control processes in children's drawing. In C. Milbrath and H. M. Trautner (eds.), *Children's understanding and production of pictures, drawing, and art: theoretical and empirical approaches* (pp. 53–85). Göttingen: Hogrefe.

(in press). A test of a neo-Piagetian model of the Water Level Task. *European Journal of Developmental Psychology*.

Morra, S., Angi, A. and Tomat, L. (1996). Planning, encoding, and overcoming conflict in partial occlusion drawing: a neo-Piagetian model and an experimental analysis. *Journal of Experimental Child Psychology*, 61, 276–301.

Morra, S., Caloni, B. and d'Amico, M. R. (1994). Working memory and the intentional depiction of emotions. *Archives de Psychologie*, 62, 71–87.

Morra, S., Gobbo, C., Marini, Z. and Sheese, R. (2008). *Cognitive development: a neo-Piagetian perspective*. New York: Erlbaum.

Morra, S., Moizo, C. and Scopesi, A. (1988). Working memory (or the M operator) and the planning of children's drawings. *Journal of Experimental Child Psychology*, 46, 41–73.

Parisi, M. and Marini, F. (1974). Il fenomeno della trasparenza nello sviluppo del grafismo infantile [The transparency phenomenon in the development of graphic skills]. Research report, Contributi dell' Istituto di Psicologia. Cagliari (Italy): Università di Cagliari.

Pascual-Leone, J. (1970). A mathematical model for the transition rule in Piaget's developmental stages. *Acta Psychologica*, 63, 301–45.

(1989). An organismic process model of Witkin's field dependence–independence. In T. Globerson and T. Zelniker (eds.), *Cognitive style and cognitive development* (pp. 36–70). Norwood, NJ: Ablex.

(2000). Reflections on working memory: are the two models complementary? *Journal of Experimental Child Psychology*, 77, 138–54.
Pascual-Leone, J. and Baillargeon, R. (1994). Developmental measurement of mental attention. *International Journal of Behavioral Development*, 17, 161–200.
Pascual-Leone, J. and Goodman, D. (1979). Intelligence and experience: a neo-Piagetian approach. *Instructional Science*, 8, 301–67.
Pascual-Leone, J. and Johnson, J. (2004). Affect, self/motivation, and cognitive development: a dialectical constructivist view. In D. Y. Dai and R. J. Sternberg (eds.), *Motivation, emotion, and cognition: integrative perspectives on intellectual functioning and development* (pp. 197–235). Mahwah, NJ: Erlbaum.
  (2005). A dialectical constructivist view of developmental intelligence. In O. Wilhelm and R. Engle (eds.), *Handbook of understanding and measuring intelligence* (pp. 177–201). Thousand Oaks, CA: Sage.
Pascual-Leone, J., Johnson, J., Baskind, S., Dworsky, S. and Severtson, E. (2000). Culture-fair assessment and the processes of mental attention. In A. Kozulin and Y. Rand (eds.), *Experience of mediated learning* (pp. 191–214). New York: Pergamon Press.
Pascual-Leone, J. and Morra, S. (1991). Horizontality of water level: a neo-Piagetian developmental review. In H. W. Reese (ed.), *Advances in child development and behaviour* (Vol. 23, pp. 231–76). San Diego, CA: Academic Press.
Phillips, W. A., Inall, M. and Lauder, E. (1985). On the discovery, storage, and use of graphic descriptions. In N. H. Freeman and M. V. Cox (eds.), *Visual order: the nature of development and representation* (pp. 122–34). Cambridge: Cambridge University Press.
Piaget, J. and Inhelder, B. (1947/1967). *La représentation de l'espace chez l'enfant*. Paris: Presses Universitaires de France (trans. as *The child's conception of space*. London: Routledge and Kegan Paul).
Picard, D. and Vinter, A. (1999). Representational flexibility in children's drawings: effects of age and verbal instructions. *British Journal of Developmental Psychology*, 17, 605–22.
Porath, M. and Arlin, P. K. (1997). Developmental approaches to artistic giftedness. *Creativity Research Journal*, 10, 241–50.
Russo Pizzo, L. (1974). La trasparenza nel disegno infantile [Transparency in children's drawing]. *Il Pisani: Giornale di Patologia Nervosa e Mentale*, 98, 179–226.
Spensley, F. and Taylor, J. (1999). The development of cognitive flexibility: evidence from children's drawings. *Human Development*, 42, 300–24.
Van Sommers, P. (1984). *Drawing and cognition: descriptive and experimental studies of graphic production processes*. Cambridge: Cambridge University Press.
Vasta, R. and Liben, L. S. (1996). The water-level task: an intriguing puzzle. *Current Directions in Psychological Science*, 5, 171–7.
Willats, J. (1977). How children learn to draw realistic pictures. *Quarterly Journal of Experimental Psychology*, 29, 367–82.
  (1985). Drawing systems revisited: the role of denotation systems in children's figure drawing. In N. H. Freeman and M. V. Cox (eds.), *Visual order: the*

nature of development and representation (pp. 78–100). Cambridge: Cambridge University Press.
  (1987). Marr and pictures: an information-processing account of children's drawings. *Archives de Psychologie*, 55, 105–25.
  (1995). An information-processing approach to drawing development. In C. Lange-Küttner and G. V. Thomas (eds.), *Drawing and looking: theoretical approaches to pictorial representation in children* (pp. 27–43). London: Pearson/Prentice Hall (distributed by www.amazon.co.uk).
Zhi, Z., Thomas, G. V. and Robinson, E. J. (1997). Constraints on representational change: drawing a man with two heads. *British Journal of Developmental Psychology*, 15, 275–90.

10 Figures in and out of context: absent, simple, complex and halved spatial fields

Chris Lange-Küttner

As in Lewin's theory of the interaction between field forces and figures in real life, Lange-Küttner explains that similar interactions occur between figures and spatial fields in pictorial space. Young children initially draw just figures in empty space with only implicit spatial relations, but gradually the spatial context becomes explicit and elaborated in an increasingly complex fashion. She thus assumes an initial object-based figure representation, which later changes into a space-based figure representation. This is illustrated by a comparison between figure drawings of young children and visual neglect patients. Lange-Küttner demonstrates empirically that figure size in children's drawings is increasingly determined by powerful pictorial rules rather than by environmental experiential factors. Her experimental studies show an emerging, systematic contingency between figure size and complexity of the spatial field, with sensitivity to spatial constraints as transitional mechanism between object-based and space-based figure representation. From an evolutionary perspective, axes systems are geometrically not more complex than spiderwebs, but while spiders continued to devour the objects caught in the net, the specifically human achievement appears to be the object permanence and apparent animation of the figures in the axes systems.

THE SPATIAL field was one of the central concepts of Lewin (1951, 1963/1982), where superior forces were impacting on figures, which could evade them by leaving the field, find ways around boundaries and barriers in order to reach a goal, or cope with field forces by overcoming pressure and frustration. Lewin's spatial model was describing social interactions taking place in a spatial field where the forces, which would demand or hamper reaching a goal in a direct and straightforward way, could be conceptualized; in this chapter it is reported how these interactions between figures and the spatial field occur systematically in pictorial space, and how in infancy and drawing these spatial fields are constructed rather than exist a priori.

Drawing is the main activity of young children to express a lasting view of objects until they can write. Young children initially depict objects floating in empty space. When large figures are drawn first, they may take up a lot of space and leave little for other figures, as an explicit spatial context which would facilitate a more planned figure placement is completely absent. However, when the spatial context of objects becomes explicit, it is structured with simple horizontal axes to denote the ground and sometimes the sky, while later entire spatial fields are constructed using more complex axes systems. As these spatial systems develop in dimensionality, they gain in impact on figure size. Hence, it is explained in this chapter how early object-driven size regulation is overtaken by axes-driven size modification in pictorial space, a development which may also have implications for our understanding of object- and space-based attention.

There is also a clinical population where drawing is often used to investigate the way in which spatial fields are constructed, i.e. stroke patients. Stroke patients have suffered a brain lesion due to blood vessels leaking into brain tissue. When this leakage occurs in a particular area responsible for visual attention, stroke patients may develop a transient or permanent syndrome called unilateral neglect of the left half of the spatial field (Bisiach and Vallar, 1988). Hence, in this chapter it is also reported how figures are constructed when visual field attention is incomplete, and how the drawing system of vulnerable stroke patients differs from that of children.

Spatial fields are constructed in actions

Adults often take for granted the left–right distinction which segments the space conveniently into two halves. However, at the very beginning of life, there does not seem to be an even spatial field for infants. When 4-month-old infants begin to 'hunt' for an object, they stiffly move both arms excitedly and simultaneously in the left and right peripheral spatial fields like rotating propellers when an object passes by in front of them, a movement also described as waving or swiping (see also Bruner and Koslowski, 1972). Thus, in reaching there is initially a *visual field triage*, periphery–centre–periphery, while in tracking a *visual neglect* of the left side could be observed (Lange-Küttner and Crichton, 1999). A bias towards the right side is also common in many animal species (Rogers, 2000). However, with the onset of one-armed, goal-directed reaching at 17 weeks and the relaxation of infants' previously stiff muscle tonus and automatic reflex system (Thelen, Corbetta, Kamm, Spencer, Schneider and Zernicke, 1993), infants of 19 weeks detected the midline of the spatial field (see also Sherick, Greenman and Legg, 1976) as well as the end points of objects' pathways. The emerging action system had changed the periphery–centre–periphery into a left–right segmentation. Furthermore, the neglect of the left side in visual tracking disappeared with the onset of reaches into the neglected field in the same way as in stroke patients, who in rehabilitation are trained to reach to the neglected left side for lasting remediation (e.g. Robertson, Nico and Hood, 1997). However, it seems that the right-side bias is only controlled, but not abolished, by more voluntary motor control, and can resurface in both children and adults under increased task demands in terms of speed (Efron and Yundt, 1996) and exhaustion (Manly, Dobler, Dodds and George, 2005).

Objects and displays

In stroke patients, the effects of the unilateral neglect are pervasive. The origins of spatial field segmentation reappear not only in the behavioural domain, e.g. when eating food only from the right side of the plate, but also in drawing, reading and writing, and in verbal descriptions of spatial arrays. The enigma of spatial neglect is that it can occur (1) in relation to objects, i.e. in an *object-centred* way when only the right-hand side of an object such as a house is drawn, or (2) in relation to a spatial field, i.e. in a *space-centred* way when only the right half of a visual field such as a market square is drawn. Thus, much discussion has focused on the question whether attention in spatial neglect is object-based or space-based, i.e. consisting of an object-recognition system and a spatial attentional system (Humphreys and Riddoch, 1993). However, an interesting third alternative is the notion that it is *display-based* (Kinsbourne, 1993). Some visual perception researchers assume an inner display on the retina, to where an inner picture is projected by an immediate, sensory memory, which integrates glances into one coherent scene, while others believe that visual attention is selective and object-based (Pylyshyn, 2003). For instance, Pylyshyn stated that 'if *anything* could count as a possible focus of attention, then the idea of attention would be devoid of explanatory value' (Pylyshyn, 2003, p. 159, italics as in the original).

However, the term display-based attention could also point to a certain artificiality of reality, as if the real world would be on display like on a monitor, showing a visually realistic image or film of the world. This image need not be on the retina; in fact there are many specialized visual brain areas which process the retinal image further, e.g. the parietal area is specialized on object movement perception (where), and the temporal area is specialized on static properties of objects such as shape and colour (what) (e.g. Mecklinger and Meinshausen, 1998; Ungerleider and Mishkin, 1982). In fact, before the invention of the camera, which mimics the light sensitivity of our eyes, a transparent display not only helped painters and draughtsman in the fifteenth century to depict in view-specific perspective, it also draws children's attention towards the actual edges and boundaries in a visual display (Lange-Küttner and Reith, 1995; Reith and Dominin, 1997). The draughtsman's display had a grid, where he could trace the contours of *whatever* fell into the squares of the grid, and then copy the content of each grid onto paper. *The spatial axes of this grid would divert attention away from objects and cut across figures.* In fact, it did not matter at all whether a contour of an object or a boundary of a spatial region had to be copied; the entire display was metrically segmented and then reproduced with the mechanical precision and accuracy of an undistorted mirror image. There has been some unease about perspective as being too unemotional and cruel (Mayer-Hillebrand, 1947), and ambivalence about a 'triumphant pursuit of power' (Panofsky, 1927/1991). Indeed, while young children until about age 7 produce better drawings when they copy a meaningful object, in older children and adults meaning was counterproductive, as abstract, geometric and meaningless models supported the depiction of a faithful, literal and accurate likeness (Mitchell, Ropar, Ackroyd and Rajendran, 2005; Sheppard, Ropar and Mitchell, 2005; see also Sheppard, Mitchell and Ropar as well as Tallandini in this volume). Figures lose meaning as they dissolve into spatial context, so much so that computer vision needs sophisticated edge-detection algorithms to find them again (Willats, 1997).

The figure and half-a-figure

However, young children still only draw complete objects in empty space. Many explanations have been offered why children initially draw only complete, non-overlapping objects without spatial context. Objects should be 'independent, small and undivided' (Tada and Stiles, 1996), distinct for identification of function (Davis, 1985) or easier counting (Towse and Hitch, 1996), or children would draw each object in its own place rather than a shared region (Goodnow, 1977; Lange-Küttner, 2006). Children would show 'shape constancy' (Deręgowski and Dziurawiec, 1996), or 'figurative, gestalt-like pseudo-conservation' (Piaget, 1969). Also in cognitive psychology, it is presumed that object parsing is an obligatory, basic process, where edges are assigned to regions in the retinal visual input, resulting in object shape descriptions (e.g. Baylis, 1998; Baylis and Driver, 1995; Logan, 1996; Treisman, 2006).

In order to investigate the contingency between object representation and segmentation, photos of full-size persons were used as a model, to draw half a person, to indicate cuts/segmentations, and as a puzzle to reconstruct the person and detect a violation (Lange-Küttner, 2000). Human figures are the earliest objects to be drawn by children (Cox, 1993). We also know since a long time that the amount of small detail is highly correlated with intelligence until adolescence (Goodenough, 1926; Goodenough and Harris, 1950). Half of the 5-year-olds and still one third of the 6-year-olds were drawing a *complete* figure, and about 20 per cent in these age-groups were only omitting a single body part, instead of drawing half a person; see also Figure 10.1.

In the perceptual task, small figure violations were detected only by a minority of 5- to 6-year-olds, but by the majority of 11-year-olds and most adults. Thus, interestingly, there was not the usual gap between perception and construction; object violations were difficult to detect and difficult to draw. Violations may have been particularly difficult as they required attention to what was *not* there. The distinction between intellectual and visual realism when defined as draw-what-you-know versus draw-what-you-see does not help to explain why violations go unnoticed and the spatial context is absent or at best implicit in young children (Light and Humphreys, 1981; Light and MacIntosh, 1980). When asked to indicate with a stick how the figure could be best cut into pieces (Lange-Küttner, 2000), children were indicating significantly more cuts than adults, but this was completely unrelated to the drawing or detection of object violation.

There is another enigma in drawing half a figure. Stroke patients with visual neglect can *only* draw half a human figure, but not a complete figure (Halligan and Marshall, 1998; see Figure 10.2), i.e. the problem is just reversed in comparison to children. Why would this be the case?

Stroke patients with visual neglect have the left side of their bodies paralysed, and thus one could assume that this half figure is just an illustration of how they feel about their body. However, as stroke patients also draw only the right side of other objects as well as of visual fields, the explanation of absent body sensations would not apply. The half figure of the adult stroke patient in Figure 10.2 shows that objects are conceptualized in an *axis-based* fashion (Driver, Baylis, Goodrich and Rafal, 1994; see also Deręgowski on body axis drawings in this volume), different from young children. Some assume that there are changes in the content of consciousness (Edelman, 2006) in stroke patients. But one would rather say that drawings by stroke patients with unilateral neglect show the same view-specific simulation of the optical impression as in the visual realism of older children, drawing *half of whatever* happens to fall into their halved field of visual attention.

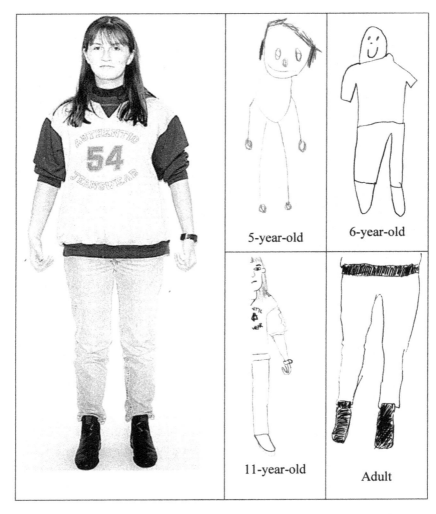

Figure 10.1 Drawing of half-a-figure, adapted from Lange-Küttner, 2000.

The figure in spatial context

So what happens to the human figure once spatial context becomes explicit in children's drawings? Geometrical objects become three-dimensional and can be depicted as overlapping, but for the human figure the more important change is from an aggregate of circles with extensions towards a smooth, view-specific figure silhouette which has become so

Figures in and out of context 201

Figure 10.2 Drawing of half-a-figure carried out by a stroke patient. Reprinted from Halligan and Marshall, 1998, p. 360, with permission from Elsevier.

detailed and specific that it tends towards a perfect likeness of a real person (Lange-Küttner, Kerzmann and Heckhausen, 2002), most perfect in the art of portraits. However, there is also the opposite trend, where figures in viewpoint perspective lose in detail and become so small that they just melt into space and become similar to texture (Lange-Küttner, 2004).

To construct sophisticated, explicit spatial axes systems in pictorial space takes many years in children's development. Longitudinal research from age 7 until 12 showed that there does not seem to be much flexibility in this development, as there was progression and stagnation in drawing pictorial spatial systems, but rarely a regression to earlier levels, mainly in terms of sparseness and a reoccurrence of empty space

(Lange-Küttner, 1994). A comparison of children in psychiatric hospitals with age-matched normal controls showed the same basic knowledge in drawing spatial systems, but a conspicuous sparseness of work-related items (Lange-Küttner, 1989). Artists who were referred to the Maudsley Psychiatric Hospital in London in the nineteenth century as mature adults did not show regression in the level of their graphic expertise; instead they concentrated on topics unconventional for artists of their time, e.g. they systematically depicted the different emotional facial expressions (for a German case study see Behr, Grohmann and Hagedorn, 1983), which became a common research topic in psychology labs more than a hundred years later.

Thus, one would predict that the ability to scale a figure according to a spatial context would also only develop with age. An evolutionary explanation for the tardy development would be that children repeat history insofar as the majority of cave paintings also depicted animals in empty space (Anati, 2002). However, these were often life-sized and could provide a very close mapping with the real object (Graff, 2006). Life-size seems to be an important aspect of information processing in ancient species, e.g. elephants can recognize themselves in life-sized mirrors, but not in smaller ones (Aldhous, 2006; Plotnik, de Waal and Reiss, 2006), while 2-year-old human infants can also recognize partial images of themselves (Nielsen, Suddendorf and Slaughter, 2006; see also Bard, this volume). However, 2-year-old infants did not use size scaling when interacting with other objects, as they make serious attempts to perform impossible actions on miniature objects (DeLoache, Uttal and Rosengren, 2004). While at 3 years, children understood the size scales of objects in the real environment (e.g. DeLoache, 1989; DeLoache, Miller and Rosengren, 1997), this is not the case in the pictorial medium, as they only just begin to draw at this age. Hence figure size is still incidental and not well regulated: pictorial objects determine each other's size in competition for the limited pictorial space on a first-come-first-served basis, with the first shape being drawn *large* and the following ones smaller, as they have to fit into the space that is left (Freeman, 1980; Thomas, 1995). Young children would draw, for instance, a dog larger than the owner, and only in 5-year-olds had size regulation become more correct (Silk and Thomas, 1986, 1988). These studies showed that *object-driven* size regulation appears to rule in the years before the emergence of complex spatial systems such as perspective. Would size continue to be regulated in this way, or would new and explicit spatial systems become important for size modification? Like astronomers, we do not content ourselves with seeing objects in empty space, but conceptualize spatial systems (Lange-Küttner, 2008).

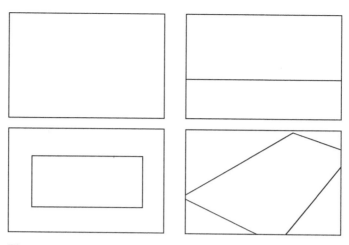

Figure 10.3 Four spatial systems (empty, horizontal, orthogonal, diagonal) were used to classify children's structuring of pictorial space, reprinted from Lange-Küttner, 2004, p. 181, with permission of Elsevier.

Object-driven and axes-driven size modification

In the first study on figure size depiction within different pictorial spatial systems, four different types of spatial systems were distinguished (Lange-Küttner, 1997; see examples of the spatial systems in Figure 10.3): (1) empty space, (2) a horizontal axis system where the lower edge of the sheet or a groundline could be used to line up figures, e.g. stripes for ground and sky, (3) an orthogonal axes system, where a large area such as a playing field was depicted, with axes at 90 degree angles, and (4) a diagonal axes system, i.e. where the vertical axes converge into viewpoint perspective.

A drawing task was given where children would draw a picture of themselves and friends at play near home or school. The sample was part of a larger, longitudinal study on social and cognitive development in Iceland, a society which underwent rapid economic change at the time (the cohort was born in 1969) (Edelstein, Keller and Schröder, 1990). Figure size was measured in centimetres and the space systems which children were constructing were rated by art historians. Children were drawing smaller, the more figures they had been drawing. This applied to small groups and crowds, but pairs of figures were not having an impact on size. Children were also drawing smaller, the more complex the spatial axes system was that they had created. And finally, children coming from agrarian communities with their large views on landscapes were drawing smaller than children from service and trade as well as from urban communities. As there were so many factors impacting on size, a multiple regression per age group was run to find the best predictor. At age 7, object-driven (number of figures) and axes-driven (space system) size reduction explained 11 per cent of the variance, but community and environment was the best predictor with 18 per cent of the variance. Although at age 9 all three factors were still significant, the weightings had changed substantially. Object-driven and axes-driven size reduction now explained 15 per cent of the variance, but community and environment was much reduced in its influence, explaining only 4 per cent of the variance. Finally, at age 12, object-driven and axes-driven size reduction explained 17 per cent of the variance and the environmental influence was reduced to nil. The shared variance between object- and axes-driven size modification was between 1 per cent and 3 per cent, thus both factors had a fairly independent influence on size. In short, individual differences due to the 'wildlife' environment were gradually phased out, and pictorial rules of size modification had become more powerful and universal amongst the children from the different communities. This certainly confirmed that the modality-specific control of pictorial space was a major factor, and that these domain-specific rules of pictorial space established themselves only gradually. Furthermore, the longitudinal design made it possible to prove that, independently of how large children were drawing at the beginning of school, size reduction followed thereafter.

This longitudinal study was replicated with a more recent cross-sectional sample (the cohort was born from 1988 on) with children from comparable communities in Scotland (Lange-Küttner, 2004). The replication was conducted because in the Icelandic study axes-driven size reduction was the best predictor at age 9, while the number of figures and thus object-driven size reduction was the best predictor for size reduction at age 12. This would not have been predicted by a model where the impact of axes systems on figure size becomes more powerful than implicit, empty space. However, in both the Icelandic and the Scottish study the overall amount of variance explained by object- and axes-driven size modification increased with age (Icelandic 11 per cent, 15 per cent, 17 per cent; Scottish 12 per cent, 9 per cent, 22 per cent) showing an increase in the use of domain-specific pictorial rules. In the more recent Scottish replication, individual differences due to community and environment did not play a role at any age, possibly because children started school very early at about $4\frac{1}{2}$ to 5 years and the school system was standardized according to a National Currriculum. At age 7, the only significant predictor for figure size was the number of figures (objects 7 per cent, systems 1 per cent). But at ages 9 and 12, axes-driven size reduction was the only significant predictor (age 9: objects 1 per cent, systems 8 per cent; age 12: objects 5 per cent, systems 17 per cent). Thus, in the Scottish replication, object-driven size modification lost in predictive power, and was superseded by axes-driven size modification. This result was more in accordance with a theory that would predict in a straightforward fashion that, according to domain-specific rules of pictorial space, the emerging spatial context would exert more influence than the individual objects in the visual scene along with increasing age.

Thereafter, the task was made more prescriptive with respect to both space system and number of figures, in order to control the results on object- and axes-driven size modification in an experimental design. As only about one-tenth of children and fewer than half of adults (Hagen, 1985; Lange-Küttner, 1994) demonstrate the ability to draw in viewpoint perspective, a booklet was created with pre-drawn spatial systems and the task to draw themselves and either one friend (pairs condition) or four friends (peers condition) playing a ball game. The design of this drawing series made it possible to test all participants' figure size in all space systems at all ages, regardless of what they would have happened to draw spontaneously (Lange-Küttner, 2004; see Figure 10.4). At age 7, the ready-made axes systems did lead to size reduction in a subtle and linear fashion along with increase of complexity in spatial systems. The spontaneously constructed spatial system on the first page with empty space was also controlled. Only in the peer condition, children who had constructed their own spatial system were drawing the smallest figures and were not reducing them any further in the drawing series. Children who had not been drawing an explicit spatial context were drawing the largest figures in empty space and decreased figure size the most thereafter during the drawing series. Thus, in 7-year-olds the presence or absence of self-invented spatial constraints appeared to be stronger than the experimental cues of the ready-made spatial systems, a remarkable impact of the own effort to spatially structure the page. In 9-year-olds size reduction was now more pronounced than in 7-year-olds, and both object-driven and axes-driven size reduction was significant. But at age 11, all factors apart from the ready-made axes systems were irrelevant. As in the Scottish replication, object-driven size reduction lost in power and axes-driven size reduction had become the only relevant factor for size modification.

Thus, there were several results to consider in their implications on a theory of the development of the pictorial space system. Schooling seems to have an influence insofar as direct perceptual impressions of the type of children's specific familiar surroundings on pictorial constructions were increasingly ruled out. The impact of the familiar 'wildlife'

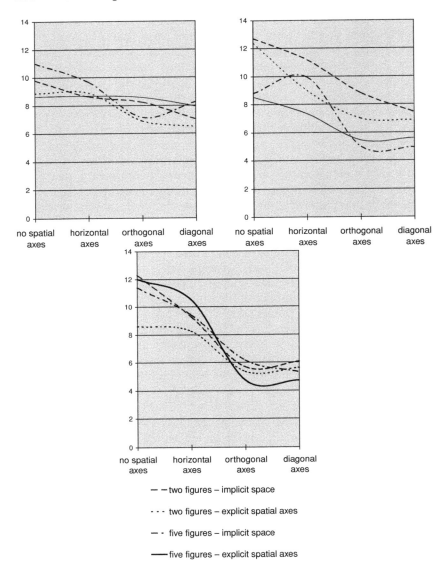

Figure 10.4 Size modification in the four spatial axes systems, adapted from Lange-Küttner, 2004, p. 185, with permission of Elsevier.

environment may have lasted longer in earlier times than nowadays. This result was very much in accordance with the European tradition of thinking, where conceptual, abstract knowledge is achieved by the purification of thought from all sensory input of the objects of thought themselves (Hegel, 1812/1975, p. 82; Kant, 1781/1980, p. 137). The studies also showed for the first time that there was a systematic contingency between object size and *all* levels of spatial axes systems, not just viewpoint perspective. The power of pictorial objects to determine size waned in middle childhood as an axial spatial system emerged which defines its extensions via a vector system, and where every point in space can be defined a priori, i.e. without objects (Lange-Küttner and Reith, 1995).

While the ready-made axes systems did reduce figure size in all age-groups, there was, however, a developmental difference in the amount of size modification. While 7-year-olds' size reduction was subtle and linear, especially 11-year-olds' size reduction was much more pronounced. Why would this be the case? Different to classification tasks where rigid ready-made objects with a constant 2D or 3D shape are used, in drawing tasks a sensorimotor factor plays an important role (Van Sommers, 1984; see also Vinter and Rosengren this volume) as entities are entirely constructed. It could be that with increasing maturity children would be able to draw smaller figures, just as they also learn to write smaller as reflected by the increasingly more narrowly lined paper used for writing. Thus, the 7-year-olds' size reduction during the drawing series may have been due just to sensorimotor practice and not to understanding of the different levels of complexity of space systems. An argument for this idea would be that a sensorimotor factor replaces age as a direct predictor for drawing from age 8 (Toomela, 2002), and because schoolchildren become more accurate in drawing both perfect geometrical forms (Lange-Küttner, 1998) and natural, irregular contours (Lange-Küttner *et al.*, 2002). However, no age differences occurred in perceptual-motor learning in a drawing task with 6- to 10-year-old children (Vinter and Perruchet, 2000; see also Vinter, Picard and Fernandez in this volume). Furthermore, it was of interest whether 7-year-olds' size reduction was dependent on the sequence which had simulated the developmental mastery of spatial systems, or whether this age-group would also reduce size when the sequence was random. One would expect that a true, powerful concept should survive the random noise in the presentation of the drawing series, while a weaker concept would be more dependent on external cues.

Habitual size and projective size

Thus it was tested whether in particular the size reduction of the 7-year-olds was dependent on the external visual cues, i.e. the logical sequence of the spatial systems gradually increasing in geometric complexity, or whether the size reduction was due to increased fine motor control during the task, as children were drawing more than twenty figures (Lange-Küttner, under revision). The task was given in three experimental conditions: (1) in a logical and (2) in a random sequence, and (3) in a practice condition where figures were only drawn in empty space. Results of the previous study were replicated. Already 7- and 9-year-olds reduced figure size along with increase of spatial system complexity, while 11-year-olds modified size much more dramatically. Importantly, the comparison with the other two conditions showed that 7- and 9-year-olds did reduce size in the logical sequence only. While this was proof that 7-year-olds could already understand all levels of space systems and adapt their figure drawings accordingly, these size modifications were not yet powerful enough to modify the embedded objects beyond the habitually drawn figure size, nor did the randomized sequence produce similar results to the logical sequence. In 9-year-olds, average size was continuously larger in the practice condition than in the random and logical sequence of axes systems, which were now constraining size consistently more than empty space. But 11-year-olds were drawing larger in the empty space and horizontal axes system, and comparably smaller in the complex axes systems, than in the practice condition. Furthermore, at age 11, size in the complex axes systems was nearly identical in the logical and the random sequence, showing that the space concept had become robust to incidental sequences. The important role of awareness of spatial constraints as a transitional mechanism at age 9 was still visible at age 11. Different from the logical sequence, in the random sequence complex axes systems could also occur in the beginning of the drawing series. The experience of the spatial constraints of complex axes systems at the beginning of the series appeared to have primed drawing of a smaller size also in spatial systems which would have otherwise allowed for drawing of a large figure size, such as empty space and groundline.

Thus, it appeared that 7-year-olds indeed understood all five different types of spatial context when logically ordered in acquisition sequence. That is, at this age children may *simultaneously* understand all space systems, different from a verbal protocol approach showing that this would develop in stages (Piaget and Inhelder, 1956; Piaget, Inhelder and Szeminska, 1960). No further conceptual development appears to be necessary, but then this early understanding of projective space had no impact on the habitually drawn figure size. In drawing research, Van Sommers (1984) called the influence of practice and habit on graphic constructions of children their 'conservatism', which has been an important research topic in recent years (e.g. Barlow, Jolley, White and Galbraith,

2003; Karmiloff-Smith, 1990, 1995; Zhang, Thomas and Robinson, 1997).

In drawing development many processes are different from cognitive reasoning processes; units of thought become more abstract and categorical; in pictorial space objects become more concrete and literally faithful to the optical impression. While, in general, speed increases in children's cognition (Kail, 1986), in drawing a sensorimotor factor becomes significant as a predictor for drawing performance for the first time (Toomela, 2002), and the fast and genius-like speed of young children slows down to make way for accuracy (Lange-Küttner, 1998). But as in logical thinking, where sufficient and necessary conditions *affect and limit* possible conclusions and all instances can be systematically exhausted (Piaget, 1981, 1983), also the pictorial space concept appears to have rules, which determine the embedded size of all instances within any one type of spatial system. Only at age 9 did children become sensitive to spatial constraints which *limited* size, and at age 12 figure size could be *enlarged or shrunk* as if using a zoom (see also Kosslyn, 1994, p. 368) and was robust to random sequence of space systems. From a perspective of childhood, at this rather mature age the pictorial space concept had become more *powerful* in its impact on objects, more *flexible* in its reaction towards different types of axes systems, and more *robust* to noisy input. Thus, could we not say that children's space concept has developed from some ancestral object-focused representation to a space-based hi-tech modern radar screen on which objects have become targets which can be identified even if of very small size? The ability of size modification would be crucial to equate a small dot on the radar screen with a full-size target such as a war ship.

Spatial axes systems in other species

I would like to close the chapter with a note about axes systems in evolution. While monkeys and humans are often compared with respect to their mental abilities due to their similar brain size, their actual productivity seems sparse compared with humans. Spiders belong to an ancient animal species which is very productive in technically highly sophisticated ways, so much so that the fibres they produce are employed as models for microfibres used for clothes and outdoor equipment (Emile, Floch and Vollrath, 2006). Spiderwebs as we know them have existed for approximately 200 million years, and constitute 'superb examples of extended anatomy' (Vollrath, 2005, p. 364), because the geometric design and size of the web construction is dependent on internal factors such as body weight and leg length. Larger spiders build larger (Risch, 1977; Venner, Bel-Venner, Pasquet and Leborgne, 2003), and faster (Rayor and Uetz,

2000), and have increased bodily resources of bio-polymer silk (Vollrath, Downes and Krackow, 1997). But external factors also matter, such as the available space, wind and humidity (Vollrath et al., 1997). While spiders were constructing sophisticated diagonal axes systems, humans were still depicting themselves and their cattle in implicit space, albeit sometimes in a rotated fashion (Lange-Küttner and Green, 2007). Spiders would build their web around a hub, which functions literally like a viewpoint, as this is the place from where they monitor their prey; then they build the axes (radii) and the frame, and finally they construct the spiral mesh to capture their prey (Foelix, 1996).

Neurotoxins have effects on cognitive and motor components in spiders. Anaesthesia increased the stiffness of the web fibre and reduced flexibility (Pérez-Rigueiro, Elices, Plaza, Real and Guinea, 2006). Amphetamine and caffeine had pronounced effects on the geometry of the web: amphetamine reduced the mesh, while caffeine reduced the size of the entire axes system (Hesselberg and Vollrath, 2004; see Figure 10.5). Thus, the axes systems of spiderwebs provide a frame where there was nothing before, which delineates and structures space, and may be reduced in scope owing to external interference or limited resources. It seems like a small geometric difference between the axes system of a spiderweb and a pictorial vector axes system, but still children need years until in their drawings, as in spiderwebs, the context of axes systems increasingly weaves objects into the surface structure. Objects now become 'framed' into a display and gradually the spatial system logic applies to them, making them sizeable along a scale, rotated around a body axis, and view-specific.

Why would the construction of an explicit spatial context take so long in human development, if already a much smaller organism such as an arthropod spider can create spatial axes systems? A hypothesis would be that the main difference between spider axes systems and graphic vector axes systems is not the geometry, but that initially one of the primary objectives of children is to make objects permanent, as some of our ancestors in their caves successfully did, creating images which lasted for generations, thousands of years later, while spiders continued to annihilate and devour their objects leaving no trace of them. Thus, the uniquely human activity in drawing would initially consist of the creation of a permanent and unambiguous object representation, and only thereafter develop a space-based real-life 3D simulation in which these 'permanent' objects could become axis-based figures which are allocated an a priori defined position in a spatial plan and become modified as if animated. It may be that this two-tiered development from an object-based to a space-based approach in children's pictorial representation could also contribute to

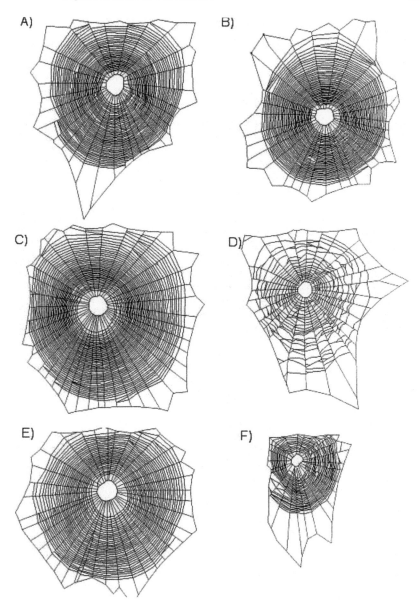

Figure 10.5 Repeated spiderwebs (row 1), spiderweb after intake of amphetamine (row 2), spiderweb after intake of caffeine (row 3). Reprinted from Hesselberg and Vollrath, 2004, p. 521, with permission from Elsevier. The figure was made available courtesy of the author Thomas Hesselberg.

the ongoing debate in cognitive psychology about how visual memory traces of objects are encoded in the mind.

REFERENCES

Aldhous, P. (2006). Elephants recognize their mirror image. *New Scientist*, 192, 17.
Anati, E. (2002). *Höhlenmalerei* [*Cave paintings*]. Düsseldorf: Albatros.
Barlow, C. M., Jolley, R. P., White, D. G. and Galbraith, D. (2003). Rigidity in children's drawings and its relation with representational change. *Journal of Experimental Child Psychology*, 86, 124–52.
Baylis, G. C. (1998). Visual parsing and object-based attention: a developmental perspective. In J. E. Richards (ed.), *Cognitive neuroscience of attention: a developmental perspective* (pp. 251–86). Mahwah, NJ: Erlbaum.
Baylis, G. C. and Driver, J. (1995). One-sided edge-assignment in vision: 1. Figure–ground segmentation and attention to objects. *Current Directions in Psychological Science*, 4, 140–6.
Behr, H.-G., Grohmann, H. and Hagedorn, B.-O. (1983). *Charakter-Köpfe: Der Fall F. X. Messerschmidt* [Heads with character: the case of F. X. Messerschmidt]. Basel and Weinheim: Beltz.
Bisiach, E. and Vallar, G. (1988). Hemineglect in humans. In F. Boller and J. Grafman (eds.), *Handbook of neuropsychology* (pp. 195–222). Amsterdam: Elsevier.
Bruner, J. S. and Koslowski, B. (1972). Visually preadapted constituents of manipulatory action. *Perception*, 1, 3–14.
Cox, M. V. (1993). *Children's drawings of the human figure*. Hove: Erlbaum.
Davies, A. (1985). Conflict between canonicality and array-specificity in young children's drawings. *British Journal of Developmental Psychology*, 3, 363–72.
DeLoache, J. S. (1989). Young children's understanding of the correspondence between a scale model and a larger space. *Cognitive Development*, 4, 121–39.
DeLoache, J. S., Miller, K. F. and Rosengren, K. S. (1997). The credible shrinking room: very young children's performance with symbolic and nonsymbolic relations. *Psychological Science*, 8, 308–13.
DeLoache, J., Uttal, D. and Rosengren, K. S. (2004). Scale errors offer evidence for a perception–action dissociation early in life. *Science*, 304, 1027–9.
Deręgowski, J. B. and Dziurawiec, S. (1996). The puissance of typical contours and children's drawings. *Australian Journal of Psychology*, 48, 98–103.
Driver, J., Baylis, G. C., Goodrich, S. J. and Rafal, R. D. (1994). Axis-based neglect of visual shapes. *Neuropsychologia*, 32, 1353–65.
Edelman, G. M. (2006). The embodiment of mind. *Daedalus*, 135, 23–32.
Edelstein, W., Keller, M. and Schröder, E. (1990). Child development and social structure: a study of individual differences. In R. M. Lerner (ed.), *Life-span development and behaviour* (pp. 152–87). Hillsdale, NJ: Erlbaum.
Efron, R. and Yundt, E. W. (1996). Spatial non-uniformities in visual search. *Brain and Cognition*, 31, 331–68.
Emile, O., Floch, A. L. and Vollrath, F. (2006). Biopolymers: shape memory in spider draglines. *Nature*, 440, 621.

Foelix, R. F. (1996). *Biology of spiders*. Second edition. Oxford: Oxford University Press.
Freeman, N. H. (1980). *Strategies of representation in young children*. London: Academic Press.
Goodenough, F. L. (1926). *Measurement of intelligence by drawings*. New York: World Book Company.
Goodenough, F. L. and Harris, D. B. (1950). Studies in the psychology of children's drawings. II. *Psychological Bulletin*, 47, 369–433.
Goodnow, J. J. (1977). *Children's drawings*. London: Fontana.
Graff, J. (2006). Saving beauty. Mold and bureaucracy threaten France's Lascaux cave. *Time*, 167, 36–42.
Hagen, M. A. (1985). There is no development in art. In N. Freeman and M. V. Cox (eds.), *Visual order* (pp. 78–100). Cambridge: Cambridge University Press.
Halligan, P. W. and Marshall, J. C. (1998). Neglect of awareness. *Consciousness and Cognition*, 7, 356–80.
Hegel, G. W. F. (1812/1975). *Wissenschaft der Logik. Erster Band: Die objective Logik [Science of logic. First volume: The objective logic]*. Hamburg: Felix Meiner [reprint of the first edition by Schrag, Nuremberg].
Hesselberg, T. and Vollrath, F. (2004). The effects of neurotoxins on webgeometry and web-building behaviour in *Araneus diadematus* Cl. *Physiology and Behaviour*, 82, 519–29.
Humphreys, G. W. and Riddoch, M. J. (1993). Interactions between object and space systems revealed through neuropsychology. In D. E. Meyer and S. Kornblum (eds.), *Attention and performance XIV: synergies in experimental psychology, artificial intelligence, and cognitive neuroscience* (pp. 143–75). Cambridge, MA: MIT Press.
Kail, R. (1986). Sources of age differences in speed of processing. *Child Development*, 57, 969–87.
Kant, I. (1781/1980). *Kritik der reinen Vernunft [Critique of pure reason]*. Frankfurt am Main: Suhrkamp.
Karmiloff-Smith, A. (1990). Constraints on representational change: evidence from children's drawings. *Cognition*, 34, 57–83.
  (1995). *Beyond modularity: a developmental perspective on cognitive science*. Cambridge, MA: MIT Press.
Kinsbourne, M. (1993). Orientational bias model of unilateral neglect: evidence from attentional gradients within hemispace. In I. H. Robertson and J. C. Marshall (eds.), *Unilateral neglect: clinical and experimental studies* (pp. 63–86). Hove: Erlbaum.
Kosslyn, S. M. (1994). *Image and brain*. Cambridge, MA: MIT Press.
Lange-Küttner, C. (1989). *Raumbegriff und Objektbeziehungen beim Kind [Space concept and object relations in the child]*. Frankfurt am Main: Lang.
  (1994). *Gestalt und Konstruktion: die Entwicklung der grafischen Kompetenz beim Kind [Gestalt and construction: the development of graphic competence in the child]*. Berne: Huber.
  (1997). Development of size modification of human figure drawings in spatial axes systems of varying complexity. *Journal of Experimental Child Psychology*, 66, 264–78.

(1998). Pressure, velocity and time in speeded drawing of basic graphic pattern by young children. *Perceptual and Motor Skills*, 86, 1299–1310.

(2000). The role of object violations in the development of visual analysis. *Perceptual and Motor Skills*, 90, 3–24.

(2004). More evidence on size modification in spatial axes systems of varying complexity. *Journal of Experimental Child Psychology*, 88, 171–92.

(2006). Drawing boundaries: from individual to common region – the development of spatial region attribution in children. *British Journal of Developmental Psychology*, 24, 419–27.

(2008). Size and contour as crucial parameters in children drawing images. In C. Milbrath and H. M. Trautner (eds.), *Children's understanding and production of pictures, drawing, and art: theoretical and empirical approaches* (pp. 89–106). Göttingen: Hogrefe.

(under revision). Habitual size and projective size: the logic of spatial systems in children's drawings.

Lange-Küttner, C. and Crichton, M. T. (1999). Change of spatial field effects in 16- to 20-week-old infants. *Brain and Cognition*, 39, 75–92.

Lange-Küttner, C. and Green, H. (2007). What is the age of mental rotation? *Proceedings of the 6th IEEE International Conference on Development and Learning*, pp. 259–63.

Lange-Küttner, C., Kerzmann, A. and Heckhausen, J. (2002). The emergence of visually realistic contour in the drawing of the human figure. *British Journal of Developmental Psychology*, 20, 439–63.

Lange-Küttner, C. and Reith, E. (1995). The transformation of figurative thought: implications of Piaget and Inhelder's developmental theory for children's drawings. In C. Lange-Küttner and G. V. Thomas (eds.), *Drawing and looking* (pp. 75–92). London: Pearson/Prentice Hall (distributed by www.amazon.co.uk).

Lewin, K. (1951). *Field theory in social science*. New York: Harper Brothers.

(1963/1982). *Feldtheorie: Kurt-Lewin-Werkausgabe, Band 4* [*Field theory. Kurt Lewin Collected Writings, Vol. 4*]. Berne and Stuttgart: Huber and Klett-Cotta.

Light, P. H. and Humphreys, J. (1981). Internal spatial relationships in young children's drawings. *Journal of Experimental Child Psychology*, 31, 521–30.

Light, P. H. and MacIntosh, E. (1980). Depth relationships in young children's drawings. *Journal of Experimental Child Psychology*, 30, 79–87.

Logan, G. D. (1996). The CODE theory of visual attention. An integration of space-based and object-based attention. *Psychological Review*, 103, 603–49.

Manly, T., Dobler, V. B., Dodds, C. M. and George, M. A. (2005). Rightward shift in spatial awareness with declining alertness. *Neuropsychologia*, 43, 1721–8.

Mayer-Hillebrand, F. (1947). Die Perspektive in psychologischer Betrachtung. *Wiener Zeitschrift für Philosophie, Psychologie und Pädagogik*, 1, 141–61.

Mecklinger, A. and Meinshausen, R.-M. (1998). Recognition memory for object form and object location: an event-related potential study. *Memory and Cognition*, 26, 1068–88.

Mitchell, P., Ropar, D., Ackroyd, K. and Rajendran, G. (2005). How perception impacts on drawings. *Journal of Experimental Psychology: Human Perception and Performance*, 31, 996–1003.

Nielsen, M., Suddendorf, T. and Slaughter, V. (2006). Mirror self-recognition beyond the face. *Child Development*, 77, 176–85.
Panofsky, E. (1927/1991). *Perspective as symbolic form*. New York: Zone.
Pérez-Rigueiro, J., Elices, M., Plaza, G. R., Real, J. I. and Guinea, G. V. (2006). The influence of anaesthesia on the tensile properties of spider silk. *Journal of Experimental Biology*, 209, 320–6.
Piaget, J. (1969). *The mechanisms of perception*. London: Routledge and Kegan Paul.
  (1981). *Le possible et le nécessaire I. L'évolution des possibles chez l'enfant* [*The possible and the necessary I: the evolution of thinking the possible in the child*]. Paris: Presses Universitaires de France.
  (1983). *Le possible et le nécessaire II. L'évolution du nécessaire chez l'enfant* [*The possible and the necessary II. The evolution of thinking the necessary in the child*]. Paris: Presses Universitaires de France.
Piaget, J. and Inhelder, B. (1956). *The child's conception of space*. London: Routledge and Kegan Paul.
Piaget, J., Inhelder, B. and Szeminska, A. (1960). *The child's conception of geometry*. London: Routledge and Kegan Paul.
Plotnik, J. M., de Waal, F. B. M. and Reiss, D. (2006). Self-recognition in an Asian elephant. *Proceedings of the National Academy of Sciences of the United States of America*, 103, 17053–7.
Pylyshyn, Z. (2003). *Seeing and visualizing: it's not what you think*. Cambridge, MA: MIT Press.
Rayor, L. S. and Uetz, G. W. (2000). Age-related sequential web building in the colonial spider *Metepeira incrassata* (Araneidae): an adaptive spacing strategy. *Animal Behaviour*, 59, 1251–9.
Reith, E. and Dominin, D. (1997). The development of children's ability to attend to the visual projection of objects. *British Journal of Developmental Psychology*, 15, 177–96.
Risch, P. (1977). Quantitative analysis of orb web patterns in four species of spiders. *Behavioral Genetics*, 7, 199–238.
Robertson, I. H., Nico, D. and Hood, B. M. (1997). Believing what you feel: using proprioceptive feedback to reduce unilateral neglect. *Neuropsychology*, 11, 53–8.
Rogers, L. J. (2000). Evolution of side bias: motor versus sensory lateralization. In M. K. Mandal, M. B. Bulman-Fleming and G. Tiwari (eds.), *Side bias: a neuropsychological perspective* (pp. 3–40). Dordrecht: Kluwer.
Sheppard, E., Ropar, D. and Mitchell, P. (2005). The impact of meaning and dimensionality on the accuracy of children's copying. *British Journal of Developmental Psychology*, 23, 365–81.
Sherick, I., Greenman, G. and Legg, C. (1976). Some comments on the significance and development of midline behaviour during infancy. *Child Psychiatry and Human Development*, 6, 170–83.
Silk, A. M. J. and Thomas, G. V. (1986). Development and differentiation in children's figure drawings. *British Journal of Psychology*, 77, 399–410.
  (1988). The development of size scaling in children's figure drawings. *British Journal of Developmental Psychology*, 6, 285–99.
Tada, W. L. and Stiles, J. (1996). Developmental change in children's analysis of spatial patterns. *Developmental Psychology*, 32, 951–70.

Thelen, E., Corbetta, D., Kamm, K., Spencer, J. P., Schneider, K. and Zernicke, R. F. (1993). The transition to reaching: mapping intention and intrinsic dynamics. *Child Development*, 64, 1058–98.

Thomas, G. V. (1995). The role of drawing strategies and skills. In C. Lange-Küttner and G. V. Thomas (eds.), *Drawing and looking* (pp. 107–22). London: Pearson/Prentice Hall (distributed by www.amazon.co.uk).

Toomela, A. (2002). Drawing as a verbally mediated activity: a study of relationships between verbal, motor, and visuospatial skills and drawing in children. *International Journal of Behavioural Development*, 26, 234–47.

Towse, J. N. and Hitch, G. J. (1996). Performance demands in the selection of objects for counting. *Journal of Experimental Child Psychology*, 61, 67–79.

Treisman, A. (2006). How the deployment of attention determines what we see. *Visual Cognition*, 14, 411–43.

Ungerleider, L. G. and Mishkin, M. (1982). Two cortical visual systems. In D. J. Ingle, M. A. Goodale and R. J. W. Mansfield (eds.), *Analysis of visual behaviour* (pp. 549–86). Cambridge, MA: MIT Press.

Van Sommers, P. (1984). *Drawing and cognition: descriptive and experimental studies of graphic production processes*. Cambridge: Cambridge University Press.

Venner, S., Bel-Venner, M. C., Pasquet, A. and Leborgne, R. (2003). Body-mass dependent cost of web-building behaviour in an orb weaving spider, *Zygiella x-notata*. *Naturwissenschaften*, 90, 269–72.

Vinter, A. and Perruchet, P. (2000). Implicit learning in children is not related to age: evidence from drawing behaviour. *Child Development*, 71, 1223–40.

Vollrath, F. (2005). Spiders' webs. *Current Biology*, 15, R364–R365.

Vollrath, F., Downes, M. and Krackow, S. (1997). Design variability in web geometry of an orb-weaving spider. *Physiology and Behaviour*, 62, 735–43.

Willats, J. (1997). *Art and representation: new principles in the analysis of pictures*. Princeton, NJ: Princeton University Press.

Zhi, Z., Thomas, G. V. and Robinson, E. J. (1997). Constraints on representational change: drawing a man with two heads. *British Journal of Developmental Psychology*, 15, 275–90.

11 Spatial and symbolic codes in the development of three-dimensional graphic representation

Maria A. Tallandini and Luisa Morassi

Tallandini investigates the dissociation of the spatial code and the semantic (or symbolic) code in drawing. She tested a model of drawing which assumes two pathways of attention to the real object. Children could either draw only paying attention to the surface properties (spatial code) which should enhance visually realistic drawing, or they would draw more meaningful objects (semantic code) where attention is diverted between spatial and semantic aspects, and thus the more early intellectually realistic drawing style should pervade. Tallandini asked children and adults to copy aggregates of cubes in different conditions, (1) plain and purely geometrical, (2) with features of a doll, (3) with a part (the head) rotated, (4) with the entire figure rotated. Using a 7-point Q3DS-scale, she found that the more complex the spatial aspects, i.e. object orientation and position, and the less semantic aspects, the better the quality of the level of the projective system, in both children and adults. It is concluded that semantic content, the 'what', interfered with the construction of spatially complex figure constructions, the 'how', a clear dissociation between the spatial and the semantic code in drawing.

FROM A historical perspective, Piaget (1977) identified two inextricable aspects of knowledge (Feldman, 2000): the 'figurative', which concerns an object's physical reality (e.g. colour, texture, position, size, weight, etc.) and the 'operative', which corresponds to the ways in which that object is understood. The 'figurative' component of knowledge is associated with the spatial and physical aspects of objects and, more generally, with the world's physical characteristics, and it therefore denotes what is called the 'spatial code'. The operative aspect of knowledge concerns an object's semantic characteristics and instruments for interpreting the information that is available in a given context and is therefore associated with the 'symbolic code'.

Piaget theorized that spatial (figurative) aspects, which are experienced through the senses, and symbolic-semantic (operative) aspects, which underlie the cognitive processes of comprehension and interpretation, are invariant functions within the same system and that they operate in an interplay of construction and re-construction, as children attempt to understand the world. Feldman (2000) later underscored how the figurative, or spatial, aspects of knowledge tend to reflect *bottom-up* cognitive and perceptual procedures, whereas operative structures refer to what are defined as higher-order or *top-down* learning processes.

One problem facing researchers on drawing production is to understand how drawers identify equivalents to properly represent objects endowed with volume and meaning, on a flat page (Cannoni, 2003; Goodnow, 1977). The acquisition of equivalents represents a constant process in our lives, in that it occurs every time we learn and accurately apply the terms 'equal' or 'different'. For example, when we draw, we use many geometric and symbolic equivalents: an upturned mouth is the equivalent of a 'happy' feeling; the bottom of a page is the equivalent of 'the ground'; an object drawn in the upper part of a page indicates that it is farther away than an object drawn in the middle of the page, etc. According to the renowned art critic Gombrich (1960), in fact, an artist transmits the semantic valence[1] of a representation to the viewer by following consolidated iconographic rules, which allow for the transmission of socially shared meaning.

Moreover, Gombrich (1960) maintained that perceptual processes rely on the same rhythm that governs representation: the rhythm of schema and adaptation based on the process of attribution of meaning to what we see. This rhythm is based on the continuous elaboration of hypotheses, and therefore on a process that modifies the meaning of reality as derived from our own experience. The most effective strategy in proceeding by trial and error is to start from the simplest assumptions. Without them, we would be unable to derive any sense from the manifold ambiguous stimuli that compose our world. As Gombrich maintained, making sense of things frequently means transforming them.

Yet, we might wonder whether this process is also active in three-dimensional (3D) drawing. More specifically, when we draw a 3D object, does the object's meaning influence its graphic representation, and if so, to what extent? There is a general consensus that a process of adapting lines drawn on a page to iconographic rules occurs over the course of development. In fact, drawing on the spatial level is based on the ability to portray things as they appear to us and it is only by drawing non-real shapes and proportions for an object that we can achieve a proper representation of it.

On the semantic level, conversely, the meaning of the stimuli can influence graphic representation because we often try to adapt the images we see to what we know about them, and this process can lead us to modify our drawings. The question that remains unanswered then is how the spatial and semantic systems interact in 3D drawing.

Many studies have analysed the processes that are used to represent a 3D object, but few have investigated the influence of semantic valence in 3D representation; and none has dealt with the relation that exists between a 3D object's meaning and its relative graphic representational techniques. The research that has examined the meaning–object representation relationship can be divided into three main strands focusing on the copy of 2D geometric figures, non-geometric stimuli and solids.

The copying of flat geometric shapes

Phillips, Hobbs and Pratt (1978) investigated the conflict between semantic valence and 2D representation by asking 6- to 9-year-old children to copy pictures of cubes and non-objects (non-existent geometrical figures) that had the same number of lines and visible sides as the cubes. Their paradigm presented two experimental conditions: one in which children were able to see both the model and their own drawings as they drew, and one in which the participants were required to look continuously at the model and were prevented from seeing their own drawings, which were hidden by a specifically designed apparatus. The authors hypothesized that viewing the model would positively influence performance in the condition in which the children were able to keep visual track of their own graphic production. They also hypothesized that the stimulus with meaning would lead to an accentuated use of intellectual realism. (The stimuli were drawings; thus the 3D–2D translation had already been carried out.) Results from both experimental situations showed that children represented familiar geometric figures in a less spatially accurate way and with greater intellectual realism than they did non-figures. The authors proposed that the translation of an 'internal visual description' into a graphic representation is a more complex process when it involves an object with known semantic valence, given that the act of copying an object with clear-cut meaning also automatically activates its relative graphomotor scheme. It was thought that this phenomenon does not occur in the drawing of non-object models, because they are less influenced by intellectual realism-induced modifications.

The influence of semantic valence on 2D representation was also studied by Vinter (1999), who asked 6- to 10-year-old children and adults to copy Van Sommers' (1984) drawing-stimuli. Her aim was to investigate the relation between the semantic valence of a stimulus and the routines individuals implement to draw it. The experimental paradigm called for the presentation of two-dimensional drawings, each of which had two meanings attributed (e.g. a glass or a person) through two different types of instructions. The two stimuli were graphically identical, but being presented with different semantic valence, they could be perceived as representing two different objects/situations. Vinter's purpose was to verify whether the variation in meaning of a visually ambiguous stimulus could lead to differences in the routine sequence used to re-produce it and to examine how graphic syntax is articulated through sub-routines of composition that were hypothesized to differ in function of a given assigned meaning. She concluded that stimuli meaning modified the graphic sequence in both children's and adults' drawings.

Vinter acknowledged Phillips et al.'s (1978) idea concerning the role of internal representations modifying the planning of drawings, but also maintained that the way in which this process unfolds is a function of two factors: (1) competition between geometric executive constraints (bottom-up factors) and semantic constraints (top-down factors), and (2) the nature of the internal representations that are tapped to plan the drawing. She proposed that it is bottom-up forces that prevail over top-down processes, whenever there is a conflict between the two, but also that this situation evolves as children develop. Specifically, she maintained that the strong dominance of certain graphic rules in children (6–7 years) can prevent them from modifying the strategies they use to express different meanings in graphic representation, and it is only when the spatial component of representation has achieved a certain flexibility (at the age of approximately 8–9 years) that semantic influences can start modifying children's graphic routines.

This second explanatory factor, which is influenced by participant age, concerns the representational units children are able to process and apply in planning the movements they make when drawing. Vinter's results (1999) showed, in fact, that the meaning effect was weaker for stimuli that were more difficult to decompose. Indeed, the strongest semantic effect was obtained with geometric models, although one intuitively would have expected a greater meaning effect with stimuli having a greater symbolic connotation, such as the stimulus representing a glass with a cherry inside versus a person with a spyglass.

The above-described body of research found a meaning effect for the graphic representation of drawings of two-dimensional stimuli, and a recent study by Sheppard, Ropar and Mitchell (2005) delved deeper into the same topic with a sample of 6- to 9-year-old children. The study was aimed at verifying three aspects of the object meaning–object drawing relation: (1) whether children can produce more accurate copies of drawings of two-dimensional stimuli than they can of drawings of three-dimensional stimuli; (2) whether drawings are more accurate when stimuli are devoid of meaning or when a semantic effect is operating; and (3) what type of interaction exists between a stimulus' meaning and its spatial characteristics. The authors presented participants with 2D stimuli (line drawings only) of a 3D object endowed with meaning, 2D representations of the same object with no 3D cues – i.e. 2D and 3D variations on drawings of a cake, a truck, a wrapped present and a television – and 2D and 3D drawings of non-existent objects of equivalent graphic complexity. Participants' drawings were evaluated in terms of the graphic accuracy of three indices: length, position and line orientation. Results showed that older children drew all the stimuli more accurately than the younger children did and that, contrary to findings from previous research (Phillips et al., 1978), stimuli meanings interacted positively with their spatial characteristics – but only in the copy of two-dimensional objects: the presence of meaning in a to-be-drawn stimulus led to performance improvement in both age-groups, but did not improve spatial organization for three-dimensional stimuli. Moreover, and contrary to findings from previous research (Phillips et al., 1978), the study demonstrated that, in tasks of copying a previously drawn object, a model's meaning can contribute to a better quality of representation.

The copying of non-geometric figures

Willats' seminal work on the drawing of non-geometric objects (Willats, 1985, 2003, 2005) led him to underscore the importance of examining both the symbolic and the geometric aspects of stimuli. He reached this conclusion after becoming aware of the limits of his previously theorized *projection* systems (Willats, 1977), which had hitherto illustrated only the 'spatial code'. He subsequently elaborated *denotation systems* to analyse drawing contexts in which both dimensional and extensional cues convey meaning.

His denotation systems represent the characteristics of the real world – or primitive scene – in the corresponding elements of a representation. He agreed with Marr (1982) in maintaining that the 'primitive' of a representation consists in the most basic units of information concerning shape that are available in that representation. He also used the denotation systems to examine a type of representation he called 'smooth edges' (figures with no corners), by typically referring to an adult's drawing of two sausages – one curved and turned in upon itself and the other straight, with no curves. The first instance presents an obvious contour occlusion that is not visible in the drawing of the straight sausage and is not achieved by the representation of corners or angles. He therefore concluded that a simple line can represent both a three-dimensional surface and a partial occlusion. In fact, we can note in our phenomenological experience how it is impossible fully to view all of the objects that are actually present in a given scene: some are partially, or even totally, hidden (occluded) by others. Furthermore, even discrete objects are only partially seen, given that their bases and their far sides are occluded.

Yet, Willats wondered whether the lines in children's drawings of 'smooth shapes' might also represent occluded contours or three-dimensional figures. He therefore carefully used his denotation systems to analyse drawings in which children had drawn an area to represent a volume, or areas to denote the sides of solids, or lines for edges. He also worked out an extension index (1985) to describe a given line's extension into the dimensions of space (length, height and depth).

His findings led him to consider two complementary types of accounts for the development of graphic representation in children: one in terms of motor control, 2D figure drawing and drawing processes, and the other in terms of meaning and, therefore, of semantic knowledge.

Hence, as mentioned previously, his 'projection systems' refer only to the spatial code, i.e. to the geometric aspects of objects, and therefore to a restricted part of the information contained in a drawing, but his more recently developed denotation systems represent the meaning a drawing conveys, and are related to a drawer's representational style. He therefore concluded that the development of graphic representation is characterized by the progressive discovery of rules for 'unifying' these projective and denotative systems of representation, in a drawer's pursuit of ever more efficacious combinations to produce realistic drawings.

Findings from the research of Lange-Küttner, Kerzmann and Heckhausen (2002) in fact confirmed the existence of a parts–all integration process, which is present from the age of 6 years upward and is characterized by a great deal of interindividual variability. These authors furthermore maintained that the processes of part differentiation and integration in human figure drawing represent the most important transition that occurs in the development of the figurative drawing.

The integration process is therefore thought to involve the interaction of spatial knowledge, cognitive processing, planning abilities (Freeman, 1980; Morra, Moizo and Scopesi, 1988), motor control (Toomela, 2002) and attention to perceptual details (Lange-Küttner, 2000), with results characterized, however, by a marked interindividual variability

(Lange-Küttner, 2000; Lange-Küttner *et al.*, 2002). Davis (1985) found that children tap two main sources of information when asked to copy a stimulus: orientation, linked to the drawing's spatial code and familiarity, linked to the object's meaning (i.e. to the semantic code).

A concept that can account for both of these processes is canonicity. The term refers to an object's conventional image in its most readily recognizable orientation, which simultaneously conveys the greatest amount of information possible concerning its structure. For instance, the human figure is typically drawn in a vertical, frontal position; but cars, fish or dogs are generally depicted from the side; and a cup is usually drawn with a fully visible handle.

An explanation for the phenomenon of canonicity can be found in a developmental transition identified by Luquet, i.e. the intellectual-to-visual realism transition (Luquet, 1927). During the phase of intellectual realism, children represent what they know about a particular object (i.e. with its semantic aspects predominating), and during the visual realism phase they start drawing objects how they actually see them (and an object's spatial aspects are integrated with its semantic aspects).

Yet, it is important to note that Luquet did not investigate the presence–absence of symbolism in drawing: his perspective was that children always try to render their drawing as realistic as possible and that the function of drawing itself is exclusively to represent something as recognizable as possible. He was therefore interpreting the development of graphic representation in terms of an increase in representational adherence to reality.

Barrett and Light (1976) later conducted a study attempting to complement this vision and proposed a modification in Luquet's (1927) sequence by identifying a Symbolism stage that takes place before Intellectual Realism and Visual Realism – i.e. a stage during which children draw what they *know* about the category to which an object belongs.

Furthermore, Tallandini and Valentini (1990) found that when children first start drawing, they tend to use the same type of prototypic symbolic representation for a model from the category for which that prototype is the most representative, but that later on during development children are able to differentiate specific subcategories from these general categories.

In Tallandini and Valentini's research (1991), children were asked to draw a prototypical school ('a school') and an exemplar school (their 'own school'), and three types of symbolism emerged: *failed symbolism* (5–6 years), in which the main pictorial components of the school either were not depicted or were unrecognizable; *generic symbolism* (5–7 years), when children drew prototypes with highly general characteristics;

specific symbolism (present in all age-groups), when the stimulus' pictorial elements were represented in such a way that what appeared on the page was seen as a school building. Tallandini and Valentini (1991) concluded that children are able to use different representative strategies and select the ones they consider the most appropriate, based on the instructions they receive. The authors also maintained that children's drawing shows a selection of strategies distinguishing prototypical versus realistic tasks.

The 'spatial' and 'symbolic' codes in drawing were also studied by Reith (1990), who used tasks requiring children to reproduce two spatially similar, non-geometric 3D stimuli (one with meaning and one without) to classify other children's drawings. Results showed that children with high levels of graphic performance also manifested greater representational awareness and that children's drawing quality depended on their ability to differentiate form and content. These findings therefore indirectly concerned the question of spatial–symbolic code integration (Ingram, 1985; Sheppard et al., 2005).

Another study investigating the graphic representation of familiar objects was conducted by Tallandini and Varesano (2003), who examined flexibility in graphic routines. In a preliminary experiment aimed at obtaining a baseline measure for participants' graphic routines, 4- to 5-year-old children and adults were asked to produce freehand drawings of a cup, a house and a church. In a second experiment, the same participants were asked to complete two different pre-drawn stimuli for each of the previously listed objects. In one condition, the pre-drawn picture represented the starting point for a routine; in the second condition the drawing was constructed as the central part of a routine. Results showed that the 4-year-olds were more anchored to their own routines than the other two age-groups were; 5-year-old children showed an ability to adapt their own graphic syntax to the task-imposed limits; and adults performed more flexibly than the two children's groups did.

In agreement with Van Sommers (1984), the authors proposed that the lack of flexibility observed in the younger children most probably depends on mechanisms pertaining to the drawing process itself. Specifically, they hypothesized that what is maintained throughout development is not an executive or motor routine, but an abstract image of a visual form that is produced during the executive process – i.e. a mental representation that simultaneously contains both the spatial aspects of an object (shape, orientation, position, etc.) and its semantic aspects (what it is, what it is used for, etc.). It therefore follows that the difficult access to representative flexibility observed in younger children's drawing might be linked to a difficulty in their integrating the spatial and symbolic aspects of stimuli.

Hence, models of the development of children's graphic ability should offer more sophisticated and flexible solutions that can also specifically account for the integration of the spatial and symbolic aspects of reality.

The copying of geometric solids

The drawing of geometric solids was investigated by Chen and Cook (1984), who used the tasks of copying from a real model, a photograph and drawings of geometric solids (a cube, a cylinder, a pyramid and a cone). They observed an interference effect between structure-representation (concerning the geometric aspects of a stimulus) and content-representation (its semantic aspects). Whereas most 5- to 7-year-old children drew with a structure-oriented strategy, 7- to 9-year-olds used a content-oriented strategy. All age-groups showed greater difficulty in copying from true models than they did in copying from line drawings. Yet, variation in performance quality was observed in function of the model proposed and nature of the task. In particular, and contrary to what might be expected, no significant modification in drawing quality emerged when the cube and the cone were presented as two-dimensional stimuli.

More recently, Bremner, Morse, Hughes and Andreasen (2000) used three different tasks to examine cube-drawing (drawing from a model, and tracing and copying a previously made drawing) and demonstrated how the abilities of copying and drawing are not wholly independent. They also showed that the task of copying (versus tracing) allows drawers to focus their attention on the structure of a represented object.

We believe that this copying–drawing relation can be explained in part by Chen and Cook's (1984) distinction between content-directed strategy and structure-directed strategy. In fact, Bremner et al. (2000) found that a drawer's need to pay close attention to line-by-line sequence (as required by the task to copy a line drawing of a cube) helps improve performance. Conversely, when participants are asked to copy from a solid, they focus their attention on reproducing the object's surfaces (the cube faces and their interaction).

Another experiment examining the relation between spatial and semantic aspects in the development of graphic representation was conducted by Ingram (1985), who used two stimuli with the same geometric shape (two wooden cubes connected by a parallelepiped), but having a different semantic valence, in that one stimulus was neutral and the other conveyed the meaning of a human figure (a 'doll'). The author evaluated participants' drawings in terms of outcomes in the representation of occlusion and canonicity, and results confirmed the simultaneous presence of two types of coding processes in children: a symbolic code, linked to the meaning of a stimulus, and a spatial code concerning the geometric and spatial relations of a stimulus' orientation. An age difference in the performance of Ingram's child participants led him to propose that these processes are present from the age of 3 years and that they integrate between 5 and 7 years of age.

Given that Ingram's (1985) experimental paradigm focused on the relevance of the symbolic meaning in children's drawings, we found it to be consonant with our own research needs. Our more recent work (Tallandini et al., 1999; Tallandini and Morassi, 2002, 2005) has therefore employed Ingram's experimental setting, and it has also examined aspects of 3D drawing techniques he did not investigate (1985). We have therefore been focusing on interrelations between the 'how' and the 'what' level in 3D drawing.

In fact, the graphic techniques children use to translate 3D onto a page are indicators of 'how' they work to produce a drawing, how their mental schema are organized, and whether certain representational strategies are already active or whether the children must create new ones for that specific task. The drawing-product provides information on the 'what' level as to children's internal representations of the geometric and semantic aspects of the objects they draw. It therefore provides evidence of the relations that exist between spatial and symbolic components in a child's surrounding world.

As explained previously, one aspect that has always intrigued researchers interested in the drawing process is the fact that graphic representation implies the simultaneous translation of an object's semantic and spatial valence into information that can be represented graphically.

Another challenge for researchers of realistic drawing is to understand how an expert drawer produces an image that is spatially similar to one portrayed by a camera. It is even more difficult to understand how a novice manages to capture an object's meaning in a 2D graphic representation. Hence, the question is: When people want to replicate a retinal image, must they somehow renounce their desire to transmit the image's meaning or do they always manage to integrate the dual aspect of reality composed of space as well as meaning? The literature on the topic provides evidence for the existence of a separation between spatial and semantic systems, the integration of which, however, can be quite complex (Ingram, 1985; Morassi and Tallandini, 2006; Sheppard et al., 2005; Tallandini, Morassi and Gerbino, 1999; Vinter, 1999; Willats, 2003, 2005).

The same type of difficulty reported in drawing research also occurs for research on praxic abilities (Rothi, Ochipa and Heilman, 1991) and action imitation (Tessari and Rumiati, 2004). In particular, Rothi et al. (1991) proposed a model concerning praxic processes and their relations to the semantic system, in which motor ability is thought to be mediated by two components: one conceptual and one production-related. The conceptual component is linked to the semantic system, which inevitably renders the input pathway longer and more convoluted. The non-conceptual component, however, is linked directly to sensorimotor modalities and produces output through a shorter route. Tessari and Rumiati's (2004) action imitation model also presents a dual pathway structure and posits that input can be processed either through a direct route or through a more intricate, semantic route.

Hence, generally speaking, each individual's processing of input (whether auditory, verbal, visual or praxic) has two routes available: a bottom-up path, consisting of figurative, spatial and perceptual procedures, and another, top-down pathway, whose functioning is predominantly linked to semantics and to the symbolic domain. The first route is a short pathway (the 'direct route'), but the second is linked to semantic memory and to the meaning of things and is therefore more elaborate (the 'semantic route') (Rothi et al., 1991; Tessari and Rumiati, 2004).

We believe that a similar set of processes can be hypothesized for drawing (Morassi and Tallandini, 2006; Tallandini and Morassi, 2005). A stimulus with neutral valence (Ingram, 1985) should elicit a drawing with more highly developed 3D characteristics than an identical object with greater symbolic valence does, by taking a shorter cognitive pathway (the direct route) and bypassing the semantic filter. Conversely, a stimulus with strong semantic valence (Ingram, 1985) should activate the passage of input through the semantic route, which sets off more complex executive processes and leads to diminished procedural flexibility and to a decline in 3D graphic performance (the 'meaning effect'). We therefore propose that this latter effect can occur with stimuli having strong semantic impact (e.g. with the doll used by Ingram, 1985), but not with objects presenting an identical spatial composition but lacking well-defined symbolic valence (Tallandini and Morassi, 2005).

The relation between spatial and symbolic codes in 3D drawing

The above-described research illustrates how individuals drawing a three-dimensional object find themselves having to cope with various types of problems. One concerns the difficulty involved in portraying the three-dimensionality of a model on a two-dimensional surface. Another is linked to an individual's ability to re-construct graphically the meaning of a stimulus in an image. As illustrated in the previous section, there is now evidence that these processes go hand in hand and mutually influence each other in the selection of strategies required to produce a finished drawing.

We therefore aimed at investigating this specific and not yet fully explored relation between spatial and symbolic content in child and adult 3D representation.

The spatial code

We based our study (Tallandini and Morassi, 2005) on Ingram's procedure: each participant was asked to draw two stimuli, both of which were made up of two wooden cubes linked by a parallelepiped; one stimulus was 'neutral' (stimulus A); the other had the same geometrical structure, but with human features added (stimulus B: the 'doll' stimulus) (Figure 11.1). Each stimulus was presented in two different orientations (vertical asset (VA) and horizontal asset (HA)) and in two different positions for each orientation (large cube beneath (VA1), large cube on top (VA2); and large cube in front (HA1), large cube behind (HA2) (Figure 11.2).

The study was conducted along two main lines, i.e. by examining the development of graphic representational ability (the *how* level) and the relation between spatial and symbolic encoding processes (the *what* level). Integration of the two areas of study was made possible by conducting within-comparisons of participants' 3D performance using the 'Quality of Three-Dimensional Representation Scale' (Q3DS).

We had developed this instrument for our study with the aim of identifying different levels of 3D ability in our participants' drawings. The coding categories comprising the Q3DS were first formulated by careful examination of collected drawings and in light of the assessment criteria that is currently available in the literature (Bremner and Batten, 1991; Bremner *et al.*, 2000; Cannoni, 2003; Cox and Perara, 1998; Nicholls and Kennedy, 1992, 1995; Toomela, 1999; Willats, 2005).

Although we were also aware of other, diverging theoretical positions (Arnheim, 1974; Freeman and Cox, 1985; Golomb, 2002), we grounded our analysis of development of 3D representational ability on the theoretical assumption that three-dimensional representation in Western cultures is based on projective techniques that are used as a set of commonly shared rules for representing reality (Chen and Cook, 1984; Nicholls and Kennedy, 1992, 1995; Tallandini and Morassi, 2002, 2005; Willats, 2005).

Quality of Three-Dimensional Representation Scale

The Q3DS was developed by first pinpointing and then categorizing the different drawing techniques participants had used. Specifically, assessing

Spatial and symbolic codes in 3D representation 229

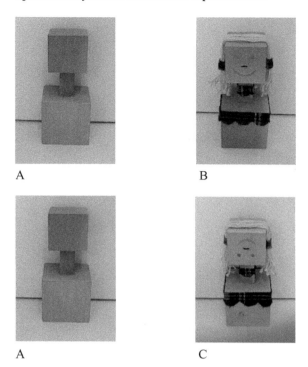

Figure 11.1 Stimuli used. Experiment 1: neutral stimulus (A) and symbolic stimulus (B); Experiment 2: neutral stimulus (A) and blurred stimulus (C).

criteria were identified for 2D, then for 3D techniques, and lastly for strategies deriving from the simultaneous use of two or more techniques.

The resulting graphic techniques were as follows:

- the 'Flat technique': referring to two-dimensional figures, with elements of intellectual realism and an absence of depth relations (Chen and Cook, 1984); this technique corresponds to Willats' *no projection* and *orthographic projection* drawing systems (1977, 1985).
- the 'Axonometric technique': in-depth edges are represented with oblique parallel lines – i.e. Willats' (1977, 1985) *oblique projection* and Nicholls and Kennedy's (1992) *square with obliques*.
- the 'Frontal technique': sides receding into depth are produced by vertical parallel lines (Tallandini and Morassi, 2002). Individuals using this technique attempt to produce a projection of a similar orthogonal stimulus on the frontal plane – a technique corresponding to *vertical oblique projection* (Willats, 1977, 1985).

230 *Maria A. Tallandini and Luisa Morassi*

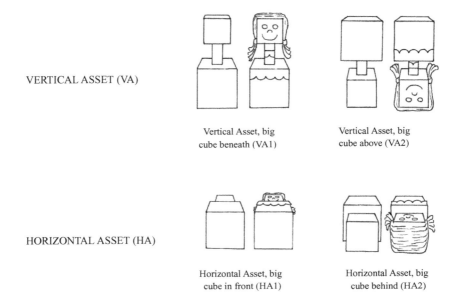

Figure 11.2 Stimuli assets and positions for experiment 1 and 2.

- the 'Prospective technique': in-depth edges are represented by converging lines. This classification contemplates the use of convergence and therefore reunites Willats' *perspective* and *naive perspective* (Willats, 1977, 1985).
- 'Mixed techniques': referring to drawings that present two or more of the above-listed techniques. Willats made no mention of this phenomenon, which was observed, rather, by Lee and Bremner (1987) and by Bremner and Batten (1991).

The coding system described herein also distinguishes between two types of mixed techniques: 'Mixed level 1', in which the flat technique is present, with oblique edges to indicate the third dimension, but with the use of incomplete sides; and 'Mixed level 2', where the 'Frontal technique' (vertical parallel lines) and the 'Prospective technique' (converging lines) are simultaneously present.

The above-described classification yielded a three-dimensional assessment scale (the Q3DS) – a 7-point scale, with 7 indicating the use of linear perspective and 1 denoting a complete lack thereof (Bremner and Batten, 1991; Chen and Cook, 1984; Cox and Perara, 1998; Lee and Bremner, 1987; Nicholls and Kennedy, 1992; Tallandini and Morassi, 2002; Toomela, 1999; Willats, 2005).

Table 11.1 *Experiment 1: neutral stimulus versus symbolic stimulus: means and standard deviations for the three participant groups considered, younger children, older children and adults*

	Exp. 1			
	Neutral stimulus		Symbolic stimulus	
Participants	M	SD	M	SD
Younger children	0.822	0.116	0.715	0.183
Older children	1.496	1.126	1.212	0.535
Adults	4.090	1.272	3.960	1.198

Our results for the spatial coding of 3D drawing replicated results from previous research showing that older children produce drawings with better three-dimensional graphic quality than younger children do (Bremner et al., 2000; Cannoni, 2003; Nicholls and Kennedy, 1992, 1995; Sheppard et al., 2005; Willats, 1977, 2003, 2005) (Table 11.1).

In fact, we observed a significant correlation between child age and scores on the Q3DS scores: children under age 5 mostly used 2D drawing. Slightly older children used strategies involving the use of parallel oblique and frontal lines (including 'mixed' techniques) (Bremner and Batten, 1991; Tallandini and Morassi, 2002; Tallandini et al., 1999), and the phenomenon was even more marked between the age of 6 and 7 years (Chen and Cook, 1984). Lastly, prospective techniques were observed to have been acquired after the age of 7 years – as also described in leading studies concerning three-dimensional drawing (Bremner and Batten, 1991; Case and Okamoto, 1996; Nicholls and Kennedy, 1992; Willats, 1977, 2005).

Willats (1977) held that, in order to develop three-dimensionality, children must first consolidate their representational abilities through 2D drawing and must then acquire different and increasingly difficult *drawing systems*. Nicholls and Kennedy (1992), however, proposed a simpler 3-phase developmental progression: 2D drawing, drawing with parallel lines and then drawing with converging lines. Both accounts were confirmed by aspects of our data. We also observed that object orientation and object position also significantly influenced the quality of our child participants' drawings.

The adults also had difficulties in our 3D representation task, especially with the doll presented in the canonical position (vertical, with the head on top). In fact, more than 90 per cent of the adult participants used strategies relying mostly on axonometric, frontal or mixed

232 Maria A. Tallandini and Luisa Morassi

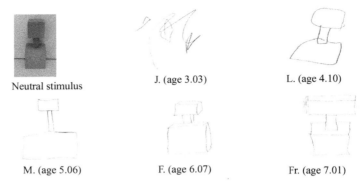

Figure 11.3a. Drawing of the *neutral stimulus* in VA1.

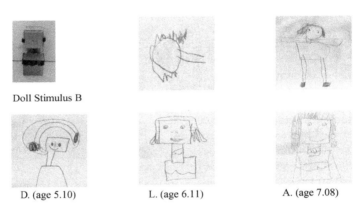

Figure 11.3b. Drawing of the *symbolic stimulus* in VA1.

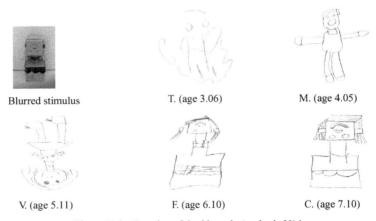

Figure 11.3c. Drawing of the *blurred stimulus* in VA1.

Figure 11.3 Examples of children's performances at different ages of the neutral (11.3a), symbolic (11.3b) and blurred stimulus (11.3c) in position VA1.

The symbolic code in 3D drawing

The most important result concerning the stimulus meaning–drawing relation was the observed influence of the symbolic code on children's three-dimensional drawing (Table 11.1). When children were presented with stimuli having neutral or symbolic valence, their drawings showed what we call 'the meaning effect', in that the influence of the stimulus' semantic component was expressed through poorer 3D performance (ANOVA stimulus (2 levels) × age (3 levels): $F(1,117) = 5.941; p < .02$) (Table 11.1 and Figures 11.3a and 11.3b). Curiously, a 'meaning effect' was also observed for adults when the stimulus representing a person was presented in the canonical position, in that the influence of the symbolic aspect overrode the spatial component. One can account for these results in two ways: by considering that drawing a model with highly evident meaning (as used in our experiment) leads to the separation of symbolic and spatial components. The other type of account refers to the varying complexity of stimuli, by which the greater number of features in the symbolic stimulus might have rendered its graphic execution more difficult.

We put these two possible explanations to the test in a second experiment, keeping the same experimental structure but presenting the neutral stimulus in contrast with another stimulus that had an equivalent degree of figure complexity, with a diminished semantic valence (stimulus C, see Figure 11.1). Specifically, the facial features used in stimulus B were reversed, but the general spatial asset of the stimulus remained the same[2] (Rakover, 2002).

We based our choice of these two stimuli on the hypothesis that, if stimulus C (blurred semantic valence) were drawn with a worse 3D quality than neutral stimulus A (as had occurred for stimulus B in the first experiment), then the result would be due not to the hypothesized 'meaning effect', but to stimulus complexity. By contrast, results of stimulus C being drawn with an equal or a better 3D quality than stimulus A would provide support for the meaning effect hypothesis.

We found that both children's and adults' drawings yielded highly similar 3D representation quality for both types of stimuli (A and C) ($F(1, 64) = 0.099; p = 0.754$) (Table 11.2).

These results therefore provided no support for the stimulus complexity hypothesis, but pointed to an interpretation linked to the semantic component.

Table 11.2 *Experiment 2: neutral stimulus versus blurred stimulus: means and standard deviations for the three participant groups considered, younger children, older children and adults*

Participants	Exp. 2			
	Neutral stimulus		Blurred stimulus	
	M	SD	M	SD
Younger children	0.839	0.133	0.822	0.188
Older children	1.696	1.026	1.758	0.747
Adults	4.750	1.108	4.637	1.003

Our findings pertaining to 3D drawing reflect Vinter's (1999) conclusions concerning the processes of graphic syntax in the copy of 2D drawings. In fact, our data also showed that the meaning of a stimulus modifies the use of 3D graphic techniques, given that in the instance of conflict between spatial and symbolic codes, symbolic-semantic (top-down) constraints prevailed over spatial and geometric (bottom-up) constraints (Figure 11.3).

Vinter (1999) maintained that when geometric representation reaches a certain degree of flexibility (after the age of 6 or 7 years) semantic forces can intervene in children's graphic routines. Our preschoolers drew the neutral stimulus with a better 3D graphic quality than they drew the symbolic stimulus. Whereas Vinter's younger participants (6 to 7 years old) did not change their graphic syntax, our own 3- to 5-year-old participants, who were younger than the children Vinter examined, were strongly influenced by the object's meaning and changed the spatial characteristics of their drawings as a consequence.

These findings are only apparently contradictory, however, because we propose that when our younger participants were presented with the doll stimulus, they produced their own previously established model of the human figure, indicating a lack of flexibility thereby. Our view is therefore that they performed differently from adults and older children because they were unable to integrate the spatial and symbolic codes in their drawings (Figure 11.3). This difficulty was observed not only with children, but also with our adult participants. This finding could be viewed as an indication of an underlying diversification in spatial and symbolic processes, whose integration is never fully achieved – an interpretation that also corroborates Vinter's (1999) finding of global sensitivity to meaning, which is active at all ages, as a function of the type of analysis a model's semantics induces.

Conclusions

In conclusion, our findings suggest that the ability to use increasingly complex 3D graphic techniques (the *how* system) is linked to developmental processes that are also influenced by stimulus meaning (the *what* system).

In fact, age influences 3D drawing performance quality, in the sense that older children draw significantly more 3D elements than younger drawers do, and adults show a higher quality of three-dimensional graphic performance than children do. At the same time, however, variation in a model's meaning can influence 3D drawing quality – both in children and, to a lesser extent, in adults (the 'meaning effect').

Our observation of this phenomenon leads us to propose that the complete integration of the spatial and symbolic aspects of reality represents a great challenge for children as they develop their three-dimensional drawing ability, but it also poses difficulty even into adulthood.

Moreover, the findings reported herein suggest that the meaning of a stimulus is cognitively processed through separate systems. Specifically, when a to-be-drawn model presents strong semantic content, a conflict arises between the stimulus' geometrical structure (the spatial code) and its meaning (the symbolic code) – i.e. the 'what' interferes with the 'how' – and input processing becomes a more complex procedure (i.e. via the *semantic route*). In fact, when the semantic content of a stimulus is blurred, no conflict between the two codes arises, and 3D graphic representation in this instance is similar to the type of representation that is used for a geometrically identical stimulus (when processing occurs via the *direct route*).

NOTES

1. The present work uses the terms 'symbolic' and 'semantic' interchangeably.
2. Rakover (2002) studied the perception and memory of faces whose distinctive characteristics, their size and their distribution had been manipulated. Our own stimulus C represented a compromise between Rakover's 'jumbled face' and 'holistic invertion'. The 'jumbled face' presents variations on the spatial relations of facial features; the 'holistic invertion' involves an inversion being applied to the entire face (hair included), but with unvaried spatial relations. The characteristics of our stimulus C face were therefore inverted by following Rakover's 'holistic invertion' rules (but excluding the hair), rendering the suggestion of semantic discrepancy thereby.

REFERENCES

Arnheim, R. (1974). *Art and visual perception: a psychology of the creative eye*. Berkeley: University of California Press.

Barrett, M. D. and Light, P. H. (1976). Symbolism and intellectual realism in children's drawings. *British Journal of Educational Psychology*, 46, 198–202.

Bremner, J. G. and Batten, A. (1991). Sensitivity to viewpoint in children's drawings of objects and relations between objects. *Journal of Experimental Child Psychology*, 52, 375–94.

Bremner, J. G., Morse, R., Hughes, S. and Andreasen, G. (2000). Relations between drawing cubes and copying line diagrams of cubes in 7 to 10-years-old children. *Child Development*, 71, 621–34.

Cannoni, E. (2003). *Il disegno dei bambini [The drawings of children]*. Rome: Carocci.

Case, R. and Okamoto, Y. (1996). The role of central conceptual structures in the development of children's thought. *Monographs of the Society for Research in Child Development (SRCD)*, 61, 1–2.

Chen, M. J. and Cook, M. (1984). Representational drawings of solid objects by young children. *Perception*, 13, 377–85.

Cox, M. V. and Perara, J. (1998). Children's observational drawings. A nine-point scale for scoring drawings of a cube. *Educational Psychology*, 18, 309–17.

Davis, A. M. (1985). The canonical bias: young children's drawing of familiar objects. In N. H. Freeman and M. V. Cox (eds.), *Visual order: the nature and development of pictorial representation* (pp. 202–13). Cambridge: Cambridge University Press.

Feldman, D. H. (2000). Figurative and operative processes in the development of artistic talent. *Human Development*, 43, 60–4.

Freeman, N. H. (1980). *Strategies of representation in young children: analysis of spatial skills and drawing processes*. London: Academic Press.

Freeman, N. H. and Cox, M. V. (eds.) (1985). *Visual order: the nature and development of pictorial representation*. Cambridge: Cambridge University Press.

Golomb, C. (2002). *Child arts in context: a cultural and comparative perspective*. Washington, DC: American Psychological Association.

Gombrich, E. H. (1960). *Art and Illusion: a study in the psychology of pictorial representation*. London: Pantheon Books.

Goodnow, J. J. (1977). *Children's drawing*. London: Open Books.

Ingram, N. (1985). Three into two won't go: symbolic and spatial coding processes in young children's drawings. In N. H. Freeman and M. V. Cox (eds.), *Visual order: the nature and development of pictorial representation* (pp. 231–47). Cambridge: Cambridge University Press.

Lange-Küttner, C. (2000). The role of object violation in the development of visual analysis. *Perceptual and Motor Skills*, 86, 1299–1310.

Lange-Küttner, C., Kerzmann, A. and Heckhausen, J. (2002). The emergence of visually realistic contour in the drawing of the human figure. *British Journal of Developmental Psychology*, 3, 439–63.

Lee, M. and Bremner, J. G. (1987). The representation of depth in children's drawings of a table. *Quarterly Journal of Experimental Psychology*, 39A, 479–96.

Luquet, G. H. (1927). *Le dessin enfantin [Children's drawings]*. Paris: Alcan.

Marr, D. (1982). *Vision*. San Francisco, CA: Freeman.

Morassi, L. and Tallandini, M. A. (2006). Graphic representation: a model of interaction between the spatial and the symbolic component. Paper presented at the XIVth Symposium of Perception and Cognition. Trieste, Italy.

Morra, S., Moizo, C. and Scopesi, A. (1988). Working memory (or the M operator) and the planning of children's drawings. *Journal of Experimental Psychology*, 46, 41–73.
Nicholls, A. L. and Kennedy, J. M. (1992). Drawing development: from similarity of features to direction. *Child Development*, 63, 227–41.
(1995). Foreshortening in cube drawings by children and adults. *Perception*, 24, 1443–56.
Piaget, J. (1977). The role of action in the development of thinking. In F. W. Overton and J. MacCarthy Gallagher (eds.), *Knowledge and Development*. Vol. 1, *Advances in Research and Theory* (pp. 17–42). New York: Plenum Press.
Phillips, W. A., Hobbs, S. B. and Pratt, F. R. (1978). Intellectual realism in children's drawings of cubes. *Cognition*, 6, 15–33.
Rakover, S. S. (2002). Featural vs configurational information in faces: a conceptual and empirical analysis. *British Journal of Psychology*, 93, 1–30.
Reith, E. (1990). Development of representational awareness and performance in drawing production. *Archives de Psychologie*, 58, 369–79.
Rothi, L. J., Ochipa, C. and Heilman, K. M. (1991). A cognitive neuropsychological model of limb praxis. *Cognitive Neuropsychology*, 8, 443–58.
Sheppard, E., Ropar, D. and Mitchell, P. (2005). The impact of meaning and dimensionality on the accuracy of children's copying. *British Journal of Developmental Psychology*, 23, 365–81.
Tallandini, M. A. and Morassi, L. (2002). Modalità di rappresentazione proiettiva nel disegno infantile [Types of projective representation in children's drawing]. In G. Di Stefano and R. Vianello (eds.), *Psicologia dello sviluppo e problemi educativi* [*Developmental psychology and educational issues*]. Florence: Giunti.
(2005). The relation between spatial and symbolic components in children's drawing. Paper presented at the 12th European Conference on Developmental Psychology, 24–28 August.
Tallandini, M. A., Morassi, L. and Gerbino, W. (1999). *The development of representation of tridimensional objects and the relation between spatial and symbolic code*. Biennal Meeting of Society for Research in Child Development (SRCD), Albuquerque, New Mexico.
Tallandini, M. A. and Valentini, P. (1990). Lo sviluppo del disegno infantile: teorie studiali [The development of drawing in children: theoretical studies]. *Età Evolutiva*, 37, 92–105.
(1991). Strategie rappresentative nel disegno infantile di un oggetto sociale. [Representational strategies in the drawing of a social object in children]. In G. Di Stefano and M.A Tallandini (eds.), *Meccanismi e processi di sviluppo: l'interpretazione postpiagetiana* [*Mechanisms and processes of development: a post-Piagetian perspective*]. Milan: Cortina.
Tallandini, M. A. and Varesano, E. (2003). Il processo produttivo nella rappresentazione grafica [The production processes in graphic representations]. *Età Evolutiva*, 76, 64–71.
Tessari, A. and Rumiati, R. I. (2004). The strategic control of multiple routes in imitation to actions. *Journal of Experimental Child Psychology: Human Perception and Performance*, 30, 1107–16.

Toomela, A. (1999). Drawing development: stages in the representation of a cube and a cylinder. *Child Development*, 70, 1141–50.

(2002). Drawing as a verbally mediated activity: a study of relationships between verbal, motor, and visuo-spatial skills and drawing in children. *International Journal of Behavioral Development*, 26, 234–47.

Van Sommers, P. (1984). *Drawing and cognition: descriptive and experimental studies of graphic production processes*. Cambridge: Cambridge University Press.

Vinter, A. (1999). How meaning modifies drawing behaviour in children. *Child Development*, 70, 33–49.

Willats, J. (1977). How children learn to draw realistic pictures. *Quarterly Journal of Experimental Psychology*, 29, 367–82.

(1981). What do the marks in the picture stand for? The child's acquisition of systems on transformation and denotation. *Review of Research in Visual Arts Education*, 13, 18–33.

(1985). Drawing systems revisited: the role of denotation systems in children's figure drawings. In N. H. Freeman and M. V. Cox (eds.), *Visual order: the nature and development of pictorial representation* (pp. 78–100). Cambridge: Cambridge University Press.

(2003). Optical laws or symbolic rules? The dual nature of pictorial systems. In H. Hecht and R. Schwartz (eds.), *Looking into pictures: an interdisciplinary approach to pictorial space* (pp. 125–43). Cambridge, MA: MIT Press.

(2005). *Making sense of children's drawing*. London: Lawrence Erlbaum.

12   On contours seen and contours drawn

Jan B. Derȩgowski

Derȩgowski describes the ambiguities of object representations in pictorial space, in terms of dimensionality as well as view-specificity. On the basis of models of visual perception, he distinguishes between boundary contours, which result from the interaction of the solid and the background, and typical contours, which are inherent characteristics of the object itself. In several studies, he demonstrates empirically that typical contours can facilitate recognition if the object is in a fronto-parallel plane and thus this view is the most commonly depicted. However, several typical contours may compete for attention, in particular in children and illiterate adults. One solution was to depict several views of the object simultaneously in a co-planar fashion, as is demonstrated in several examples from ancient art and children. Another instance of the conflict between boundary and typical contour is the depiction of eyes (eye spots) in the fronto-parallel plane versus in profile, or, when in conflict, in a mixed version with eyes depicted en face but with the face contours in profile. Derȩgowski finally concludes that whereas canonical contours establish themselves with experience, typical contours could be specified also for novel objects, and typical contour therefore seems the more satisfactory concept.

On contours seen

Each object within the observer's field of view furnishes a great variety of cues from which, combined and blended, his percept of the object arises.[1] The visual cues as to the *shape* of the object fall into two distinct categories: (i) the outline of the object as seen against its background, and (ii) the cues deriving from the visible surface of the object. Both categories derive from the same source to which Gibson (1950) and his followers attended with such zest – the texture gradients.

239

240 *Jan B. Deręgowski*

Figure 12.1(a) A camouflaged bird.

Figure 12.1(b) The camouflage improved by removal of the contours within the typical contour. The figure in the bottom right-hand corner shows the bird as it appears in Figure 12.1a.

A texture gradient of an object is normally different from that of its background and this difference is seen as the object's edge or outline. When it is absent the object and the background merge; the object is camouflaged. Such is the case with the bird shown in Figure 12.1a. Its concealment is, however, not perfect because cues of the second kind,

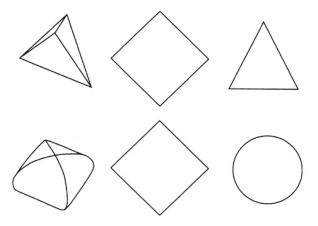

Figure 12.2 A tetrahedron and two projections of its boundary contour, and immediately below a clegg and its corresponding projections.

those deriving from its surface, are there. Removal of these cues would, as Figure 12.1b shows, strengthen the camouflage. The insert in Figure 12.1b shows the enlargement of the bird shown in Figure 12.1a.

The boundary line between the two texture gradients, that of the background and that of the object, will be called a *boundary contour.*

The shape of the boundary contour depends on the orientation of the object. The bird's boundary contour would be quite different if it were photographed from a different angle. Indeed, two distinct solids can project similar boundary contours. For example, the tetrahedron (a solid having four triangular faces, Figure 12.2) can project a square boundary contour, and so can the *clegg* (a solid formed by the orthogonal intersection of two cylinders) shown below it. These two solids can also project quite distinct shapes: a tetrahedron as a triangle and a clegg as a circle.

Boundary contours, therefore, do not offer infallible means for identification of a shape. Further contours which are present within the area delimited by the boundary facilitate identification, as figures showing both the tetrahedron and the clegg demonstrate.

These additional contours are attributes of the solid alone and are created by the texture gradients of the solid's surface. They indicate a rapid change in the shape of the surface, and are termed *typical contours.* The essential difference between the two types of contours, boundary and typical, is that whilst the former is the result of interaction of the solid and its background, the latter is an inherent characteristic of the solid.

Figure 12.3 One of the stimuli used in the discrimination learning task.

Solids differ in cogency of their typical contours. The sphere is at the very extreme of the range, having no typical contour at all. It is the only solid defined solely by the shape of its boundary contour and the uniformly changing texture gradient within the contour. In contrast a flat lamella has a very pronounced typical contour which runs along its edge. The edge of the lamella and its background jointly determine the shape of its boundary contour, the shape of which depends on the lamella's orientation; when the lamella is in the observer's fronto-parallel plane its boundary contour has identical shape with that of its typical contour; the contours are geometrically congruent.

If contours of solids have perceptual significance as suggested above, then one would expect models with different contours and models differing in visibility of contours to evoke distinct percepts.

In order to investigate this, models which were unlikely to be familiar to subjects were used (Deręgowski, Parker and Dziurawiec, 1996). The subjects were young children. They were seated in front of the apparatus but were not otherwise restricted. The method was that of discrimination learning whereby the difficulty of identifying one of the paired stimuli is measured. The models (Figure 12.3) had either two pronounced contours, one in each of the orthogonal vertical planes, one of the contours (the principal contour) was much more pronounced than the other (the minor contour), or only one (either principal or minor) contour. The models were presented so oriented that either the principal contour was identical with the boundary contour, or the minor contour was identical with the boundary contour, or neither of the contours was identical with the boundary contour as the planes containing them were at 45° to the observer's fronto-parallel plane. The results obtained are summarized below in terms of difficulty of discrimination within pairs of models. (Higher numbers indicate greater difficulty.) Difficulty of discrimination when both contours differ and the principal contour is in the observer's fronto-parallel plane (the condition in which fewest difficulties occurred) is taken as unity.

When the stimuli are presented with their differing contours in the observer's fronto-parallel plane and differ only in their principal contours, the score is 5; when they differ only in their minor contours, the score is 9. This confirms that the contours differ in cogency.

When stimuli differing in their principal contours only are presented at an angle to the observer's fronto-parallel plane, the difficulties increase with the increase of the angle. Stimuli at 45° yield a score of 7, those at 90° a score of 11. The orientation of the typical contour seems therefore of consequence. All the results are summarized in Figure 12.4.

The role of the principal typical contour was further investigated using subjects drawn from the same population. Each subject was shown an unfamiliar geometric model on a turntable so that it was displayed in the round, and following this, three replicas of that stimulus were set in different orientations; the subject was then invited to point to the replica which looked most like the rotating stimulus. Subjects chose stimuli which had either the principal or the minor typical contour in the fronto-parallel plane more frequently than those which were presented with those contours at 45° to that plane. The importance of the fronto-parallel plane was thus confirmed.

In order to find out whether the effect of the fronto-parallel plane is also to be found in adults a different procedure was used (Deręgowski and McGeorge, 1998a). Subjects were briefly shown vertical pentagonal lamellae in a 3 × 3 array and were required to reproduce the arrangement on an identical display board. The orientation of the lamellae of the stimulus display was varied. It was found, as would be expected, that lamellae corresponding to those whose typical contours lie outwith the fronto-parallel plane were placed with their typical contours closer to the fronto-parallel plane than the initiating stimuli. The tendency to encode stimuli as if their typical contours were in the fronto-parallel plane is also present in adults. Another experiment involving adults (Deręgowski and McGeorge, 1998b) showed that the distinctiveness of typical contours affects significantly the perceived similarity of solids.

It seems unlikely that such a striking perceptual characteristic as contours would not affect the manner in which the artist draws his percept

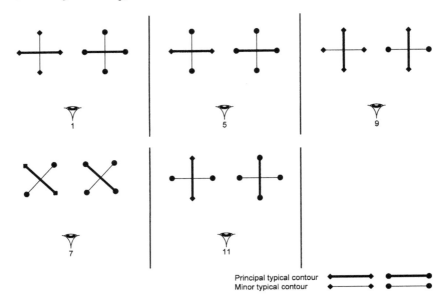

Figure 12.4 Results of the discrimination learning task. The two planes containing the typical contours are shown by two lines (major contour by a thicker line) and the line ending, indicating either similarity or difference of the shapes of contours. The position of the observer is shown by the 'eye'. The number below the eye is the difficulty score. The larger the number, the more difficult the discrimination.

of the object, and indeed there are data showing that, as far as perspective is concerned, the same perceptual mechanisms operate in the case of three-dimensional models and drawings of those models (Deręgowski, Shepherd and Slaven, 1997).

The role of typical contours in depictions will now be considered.

On contours drawn

Depictions, be they rock engravings, finger tracings or paintings, are the enduring documents of human cognitive activity, extending further back in time than any comparable artefacts. The artist's task was then and still is to create an object such that its percept is in some way reminiscent of the percept of the model; in the case of a draughtsman or a painter to create such a depiction. This can be done either by re-creating the cues provided by the original model, or by means of a perceptual shortcut, by creating derivative cues such as are present in the percept of the model.

On contours seen and contours drawn 245

Figure 12.5 Palaeolithic portrait of a mammoth.

It has been shown that in three-dimensional models such derivative cues are associated with lines which occur whenever the texture gradient changes markedly. This chapter will be concerned with depiction of objects by means of such lines, a device accessible to an artist equipped with the simplest of implements, a pencil, a stylus or even just a finger.

A stone age artist drew the figure shown above (Figure 12.5), using such a simple implement. The noteworthy fact about this figure is that it is immediately recognizable as portraying a mammoth. The typical contour of the animal's back depicted by the artist is sufficient to convey this information. The typical contour is at its most telling, as studies of perception show, when in the fronto-parallel plane. This, therefore, is the line to draw and this is what the stone age artist did when he drew the shape of the mammoth's spine. Such portrayal is a considerable achievement, for it is unlikely that the mammoth posed for the artist, patiently presenting his spine in the fronto-parallel plane. The artist must have abstracted its shape in the course of observations made in occasional encounters, just as children abstracted the percept of an unfamiliar geometrical model in the experiment described above.

Sometimes identification of the contour to be depicted may be difficult. The artist may have to decide which of the typical contours is characteristic of the model, and which is merely a minor inconsequential detail. The task is relatively easy in the case of the axe shown in Figure 12.6, where minor typical contours showing the roughness of its face are readily dismissible, so that its edge (just like the edge of a lamella) is clearly the dominant typical contour to be portrayed. The task is much more difficult when the minor typical contour is associated with a particularly important feature. In the case of the human head eyes are such a feature,

Figure 12.6 A stone age axe.

and as Swindler (1931) has shown, it took the ancient Greek vase painter considerable time to learn to treat the typical contour of the eye as a minor feature of the human head, so that the dominant typical contour, the profile, remained unchallenged.

The decision as to how to depict competing contours is particularly difficult when the choice has to be made from several typical contours of equal cogency and in distinct planes, as is the case of a cube. Bartel found (1927; for a brief summary of these findings see Deręgowski, 1986; for general background to Bartel see Deręgowski, 1994) that both children and illiterate adults find it difficult to draw cuboids. Some drawings made by illiterate adults are shown in Figure 12.7. These are the more complex depictions of a simple rectangular box. The most common depiction consisted simply of a rectangle, and the next most common, of two rectangles, one within another. Over 80 per cent of drawings fell into these two categories.

Children from a primary school in Kenya (Deręgowski, 1976) drew a cube on display as assemblies of quadrilaterals, just as Bartel's subjects did, but did not do so when shown a *picture* of a cube, showing their drawings of the cube to be a consequence not of motor but of perceptual abilities, and that non-co-planarity of typical contours of the cube was probably responsible for the result.

Fortunately for Palaeolithic artists, equines and bovines presented no comparable difficulties. Not only do these animals have pronounced

Figure 12.7 Drawings of an oblong box done by illiterate adult men. (After Bartel, 1927)

planar typical contours which run along their spines, but such contours are generally seen in the vertical plane. It is therefore not surprising that depictions of these animals are commonplace in early art. Pictures of perceptually difficult animals who lack such attributes are rare, as are pictures of humans. Felines are difficult to depict because they lack stable typical contours. Photographs of a cat taken within ten minutes (Figure 12.8) show the extent of changes of its shape, and although in each position its body has contours, these vary to such an extent from position to position that it is impossible to decide which shape represents the cat. Its spine is now convex, now concave, now s-shaped. When asked to draw a cat from memory one is inclined to ask 'Which cat?' And so Leroi-Gourhan (1982) reports that the ratio of felines to other animals in rupestral art of the Dordogne is 1:60.

Even in ancient Egypt, a culture favourably disposed to cats (Germond and Livet, 2001; Keller, 1909) pictures of cats were not numerous. One can, of course, portray a cat by depicting it in one of its poses, choosing either a pose shared with other animals or an anthropomorphic pose, and

248 *Jan B. Deręgowski*

Figure 12.8 Does a cat have a shape? Eight poses of Belzebub photographed within 10 minutes.

incorporating in the picture such an unmistakable feature as, say, the tail. This was, indeed, done on a very whimsical *ostrakon* (a drawing done on a flake of limestone) which contrasts pleasantly with the contemporary ancient Egyptian hieratic art. A cat is handing a fish to a mouse seated on a stool (Figure 12.9). The mouse holds in one of his paws a skeleton of a fish he has just eaten and in the other a *phial*. He is being invited by the cat to continue his un-mouse-like repast. All the elements of the picture are shown by their combination of typical and boundary contours, in accordance with the rule that in the fronto-parallel plane typical contours convey the depicted items most clearly, the very fact that is responsible for the use of silhouettes, by ancient Greek vase painters and much later by the great silhouette cutters such as M. August Edouart, who travelled the world snipping silhouettes of the famous early in the nineteenth century (Deręgowski, 1984).

There are animals whose bodies have unchanging planar typical contours, but these contours lie in planes at an angle to each other. This is so in the case of horned animals; the typical contour of the animal's back is in a plane orthogonal to the plane of its horns. The artist is therefore faced

Figure 12.9 Ancient Egyptian ostrakon. (After Swindler, 1931)

Figure 12.10 The La Grèze bison. (After Swindler, 1931)

with a problem similar to that facing a child drawing a cube (Freeman, 1986). The solution adopted by the author of the La Grèze bison (Figure 12.10), and later enshrined in formal ancient Egyptian art (Michałowski, 1969), is to portray both typical contours as if they were co-planar. The same solution was adopted by Australian Aborigine artists for depiction of crocodiles. The crocodile depicted in Figure 12.11 is clearly

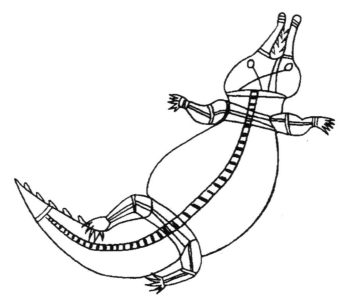

Figure 12.11 A crocodile. A traditional Australian portrayal. (After Spencer, 1904 and Chaloupka, 1983)

uncomfortably twisted but the typical contours of its three concatenated body parts lie in the same plane, the plane of the picture.

Inspired by the Australian pictures, Dziurawiec and Deręgowski (1992) presented children with tripartite models and requested that these be drawn. The three elements of the models, the head, the body and the tail, could lie either in the same plane or in orthogonal planes. They found that, like Australian artists, children tended to draw the models so that the typical contours of the three parts lay in the plane of the picture.

In a further study (Deręgowski and Dziurawiec, 1994) young children were presented with specially made models and required to draw them. Each model consisted of a sphere with one or more tangential square lamellae attached to it. The space between the lamellae and the sphere was filled in so as to obtain a smooth transition. When more than one lamella was used the lamellae were mutually orthogonal. The models were always presented with one of the square faces at 45° to the child's fronto-parallel plane. Analysis of drawings obtained showed a very strong tendency (92 per cent of responses) to draw models with only one square surface as if the square typical contour lay in the fronto-parallel plane. This tendency to depict squares by squares declined markedly with the increase of the number of square surfaces and therefore with the increase of non-co-planar typical contours. The corresponding scores were: for the solid having two square faces, 55 per cent; for the solid having three square faces, 37 per cent; and for the control cube, 28 per cent. Thus children depicting these solids used the typical contours, and presentation of non-co-planar contours obliged them to abandon the stratagem of drawing these contours 'as they really are', and to introduce distortions which can be thought of as perspective-like. This effect was more pronounced in the responses of older children. Whether this is the effect of ageing or of learning is uncertain, but a drawing obtained by Bartel from illiterate adults and Serpell's (1979) African data favour the latter interpretation.

It has been shown by Binet (1890) that children are not disturbed by incoherence of depicted animals, such as, for example, giraffes with dogs' heads, but simply name them by reference to one of their parts. It has also been shown (Young and Deręgowski, 1981) that such tolerance of inconsistency also occurs when 'impossible' figures (such as a two-pronged trident) are presented; children perceive correctly the apparent three-dimensionality of the elements, but fail to perceive that distinct elements are spatially mutually contradictory. They attend, it would appear, to one element at a time.

These observations may also apply to the actions of the artist drawing the Australian crocodile – he draws one typical contour at a time, and he draws it as if it were in the pictorial plane. He is not in the least concerned with the fact that the separate elements, which are not co-planar, are shown as such. One would, indeed, expect the very act of drawing, since the elements are drawn one at a time, to reinforce the tendency to treat the elements as being independent. As a result occasionally striking and puzzling pictures appear, such as those of elephants, one from Shiraz, Iran, and one from China (Figure 12.12). In the case of each elephant both front legs are on the same side of the body. (One can but admire the canniness of the artist who drew the mammoth in Figure 12.5. By not drawing the legs he conveyed his meaning and avoided this trap.)

An even more striking instance of the phenomenon is provided by the fifteenth-century decorator of Boccacio's *De claris mulieribus*, who unwittingly, one suspects, anticipated many geometric figures to be found in the learned twentieth-century treatises on perception (Figure 12.13).

Artists can also create depictions which consist of a blend of typical contours and purely linear elements. This is so in a rock engraving from Bohuslän in Sweden from about 500 BC (Figure 12.14). The two oxen, whose horns show that they are viewed from above, pull a four-wheeled cart, whose wheels show that it is viewed laterally. The bodies of the oxen are not, however, shown by their typical outlines. They have been reduced to mere lines, as have their legs, and it is the juxtaposition of

252 *Jan B. Deręgowski*

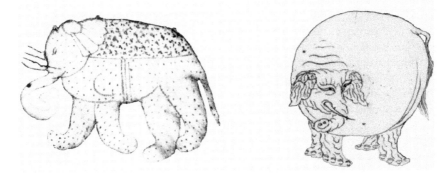

Figure 12.12 A Persian and a Chinese portrayal of an elephant.

Figure 12.13 A weaver working at an impossible loom (detail).

these elements and the horns that conveys what animals these are. Such reduction to purely linear form and abandonment of typical contours carries a penalty of losing the ability to distinguish among certain species of animals. Man, whose upright posture distinguishes him from all other animals, remains clearly identifiable even in such minimalist depictions

Figure 12.14 An engraving from Bohuslän.

as a finger drawing done in a tray of sand by a Bushman (Reuning and Wortley, 1973) or those done by Tale who had never drawn before (Fortes, 1940, 1981).

This is, indeed, an ingenious solution of a very complex problem of drawing a man, an object with several distinct typical contours, the profile of the head, the shape of the eye, the shoulders and the feet. Ancient Egyptians solved it by rigidly adhering to typical contours. Palaeolithic artists eschewed it; and in spite of their intrinsic interest to the artist, anthropomorphic depictions in the Dordogne constitute less than 5 per cent of the total number (Leroi-Gourhan, 1982). Man is a difficult beast to draw.

Other factors than mere shape of the typical contours may affect recognition of objects. Familiarity with objects is such a factor. It is, however, a factor remote from pure perception. Eyespots are a purely perceptual vector which affects both depiction and recognition of animate objects and which derives not from the shape of the model, but from the importance attached to one particular feature. There is ample evidence that animals respond to eyes and to eyespots in a specific manner. Garter snakes strike decoys with eyespots and ignore those without (Bern and Herzog, 1994). The northern pygmy owl has eyespots on the nape which serve to deflect mobbing birds in such a way as to make it easier for the owl to catch them (Deppe, Holt, Tweksbury, Broberg, Petersen and Wood, 2003). Responses of children to models are affected by eyespots, and eyespots within the outline of a head affect the perceived orientation of the outline (Dziurawiec and Deregowski, 2002, 2007).

The problem of picture makers is twofold and concerns both depiction of a single eye and depiction of a pair of eyes. The difficulties experienced by the Greek vase painters when depicting an eye in a face drawn in profile have already been described. The difficulties associated with depiction of two eyes arise because eyes of many creatures, human beings included, are in a different plane from the dominant typical contour of the head. A

Figure 12.15 A Spanish medieval beast.

solution sometimes used is the same as that used when depicting the horns of a bovine: the eyes are drawn as if they were co-planar or very nearly so with the dominant typical contour. Thus the same solution is used, although the origins of the perceptual difficulties are different, being in the one case the non-co-planarity of pronounced typical contours, and in the other, primarily, the suasion of the eyespots. The device was used by a medieval Spanish artist who drew an apocalyptic beast (depicted in Figure 12.15) and by Picasso in his portrait of Marie-Thérèse. Young children of the early twentieth century have, as Wilson and Wilson (1982) show, favoured this solution, but later generations have, for reasons unknown, abandoned the profile in favour of the eyes, so that by far the most frequent response to the draw-a-man task is the face as seen from the front.

The ancient Egyptian artists also showed a lurking liking for *en face* portrayals. Their professional code required that heads be shown in profile, but in circumstances where its application could be relaxed, as when portraying men of inferior status, heads were occasionally depicted *en face*. Thus in a melee presented on Tutankhamen's ornate chest (Figure 12.16) about a fifth of the defeated, fleeing enemies look squarely at the viewer, but the victorious Egyptians invariably advance showing only their profiles. Depictions of the faces of the vanquished are therefore bimodally distributed, as the two perceptual vectors, the typical contour and the eyespots, would lead one to expect.

Envoi

Contours are characteristic of all solid objects, which enable observers to distinguish between objects and to depict objects. The notion of a typical contour, a *physical* characteristic of an object, which is in principle

Figure 12.16 An ancient battle as portrayed on Tutankhamen's chest (detail).

determinable, implies that one can, by examining an object in the round, determine how it should be presented and how it should be depicted to ensure optimal recognition. This seems a more satisfactory notion than that of the canonical view which accepts that objects are more easily recognized from certain stances than from others, but does not define precisely how these stances are determined – the canon of the canonical view does not seem to be readily accessible.

It may well be that familiarity with objects and their depiction establishes certain aspects of these objects as canonical, but the process involved in this is that of perceptual learning, rather than that of simple perception, and as such is likely to be influenced by the culture and the environment of the learner, but it is impossible to determine, a priori, the canonical aspects of novel objects. In contrast, the notion of typical contours applies equally to all objects, familiar and unfamiliar.

The notion of typical contours also seems more satisfactory than any notion based on analysis of a solid into basic geometric components, because it does not call for categorization or 'rounding off' of stimuli with unusual shapes, as in Figure 12.3, in order to make them fit into a framework of postulated geometrical entities.

However, Deręgowski and McGeorge's studies (1998a, 1998b) suggest that depiction of an object by means of its dominant typical contour carries with it an implication of flatness; and since depictions by means of typical contours are obtained when the draughtsman draws 'from memory', unanswered questions arise: Are mental representations flattish? Are they 'compressed' so that the dominant contour remains unchanged, but other less salient features are distorted?

This chapter is concerned with simple linear portrayals. It does not treat on all the vectors affecting perception and depiction. It shows how texture gradients 'create' contours. These, however, are not the only factors forming the percept. Perception is not a purely 'optical' process – it depends on the 'preparedness of mind' (Arber, 1954), and as does perception, so does depiction.

NOTE

1. The author is indebted to Mr P. Bates for preparation of all the figures. He is also indebted to the Gulbenkian Museum of Lisbon for photographs of dishes, elements of which were used to compose Figure 12.12.

REFERENCES

Arber, A. (1954). *The mind and the eye*. Cambridge: Cambridge University Press.
Bartel, K. (1927/58). *Perspektywa malarska* [Painterly perspective]. Warsaw: Panstwowe Wydawnictwo Naukowe.
Bern, C. and Herzog, H. A. (1994). Stimulus control of defensive behaviours of garter snakes (*Thamnophis sirtalis*): Effects of eyespots and movement. *Journal of Comparative Psychology*, 108, 353–7.
Binet, A. (1890). Perception d'enfant [Children's perception]. *Revue Philosophique*, 30, 47–72.
Chaloupka, G. (1983). *From palaeoart to casual painting*. Darwin Northern Territory Museum of Arts and Sciences.
Deppe, C., Holt, D., Tweksbury, J., Broberg, L., Petersen, J. and Wood, K. (2003). Effect of northern pygmy owl (*Glaucidium gnoma*) eyespots on avian mobbing. *The Auk*, 120, 765–71.
Deręgowski, J. B. (1976). Coding and drawing of simple geometric stimuli by Bukusu school-children in Kenya. *Journal of Cross-Cultural Psychology*, 7, 195–208.
  (1984). *Distortion in art: the eye and the mind*. London: Routledge and Kegan Paul.

(1986). Kazimierz Bartel's observations on drawings of children and illiterate adults. *British Journal of Developmental Psychology*, 4, 331–3.
(1994). Bartel, K. (1882–1941). *Psychologie und Geschichte*, 5, 246–60.
Deręgowski, J. B. and Dziurawiec, S. (1994). Perceptual impulsions and unfamiliar solids: evidence from a drawing task. *British Journal of Psychology*, 85, 1–15.
Deręgowski, J. B. and McGeorge, P. (1998a). The role of typical contours in encodement of objects in three-dimensional arrays. *Perception*, 27, 283–94.
(1998b). Perceived similarity of shapes is an asymmetrical relationship. *Perception*, 27, 35–46.
Deręgowski, J. B., Parker, D. M. and Dziurawiec, S. (1996). The role of typical contours in object processing by children. *British Journal of Developmental Psychology*, 14, 425–40.
Deręgowski, J. B., Shepherd, J. and Slaven, G. A. (1997). Sex differences on Bartel's test. *British Journal of Psychology*, 88, 637–51.
Dziurawiec, S. and Deręgowski, J. B. (1992). Twisted perspective in young children's drawings. *British Journal of Developmental Psychology*, 10, 35–49.
(2002). The eyes have it: perceptual investigation of eyespots. *Perception*, 31, 1313–22.
(2007). The perceptual effect of eyespots, or the devil may seem closer than she really is. *Australian Journal of Psychology*, 59, 101–7.
Fortes, M. (1940). Children's drawings among the Tallensi. *Africa*, 13, 293–5.
(1981). Tallensi children's drawings. In B. Lloyd and J. Gay (eds.), *Universals of human thought*. Cambridge: Cambridge University Press.
Freeman, N. H. (1986). How should a cube be drawn? *British Journal of Developmental Psychology*, 4, 317–22.
Germond, P. and Livet, J. (2001). *An Egyptian bestiary*. London: Thames and Hudson.
Gibson, J. J. (1950). *The perception of the visual world*. Boston: Riverside Press.
Keller, O. (1909). *Die antike Tierwelt, I* [*The antique animal world, I*]. Leipzig: Engelmann.
Leroi-Gourhan, A. (1982). *The dawn of European art*. Cambridge: Cambridge University Press.
Michałowski, K. (1969). *Art of ancient Egypt*. London: Thames and Hudson.
Reuning, H. and Wortley, W. (1973). Psychological studies of the Bushmen. *Psychologia Africana Monographs*. Supplement No. 7.
Serpell, R. (1979). How specific are perceptual skills – study of pattern reproduction. *British Journal of Psychology*, 70, 365–80.
Spencer, B. (1904). *The northern tribes of central Australia*. London: Macmillan.
Swindler, M. H. (1931). *Ancient painting*. New Haven, CT: Yale University Press.
Young, A. W. and Deręgowski, J. B. (1981). Learning to see the impossible. *Perception*, 10, 91–105.
Wilson, M. and Wilson, B. (1982). The case of disappearing two-eyed profile: or how little children influence drawings of little children. *Research in Visual Arts Education*, 15, 19–32.

Part III

Aging, blindness and autism

13 Benefits of graphic design expertise in old age: compensatory effects of a graphical lexicon?

Ulman Lindenberger, Yvonne Brehmer, Reinhold Kliegl and Paul B. Baltes

The research of Lindenberger, Brehmer, Kliegl and Baltes into the cognitive decline-compensating effects of expertise is based on the difference between fluid and crystallized intelligence. While fluid intelligence measures such as speed and capacity are more biologically determined and thus decline with age, crystallized intelligence measures encompass culture-based skills and factual knowledge, and are more resilient to ageing-induced decline. Would the graphic expertise of professional older designers protect them against cognitive decline compared to young designers and two age- and intelligence-matched control groups? This was tested in a training study using the Method of Loci where visualization and imagery is essential, as recall of words is cued by previously associated landmarks. As expected, graphic designers showed better performance on spatial tests than controls, but this was even more pronounced in the older group, where the designers had consistently higher scores than their age peers. While older graphic designers could not match the performance of the young groups, they did fare better than their age-matched controls in the post-training Method of Loci memory assessment. It is concluded that although graphic expertise could not entirely compensate for the biologically determined reduction in fluid intelligence, there was a positive effect on episodic memory.

COGNITIVE functioning in later periods of the adult lifespan is characterized by a dynamic interdependence between knowledge-related increments and senescent declines. To capture this interdependence, two-component models of cognition separate a biology-based component from a culture-based component of intellectual functioning (e.g. Baltes, 1987; Cattell, 1971). According to Baltes (1987), the 'mechanics' of cognition reflect the speed, accuracy and coordination of elementary cognitive processes, such as processing speed, inhibition, attention, memory capacity and reasoning. The efficacy of this component shows a monotone decrease during adulthood and early old age, and an accelerated decline in old age, probably because of aging-related changes in the brain. In contrast, the cognitive pragmatics reflect biographically acquired culture-based skills and factual knowledge, such as verbal fluency or mental arithmetic. Performance on tasks assessing this component remains invariant or even increases further with age during adulthood. In contrast to the mechanics of cognition, this component is more resilient to the effects of brain aging (Baltes, 1987; Li, Lindenberger, Hommel, Aschersleben, Prinz and Baltes, 2004).

Within the pragmatics, normative bodies of knowledge that are taught in school and relevant for all members of society, such as verbal knowledge and number facility, can be set apart from more specialized bodies of knowledge reflecting professional expertise or other less invariant aspects of a person's biography. Research in the domains of cognitive aging and expertise has emphasized the influence of these non-normative or idiosyncratic forms of pragmatic knowledge to between-person (interindividual) differences and within-person (intraindividual) changes in cognitive functioning. Age-comparative studies with individuals differing in their levels of expertise have been conducted in such diverse domains as typewriting (Bosman, 1993; Salthouse, 1984), chess (Charness, 1981, 1989; Jastrzembski, Charness and Vasyukova, 2006), Go playing (Masunaga and Horn, 2001), air-traffic control and piloting (Morrow and Leirer, 1997; Morrow et al., 2003), Mastermind (Maylor, 1994), crossword-puzzle solving (Rabbitt, 1993), management skills (Walsh and Hershey, 1993), piano playing (Krampe, Engbert and Kliegl, 2001; Krampe and Ericsson, 1996) and visual identification (Viggiano, Righi and Galli, 2006). In addition to questions regarding the causes and origins of expert knowledge and expert performance in specific domains of functioning, two issues have attracted the interest of developmental researchers: (a) Do individual differences in person-specific pragmatic and expert knowledge influence the developmental pathway of the mechanics of cognition (Krampe and Ericsson, 1996; Salthouse, 1991)? (b) To what extent does biographically acquired knowledge compensate for declines in the mechanics of cognition in old age (Bosman and Charness, 1996; for review, see Krampe, 2002; Krampe and Baltes, 2003)?

In this chapter, we report and further analyse and interpret results from an age-comparative memory training study that investigated graphic design expertise in relation to episodic memory performance (Lindenberger, Kliegl and Baltes, 1992). Lindenberger et al. (1992) investigated younger and older expert graphic designers' serial word recall after instruction and training in the use of an imagery-based mnemonic strategy, the Method of Loci. This strategy involves the use of a highly familiar ordered sequence of locations (i.e. a mental map) as a cognitive structure for encoding and retrieving new information (cf. Bower, 1970; Kliegl, Smith and Baltes, 1989). To-be-encoded items are successively linked with locations from the mental map through the use of visual imagery. At recall, the ordered locations are mentally revisited, and the visualized items are retrieved and decoded if necessary. Evidence from different lines of research suggests that the effective use of visual imagery is a critical component in memory functioning with the Method of Loci (e.g. Baddeley and Lieberman, 1980; Kliegl, Smith and Baltes, 1990; Logie, 1986; Richardson, 1985). In comparison to the original report provided by Lindenberger et al. (1992), we will take a closer look at two covariates administered in the original study, a subtest of the Torrance Tests of Creative Thinking: Thinking Creatively with Pictures (Torrance, 1966a, 1966b) and the Card Rotation Test from the ETS battery (Ekstrom, French and Harman, 1976). We will argue that the Torrance test of visual creativity was well suited to capture central aspects of graphic designers' expert knowledge of graphical forms, and will speculate about the compensatory function of this knowledge in old graphic designers.

During the past three decades, several studies have investigated lifespan gradients in the cognitive mechanics of episodic memory with a testing-the-limits approach to instruction and training of the Method of Loci (Baltes and Kliegl, 1992; Brehmer, Li, Müller, Oertzen and Lindenberger, 2007; Kliegl, Smith and Baltes, 1986, 1989; Lindenberger and Baltes, 1995; Lindenberger et al., 1992; Stigsdotter Neely and Bäckman, 1993; Verhaeghen and Marcoen, 1996). From a developmental perspective, the testing-the-limits procedure aims at 'compressing' time by providing a high density of experience and arranging for an improved measurement context in order to identify an individual's latent potential in a particular domain of functioning. Typically, individuals of different ages are first given instructions for a performance-enhancing memory strategy that they were not familiar with beforehand. After large amounts of training and practice, interindividual differences in upper limits of performance (developmental reserve capacity) can be estimated with some confidence.

With respect to episodic memory, testing-the-limits studies have shown (a) that cognitively healthy younger and older adults (at least up to their 80s) can improve their performance relative to a no-instruction baseline; and (b) that performance gains and maximum performance levels decrease substantially with advancing adult age (Baltes and Kliegl, 1992; Brehmer et al., 2007; Kliegl et al., 1989, 1990; Rose and Yesavage, 1983; Singer, Lindenberger and Baltes, 2003; Thompson and Kliegl,

1991). Because negative adult age differences were magnified after training, Kliegl *et al.* (1989) concluded that the effects of cognitive aging may be more clearly identifiable at performance conditions near the upper limits of reserve capacity, or cognitive plasticity, than at baseline performance conditions (Baltes and Kliegl, 1992).

The Lindenberger *et al.* (1992) study, which is summarized and further interpreted in the present report, combined the testing-the-limits paradigm with research on the relation between professional expertise and adult age changes in cognitive functioning. To this end, the authors investigated older adults with a high amount of task-relevant pre-experimental practice, knowledge and ability ('talent') in order to investigate whether the combination of professional expertise and talent is able to mitigate or even eliminate negative adult age differences in upper limits of episodic memory performance (Baltes and Kliegl, 1992; Kliegl *et al.*, 1989).

Assuming that visual imagery is a critical component in memory functioning with the Method of Loci, Lindenberger *et al.* searched for a profession that places a high emphasis on the generation of visual images in the context of verbal material. The profession of *graphic design* was deemed to meet this requirement. Graphic designers working as freelance artists create posters, art catalogues, and advertisements in newspapers and news magazines, as well as other kinds of pictorial representations. They communicate pictorial representations both verbally and visually, and are experts in integrating desired information into their design. Frequently, they need to create easily detectable and recognizable pictograms that tie concepts and emotional states to the target product. It appeared plausible to assume that the kind of creative visual imagery needed to achieve expert levels of performance in this type of professional activity would facilitate the acquisition and use of an imagery-based mnemonic strategy such as the Method of Loci.

In summary, the goal of the study of Lindenberger *et al.* (1992) was to investigate whether a group of older experts with lifelong experience in the production of visual images on the basis of verbal material would be able to reach the level of performance of younger adults with or without similar task-relevant experience. To investigate this question, age and expertise were examined at two levels in a fully crossed quasi-experimental design (i.e. younger adults versus older adults, and experts versus normal 'control' individuals). In addition to memory functioning with the Method of Loci, standard marker tests of spatial visualization and visual creativity were conducted to support the legitimacy of the contrast between experts and controls.

The inferential limitations related to the quasi-experimental design of this study should be noted at the outset. A possible superiority of expert graphic designers over 'control' individuals may reflect professional expertise, superior ability or an interaction of the two (e.g. 'nurtured nature'). That is, it may reflect the accumulation of task-relevant experience and its coordination into a body of factual and procedural knowledge that can be brought to bear upon the task, but it may also reflect initial differences in talent or task-relevant 'abilities', or, in the case of older graphic designers, the fortunate biographical constellation of individuals who have been dwelling on their strengths throughout their professional lives. The latter effects may have been further accentuated by selective survival in the profession, as only people with certain talents may have been able to stay active in this highly demanding job into old age. Clearly, the present study cannot resolve these interpretational ambiguities.

Six older graphic designers (ages 64–81, $M = 69.9$ years), six normal older control adults (ages 64–80, $M = 70.5$ years), six younger graphic design students (ages 22–24, $M = 23.0$ years) and six normal younger control students (ages 21–24, $M = 22.6$ years) participated in the experiment, with three women and three men in each of the four groups. Except for two older graphic designers and two older normal participants with nine years of schooling, all research participants had completed approximately thirteen years of schooling. At the time of testing, all younger participants were undergraduates at Berlin universities. Those not specializing in graphic design were studying at other departments of the Free University of Berlin. Of the six younger graphic designers, five were at the end of their second year at the graphic design department of the Berlin School of Arts (Fachbereich Visuelle Kommunikation der Hochschule der Künste Berlin). The sixth participant had just completed her degree as a graphic designer at another Berlin graphic design school (Berufsfachschule für Fotografie, Grafik und Mode). All six older graphic designers were 'experts' in the sense that they had been, or continued to be, highly successful professionals. At the time of testing, five designers were still active in their fields; for more information, see Lindenberger et al. (1992).

Location–word pairs were used to assess episodic memory performance. The same set of twenty well-known Berlin landmarks served as location cues for all participants. The sequence of locations was geographically meaningful and corresponded to a fictitious sightseeing tour. A city map and photographs of the landmarks were used in training. A total of nine different non-overlapping twenty-item noun lists were used as to-be-learned words. The nouns of these lists had an imagery rating above 6.00 on a 7-point scale according to the norms provided by Baschek, Bredenkamp, Öhrle and Wippich (1977; see also Paivio, Yuille and Madigan, 1968). To avoid effects related to cohort, care was taken that the nouns were neither 'dated' nor 'modern'.

In contrast with most other studies with the Method of Loci, recall was cued presenting the landmarks in the same serial order as at encoding. It was assumed that graphic designers had large amounts of professional experience in *generating* visual images on the basis of verbal material, but not in *retrieving* these images without the help of external cues. Therefore, the provision of such cues was expected to maximize the beneficial effects of graphic design expertise on serial word recall with the Method of Loci. Within groups, half of the participants received the sequence of Berlin landmarks in reverse order. For the entire duration of the experiment, it was ensured that a given landmark–noun combination was never presented more than once to a participant to avoid repetition effects.

Training programme

Participants were scheduled to participate in twenty-one sessions lasting from 60 to 90 minutes each. Sessions were administered on different days, with a minimum of one day between sessions and a maximum generally not exceeding four days.

Assessment of covariates (Sessions 1 and 2). Psychometric assessment served two main purposes: (a) to test the expectation that graphic designers would perform above the level of normal control adults on measures of criterion-relevant intellectual abilities (visual creativity and spatial visualization); (b) to check whether graphic designers and controls were comparable in general (i.e. not directly expertise-related) aspects of intelligence. In the first session, the 'Parallel Lines' subtest of the Torrance Test of Creative Thinking: Thinking Creatively with Pictures was administered (Torrance, 1966a, 1966b; for a recent review, see Kim, 2006). The second session started with tests from the Hamburg-Wechsler Intelligence Test for Adults in the following order: Forward Digit Span, Backward Digit Span, Vocabulary, and Digit Symbol Substitution (Wechsler, 1964). Thereafter, two tests of spatial visualization, Card Rotation and Surface Development, were given (Ekstrom *et al.*, 1976).

Instruction in the Method of Loci (Session 3). At the beginning of Session 3, participants were introduced in detail to the Method of Loci. First, they were told about the historical origins of the method. Then, the functioning of the method was explained to them using concrete examples. The generation of interactive visual images between landmark cues and to-be-learned words was highlighted as the critical feature of the method. Graphic designers were asked to recollect aspects of their work performance that involved different forms of interactive visual imagery, and it was suggested to them that they consider the acquisition of the Method of Loci as a task that is related to their professional expertise. Other participants were asked to think of situations in which they used interactive visual imagery. They were told that they were expected to engage in this kind of activity in the following sessions. Next, all participants were given a form with the twenty Berlin landmarks in experimental sequence (which served as memory loci in the later sessions) and were told about their function in the Method of Loci. The experimenter provided a city map of Berlin, and participants were asked to locate the landmarks on the map in correct order.

Training assessment (Sessions 4–9). Five different lists of high-imagery nouns (i.e. twenty to-be-learned words each) were administered in each session. Within sessions, each of the five lists appeared only once. Two different presentation times (the time available to form an interactive image, linking the location cue and the to-be-learned word) were used during training (i.e. 4.5 s and 7.5 s per word). After the recall phase, the tutor commented on the participant's performance, and made suggestions for further improvement. For instance, the tutor stressed the importance of creating interactive visual images that combined landmark and noun information, and encouraged the participant to concentrate ('zoom in') on those aspects or details of a location that the participant considered to be most imageable.

Post-training assessment (Sessions 10–21). In each session, four different twenty-item noun lists were presented at one of three different presentation times (i.e. 7.5, 4.5 or 1.5 s per word). During the twelve sessions of post-training assessment, each combination of word lists and presentation times was administered four times (for details, see Lindenberger et al., 1992).

Results are provided in three sections. First, group differences in psychometric tests are reported. Second, data from the training sessions (sessions 4–9) are examined to check whether participants in all groups profited from training and were able to use the mnemonic technique under easy task conditions. Third, post-training group differences in post-training assessment (sessions 10–21) are analysed to investigate whether older graphic designers were able to reach the performance level of younger participants. We focus our presentation of results on expertise-related results.

Graphic fluency and Card Rotation expertise effects

Table 13.1 displays the means and standard deviations as well as relevant statistical tests for the psychometric measures. In line with findings of large-scale normative studies of cognitive aging (cf. Salthouse, 1982;

Table 13.1 *Means, standard deviations and F values for the covariates assessed in the Lindenberger et al. (1992) experiment*

	Younger adults				Older adults				F values		
	Control		Designers		Control		Designers				
Tests	M	SD	M	SD	M	SD	M	SD	Age	Expertise	Age × expertise
Criterion-relevant tests											
Torrance Visual Creativity	43.7	5.0	55.6	8.2	42.4	4.4	58.3	10.5	0.06	**20.93**	0.45
Surface Development	18.2	4.5	26.7	3.0	3.4	2.1	13.8	6.5	**59.24**	**27.63**	0.22
Card Rotation	64.5	13.6	68.8	9.9	25.2	8.2	50.2	13.4	**38.14**	**9.76**	**4.84**
Wechsler tests											
Digit Symbol Substitution	60.0	3.1	60.6	8.4	47.7	9.4	45.4	6.6	**21.51**	0.08	0.23
Vocabulary	70.3	2.1	67.7	7.0	70.3	8.0	63.3	7.8	0.63	3.13	0.44
Forward Digit Span	7.5	0.8	7.8	1.2	6.3	1.0	6.5	0.8	**9.78**	0.39	0.04
Backward Digit Span	6.2	0.8	6.7	1.4	6.5	0.8	6.3	1.0	3.62	0.58	0.14

Note. In all four age-groups, N = 6; for all F values, dfs = 1,20. Values significant at the .05 level are in bold. Raw scores are reported for all measures except for the Torrance Visual Creativity test. Scores on the latter measure represent the T-transformed (i.e. M = 50, SD = 10) unweighted composites of the scoring dimensions of fluency, flexibility and elaboration (cf. Torrance, 1966a, 1966b).

Li et al., 2004) younger adults had higher scores than older adults on indicators of the mechanics of cognition (i.e. Digit Symbol Substitution, Forward Digit Span, and marginally also for Backward Digit Symbol Span), and on both tests of spatial visualization. As expected, negative adult age differences were absent for the marker test of the pragmatics (i.e. Vocabulary). The absence of significant age differences in the Torrance Visual Creativity Test contrasts with earlier studies that report adult age differences in creative performance favouring the young (Alpaugh and Birren, 1977; Ruth and Birren, 1985).

Of particular interest is the investigation of possible expertise effects in criterion-relevant and more general measures of intellectual functioning. Graphic designers scored significantly higher on the two tests of spatial visualization and the Torrance Visual Creativity Test than control participants. With the exception of Card Rotation in younger participants, group differences between graphic designers and control participants were also significant when tested within age-groups. No significant effects of expertise were found on the Wechsler tests. The presence of differences between experts and control participants on the criterion-relevant ability markers, together with the absence of such differences on other measures of intellectual ability, was consistent with our expectations.

The inspection of raw data from the 'Parallel Lines' subtest of the Torrance Tests of Creativity is especially instructive, as expertise effects were particularly pronounced for this test, whereas age effects were not reliable. Participants were asked to provide as many different meanings to two parallel lines as possible, either by adding detail, giving the lines a verbal title, or both. The participant with the highest score, and whose test sheet is reproduced in Figure 13.1, was an older graphic designer, and three of the four best-performing individuals were older graphic designers (see Figure 13.2). Possible mechanisms that may explain older graphic designers' remarkable levels of graphical fluency will be addressed in the discussion.

For the other criterion-relevant test, Card Rotation, we observed main effects of age (higher performance in younger adults compared to older adults) and expertise (higher performance of graphic designers compared to normal controls). Interestingly, the Age × Expertise interaction was also reliable, reflecting larger expertise effects among older adults than among younger adults (see Figure 13.3). Though a firm inference is rendered impossible by the cross-sectional nature of the data, this pattern of findings is consistent with the claim that professional expertise may attenuate age-related decline in those aspects of the mechanics that are presumably closely related to professionally relevant skills.

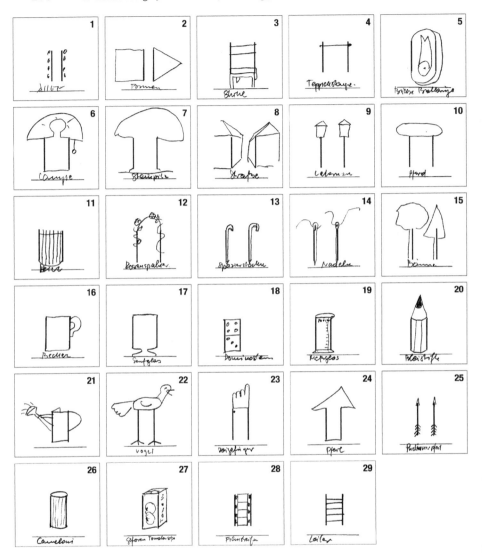

Figure 13.1 The performance of one older graphic designer in the Parallel Lines subtest of the Torrance Test of Creative Thinking: Thinking Creativity with Pictures, Form A (Torrance, 1966a, 1966b). The participant obtained the highest score on this test (see Figure 13.2).

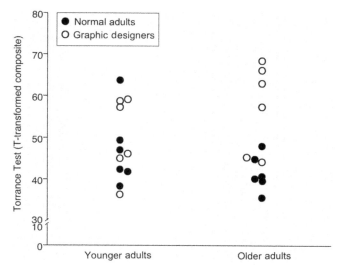

Figure 13.2 Performance of the Torrance Visual Creativity Test as a function of age-group and expertise. Scores represent T-transformed unweighted composites of the scoring dimensions of fluency, flexibility, originality and elaboration (cf. Torrance, 1966a, 1966b). Each dot refers to one participant.

Acquisition of mnemonic skill

Participants in all groups improved their performance in the course of the seven training sessions. Time did not interact with age-group or expertise, indicating that gains in recall performance did not differ across groups. Average performance levels across the training phase showed that younger control participants (M = 17.6, SD = 1.4), younger graphic designers (M = 17.4, SD = 1.0) and older graphic designers (M = 12.3, SD = 2.0) were profiting from the use of the mnemonic strategy because their performance levels after training were clearly above the range of performance in cued serial word recall generally found in adults without instruction and training in a memory skill. The situation is somewhat less clear in the case of the older control participants, who recalled on average 6.3 words (SD = 3.0) in correct serial position. This level of performance is somewhat higher than the level observed in older samples under similar task conditions but without imagery instructions (cf. Kliegl et al., 1989; Treat and Reese, 1976). For instance, Kliegl et al. (1989) found that a comparable sample of older adults recalled about 4 out of 30 words prior to mnemonic instructions under very similar task conditions.

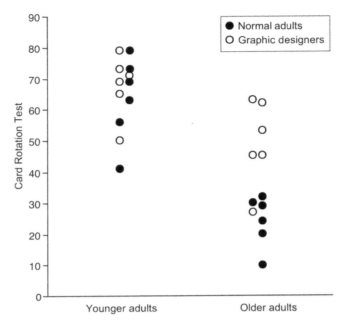

Figure 13.3 Performance of the Card Rotations Test from the ETS as a function of age-group and expertise. Each dot refers to one participant.

Group differences in cued recall

We now turn to the question whether older graphic designers were able to reach the level of recall performance of younger adults. Data from the twelve post-training sessions were used to address this question. Figure 13.4 shows the average performance in post-training assessment for each of the twenty-four research participants. Cronbach's alpha for this score, which was based on forty-eight trials (12 sessions × 4 lists each session), was .99 in the total sample, .95 in younger control participants, .93 in younger graphic designers, .98 in older control participants, and .87 in older graphic designers.

Younger participants recalled more words in correct serial position than older participants, and graphic designers recalled more words correctly than control subjects. The interaction was not significant. In follow-up t-tests, it was found that older graphic designers performed above the level of older control participants, but below the level of younger control participants; see Table 13.2. The difference between younger graphic designers and younger control participants was not significant.

Benefits of graphic design expertise in old age

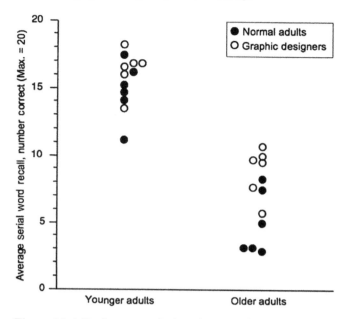

Figure 13.4 Performance during the test phase of mnemonic training as a function of age-group and expertise. Each dot refers to one participant.

An inspection of the data shown in Figure 13.4 reveals that none of the older graphic designers was able to reach the level of performance of younger adults. This perfect separation is highly unlikely by chance, $p = (1/18!) \times (12! \times 6!) = 5.39^{-5}$. The highest-scoring older graphic designer remembered an average of 11.1 words in correct serial position, whereas the lowest-scoring younger subject remembered 11.3 words. Note, however, that the four older adults with the best scores were graphic designers (see Figure 13.4). Also, though the corresponding interaction was not reliable, it seems that the performance of younger experts and younger control subjects was much more intermixed than the performance of older experts and older control subjects.[1]

Two further results deserve to be mentioned. First, the pattern of group differences was stable throughout post-training assessment. The stability of individual differences within and across groups (indexed by the high internal consistencies reported earlier) and the absence of group-by-session interactions in post-training assessment render it unlikely that additional exposure to the Method of Loci would have allowed older graphic designers or older adults in general to reach the level of cued

Table 13.2 *Means, standard deviations and post hoc t-tests for cued serial recall of twenty-item noun lists during the twelve-session test phase of the Lindenberger et al. (1992) experiment*

| | Younger adults | | | | Older adults | | | | t values | |
| | Normal | | Designers | | Normal | | Designers | | Older graphic designers versus younger control participants | Older graphic designers versus older control participants |
Rate	M	SD	M	SD	M	SD	M	SD		
7.5 s/word	17.3	1.8	18.6	1.1	6.6	3.0	12.4	2.3	−4.13***	3.73***
4.5 s/word	16.9	2.5	18.3	1.0	5.7	3.0	10.3	2.2	−4.86***	3.14**
1.5 s/word	10.7	2.4	12.0	2.5	2.9	1.4	4.4	1.3	−5.71***	1.88*

* $p < .10$. ** $p < .05$. *** $p < .01$

serial word recall displayed by younger adults. Second, the authors compared older graphic designers with older control adults to investigate whether group differences in recall performance difference were related to individual differences in criterion-relevant tests of visual creativity and spatial visualization. Statistical control for differences in visual creativity or spatial visualization turned out to eliminate group differences in cued serial recall between the two groups completely. This finding supports the hypothesis that the recall advantage of older graphic designers over older normal adults was related to the visual image generation component of the Method of Loci.

Revisiting the two-component model: disentangling expertise effects on the mechanics and pragmatics of cognition

This study explored relations between adult age, professional expertise and skilled memory performance after instruction and training in an imagery-based mnemonic skill. Concluding, we would like to summarize the main findings of this study, and point to open questions that need to be addressed in future work.

The main finding from the Lindenberger et al. (1992) study is that age-related declines in upper limits of episodic memory performance during adulthood are not easily altered by task-relevant lifelong experience. The choice of graphic designers as the expert group in the Lindenberger et al. (1992) study was based on evidence suggesting that interactive visual imagery is an important mediator affecting memory functioning using the Method of Loci (Baddeley and Lieberman, 1980; Richardson, 1985). Of course, we cannot exclude that a different group of older experts would have reached higher levels of mnemonic skill. For example, older professional mnemonists may show more substantial expertise-related experiential benefits in episodic memory performance than older graphic designers. In the former case, however, the domain of expertise would be almost identical to the criterion task, so the scope of the assessed expertise effect would be very narrow.

On a more positive note, graphic designers, and especially older graphic designers, showed higher levels of performance than age-matched control participants on tasks assumed to benefit from graphic design expertise, and they reached higher levels of skilled episodic memory performance using an imagery-based memory skill than their same-aged peers. Overall, graphic designers appear to be better able to produce and transform visual representations than their age-matched control participants. On the Card Rotation and Surface Development tests from the ETS, older graphic designers did not show the typical very low levels of performance commonly observed in this domain of performance among older adults (e.g. Jenkins, Myerson, Joerding and Hale, 2000). On the Parallel Lines subtest of the Torrance, differences between graphic designers and control participants were substantial, and age-based differences were not reliable.

Given the selective advantages of graphic designers over control participants, one may wonder how these differences map onto the two-component model of lifespan cognition introduced before. Unfortunately, the cross-sectional nature of the data and the lack of process models for the target tasks (cf. Krampe, Engbert and Kliegl, 2001; Krampe and Ericsson, 1996) does not permit an unambiguous attribution of expertise-related differences to the mechanics or the pragmatics of cognition. Nevertheless, we would like to offer some speculations and suggestions for further research.

In principle, two scenarios are possible. According to the first, the advantageous performance profile of older graphic designers reflects, to some extent, experience-induced alterations in the mechanics of cognition. In our judgement, the performance of older graphic designers on the Card Rotation test is most amenable to this kind of interpretation. The constant need to image and spatially transform visual representations in working memory may have helped graphic designers to attenuate some of the normative losses in mental rotation abilities. Recent neuroimaging findings of structural changes of the brain as a function of visuo-spatial experience suggest that such experience-dependent modulations of the mechanics of cognition may in fact be possible (cf. Draganski et al., 2004; Maguire et al., 2000).

According to the second scenario, older graphic designers have acquired a rich body of factual and procedural knowledge that attenuates the adverse consequences of mechanic decline in expertise-relevant functional domains without altering the course of this decline itself. In addition to episodic memory performance itself, older graphic designers' impressively high levels of performance on the Parallel Lines subtest of the Torrance is consistent with this interpretation. Specifically, we would like to propose that graphic designers have acquired a 'lexicon' of graphical forms to express and promote concepts and ideas, and have stored this repertoire of concept–form associations in long-term memory. Thus, when working on the Torrance test, graphic designers had less need to create such associations on the spot than control participants because instead they were able to retrieve such associations from long-term memory (see also Patterson and Erzinclioğlu, this volume, for the opposite extreme).

Whereas the first scenario emphasizes the experience-dependent malleability of mechanic decline, the second scenario emphasizes the compensatory function of pragmatic knowledge. It is likely that the two options co-exist and interact with each other and with maturational and senescent changes in the course of lifespan development (e.g. Lindenberger, Li and Bäckman, 2006; Li and Lindenberger, 2002). Future studies need to identify the mechanisms through which experience alters mechanic declines, attenuates their consequences, or both. The present results suggest that the experience-dependent modulation of visuo-spatial skills offers a fertile testing ground for investigating this issue.

NOTE

1. Given that older and younger participants differed in Digit Symbol Substitution performance, one may argue that the observed age differences reflected the use of speeded encoding conditions throughout the post-training assessment (i.e. 1.5, 4.5 and 7.5 s/word). However, based on further analyses reported by Lindenberger et al. (1992), this explanation seems unlikely, as age differences did not decrease with longer encoding times.

REFERENCES

Alpaugh, P. K. and Birren, J. E. (1977). Variables affecting creative contributions across the adult life span. *Human Development*, 20, 240–8.
Baddeley, A. D. and Lieberman, K. (1980). Spatial working memory. In R. S. Nickerson (ed.), *Attention and performance* (Vol. 3, pp. 521–39). Hillsdale, NJ: Erlbaum.
Baltes, P. B. (1987). Theoretical propositions of life-span developmental psychology: on the dynamics between growth and decline. *Developmental Psychology*, 23, 611–26.
Baltes, P. B. and Kliegl, R. (1992). Further testing of limits of cognitive plasticity: negative age differences in a mnemonic skill are robust. *Developmental Psychology*, 28, 121–5.
Baschek, I.-L., Bredenkamp, J., Oehrle, B. and Wippich, W. (1977). Bestimmung der Bildhaftigkeit (I), Konkretheit (C) und der Bedeutungshaltigkeit (m') von 800 Substantiven [Determination of imageability (I), concreteness (C) and meaningfulness (m') for 800 nouns]. *Zeitschrift für Experimentelle und Angewandte Psychologie*, 24, 353–96.
Bosman, E. A. (1993). Age-related differences in the motoric aspects of transcription typing skill. *Psychology and Aging*, 8, 283–308.
Bosman, E. A. and Charness, N. (1996). Age-related differences in skilled performance and skill acquisition. In F. Blanchard-Fields and T. M. Hess (eds.), *Perspectives on cognitive change in adulthood and aging* (pp. 428–53). New York: McGraw-Hill.

Brehmer, Y., Li, S.-C., Müller, V., Oertzen, T. von and Lindenberger, U. (2007). Memory plasticity across the lifespan: uncovering children's latent potential. *Developmental Psychology*, 43, 465–78.

Bower, G. H. (1970). Analysis of a mnemonic device. *American Scientist*, 58, 496–510.

Cattell, R. B. (1971). *Abilities: their structure, growth, and action.* Boston, MA: Houghton Mifflin.

Charness, N. (1981). Aging and skilled problem solving. *Journal of Experimental Psychology: General*, 110, 21–38.

(1989). Age and expertise: responding to Talland's challenge. In L. W. Poon, D. C. Rubin and B. A. Wilson (eds.), *Everyday cognition in adulthood and late life* (pp. 437–56). Cambridge: Cambridge University Press.

Draganski, B., Gaser, C., Busch, V., Schuierer, G., Bogdahn, U. and May, A. (2004). Changes in grey matter induced by training. *Nature*, 427, 311–12.

Ekstrom, R. B., French, J. W. and Harman, H. H. (1976). *Manual for kit of factor-references cognitive tests.* Princeton, NJ: Educational Testing Service.

Jastrzembski, T. S., Charness, N. and Vasyukova, C. (2006). Expertise and age effects on knowledge activation in chess. *Psychology and Aging*, 21, 401–5.

Jenkins, L., Myerson, J., Joerding, J. A. and Hale, S. (2000). Converging evidence that visuospatial cognition is more age-sensitive than verbal cognition. *Psychology and Aging*, 15, 157–75.

Kim, K. H. (2006). Can we trust creativity tests? A review of the Torrance Tests of Creative Thinking (TTCT). *Creative Research Journal*, 8, 3–14.

Kliegl, R., Smith, J. and Baltes, P. B. (1986). Testing-the-limits, expertise, and memory in adulthood and old age. In F. Klix and H. Hagendorf (eds.), *Human memory and cognitive capabilities* (pp. 395–407). Amsterdam: North-Holland/Elsevier.

(1989). Testing-the-limits and the study of adult age differences in cognitive plasticity of a mnemonic skill. *Developmental Psychology*, 25, 247–56.

(1990). On the locus and process of magnification of age differences during mnemonic training. *Developmental Psychology*, 26, 894–904.

Krampe, R. T. (2002). Aging, expertise, and fine motor movement. *Neuroscience and Biobehavioral Reviews*, 26, 769–76.

Krampe, R. T. and Baltes, P. B. (2003). Intelligence as adaptive resource development and resource allocation: a new look through the lenses of SOC and expertise. In R. J. Sternberg and E. L. Grigorenko (eds.), *Perspectives on the psychology of abilities, competencies, and expertise* (pp. 31–69). New York: Cambridge University Press.

Krampe, R. T., Engbert, R. and Kliegl, R. (2001). The effects of expertise and age on rhythm production: adaptations to timing and sequencing constraints. *Brain and Cognition*, 48, 179–94.

Krampe, R. T. and Ericsson, K. A. (1996). Maintaining excellence: deliberate practice and elite performance in young and older pianists. *Journal of Experimental Psychology: General*, 125, 331–59.

Li, S.-C. (2003). Biocultural orchestration of developmental plasticity across levels: the interplay of biology and culture in shaping the mind and behaviour across the lifespan. *Psychological Bulletin*, 129, 171–94.

Li, S.-C. and Lindenberger, U. (2002). Co-constructed functionality instead of functional normality. *Behavioral and Brain Sciences*, 25, 761–2.

Li, S.-C., Lindenberger, U., Hommel, B., Aschersleben, G., Prinz, W. and Baltes, P. B. (2004). Transformations in the couplings among intellectual abilities and constituent cognitive processes across the life span. *Psychological Science*, 15, 155–63.

Lindenberger, U. and Baltes, P. B. (1995). Testing-the-limits and experimental simulation: two methods to explicate the role of learning in development. *Journal of Human Development*, 38, 349–60.

Lindenberger, U., Kliegl, R. and Baltes, P. B. (1992). Professional expertise does not eliminate age differences in imagery-based memory performance during adulthood. *Psychology and Aging*, 7, 585–93.

Lindenberger, U., Li, S.-C. and Bäckman, L. (2006). Delineating brain-behaviour mappings across the lifespan: substantive and methodological advances in developmental neuroscience. Editorial. *Neuroscience and Biobehavioral Reviews*, 30, 713–17.

Logie, R. H. (1986). Visuo-spatial processing in working memory. *Quarterly Journal of Experimental Psychology*, 38A, 229–47.

Maguire, E. A., Gadian, D. G., Johnsrude, I. S., Good, C. D., Ashburner, J., Frackowiak, R. S. J., et al. (2000). Navigation-related structural change in the hippocampi of taxi drivers. *Proceedings of the National Academy of Sciences USA*, 97, 4398–4403.

Masunaga, H. and Horn, J. (2001). Expertise in relation to aging changes in components of intelligence. *Psychology and Aging*, 16, 293–311.

Maylor, E. A. (1994). Ageing and retrieval of specialized and general knowledge: performance of "Masterminds". *British Journal of Psychology*, 85, 105–14.

Morrow, D. G. and Leirer, V. O. (1997). Aging, pilot performance, and expertise. In A. D. Fisk and W. A. Rogers (eds.), *Handbook of human factors and the older adult* (pp. 199–230). New York: Academic Press.

Morrow, D. G., Ridolfo, H. E., Menard, W. E., Sanborn, W. E., Stine-Morrow, E. A. L., Magnor, C. et al. (2003). Environmental support promotes expertise-based mitigation of age differences in pilot communication tasks. *Psychology and Aging*, 18, 268–84.

Paivio, A., Yuille, J. C. and Madigan, S. A. (1968). Concreteness, imagery, and meaningfulness values for 925 nouns. *Journal of Experimental Psychology*, 76, 1–25.

Rabbitt, P. M. A. (1993). Crystal quest: a search for the basis of maintenance of practised skills into old age. In A. Baddeley and L. Weiskrantz (eds.), *Attention: selection, awareness, and control* (pp. 188–230). Oxford: Clarendon.

Richardson, J. T. E. (1985). Converging operations and reported mediators in the investigation of mental imagery. *British Journal of Psychology*, 76, 205–14.

Rose, T. L. and Yesavage, J. A. (1983). Differential effects of a list-learning mnemonic in three age-groups. *Gerontology*, 29, 293–8.

Ruth, J.-E. and Birren, J. E. (1985). Creativity in adulthood and old age: relations to intelligence, sex and mode of testing. *International Journal of Behavioral Development*, 8, 99–109.

Salthouse, T. A. (1982). *Adult cognition: an experimental psychology of human aging*. New York: Springer.

   (1984). Effects of age and skill in typing. *Journal of Experimental Psychology: General*, 11, 345–71.

   (1991). Expertise as the circumvention of human processing limitations. In K. A. Ericsson and J. Smith (eds.), *Towards a general theory of expertise: prospects and limits* (pp. 286–300). Cambridge: Cambridge University Press.

Singer, T., Lindenberger, U. and Baltes, P. B. (2003). Plasticity of memory for new learning in very old age: a story of major loss? *Psychology and Aging*, 18, 306–17.

Stigsdotter Neely, A. and Bäckman, L. (1993). Long-term maintenance of gains from memory training in older adults: two $3^1/_2$-year follow-up studies. *Journal of Gerontology: Psychological Sciences*, 48, P233–P237.

Thompson, L. A. and Kliegl, R. (1991). Adult age effects of plausibility on memory: the role of time constraints during encoding. *Journal of Experimental Psychology: Learning, Memory, and Cognition*, 17, 542–55.

Torrance, E. P. (1966a). *Torrance Tests of Creative Thinking: directions manual and sorting guide*. Princeton, NJ: Personnel Press.

   (1966b). *Technical-norms manual for the Torrance Tests of Creative Thinking: research edition*. Princeton, NJ: Personnel Press.

Treat, N. J. and Reese, H. W. (1976). Age, pacing, and imagery in paired-associative learning. *Developmental Psychology*, 12, 119–24.

Verhaeghen, P. and Marcoen, A. (1996). On the mechanisms of plasticity in young and older adults after instruction in the Method of Loci: evidence for an amplification model. *Psychology and Aging*, 11, 164–78.

Viggiano, M. P., Righi, S. and Galli, G. (2006). Category-specific visual recognition as affected by aging and expertise. *Archives of Gerontology and Geriatrics*, 42, 329–38.

Walsh, D. A. and Hershey, D. A. (1993). Mental models and the maintenance of complex problem solving skills in old age. In J. Cerella, J. Rybash, W. Hoyer and M. L. Commons (eds.), *Adult information processing: limits on loss* (pp. 553–84). San Diego, CA: Academic Press.

Wechsler, D. (1964). *Der Hamburger-Wechsler-Intelligenztest für Erwachsene (HAWIE)*. Berne: Huber.

14   Drawing as a 'window' on deteriorating
      conceptual knowledge in neurodegenerative
      disease

Karalyn Patterson and Sharon W. Erzinçlioğlu

Patterson and Erzinçlioğlu discuss drawing as one technique for investigating the nature of semantic memory and its disorders. Semantic dementia (SD) is a neurodegenerative condition characterized by gradual degradation of central conceptual knowledge. Given that patients with SD have (a) well-preserved perceptual and motor skills (which means that they can easily copy drawings with the model present) and (b) reasonable preservation of at least some aspects of short-term and episodic memory, the technique of delayed copy drawing can be employed. A line drawing of a familiar object is presented for the patient to study; it is then removed and the patient does something else for 10 or 15 seconds, and is finally asked to draw what she or he was looking at. Because literal visual memory is fragile even in the normal cognitive system, the delayed-copy task evokes and relies on a combination of short-term visual memory and long-term conceptual knowledge. Thus normal individuals, in delayed copy drawing of a rhinoceros, draw it with horns and 'armoured' skin not only because they remember seeing these specific features but also because their conceptual knowledge of rhinos demands these features in the reproduction. The degraded knowledge in SD patients means that they cannot recognize this thing as a rhinoceros; they only know it is some sort of animal. The impoverished drawings that they produce a mere 10 seconds after studying the targets provide an informative window on the quality of their conceptual knowledge.

> Ring the bell that still can ring
> Forget your perfect offering
> There's a crack, a crack in everything . . .
> It lets the light in.
>
> From *Anthem* by Leonard Cohen

Whose drawing?

AS THIS book clearly attests, drawing – as a technique employed by cognitive psychologists to study children's conceptual knowledge – yields a wealth of intriguing insights into the developing mind. This chapter, however, is concerned not with drawing as a reflection of the gradual development, generalization and differentiation of concepts in children, but rather as one method of observing the disintegration of concepts, in adults who (presumably) were completely normal prior to brain injury or disease. There are several aetiologies that can disrupt conceptual knowledge or semantic memory, including cerebrovascular accident (stroke), viral encephalitis and neurodegenerative diseases with prominent cognitive sequelae. The most common and best-known instance of this latter category is Alzheimer's disease (AD); but there is another degenerative condition that, whilst far less prevalent than AD, is also more theoretically informative because of its relatively selective impact on semantic memory. Semantic dementia (SD), one of the manifestations of Pick's disease or fronto-temporal dementia (Hodges, Patterson, Oxbury and Funnell, 1992; Hodges, Graham and Patterson, 1995; Neary et al., 1998), results from a degenerative brain process that almost invariably begins in the anterior, inferior temporal lobes (Nestor, Fryer and Hodges, 2006). Patients who receive appropriate medical investigation early in the course of the disease may appear, on simple inspection of structural brain images, to have unilateral loss of brain tissue, i.e. in either the left *or* the right temporal lobe; but the disease inevitably affects both sides, even if asymmetrically. With time, the disease process tends to spread either forward, into the frontal lobes, or back into the posterior temporal lobes, or both; and, as a result, the cognitive consequences may also become more widespread and less specific; but for a considerable period of time, perhaps 3–4 years depending on the stage at which the patient is diagnosed, it is possible to observe and assess gradual deterioration of conceptual knowledge in SD without much else going wrong. The condition, which as yet has no known effective treatment, is of course devastating to sufferers and carers, and indeed to neurologists and neuropsychologists who observe the decline without being able to provide significant help other than information and advice. The nature of semantic deterioration in SD is, however, also a source of considerable insight into the structure and organization of conceptual knowledge in the brain.

The status of a patient's knowledge of concepts is most frequently assessed, in SD and other acquired disorders, via tests based entirely, or in part, on words as stimuli or responses or both. Thus, patients are asked (a) to name objects or pictures of concepts that can be represented pictorially (non-verbal stimuli, verbal responses), (b) to point to pictures corresponding to the spoken names of objects (verbal and non-verbal stimuli, non-verbal response), (c) to define either concrete (e.g. 'asparagus') or abstract (e.g. 'sympathy') concepts from their spoken names (verbal stimuli and responses), etc., etc. Given the omnipresence of language in human conceptual behaviour, purely non-verbal tests are harder to design. Most rely on the selection of a response picture, from amongst two or more alternatives, to match a target picture on a conceptual rather than a visual basis. For example, in the Pyramids and Palm Trees Test (Howard and Patterson, 1992), the item that gives the test its name requires the participant to select the picture of a palm tree rather than a pine tree as a match for the target picture of an Egyptian pyramid. There is no more visual similarity between a palm tree and a pyramid than between a pine tree and a pyramid; one makes the correct choice by virtue of knowing what kind of vegetation is found in the vicinity of the pyramids. Tests of this kind are useful, but can only take the neuropsychologist so far in the investigation of conceptual knowledge. This is primarily because the response of the patient – simply matching up two pictures selected by the test designer as related on some specific dimension (e.g. geographical location in the case of the pyramid and palm tree; what kinds of clothing we traditionally put on different parts of the body in the case of matching a pair of mittens to the hands rather than the feet) – leaves so little scope for the expression of what the patient still knows about the concepts in question.

Drawing seems to offer precisely the desired expressive scope; but the standard technique for assessing knowledge via drawing – e.g. 'Please draw a picture of a giraffe' (or whatever) – turns out not to be of much use in SD, because it requires comprehension of the concept words. Semantic dementia corresponds to deterioration of central conceptual knowledge, not to degraded knowledge of words; but there is typically an asymmetry in the extent of comprehension deficit for verbal in contrast to pictorial stimuli, with an advantage for the latter (Lambon Ralph, Graham, Patterson and Hodges, 1999). This discrepancy does not, or at least certainly need not, reflect separate systems in the brain for the representation of verbal and non-verbal information. It can arise purely from an inherent difference in the nature of the mapping from words versus pictures to the corresponding amodal conceptual representations (Rogers et al., 2004a). Apart from bound morphemes like the English affix –s, which at the end of a noun typically signifies more than one, or the English prefix dis-, which at the beginning of a word often indicates a kind of reverse action, as in 'discharge' or 'disarm' (although not always: 'display' is not the reverse of play, and 'distance' is not a prefixed word at all), components of words give virtually no hint to the meaning of the whole word. No individual letters or combinations of letters in the word 'giraffe' have any meaning; and in words coincidentally composed of chunks that do have meaning, those chunks would typically only mislead as to the meaning of the whole (a 'cabinet' contains no cab, bin or net). Nor does the general 'shape' of a spoken or written word reveal anything about its nature. Objects (or pictures of them) are a different kettle of fish: their components, such as the legs, eyes, ears of the giraffe, do provide substantial clues to their meanings, as do their general shapes (a natural-kind or biological shape for a giraffe, a man-made artefact shape for a cabinet). Fairly late in the progression of SD, patients who do not exceed chance-level performance in classifying spoken or written words as the names of living versus man-made things often still succeed fairly well at the classification task with pictures of the same objects (Hodges, Patterson and Tyler, 1994). Given that they fail other semantic tasks requiring precise knowledge of those pictures, it seems likely that they achieve their above-chance picture classification into living versus man-made on the basis of such clues from component features and general shape.

The implication of this discrepancy between verbal and non-verbal comprehension for the current topic is this: if the researcher interested in SD were to employ only the typical method of eliciting drawings – i.e. telling the patient the name of each object concept to be drawn – drawing would not be a fruitful method of investigation, because the patient's response would frequently be no more than 'What's a giraffe?' A different technique is required.

What drawing task?

Following Franklin, Van Sommers and Howard (1992) and Lambon Ralph and Howard (2000), the procedure upon which we have settled for obtaining drawing responses with informative content from patients with semantic dementia (SD) is a task called delayed copy drawing. Recall the claim above that SD involves a relatively selective deterioration of semantic memory, at least until late in the disease process. Accordingly, SD patients before this late stage have no notable impairment in either perceptual or motor abilities; and, therefore, when asked to copy a drawing of either a meaningful or a meaningless figure with the model in front of them, they typically do so as well as any neurologically intact adult. Furthermore, they have no notable impairment in remembering that they have seen a particular object or drawing recently. If, for example, an SD patient fails to name a picture of a giraffe (and he or she *would* typically fail, responding either 'I don't know' or 'Is that a horse?' or some such), and the giraffe then reappears later in the series of pictures to be named, the patient will very often comment 'I didn't get that one before, and I still can't.' (This would almost never happen in a patient with Alzheimer's disease, where the primary deficit is precisely in this kind of encoding and retrieval of new experiences.)

One of the standard tests used to assess neurological patients' abilities in all three of these domains – visual perception, motor processing and non-verbal memory – is copy and recall of a complicated but meaningless geometric figure called the Rey Complex Figure (Rey, 1941). Initially the person is asked to copy this figure with it in full view, and SD patients almost invariably do this as well as age-matched controls. In the second part of the test, about half to three-quarters of an hour later, he or she is asked, without prior warning, to reproduce the figure from memory. Normal adults are far from perfect at this kind of delayed literal visual recall: on average, they accurately reproduce in the delayed condition only about 50 per cent of the Rey figure's elements that they correctly drew when copying it from the model. When asked 'Remember that funny picture that I asked you to copy a while ago? Please try to draw it again, this time from memory', a patient with AD is likely to say 'What funny picture?'; but SD patients will typically remember the event and set about trying to reproduce the figure, and will manage to do so as well, or nearly as well, as a normal person. On the basis of this observation, one might predict that they would show exactly the same behaviour when tested on line drawings of real, familiar objects. This prediction is, however, wrong, or at least half wrong: the patients' ability to copy real objects is reasonably good but their recall of them is not.

We do this experimental task in a somewhat different manner from the procedure for administering the Rey figure test (for further details of the procedure used in delayed copy drawing, see Bozeat *et al.*, 2003; Jefferies *et al.*, 2005; Lambon Ralph and Howard, 2000; Rogers *et al.*, 2004a). In one session, we ask the patients to copy line drawings of objects, such as a rhinoceros or a piano, with the stimulus picture present. On a different day, we show them each picture and let them study it for perhaps 5 seconds so that they have a good idea of what it looks like; they are not asked to name it (which they would mostly fail to do anyway), nor does the experimenter name it for them. The drawing is then removed from view and the patient counts aloud from 1 to 15, which takes patients (and controls) about 10 seconds. The patient is then asked to draw what he or she was looking at before counting (again, no name).

Figure 14.1, an example from Bozeat *et al.* (2003), illustrates the stimulus picture of a rhinoceros at the top and both an SD patient's direct copy

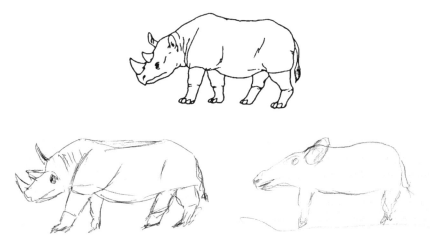

Figure 14.1 The direct (below left) and delayed (below right) copies of the picture of a rhino (above) by DS, a patient with semantic dementia.

(below on the left) and his delayed copy of it 10 seconds later (below on the right). The direct reproduction, although not perfect in every detail (e.g. the toes are rather sketchy, and the rhino's right ear has become a third horn), is a thoroughly recognizable facsimile; but the delayed copy has lost virtually all of its unique features and looks like a much more generic animal shape, perhaps a pig or a dog with a long nose.

What do we learn from delayed copy drawing in semantic dementia?

How is one to interpret the two discrepancies just described, (a) between SD patients' direct and delayed copy of meaningful objects and (b) between their delayed recall of meaningless and meaningful figures? Our explanation is that the two tasks that they perform with essentially normal accuracy are at the very perceptual end of a perceptual ↔ conceptual continuum. Direct copy of a figure can be done without reference to conceptual knowledge, as witnessed by the fact that both normal people and patients can do these tasks on nonsense figures as well as on meaningful pictures. Delayed copy of meaningless figures can be done (although not all that skilfully by either patients or controls) without reference to conceptual knowledge because it must be: there are no obvious concepts to refer to in performing this task. But delayed copy of a meaningful drawing – which would presumably be as difficult as delayed copy of a meaningless figure if it were being performed solely on the basis of literal stimulus memory – can rely on, indeed probably cannot avoid relying on, conceptual knowledge. Normal individuals, in delayed copy drawing of a rhinoceros, do not need to invoke literal visual memory in order to endow it with horns: once they have recognized the stimulus picture as a rhino (and of course remembered this 10 seconds later), semantic memory announces that it must have horns. Our hypothesis is that exactly the same reliance on semantic knowledge occurs, and similarly cannot fail to occur, in SD patients; but because their conceptual knowledge is so degraded, they have only recognized the rhino as some kind of generic animal; that is then what they remember and what their delayed reproduction represents.

This interpretation is supported by results from Jefferies et al. (2005) in a study mainly concerned with the impact of semantic degradation on auditory-verbal short-term memory. For each of five SD patients, words were individually selected to form two sets, matched as closely as possible for length and frequency: (a) words whose meanings were still relatively intact for that patient, as evidenced by good performance on these items in tasks of picture naming, word definition and synonym judgement; and (b) words whose meanings were degraded for that patient as evidenced by poor performance on the same tasks. These two sets were assembled into lists of three or four unrelated words such that any given string consisted of either 'known' or 'degraded' items, and were read aloud to the patients at a rate of one item per second (as is standard in such tasks) for immediate serial recall. The main outcome of this study was a consistent and reliable advantage in recall for the 'known' words, demonstrating an impact of semantic memory on short-term memory. What is relevant here is that, additionally, the patients were asked to perform delayed copying of pictures corresponding to the picture names used as words in the recall experiment. Jefferies et al. documented the same advantage for 'known' over 'degraded' items in delayed copying as in the short-term verbal memory task, supporting the hypothesis that the quality of semantic knowledge for a concept/picture determines how well it can be reproduced in delayed copying.

The horn-less, armour-less rhinoceros in Figure 14.1 may seem like a particularly striking example, and not all of the SD patients' delayed copy drawings are quite so unfaithful to their stimuli; but there are many other examples like the rhino, as illustrated in Figure 14.2. As for the rhinoceros in Figure 14.1, Figure 14.2 illustrates, for each of four objects (two animals, two man-made objects) and for each of three SD patients: (a) the stimulus picture presented to the patients (at the top of Figure 14.2), (b) the three patients' direct copy drawings (i.e. with the picture present) from one test session and (c) the three patients' delayed copy drawings

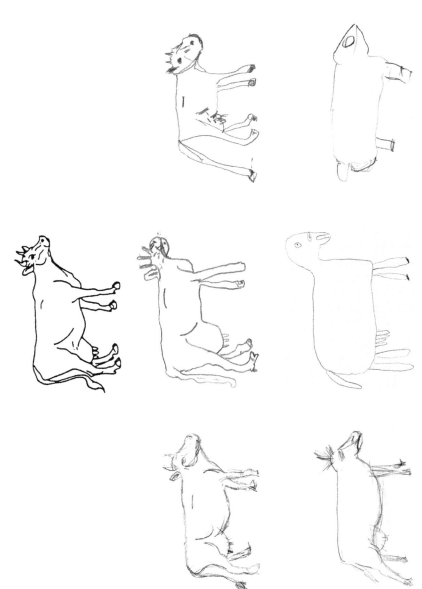

Figure 14.2 Direct copy and delayed copy drawings of two animals (cow and frog) and two man-made objects (bicycle and piano) for each of three semantic dementia patients (DS, DC and IF, always in that order). In each case the patient's delayed copy drawing is arranged beneath his or her direct copy.

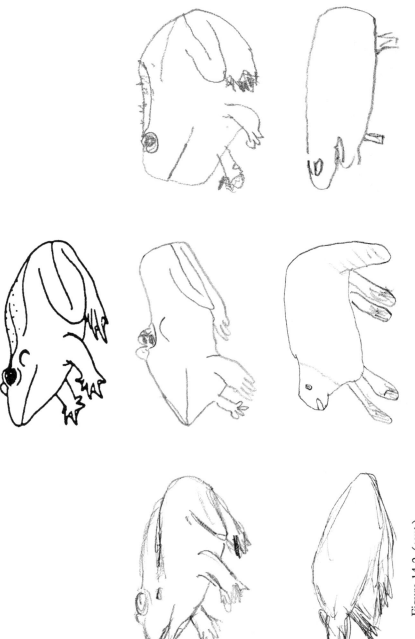

Figure 14.2 (*cont.*)

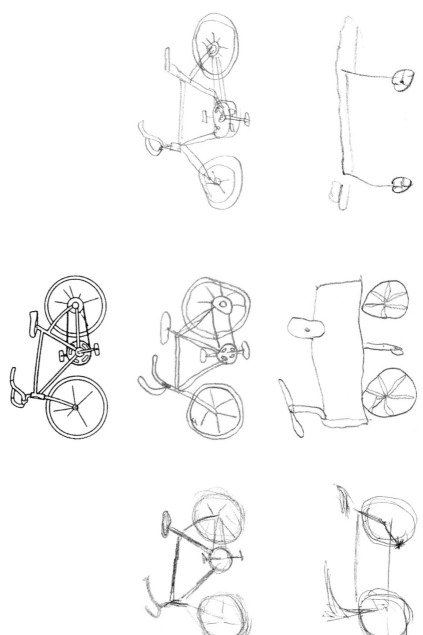

Figure 14.2 (cont.)

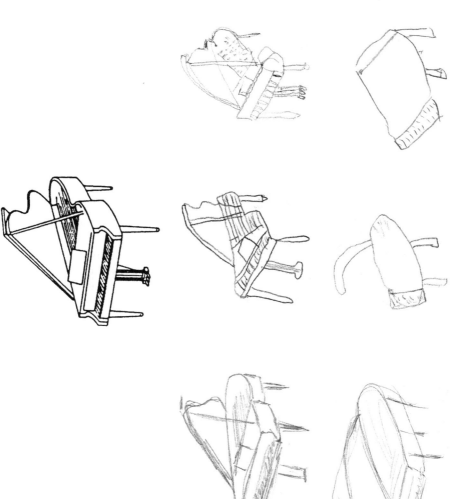

Figure 14.2 (cont.)

(produced about 10–15 seconds after the picture has been removed) from a different test session. The patients (DS, DC and IF) were all, as is typical for SD, profoundly anomic, with scores on our standard picture-naming test of 17/64 (DS), 11/64 (DC) and 1/64 (IF); age-matched controls correctly name an average of 62.3/64 pictures on this test. Other assessments of semantic memory confirmed that DS was still at a relatively mild stage of semantic deterioration, DC had a moderate semantic deficit, and IF was very severely, although still fairly selectively, impaired in semantic knowledge.

The direct copy drawings in Figure 14.2 – whilst far from fine art – are mostly adequate reproductions of the targets, in the sense that one would know without seeing the stimulus picture what object the patient was copying. This is true even for DC and IF, although there is certainly, and unsurprisingly, some observable impact of semantic severity even on immediate drawing. Note, for example, that neither DC's nor IF's directly copied frog has very adequately webbed feet, while IF produced a rather emaciated cow with a tail terminating in something like another hoof. But the main points of the examples in Figure 14.2 are (a) the 'fate' of the drawings when the stimulus picture was no longer present and the patients were thus forced to rely on what they had managed to glean about the nature of the object from looking at it a short time earlier, and (b) how this 'fate' interacts with the severity of the patient's semantic degradation. For the patient at the mildest stage of disease, DS, although the cow's horns have become somewhat more like deer antlers, and the frog has lost definition and become rather abstract, most of his delayed copy drawings in Figure 14.2 (unlike his rhinoceros in Figure 14.1) are recognizable as their targets. For the moderate-stage patient, DC, her delayed copy cow provides a hint to its identity because it has udders, but in other respects is pretty un-cow-like; the bicycle is clearly a vehicle of some sort but looks more like a wagon than a bicycle; and neither the piano nor the frog would be identifiable as such in isolation. For the most severely impaired patient, IF, it seems unlikely that any of his delayed copy drawings would be named as their targets by someone seeing them in isolation. The cow and frog are clearly animals but have no target-specific features.

One of the noteworthy things about the discrepancy between copy and delayed copy drawings in SD is that it forms an almost perfect opposite of the discrepancy between copy drawings and drawing-to-concept-name in a neuropsychological syndrome called apperceptive or visual-form agnosia. In this condition – resulting in one well-studied case from lateral-occipital-lobe damage consequent on carbon monoxide poisoning (Servos, Goodale and Humphrey, 1993) – the patient has normal semantic knowledge of objects and concepts but a fundamental visual-perceptual processing deficit. The examples of drawings in Figure 14.2 are strikingly reminiscent of those reproduced in the article by Servos *et al.* (1993), but with the conditions reversed. That is, the pattern in SD is good direct copy drawings and very impoverished drawings from memory; the pattern in visual-form agnosia is very impoverished direct copy drawings and good, or at least much better, drawings from memory (in that case, truly from semantic memory – i.e. in response to the concepts' names).

Looking at the examples in Figure 14.2 is instructive; but as researchers we need to go beyond the individual examples to some more systematic generalizations about how the delayed copies deviate from their model pictures. There are several ways in which we have attempted, or can attempt, to achieve such generalizations, and these are discussed below. Before we do so, however, it should be explained that we apply formal scoring procedures to the patients' drawings; and because drawings are complex constructions rather than simple responses that (in tests like picture naming) can be treated as correct or incorrect, the scoring procedures are always based on a comparison between the drawings produced by patients and those produced under the same experimental conditions by normal individuals who are selected to match the patients in age and educational level. Our standard technique for scoring is, first, to assemble a list of every feature produced for each object concept by any of the normal control participants. Next, we select, for each item, the subset of features produced by all, or nearly all, of the controls. Relative to this resulting target list for a concept, a patient can lose points by either (a) failing to produce a feature that is on the list (omissions) and/or (b) incorporating in his or her drawing a feature that is not on the list (intrusions). This scoring procedure can be used equally well for drawing in response to concept names; but as explained above, the latter task is less informative in SD given how often the patients fail to recognize an object name and therefore produce no drawing.

How to systematize the results of delayed copy drawing in SD

One way to go beyond the examples towards something more systematic is the main type of analysis used in the articles by Bozeat *et al.* (2003) and Rogers *et al.* (2004a). This involves a further classification of the features on each concept's target list in terms of how characteristic these features are of other exemplars from the same semantic category – not other exemplars in the drawing test but other exemplars in the real

Figure 14.3 Two examples from the Object-Decision Test of Rogers et al., 2004b.

world. The reason for the emphasis on typicality of features within an item's category is that we know from our other research on SD that typicality is one of the three most powerful determinants of SD patients' success on tests of semantic knowledge, the other two being the frequency or familiarity of the item being tested, and the extent of the individual patient's semantic deterioration. Take, for example, a test of object recognition called object decision, which involves presentation of object pictures, some of which are real and some of which have been doctored so that they are still fairly plausible but do not correspond to real-world objects. The participant's task is to decide whether a stimulus picture is a real object. SD patients are impaired relative to normal controls in object decision tests, and the extent of this impairment is strongly predicted by a combination of the three factors just mentioned: severity of the patients' semantic decline; frequency or familiarity of the real objects in the test; and the typicality of the objects and pseudo-objects. We often administer the test in a 2-alternative forced choice format, where the patient is simultaneously offered one correct and one doctored version of the same object and asked to select the real one (see Figure 14.3 for examples). SD patients will usually make the correct selection when the real object has a structure more typical of its category than the pseudo-object (e.g. in the choice between the two monkeys, one with small ears – which are not only correct for a monkey but also characteristic of most animals – and one with elephant-sized ears, which are not only incorrect for the monkey but also atypical of animal ears). By contrast, patients with moderate to severe SD tend to prefer the pseudo-object as the real one if it is more typical than the genuine object (e.g. the elephant with small versus big ears) (see Rogers, Lambon Ralph, Hodges and Patterson, 2004b, for data from this object decision test; and Patterson *et al.*, 2006 for data from six different tasks – some receptive, some expressive, some verbal, some non-verbal – demonstrating the impact of typicality on SD performance).

To return to drawing: in our previous studies of delayed copy drawing (Bozeat *et al.*, 2003; Rogers *et al.*, 2004a), each feature for each target object was assigned one of three classifications: '*shared-**domain***', '*shared-**category***' or '*distinctive*'. To illustrate this, let us take the example of a peacock. Its domain is animals, and most animals have an obvious head and eyes. These features on the peacock are therefore classed as 'shared-domain'. Its category or subgrouping is birds, and most birds (although not other animals) have two legs and a beak; these features are therefore classed as 'shared-category' for the peacock. The large fantail on a peacock is distinctive. Of course not all features of objects are as strongly shared or as strongly distinctive as the ones used here for purposes of illustration. Our criterion for a shared versus a distinctive feature was a pragmatic one: is the feature characteristic of more than or less than 50 per cent of the other members of the domain or category? Also, not all objects are so easily classifiable into domains and categories as the peacock; but all of the items in the set that we used for drawing do yield pretty well to this arrangement, because they were chosen to do so for other reasons. For example, we use the same objects when we ask the patients to do sorting tests at various levels, such that items like the peacock can be sorted into the animal domain at the top level, the bird category at an intermediate level, and various groupings at a subordinate level (e.g. domestic versus foreign). Similarly, objects like a spanner can be classed as man-made at the superordinate level, a tool at the category level, and made of metal versus wood at a subordinate level.

In classifying the patients' errors, we defined an *omission* as an absent feature that should have been there, as signalled by the fact that almost all control subjects include it when drawing the object, and an *intrusion* as an included feature that should not have been present because controls never produce it for that object. The striking finding from this analysis based on the typicality of object features was as follows. In delayed copy drawing, SD patients rarely omitted shared-by-domain features, sometimes omitted shared-by-category features, and frequently omitted distinctive features. The likelihood of intrusion errors followed precisely the reverse order: most intrusions corresponded to the addition of shared-by-domain features onto members of the domain lacking these; there were only occasional intrusions of a shared-by-category feature, and essentially none of distinctive features (see Rogers et al., 2004a, for the quantification of these results).

This pattern is precisely what would be predicted from a theoretical account of SD in which knowledge is more robust to the deterioration process if it is characteristic of a large chunk of semantic space, and more vulnerable to deterioration if it applies to only one or a few concepts in semantic space.

A second way to systematize the delayed copy results in SD would be the scheme introduced by Karmiloff-Smith (1990) in her analysis of the drawings produced by normal children aged 4–6 or 8–10. In that study, the children were first asked to draw pictures of three objects (a house, a man and an animal) and subsequently asked to draw an instance for each of the same three categories 'that does not exist'. Karmiloff-Smith categorized the changes between real and non-existent instances into six types:
1 shape and size of elements changed
2 shape of whole changed
3 deletion of elements
4 insertion of new elements
5 position/orientation changed
6 insertion of cross-category elements.

Her analysis revealed that change-types 1–3 were used frequently (and roughly equally) by the younger and older children, but types 4–6 were used essentially only by the older children.

This method of treating the data is perhaps not quite so appropriate to our delayed copy task, given that the patients have recently seen a model of what they are meant to draw, and we are asking them to reproduce that model, not to use their imaginations. Nevertheless, the analysis published by Karmiloff-Smith (1990, p. 71) can be applied to the discrepancies between the patients' immediate and delayed copies. We have done only a very approximate quantitative analysis of the proportion of delayed copy drawings with these various change types, which demonstrates (perhaps unsurprisingly) (a) that the great majority of changes can be classified as type 3, i.e. deletion of elements, (b) that change-types 1 and 2 are also relatively frequent although not as prevalent as type 3, and (c) that change-types 4–6 are much rarer than 1–3. Examples of the six types are shown in Figure 14.4 and are as follows. DC's delayed copy peacock contains elements changed in shape and size (type 1). IF's seal

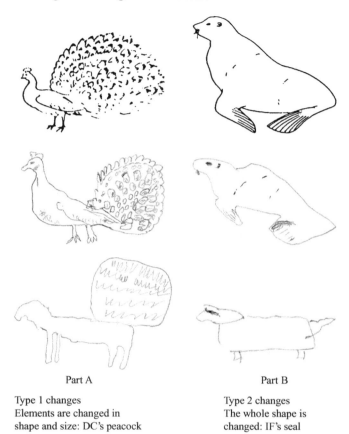

| Part A | Part B |

Type 1 changes
Elements are changed in
shape and size: DC's peacock

Type 2 changes
The whole shape is
changed: IF's seal

Figure 14.4 Examples of direct copy and delayed copy drawings from semantic dementia patients, showing how the delayed copy drawings can be systematized following the scheme of Karmiloff-Smith (1990).

has changed its whole shape (type 2). DC's kangaroo and IF's squirrel have lost their tails, DC's camel has lost its hump, and her saw has lost its hand-hold (type 3). DC's helicopter has legs rather than runners and her plug has acquired a cross-bar that would rather vitiate its function (type 4). DS's toothbrush has changed its orientation (type 5) as well as becoming a more generic brush. In line with expectations, there are few if any cross-*domain* insertions; but there are certainly things that could be identified as the insertion of cross-*category* elements (type 6): DS's duck and DC's peacock now have four (rather than two) legs; IF's seal has acquired a tail (as did DC's frog in Figure 14.2); and DC's kangaroo has adopted a rather human-like standing posture.

Part C

Part D

Type 3 changes
Loss of characteristic features:
Left: Kangaroo lost the tail; Right: Camel lost the hump

Figure 14.4 (*cont.*)

Drawing in neurodegenerative disease 299

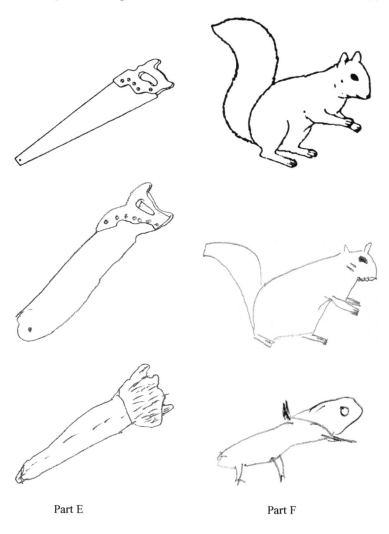

Part E   Part F

Type 3 changes
Loss of characteristics features:
Left: Saw lost teeth and grip; Right: Squirrel lost the tail

Figure 14.4 (*cont.*)

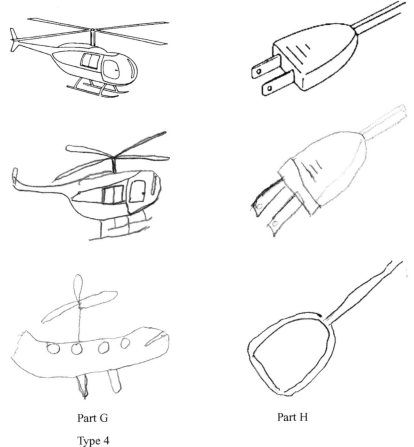

Part G

Part H

Type 4
Functional changes:
DC's helicopter has legs and the plug a cross-bar

Figure 14.4 (*cont.*)

Part I
Type 5 changes:
Orientation changes
DS's toothbrush

Part J
Type 6 changes:
Cross-category insertions of elements:
DS's duck and peacock (part A) have four legs

Figure 14.4 (*cont.*)

Concluding comments

This brief chapter has scarcely done justice to the rich world of drawing as a technique for investigating the erosion of conceptual knowledge in neurodegenerative disease. Indeed, the research on this topic that the chapter so briefly summarizes has only scratched the surface of what is bound to be a deep fund of information. What we have learned from the patients' drawings thus far mainly corroborates what we already knew, or at least suspected, from other research. It could be viewed as disappointing that the conclusions are not wholly novel; but instead we take it as reassuring that different lines of investigation yield converging evidence. The main conclusions afforded by the SD patients' drawings, in concert with the evidence from other techniques, are as follows.

Semantic dementia involves a deterioration of central conceptual knowledge that is reflected in any task requiring such knowledge, irrespective of the domain of knowledge being tapped, the modality of the stimulus employed to probe that knowledge or the modality of the response requested to display it.

The semantic deterioration in SD is, at least for a considerable period of time, highly selective, indicating that such central conceptual knowledge represents a focal component of cognitive architecture in the brain, which can be affected without major consequences for other components such as perceptual or motor ability or episodic memory.

The semantic decline, despite being inexorable and eventually profound, is always partial and graded. Concepts are not here today and gone tomorrow. The basic distinction between natural kinds or living things and man-made objects or artefacts persists for a long time.

The decline is strongly modulated by the extent to which aspects of knowledge are typical of other concepts in the same category or domain. A feature shared is a feature less vulnerable.

The semantic deterioration *is* profound. Given that the patients have the necessary perceptual, motor and memory skills needed to perform the delayed copy drawing task, what they produce under these conditions is a stark indication that they no longer really know/understand the concepts represented in the pictures that they are copying. Because anomia is such a prominent aspect of SD, it is sometimes tempting to think that, when the patients look at pictures of camels and pianos and are unable to name them, they still recognize what they are looking at and just cannot retrieve or produce the correct name. Their delayed copy drawings seem irrefutably to rule out that possibility.

We hope, indeed predict, that future investigations of drawings in SD will delve deeper into this rich source of information about the structure of conceptual knowledge as revealed by its disintegration.

Acknowledgements

We are grateful to John R. Hodges for permission to publish results from these SD patients under his care, to Sasha Bozeat for allowing us to include drawings from her studies of SD and to Simon Strangeways for help in producing the figures.

REFERENCES

Bozeat, S., Lambon Ralph, M. A., Graham, K. S., Patterson, K., Wilkin, H., Rowland, J., Rogers, T. T. and Hodges, J. R. (2003). A duck with four legs: investigating the structure of conceptual knowledge using picture drawing in semantic dementia. *Cognitive Neuropsychology*, 20, 27–47.

Franklin, S., Van Sommers, P. and Howard, D. (1992). Drawing without meaning? Dissociations in the graphic performance of an agnostic artist. In R. Campbell (ed.), *Mental lives: case studies in cognition* (pp. 178–98). Oxford: Blackwell.

Hodges, J. R., Graham, N. and Patterson, K. (1995). Charting the progression in semantic dementia: implications for the organization of semantic memory. *Memory*, 3, 463–95.

Hodges, J. R., Patterson, K., Oxbury, S. and Funnell, E. (1992). Semantic dementia: progressive fluent aphasia with temporal lobe atrophy. *Brain*, 115, 1783–1806.

Hodges, J. R., Patterson, K. and Tyler, L. K. (1994). Loss of semantic memory: implications for the modularity of mind. *Cognitive Neuropsychology*, 11, 505–42.

Howard, D. and Patterson, K. (1992). *Pyramids and palmtrees: a test of semantic access from words and pictures*. Bury St Edmunds: Thames Valley Test Company.

Jefferies, E., Jones, R.W., Bateman, D. and Lambon Ralph, M. A. (2005). A semantic contribution to nonword recall? Evidence for intact phonological processes in semantic dementia. *Cognitive Neuropsychology*, 22, 183–212.

Karmiloff-Smith, A. (1990). Constraints on representational change: evidence from children's drawing. *Cognition*, 34, 57–83.

Lambon Ralph, M. A., Graham, K. S., Patterson, K. and Hodges, J. R. (1999). Is a picture worth a thousand words? Evidence from concept definitions by patients with semantic dementia. *Brain and Language*, 70, 309–35.

Lambon Ralph, M. A. and Howard, D. (2000). Gogi aphasia or semantic dementia? Simulating and assessing poor verbal comprehension in a case of progressive fluent aphasia. *Cognitive Neuropsychology*, 17, 437–65.

Neary, D., Snowden, J. S., Gustafson, L., Passant, U., Stuss, D., Black, S., Freedman, M., Kertesz, A., Robert, P. H., Albert, M., Boone, K., Miller, B. L., Cummings, J. and Benson, D. F. (1998). Frontotemporal lobar degeneration: a consensus on clinical diagnostic criteria. *Neurology*, 51, 1546–54.

Nestor, P. J., Fryer, T. D. and Hodges, J. R. (2006). Declarative memory impairments in Alzheimer's disease and semantic dementia. *NeuroImage*, 30, 1010–20.

Patterson, K., Lambon Ralph, M. A., Jefferies, E., Woollams, A., Jones, R., Hodges, J. R. and Rogers, T. T. (2006). 'Pre-semantic' cognition in semantic dementia: six deficits in search of an explanation. *Journal of Cognitive Neuroscience*, 18, 169–83.

Rey, A. (1941). L'examen psychologique dans les cas d'encephalopathie traumatique [The psychological assessment of a case of traumatic encephalopathy]. *Archives de Psychologie*, 28, 286–340.

Rogers, T. T., Lambon Ralph, M. A., Garrard, P., Bozeat, S., McClelland, J. L., Hodges, J. R. and Patterson, K. (2004a). The structure and deterioration of semantic memory: a neuropsychological and computational investigation. *Psychological Review*, 111, 205–35.

Rogers, T. T., Lambon Ralph, M. A., Hodges, J. R. and Patterson, K. (2004b). Natural selection: the impact of semantic impairment on lexical and object decision. *Cognitive Neuropsychology*, 21, 331–52.

Servos, P., Goodale, M. A. and Humphrey, G. K. (1993). The drawing of objects by a visual form agnostic: contribution of surface properties and memorial representations. *Neuropsychologia*, 31, 251–9.

15 Drawings by a blind adult: orthogonals, parallels and convergence in two directions without T-junctions

John M. Kennedy and Igor Juricevic

Kennedy and Juricevic argue that in both normal sighted and blind people the development of drawing using spatial projection systems proceeds from an orthogonal basis to freehand versions of parallel perspective and inverse perspective, and then to viewpoint perspective in which convergence shows parallel edges in the scene. They suggest the development of visually realistic contour drawing using T-junctions for overlap occurs independently. The authors report a case study of a blind young woman, Tracy T, who has had exceptionally extensive drawing practice since childhood. In the case study, Tracy T used a raised line drawing kit to draw objects in various orientations. A verbal protocol was taken while drawing. Tracy T drew a 3D cube in perspective, objects from various directions and figures involved in actions. Most strikingly, she used two-point perspective when sketching the roof of a house from above. Sometimes her verbal comments would outstrip her graphic abilities. Notably, for Tracy T, overlap was a problem, and she left drawings requiring overlap incomplete. Improvisation helped her avoid problems in relatively free drawing tasks compared to more prescriptive ones. The study offers evidence that blind people tackle spatial drawing problems in similar ways to sighted people.

TRACY T, a blind adult, has appreciable spatial skills and an interest in drawing.[1] Here we find that her drawings generally employ orthogonals, that is, plans and elevations with correct orientation from the observer's vantage point. Occasionally they use freehand parallel, and one- and two-point projection. Tracy T does not use T-junctions for overlap, and she was unable to complete drawings of objects in three-quarter view. We argue that drawing development in both the blind and the sighted proceeds from orthogonals to freehand versions of parallel, inverse, and one-, two- and three-point perspective, and T-junctions for overlap are discovered separately from this sequence.

A report on Tracy T is an important addition to the debate about projection in drawing development (Eriksson, 1998; Golomb, 2002; Kennedy, 2003; Willats, 2003) because she has appreciable drawing skills. Previous studies of raised outline pictures with blind adults and children focused on the emergence of the most basic drawing abilities (Laursen, 2006). The abilities were thought to follow from two factors. First, lines have affinities with surface edges in touch just as they do in vision, and, second, they have directions from our vantage point in touch much as they do in vision (Kennedy and Juricevic, 2006).

Touch entails projective geometry if it detects directions from a vantage point (Cabe, Wright and Wright, 2003; Kappers and Koenderink, 2002). Hence, in drawing development we should increasingly take direction into account, whether we are sighted or blind. It is likely that early drawings copy left–right and up–down directions from our vantage point, and we advance towards use of convergence to show that receding objects subtend ever smaller angles from our vantage point (Nicholls and Kennedy, 1992, 1995).

Relatively unpractised blind children and adults identify objects such as telephones, cups and hands in raised-outline drawings that show surface edges, though, as Lederman, Klatzky, Chataway and Summers (1990) rightly stress, the identification rates are modest, ranging from about 10 per cent to about 70 per cent after many seconds of exploration, unlike vision's 100 per cent rate after a split second (D'Angiulli, Kennedy and Heller, 1998; Heller et al., 2002, 2006; Millar, 2006). Also, blind children and adults who have very little practice in drawing use lines for surface edges, drawing recognizable pictures of common objects such as tables, chairs and glasses. The drawings usually portray the facets of objects that are in front of the vantage point. They copy the orthogonal dimensions left–right and up–down as they are oriented from the observer's point of view by using the same dimensions on the picture surface. Orthogonals are also used to copy depth, for example situating the carriages of a train left-to-right on the page to depict a train rushing directly at the observer, as if the observer's vantage point had moved to the side of train.

If the drawing uses the vertical dimension on the page for depth from the vantage point, with more distant cross-ties of the train's tracks shown higher up the picture, this is an advance on using the left–right dimension for depth since the observer's vantage point has not moved, and height in the picture captures the directions of the cross-ties – the distant cross-ties are higher in direction from the vantage point.

A more sophisticated drawing system uses parallel oblique projection, in which lines diagonal to the vertical dimension of the page depict the receding tracks in the scene. Usually, the obliques rise on the picture surface to show increase in distance. In a further advance, rail tracks are depicted by lines that converge on the picture surface. The converging lines mimic the directions to the sides of the tracks narrowing as their distance increases. If the lines converge to one focus on the page this is one-point perspective. To be in perfect one-point linear perspective, the rate of convergence would need to be calculated precisely, using projective geometry.

In two-point perspective, there would be two centres of convergence for surfaces at right angles, one to the left, say, for the front wall of a house and one to the right for the end wall. In three-point perspective, the two walls and a flat roof of the house could be shown by three centres of convergence (Juricevic and Kennedy, 2006).

In inverse perspective, lines diverge to show increases in distance. In sighted children's drawings, use of 'divergent perspective' is a matter of convenience (Arnheim, 1974). It is useful to show the front and two sides of a house. The child of 9 or 10 may use parallel, convergent and divergent obliques as convenient to show parts of the object that are hidden from the observer's vantage point. Convenience takes precedence over consistency. Children of 11 or older tend to use parallels or converging lines consistently.

T-junctions can depict an overlapped surface with the I stem of the T. They can be used in orthogonal, parallel, inverse and convergent drawings and so their discovery may be independent of these projections. T-junctions show overlap in early Renaissance pictures in which parallel and divergent perspective are employed (Landerer, 2000). The overlap often conflicts with other parts of the picture. For example, T-junctions show legs of people overlapping table legs that height in the picture plane and inverse perspective depict as foreground objects. If the development of the use of T-junctions is independent of other systems for depicting depth, a radical hypothesis is that they could be missing in drawings by the blind that use many kinds of projections.

Very few early-blind people have extensive experience of drawing (Berg, 2003). We have only encountered four, including the one reported here. All four deserve detailed case study, with many tasks tackled by each subject to define the systems they use. The tasks should be relevant to depth, overlap and orientation from the participant's vantage point. Several tasks should be relevant to any general drawing strategy in question.

Static drawings cannot literally copy motion in a scene. However, just as language can use words out of place in metaphors, drawings can distort a shape to suggest motion non-literally (Kennedy and Merkas, 2000). If Tracy T can create metaphoric shapes for motion, any limits she shows in other drawing tasks are unlikely to be due to failing to be inventive.

A blind child aged 12, Gaia, from Rome, is the only blind child we have tested who had been encouraged to draw every week since preschool (Kennedy, 2003). Tracy T has had many more years of experience and should offer more sophisticated projections.

Gaia often drew objects very clearly and recognizably. Since the forms in the picture and the objects in the scene being depicted were oriented similarly from her point of view she used orthogonals. In addition, like sighted children aged 5–7 (Golomb, 2002), she portrayed depth with objects lined up vertically, bottom-of-page to top-of-page in order of distance from the observer. Gaia drew a cube as if 'folded-out' (characteristic of sighted children about 7 years old). She used parallel perspective for tables and for rows of objects. Of striking interest, on several occasions she also drew tables and rooftops in keeping with inverse perspective (like sighted children between 9 and 11). With impressive similarity to early Renaissance pictures, she used T-junctions quite inconsistently, with rear legs of tables portrayed as overlapping legs of chairs in the foreground.

Gaia was unable to use obliques systematically to complete a drawing of a house in three-quarter view, i.e. with a corner of the house in front of her. She drew the receding roof, front and end walls in oblique parallel perspective, but incompletely. This suggests Gaia is just beginning to use oblique dimensions for depth, like sighted 9–11-year-olds.

Tracy, a blind woman in New York, has drawn pictures from childhood. Hence, she and Tracy T should use the same systems.

Tracy from New York used parallel obliques. Her use of inverse perspective was quite infrequent. Her T-junctions were consistent with other depth indicators. Further, one remarkable drawing depicted receding rows of glasses on a table top with U-shapes getting progressively smaller and higher on the picture plane to represent glasses that were more distant and higher in direction from the observer's vantage point (Kennedy and Juricevic, 2003). In addition, the spaces between the glasses converged to represent increasing distance. This is one-point perspective, and highly advanced developmentally. Tracy can be compared to 11–13-year-old sighted children.

Esref, a totally blind man from Turkey, has more experience drawing than Tracy T. He is impressively advanced (Kennedy and Juricevic, 2006).

Esref drew freehand in one, two- and three-point perspective. He drew the tops, fronts and sides of houses and cubes using convergence. He made consistent use of T-junctions in pictures of tables and chairs. He compares favourably to sighted teens and adults with extensive drawing experience.

If drawing development occurs in the blind as in the sighted, Tracy T's drawings should use systems found in drawings by Gaia, Tracy and Esref. Some systems may have matured though others are emerging. If so, her drawings would show consistent, frequent use of some systems, but others would be inconsistent, and some tasks would be incomplete. If she usually relies on orthogonals, advanced tasks to do with depth should challenge her. Indeed, her drawings are incomplete in matters to do with obliques and convergence, and she omits use of T-junctions for overlap.

Drawings by Tracy T

Tracy T is employed to use spatial skills. She directs phone inquirers to appropriate offices in a large city hall. The route information she provides requires plan views, not ones with foreshortening and convergence.

Because of retinal blastomas, Tracy T has been totally blind since $2\frac{1}{2}$ years old, having lost one eye at 6 months. She has no visual memories. Her experience with pictures she describes as 'quite a bit', including drawing with crayon and pencil on paper, and with a raised-line drawing kit.

Our first meeting was a social occasion. She indicated she likes drawing. She drew a cat, an airplane, a 'smiley face' and a yacht at her own behest. Of course, these could be arbitrary formulae she has been taught. How does she respond to novel tasks to do with depth? We invited her to be interviewed formally.

Tracy T was given a raised-line drawing kit, comprising a plastic sheet on a rubber-coated board. A ballpoint pen writing on the sheet produces a raised line. She was asked to draw objects in various configurations, at a variety of orientations, and from different vantage points. Tracy T was motivated to draw. Indeed, she volunteered extra drawings during the tests. We will comment briefly here on each drawing in the order in which they were given, leaving general matters for the Discussion.

1. Crossed pencils were drawn as two lines forming an X, with no indication of overlap and the vantage point (Figure 15.1, left). The drawing uses similarity of form showing objects oriented as they were from her vantage point.

2. In the top row of Figure 15.1 a glass from the side is shown as a closed U (an elevation), and one from above is a circle (a plan view). To draw, first, a glass shown standing, second, one tilted away (at about 45 degrees) and, third, one lying down with its base towards her, she drew

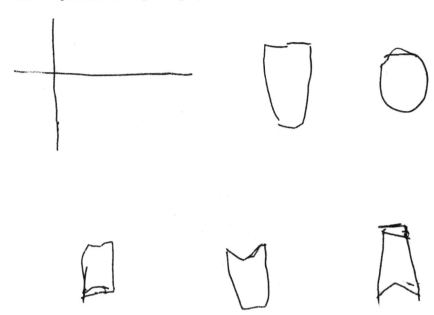

Figure 15.1 Crossed fingers, glass from the side and above, sitting on a table, lying down and upside-down.

the standing glass as an elevation with a double line for the base (bottom row, left), and the one lying down, bottom towards her, as a plan view with two U shapes, one a shallow U for the brim 'to show it is open' (bottom row middle). In keeping with her reliance on orthogonals, Tracy T said she did not know how to draw the tilted glass.

Tracy T volunteered an elevation of a glass upside down (Figure 15.1 bottom right), two lines for the base now at the top of the drawing, and a U for the brim at the bottom.

Her U for a brim could be showing half the brim in plan view (a 'disintegration-and-emphasis' drawing (Caron-Pargue, 1985), in which part of a feature is selected), a tactic which is common in drawings from sighted children aged 7–9.

3. To draw a cube and a cup at three separations Tracy T used a plan view (Figure 15.2), the cube as a single square and the cup as a circle. The cup was drawn further up the picture plane as it receded.

4. Her drawings of a hand and a hand with fingers crossed (Figure 15.3) use true form, the fingers-crossed with no hidden line elimination.

5. Requested to draw a table from the side, her vantage point was indicated by putting her hand at the level of the table top and a short distance

Drawings by a blind adult

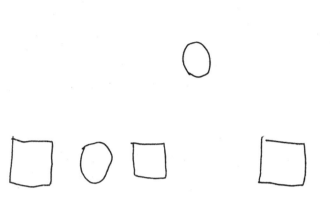

Figure 15.2 Cube and glass, with the glass at three depths.

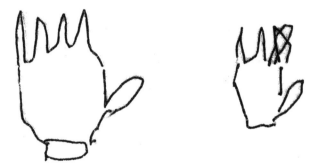

Figure 15.3 Hand and hand with fingers crossed.

from it (about 30 cm). She drew an inverted U-shape (Figure 15.4, left) with right-angled corners, with just a single line for the edge of the table, an elevation in keeping with the vantage point. Not-quite-vertical lines were added for the rear legs. In similar drawings from sighted 8- and 9-year-olds (Goodnow, 1977) the angles of lines at junctions are often modified as convenient to show features that would be occluded.

She was then asked to draw a table from a three-quarter view, putting her hand near one of the table's corners, and about 30 cm above it and about 30 cm distant from the table edge as before. In keeping with her reliance on orthogonals, Tracy T said she did not know how to draw this.

Figure 15.4 Table and microwave oven.

Figure 15.5 Person standing, walking, lying down and running.

6. Asked to draw a cube, Tracy T drew a square and said 'But it is just flat.' She then volunteered a drawing of a microwave oven, from the front (Figure 15.4 right). Her probable motive was that there are more identifying details in the oven drawing than in the cube-as-elevation drawing, which could portray a flat surface. On the right a rectangle with dots suggests the control panel. Of interest, short lines to the left suggest the left receding side, shown incompletely (Jansson, 2001).

7. Figure 15.5 shows drawings of people. One is of a person standing with L-shaped stick-figure legs, feet pointing one left, one right, a common device from sighted children aged 7–9, in keeping with orthogonals (Cox, 1992, 1993). She said, 'I had to put his feet sideways 'cause I don't know how to do frontwards.' An extra line to the right of the head rounds off the head shape. For a person walking, she drew the arms out more ('swinging'), one leg short, and 'the long one is forward', she said. (This short-leg drawing could be a precursor to foreshortening. See also Figure 15.12.) A person lying down 'would be like a profile', she said, and she drew the bottom leg straight, the top one bent ('the knee would be bent') and 'resting on the other one'. She said, 'The bottom arm would have to go in front of his body' and the upper arm 'would come down and be resting on the floor'.

8. She was asked to draw a card folded in half and standing on the table in front of her in two positions, one with the rear half folded behind

Drawings by a blind adult 313

Figure 15.6 Wheel static and spinning too fast to make out.

and occluded by the front half, and one with the rear folded out, and not occluded, but still slanting away from her, receding at about 45 degrees. She drew two V shapes, one acute, one obtuse, drawing the card from above (plan view).

9. After the card task, Tracy T was asked to draw a wheel with five spokes in different kinds of motion (Figure 15.6). Static was drawn with all spokes straight from a central point, a spinning motion with spokes bent (saying 'they're not straight – they'd be flashing by'), wobbly was drawn with wavy lines, spinning-too-fast-to-make-out as an empty oval. For a wheel with its brakes on, she said the drawing would not be different from the static-wheel drawing. She was unable to draw a wheel for jerky motion.

10. Drawing a person running (Figure 15.5, right) she said, 'Sideways, a stick person would be easy. One arm would be forward. The left arm would be back. One leg would be up and forward. The other one would be back and maybe slightly bent.' She did not know how to distinguish the legs from the vantage point of the observer. 'I don't know how to show which is which. If I drew it on top it would show which leg is which.' The head she described as a 'profile, looking towards the side of the page'. The drawing contains an extra line paralleling the rear leg, on which she did not comment. It may be a false start.

11. Asked to draw a table again, she drew an inverted U-shape once more (Figure 15.7, top left), omitting the rear legs this time. Then she was asked to draw the table from above, the side and below (Figure 15.7, top row). For 'from above' she drew a rectangle. From the side she drew an inverted U with a crossbar. The legs, she said, are 'technically one right behind the other'. She drew the table from underneath as a rectangle containing a rectangle for 'the frame inside. I don't know how to draw the legs. They'd come up.' The drawings are in parallel perspective.

12. She uses parallel projection and height in the picture in sketching two rows of glasses receding from her on the table-top, three glasses per row (Figure 15.7, bottom left). 'From the side you'd see the top of one

Figure 15.7 Table, table from above, table from side and table from underneath. Bottom: Two rows of glasses, three glasses per row, receding across the table. Two cars, one behind the other.

behind the other. You wouldn't see the bottom of this one.' Once again she said, 'I'd do a dip [small U at top] to show its open.' The drawing includes hidden-line elimination for the bottoms of glasses, but vertical lines for the sides of the rear glasses obtrude on the spaces depicting foreground glasses, and do not terminate in T-junctions.

13. She was asked to draw two cars, one behind the other (Figure 15.7, bottom right). Using orthogonals, the cars are drawn from the side and lined up left-to-right. The car on the right has two lines for the hood, a mistake she said, and the upper line 'should not be here', and the windshield should have 'more of an angle'.

14. She used orthogonals for a person facing her and a second in profile, and drew incompletely for a three-quarter view, which she was told is 'halfway in-between'. She drew (Figure 15.8) a person facing her with two eyes and a central nose and mouth. The profile has one eye, the nose and the mouth on the right. For the three-quarter view she said 'maybe you could do an eye, a nose and a part of an eye . . . but not all of the mouth' and 'most of the body but you wouldn't see all of it'. She continued, 'You'd see the right arm and the whole right leg and part of the left leg. I don't know how to do that so I'll just put part of a leg', and a short line is included. Her drawing omits a contour for the far side of the body. This omission and comments on the rear leg fit with a system relying on orthogonals without T-junctions to show overlap.

Drawings by a blind adult 315

Figure 15.8 Person standing, side on, three-quarter view.

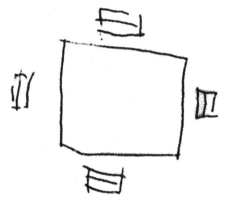

Figure 15.9 Table and four chairs.

15. For a table and four chairs around it, she used a plan view (Figure 15.9), the chairs as smaller rectangles bisected by straight lines for the back of the chairs.

16. In 'Piaget's three-mountains task' (Heller and Kennedy, 1990) three objects are set before the subject, on a rectangular mat. The objects were a sphere to the near left, a cone in the far centre and a cube to the mid right. Tracy T was asked to draw these from her vantage point,

from 180 degrees opposite, 90 degrees to the left, 90 degrees to the right and from a vantage point above the mat. The vantage points were demonstrated using a doll, head level with the objects, or, in the case of 'above the mat', centred above the mat with its feet towards her. She drew the objects in elevation as a circle (sphere), a triangle (cone) and a square (cube), except for 'above', for which she drew in plan view with the cone as a circle with a dot in the centre. The mat was drawn as a single line. The order of the objects was correct from her vantage point and she used height in the picture plane to show the depth of the objects. From other vantage points she was in error. For example, for the vantage point on the far side of the mat she retained the cone in the centre but put it high on the picture surface. From 90 degrees to the left, she did not draw the left-to-right order correctly (the sphere was not moved to the right).

17. She drew a house from several vantage points. The roof was formed by two equal rectangles meeting at a roofline equal in length to the front of the house. It did not narrow upwards. For the vantage point in front of the house, she drew a rectangle and said, 'This is the house part.' Then she said, 'I'm not sure how to show the roof is sloped from the front. I'll just put the sidelines slanted in just a little bit' and she drew the roof using converging lines (Figure 15.10, top left), narrowing towards the roofline, in one-point perspective. For the gable end (Figure 15.10, top middle) she said, 'You just draw the two lines on a slope. They peak together.' From above (Figure 15.10, top right) she drew both of the receding sides of the roof using converging lines. Indeed, about the central long line she said, 'This would be the peak.' She commented on the convergence, 'This would be the slope coming down.' This is a freehand drawing in two-point perspective.

To show the house in three-quarter view (a vantage point near a corner of the house and slightly above the top of the rectangle for the front of the house) she began with a V to show 'the left wall and the right wall', but then she said, 'I don't know how to incorporate the roof' and stopped drawing.

18. For a cube balanced on a vertex, Tracy T drew three quadrilaterals around a central Y, for the three faces and the vertex facing her (Figure 15.10, bottom), with both sides diverging, in inverse projection.

19. Tracy T drew an insect, a dog and a person as a top, a side and a front view respectively, using orthogonal schemas (Figure 15.11).

20. She was asked to draw a cube in various locations demonstrated to her by moving the cube sideways: first, on the table and directly in front, then to the right and then further to the right. She used her 'incomplete sides' device. For the cube in front, she drew a square and two short lines

Drawings by a blind adult 317

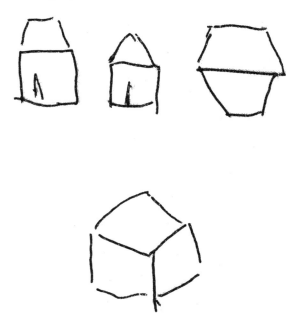

Figure 15.10 House from front, from gable end, and from above. Cube vertex pointing forwards.

upwards from its corners (Figure 15.12, top left). She said, 'I don't know how to draw the top. So I'll just draw a line in a bit.' Then to show cubes to the side, she drew a pattern three times: a tilted square with a short line to the left at its base and an inverted L at the top right corner (Figure 15.12, top right). 'The short line is for the short side – you see a little bit of it.' The L is 'to show the top'.

She was then asked to draw a set of three cubes moved vertically, initially at head height and 'level with my face', as Tracy T herself put it, second moved down with the top surface and front facing her and 'evident as you reach out', third moved up so it was above head height with the front and bottom surfaces facing her.

She used her incomplete-side device again. The head-height cube is drawn as a single square (Figure 15.12, bottom left). One rectangle stacked on top of an incomplete rectangle (Figure 15.12, bottom, second from left) is the cube moved downward. Figure 15.12, bottom middle, shows a cube above head height, with two complete sides (a 'fold-out' drawing). About the oblique lines flanking the lower square (showing the bottom of the cube) she said, 'It's the sides you would see. I don't know

Figure 15.11 Insect, dog and person.

Figure 15.12 Cube in different locations. Bottom right is a half-cube, from above and incomplete.

how to represent both.' (The drawings using only the two faces in front of the vantage point are in an orthogonal 'vertical' projection (Willats, 2003), a step beyond a full 'fold-out' drawing by implying the vantage point to select the faces.)

21. Asked to draw a block the size of half a cube, with its square face towards her she used plan views and the incomplete-side device, saying 'I can only show it straight down, which would be a rectangle' (Figure 15.12, bottom right). The incomplete rectangle indicates 'you would not see the back'.

Discussion

Tracy T chiefly uses orthogonals and on occasion she uses parallel, inverse and freehand two-point projection. That is, she mostly draws true shapes that retain the orientation of the object from her vantage point, fronts of objects in elevations, and plan views for tops of objects and their locations in depth. However, she also uses parallel projection and height in the picture plane in sketching rows of glasses and tables. Consistent with parallel projection, she described occlusion in omitting bases of glasses and rear legs of tables. Further, she used inverse projection for the cube balanced on a vertex. In an especially advanced drawing, the roof of the house was sketched in one- and two-point perspective. Her most notable omission is the use of T-junctions for overlap.

Her plans, elevations, inverse and parallel projection, flexibility with figures, addition of lines for rear table legs and side-surfaces of cubes as convenient, objects in a horizontal line to show depth, and short-line devices to show objects incompletely may be characteristic of many sighted 9- or 10-year-olds (Milbrath, 1998). Her use of freehand two-point perspective is much more advanced, by two or three years at least even in sighted teenagers familiar with many kinds of pictures. It is worthy of a great deal of attention.

When Tracy T draws objects as true forms simply by selecting one aspect, it is well chosen. It presents many relevant features (for example, in the top view of an ant, the side view of a car or a dog, and the front view of a person). In this orthogonal system, the object can be drawn in a variety of novel postures (e.g. a person lying down), or from a variety of vantage points on demand (e.g. a house from the end).

In her plans and elevations, Tracy T readily changes her vantage point from one of the major orthogonals to another around a single object such as a glass or a table. Advancing to parallel perspective, she improves the scope of the orthogonal system by adding information for depth by height in the picture plane (for the rows of glasses) and by consistently omitting features that are to the rear or project directly to the observer (such as legs of tables).

Her two-point perspective drawing of the house from above is highly advanced. Restricted to one object in one drawing, this could be her first use of this scheme. She did not apply it to suitable subjects such as the tilted glass, the folded card, the three-quarter view of the house or cubes arranged in horizontal and vertical arrays (Goodman, 1968; Hopkins, 2003; Lopes, 2003). It may have been invented on the spot in the form of a rule such as 'use convergence to indicate surfaces sloping with respect to the horizontal', missing for the moment the broad implications for any receding surface.

Tracy T deviates from true form as convenient to show table legs or cube sides which would otherwise be occluded (Freeman, 1986). Goodnow (1977) regards this as developmentally less advanced than the consistent use of one spatial scheme that accepts inconvenient consequences. The use of short lines for rear legs or side surfaces is another deviation from true form (though one that might lead her to foreshortening, we may speculate, if she began relating it to the object's orientation to the vantage point.

She is defeated by vantage points between the main orthogonals for tilts and three-quarter views. She shifts from elevation to plan view when confronted with tasks for which convergence would be suitable. Also, her coordination of height-in-the-picture and representation with the left–right axis on the picture surface is not sufficient to solve the three-mountains task, for example correctly reversing the left–right order of the objects but not realizing that what is high in the picture plane from her vantage point is low for someone opposite.

Her use of obliques is restricted. They depicted rear legs that should be occluded, receding side surfaces of a cube posed on its vertex, and a slanted roof. These may each be motivated by what Tracy T takes to be different cases.

Tracy T depicted wheels in motion using metaphoric devices. Evidently, pictorial metaphors can be produced when a system for representing all of 3D space is incomplete. Likely, a metaphoric change in shape of any part of an object, such as a spoke of a wheel, can be invented if its shape has been mastered. Tracy T's willingness to invent devices, including table legs not quite vertical, and short lines, as well as shapes of spokes, indicates that her omission of T-junctions and her leaving some tasks incomplete is not due to lack of inventiveness. Indeed, the drawings of spokes show she is willing to go beyond literal representation. Metaphoric devices put relevant features of the literal case in an unrealistic but apt context. Tracy T's motion devices are a case in point.

Gaia did not draw any metaphors, saying pictures cannot show motion. It may be that many artists with Gaia's skills are coming to terms with the limits of pictures, and are in a middle-childhood phase when the emphasis is on making good literal copies and this goal crowds out others. (Discomfiting adults, teenagers point out literal meanings of our expressions we might prefer to gloss over.)

It is remarkable that Tracy T's comments show she understands occlusion in the scene, but her drawings do not include T-junctions for overlap, and are left incomplete by her own admission. Probably, she is considering spatial relations in the scene and spatial relations on the picture surface, not primarily matching the junctions of lines on the picture surface with possible referents in the scene. The drawing of two rows of glasses receding shows the two front glasses completely and eliminates lower parts of rear glasses, but with lines that simply terminate without finishing in T-junctions.

Projections may be fairly independent from depth information from junctions in early drawing development, and consistency a late development. If so, omission or conflict between devices is to be expected in middle-childhood and in drawings by blind people whose experience in drawing is modest. Indeed, Kennedy (1993) reported that unpractised blind adults drawing crossed fingers often did not use hidden-line elimination.

One lesson from Tracy T's abilities is that the keys to drawing development are broader than any single modality. Edges, forms, vantage points and the direction of objects from observers are not specifically visual or tactile. To draw, these must be related to visual and tactile properties of the picture surface such as lines, shapes, and orthogonal and oblique axes. The developing artist may match orthogonals, then height in the vertical plane, then obliques and then converging directions of parts. We can align these via vision or touch.

Further, we may develop depiction skills in a sequence for reasons that are independent of vision or touch and largely to do with logical priority. We have to know the shape of an object before we can apply a projection to the shape. If we know a shape, and merely repeat the shape in a drawing, that is using similarity geometry. It involves no new features, no transformations. If the orientation of the object is copied, the result is an orthogonal projection. Retaining height in the picture plane, parallel projection can copy the true shapes of fronts of objects, and also align the depth in the scene with diagonals on the picture surface. It can combine orthogonals, height-in-the-picture and diagonal alignment. Linear perspective can shrink the fronts progressively to indicate increasing depth. In this respect it is parallel projection plus a transformation.

Parallel perspective is nested within linear perspective in the same way that orthogonals and height-in-the-picture are nested within parallel perspective. Hence, the blind and the sighted could be on the same developmental trajectory because for both the crux of development is that earlier skills are nested within later skills.

In sum, though many of her drawings have projective systems typical of a 9- or 10-year-old sighted child, Tracy T's use of one- and two-point convergence and short, incomplete lines could be harbingers of advances. Her modal system is orthogonal but she uses a wide range of projections. Tracy T's drawings are evidence that blind people tackle drawing tasks using the same systems as the sighted. Since much of a scene is common to touch and vision, drawing development can be similar in the blind and the sighted. In effect, advances in drawing skill entail the developing artist, blind or sighted, treating pictures as ways of demonstrating the directions to parts of the scene rather than as ways of copying true form.

NOTE

1. We thank Tracy from Toronto for her very valuable help in this research. The chapter is dedicated to picture theorists John Willats, who died in 2006, and Rudolf Arnheim, who died in 2007 in his 103rd year.

REFERENCES

Arnheim, R. (1974). *Art and visual perception*. Berkeley: University of California Press.
Berg, I. (2003). *Zeichnungen blinder und sehender Kinder im Vergleich [Comparison of drawings by blind and sighted children]*. Stuttgart: Ibidem.
Cabe, P. A., Wright, C. D. and Wright, M. A. (2003). Descartes' blind man revisited: bimanual triangulation of distance using static hand-held rods. *American Journal of Psychology*, 116, 71–98.
Caron-Pargue, J. (1985). *Le dessin du cube chez l'enfant [Children's drawings of cubes]*. Berne: Lang.
Cox, M. V. (1992). *Children's drawings*. London: Penguin.
(1993). *Children's drawings of the human figure*. Hove: Erlbaum.
D'Angiulli, A., Kennedy, J. M. and Heller, M. A. (1998). Blind children recognizing tactile pictures respond like sighted children given guidance in exploration. *Scandinavian Journal of Psychology*, 39, 187–90.
Eriksson, Y. (1998). *Tactile pictures: pictorial representations for the blind 1784–1940*. Goteberg: Goteberg University Press.
Freeman, N. H. (1986). How should a cube be drawn? *British Journal of Developmental Psychology*, 4, 317–22.
Gibson, J. J. (1962). Observations on active touch. *Psychological Review*, 69, 447–9.
Golomb, C. (2002). *Child art in context: a cultural and comparative perspective*. Washington, DC: American Psychological Association.
Goodman, N. (1968). *Languages of art*. Indianapolis: Bobbs-Merrill.
Goodnow, J. J. (1977). *Children's drawings*. London: Fontana.
Heller, M. A. and Kennedy, J. M. (1990). Perspective-taking, pictures and the blind. *Perception and Psychophysics*, 48, 459–66.
Heller, M. A., Brackett, D. E., Scroggs, E., Steffen, H., Heatherly, K. and Salik, S. (2002). Tangible pictures: viewpoint effects and linear perspective in visually impaired people. *Perception*, 31, 747–69.
Heller, M. A., Kennedy, J. M., Clark, A., McCarthy, M., Borgert, A., Wemple, L., Fulkerson, E., Kaffel, N., Duncan, A. and Riddle, T. (2006). Viewpoint and orientation influence picture recognition in the blind. *Perception*, 35, 1397–1420.

Hopkins, R. (2003). Touching, seeing and appreciating pictures. In E. Axel and N. Levent (eds.), *Art beyond sight: a resource guide to art, creativity and visual impairment* (pp. 186–99). New York: AFB Press.

Jansson, G. (2001). The potential importance of perceptual filling-in for haptic perception of virtual object form. In C. Baber, M. Faint, S. Wall and A. M. Wing (eds.), *Eurohaptics 2001. Conference Proceedings. Educational Technology Research Papers* (Vol. 12, pp. 72–5). Birmingham: Birmingham University Press.

Juricevic, I. and Kennedy, J. M. (2006). Looking at perspective pictures from too far, too close and just right. *Journal of Experimental Psychology: General*, 135, 448–61.

Kappers, A. M. L. and Koenderink, J. J. (2002). Continuum of haptic space. In L. Albertazzi (ed.), *Unfolding perceptual continua* (pp. 29–79). Philadelphia: John Benjamins.

Kennedy, J. M. (1993). *Drawing and the blind*. New Haven, CT: Yale University Press.

  (2003). Drawings from Gaia, a blind girl. *Perception*, 32, 321–40.

Kennedy, J. M. and Juricevic, I. (2003). Haptics and projection: drawings by Tracy, a blind adult. *Perception*, 32, 1059–71.

  (2006). Form, projection and pictures for the blind. In M. A. Heller and S. Ballesteros (eds.), *Haptics, blindness and neuroscience* (pp. 73–93). Mahwah, NJ: Erlbaum.

  (2006). Blind man draws using diminution in three dimensions. *Psychonomic Bulletin and Review*, 13, 3, 506–9.

Kennedy, J. M. and Merkas, C. E. (2000). Depictions of motion devised by a blind person. *Psychonomic Bulletin and Review*, 7, 700–6.

Landerer, C. (2000). Kunstgeschichte als Kognitiongeschichte: ein Beitrag zur genetischen Kulturpsychologie [History of art as history of cognition: a contribution to genetic culture psychology]. Doctoral dissertation, University of Salzburg.

Laursen, B. (2006). Tegning, cognition og innovation – om komplekse tegnekompetencer [Drawing, cognition and innovation – on complex drawing abilities]. *Billedpaedagogisk Tidskrift*, 2, 8–10.

Lederman, S. J., Klatzky, R. L., Chataway, C. and Summers, C. (1990). Visual mediation and the haptic recognition of two-dimensional pictures of common objects. *Perception and Psychophysics*, 47, 54–64.

Lopes, D. M. M. (2003). Are pictures visual: a brief history of an idea. In E. Axel and N. Levent (eds.), *Art beyond sight: a resource guide to art, creativity and visual impairment* (pp. 176–85). New York: AFB Press.

Milbrath, C. (1998). *Patterns of artistic development in children: comparative studies of talent*. Cambridge: Cambridge University Press.

Millar, S. (2006). Processing spatial information from touch and movement: implications from and for neuroscience. In M. A. Heller and S. Ballesteros (eds.), *Haptics, blindness and neuroscience* (pp. 25–48). Mahwah, NJ: Erlbaum.

Nicholls, A. and Kennedy, J. M. (1992). Drawing development: from similarity of features to direction. *Child Development*, 63, 227–41.

(1995). Foreshortening in cube drawings by children and adults. *Perception*, 24, 1443–56.

Willats, J. (1997). *Art and representation*. Princeton: Princeton University Press.

(2003). Optical laws or symbolic rules? The dual nature of pictorial systems. In H. Hecht, R. Schwartz and M. Atherton (eds.), *Looking into pictures: an interdisciplinary approach to pictorial space* (pp. 125–43). Cambridge, MA: MIT Press.

16 Differences between individuals with and without autism in copying tasks: how knowledge interferes when drawing perspective

Elizabeth Sheppard, Peter Mitchell and Danielle Ropar

Sheppard, Mitchell and Ropar investigate whether individuals with autism are less likely than control participants to use object-specific drawing schemata which do not depict the model they actually see. Self-taught savant skills are much more frequent in autistic populations, and it is assumed that these may be responsible for a less conceptual approach which allows lower-level perceptual processing to prevail. However, because the empirical results from previous research did not prove to be conclusive, Sheppard, Mitchell and Ropar in several studies used tasks where in one condition a purely geometrical form was presented, while in the other condition features were added to convey the impression of a more meaningful object from everyday life. In children and adults without autism, meaningfulness could lower or enhance the level of drawing, depending on the kind of object, while spatial complexity appeared always to make drawing more difficult. Individuals with autism, however, were better able either to overcome or to ignore conceptual object knowledge, in particular when recreating a line drawing. It is concluded that this result reflects a special ability for literal understanding in autism.

A GREAT deal of research on drawing has focused on the effects of conceptual knowledge on performance. Generally, the bulk of findings suggest that prior knowledge about the subject matter interferes with accurate depiction. It seems that participants are liable to rely upon this instead of the viewpoint-specific information projected onto the retina. In other words, people sometimes draw what they know rather than what they see. In many studies participants are invited to draw a real three-dimensional object, and an essential part of the drawing process surrounds the problem of translating from a three-dimensional world to the two-dimensional paper. Some studies, though, have involved copying from a line drawing, where the 'translation problem' is solved already. Nevertheless, even these studies find that participants make systematic errors when asked to copy, suggesting that influence from prior knowledge of the subject matter is pervasive. However, data collected from recent studies of individuals with autism indicate that they perform quite differently when drawing than when copying, which not only highlights a difference between individuals with and without autism, but also raises the possibility that subtly different cognitive mechanisms could be at work when the subject matter is a real 3D object and when it is a 2D line drawing.

In this chapter we will contrast performance of those with and without autism on tasks that involve drawing real three-dimensional objects, and tasks that involve copying line drawings that *represent* three-dimensional objects. The chapter ends with speculations on the types of representation produced in the perception of line drawings versus real objects, and we discuss possible relationships between performance on copying tasks and the ability to meta-represent.

The influence of conceptual knowledge on drawing in individuals of typical development

The idea that drawing inaccuracies occur when the artist relies on his or her concepts (or knowledge) rather than viewpoint-specific information has a long history in drawing research. The development of drawing skill has traditionally been characterized as a shift from intellectual realism (depictions that are based upon internal representations) to visual realism (depictions that preserve information consistent with the artist's viewpoint) (Luquet, 2001). Freeman and Janikoun (1972) found that children under the age of about 8 tend to draw the handle of a cup even if the subject matter was oriented such that the handle was not visible. Children above this age tended not to include the handle if they could not see it. Such a transition (from intellectual to visual realism) implies that at some point most people acquire ability to draw in a visually realistic manner. Whilst clearly there are improvements in viewpoint-specific drawing with age, adults also produce knowledge-based errors in some contexts. Gombrich (1984) argues that, when drawing an object, people draw from a memorized ideal of the subject matter, called a schema. The schema contains information about the object that is viewpoint independent, as it describes invariant properties of the object. Therefore, drawing from a schema results in inaccuracies, especially those of distorted perspective (Kubovy, 1986).

The influence of conceptual knowledge on drawing in individuals with autism

A few striking cases of savant artists, individuals with extraordinary skills of accurate depiction but otherwise average or even impaired in cognitive functioning, have attracted a great deal of attention in the wider media. Studies examining the prevalence of savant abilities show that savant skills, including drawing, are greatly overrepresented amongst populations with autism (1 in 10 individuals with autism compared with 1 in 2000 individuals with cognitive disability; Hill, 1977; Rimland, 1978). In fact, cases of savant skills in individuals exhibiting no autistic features are extremely rare. This suggests that an aspect of autism might promote the development of savant abilities.

One view says that individuals with autism have an information processing style that is less concept-driven than that of individuals without autism, which allows lower-level perceptual processing to prevail (Frith, 2003). Researchers such as Snyder and Thomas (1997) argued that this perceptual style is the key to the development of outstanding skill by some individuals with autism. This seems like a compelling suggestion given that it is already well known that typically developing individuals make errors in basing drawings upon their conceptual knowledge rather than just information projected onto the retina.

Researchers have investigated whether some drawings by children with autism show a greater degree of visual realism than drawings of comparison participants of the same mental age. Charman and Baron-Cohen (1993) administered three tasks to children with and without autism, the first of which was Freeman and Janikoun's (1972) mug task, for which the children had to draw a mug with the handle occluded. The second task involved drawing objects partly occluded by a wall, and the third task involved drawing and colouring a cube that had six painted faces, from a vantage point where only three could be seen. Surprisingly, there was no difference between groups in the number of visually realistic drawings produced, with all participants producing drawings commensurate with their mental age.

Eames and Cox (1994) argued that failures to find precocious visual realism in previous studies could have resulted from children with autism being matched inappropriately with developmentally advanced comparison participants. Eames and Cox carried out a range of tasks to assess visual realism in children with autism, those with Down's syndrome, and typically developing children, all carefully matched according to mental age. In accordance with previous studies, though, the children with autism were still not more likely to produce visually realistic drawings than the comparison participants, and, if anything, their overall performance was below that of mental-age-matched children of typical development. From this study, Eames and Cox concluded that there is no autism-specific propensity for visually realistic drawings.

The studies described here led to the conclusion that there are no differences between the drawings of non-savant individuals with autism and other individuals of the same mental age. This has been interpreted as evidence that savant artists form a distinct subgroup within the autistic spectrum, and that there is no sign of incipient visual realism in the wider population of autism.

The influence of conceptual knowledge on copying in individuals of typical development

The kinds of knowledge-based errors that people make when drawing are observed on copying tasks. Chen (1985) argues that to draw from a real object, such as a cube, it is necessary to overcome one's knowledge about the object, and also to have appropriate drawing devices (so they know how to depict the cube). These devices are needed to overcome the problem of translating from the real three-dimensional object to the two-dimensional medium. However, the devices are not needed for copying where a solution to depicting 3D on a 2D surface is already presented. Hence, to succeed on a copying task, Chen argues that one *only* need overcome knowledge about the object, especially of its spatial structure. A 'structure-directed strategy' can be used, by accurately reproducing each line in the stimulus, without considering what it is meant to represent. This fact makes it all the more remarkable that both children and adults have been observed to make systematic errors when copying a line drawing of a 3D object.

We carried out one such task with adults (Mitchell, Ropar, Ackroyd and Rajendran, 2005), who were asked to copy two versions of the Shepard illusion (Figure 16.1). The shape and area of the two parallelograms are identical, even though the one on the right looks squarer. The illusion assumes greater potency when we add legs to make the parallelograms look like the tops of tables. These additional features suggest to us that we are viewing the surface of the tables from an oblique perspective. In contrast, the cues to vantage point are not so strong when the legs are missing, as in the top part of the figure. In this case, the illusion probably depends to a large extent on low-level perceptual mechanisms of the kind involved in the horizontal–vertical illusion. Namely, we tend to overestimate the length of vertical lines relative to horizontal lines, making the right-hand parallelogram seem squarer than the left-hand figure. In short, the illusion associated with parallelograms is associated with basic perceptual processes, while the illusion associated with the tables is associated additionally with 3D cues. Consequently, we might be tempted to say that the 'real' shape of the table is squarer than it appears in the right-hand part of the illusion, and that there is thus a

Individuals with and without autism in copying tasks 329

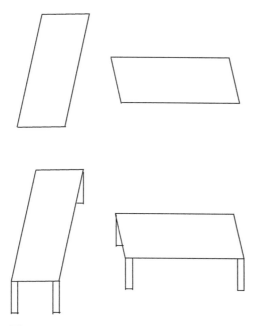

Figure 16.1 Shepard parallelograms and tables.

contrast between 'real' and 'projected' shape. There is no such contrast for the parallelogram version of the illusion.

According to Cohen and Bennett (1997), when drawing a perceptually low-level illusion like that induced by the parallelograms, participants will draw accurately. This happens even though participants fall for the illusion and therefore intend to draw the right-hand parallelogram squarer than the left-hand one. In doing the drawing, the illusion is re-created as the participants lay down the pencil lines and so, ironically, they actually draw the figure in a physically accurate way: they would insist that they had made the right-hand parallelogram squarer than the left-hand one, just like in the target figure, and yet unwittingly they would have made a physically accurate drawing such that the two parallelograms are identical!

But when drawing the parallelograms that form the surfaces of tables, we might expect to find not only that participants are susceptible to the illusion but also that they draw the right-hand table such that it is physically squarer than the left-hand table. This is because there is a contrast between the shape that is apparently being projected and the 'real' shape that the participant infers the table to have: the real shape is much squarer

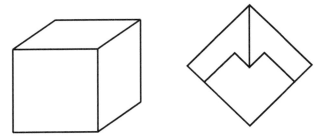

Figure 16.2 Object and non-object used by Phillips *et al.* (1978).

than the projected shape. The resultant knowledge of real shape then seems to contaminate the participants' estimation of the appearance of the table-top, leading them to draw a table that is squarer than it ought to be considering the vantage point. As predicted, we found that participants made systematic errors in their drawings of the table stimuli, but not the parallelograms, which were copied accurately. Also, there was a strong correlation between measures of susceptibility to the table illusion and systematic error in drawing, while there was no such correlation for the parallelogram illusion. In other words, susceptibility to the illusion statistically 'explained' systematic drawing errors of the table figures.

Whilst adults make systematic knowledge-based errors when copying, the inaccuracies that children produce are even more dramatic. Phillips, Hobbs and Pratt (1978) asked typically developing children aged 7 and 9 years to copy a line drawing of a cube in oblique perspective (i.e. depicting depth with parallel oblique lines) and an abstract non-object design of roughly the same complexity (Figure 16.2). The children were much poorer at copying the cube than the non-object design, and although their copies included many features of the model, they also revealed a number of characteristic errors, including extra faces, making all angles into right angles, and extending all lines to a common baseline.

These errors appear to reflect children's knowledge of the properties of cubes; however, it is possible that the errors were the result of figural biases, such as the perpendicular bias (a tendency to make obtuse and acute angles into right angles; Bremner, 1984). This suggestion was refuted by another copying experiment carried out by Lee (1989). She asked children to copy line drawings of simple shapes, based on parallelograms and trapeziums. In one experiment, participants were told that the stimuli represented parts of tables; in another the same stimuli were used but participants were not told what they represented. Children who interpreted the stimuli as parts of tables made more drawing errors than those given no interpretation for the stimuli, implying that interpreting items to be drawn influences drawing accuracy adversely.

Whilst the results of Phillips *et al.* and Lee imply that conceptual knowledge has a detrimental effect on drawing accuracy, Phillips *et al.* point out that it is not entirely clear which aspects of object knowledge are responsible for children's difficulties drawing the cube. They make the distinction between (1) translating between a three-dimensional internal model and the required two-dimensional output, and (2) activation of data-structures associated with object properties (behaviour, function, etc.). Phillips *et al.* (1978) appear to be saying that children may struggle either because (1) the apparent projected shape contrasts with 'real' shape – as in the example of the table version of the Shepard illusion – or (2) knowledge of the features of this kind of object intrudes upon the process of depiction – as when a child includes the handle of a cup even though it is not visible from the child's vantage point.

In that case, will children find it difficult to copy a line drawing of an object without a three-dimensional interpretation, where they will nevertheless have associated featural knowledge but no 3D or depth information? Conversely, will children find it difficult to draw an item that allows a 3D interpretation, even if it is unfamiliar such that the child has no featural knowledge?

With these questions in mind, we designed an experiment that attempted to examine the effects of three-dimensionality and object familiarity relatively independently (Sheppard, Ropar and Mitchell, 2005). Children aged 7 and 9 years were asked to copy meaningful and non-meaningful two-dimensional and three-dimensional line drawings (Figure 16.3) constructed from the same lines, to control for motor demands. Analyses showed a strong effect of dimensionality, where children in both ages produced much poorer drawings of three-dimensional than two-dimensional objects. However, somewhat surprisingly, 7-year-olds produced copies of the meaningful items superior to those of the non-meaningful ones. By 9 years, meaningfulness was still beneficial but not significantly so. These results imply that different conceptual aspects of objects exert different effects on drawing performance. In this case, perceiving the drawing as three-dimensional makes drawing more difficult, but meaningfulness may actually assist young children to draw more accurately. This may be because their object knowledge aids planning, to isolate important structural units, and to include details based on expectation of their presence (e.g. the window on the truck).

Our study suggested that some forms of object knowledge (three-dimensionality) are harmful to copying performance, whilst others (meaningfulness) can actually improve copying accuracy. The fact that

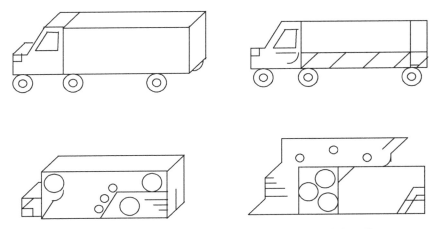

Figure 16.3 Example stimuli used by Sheppard *et al.* (2005).

stimulus factors like meaningfulness and three-dimensionality influence performance in copying indicates that adults and children alike are compelled to make a conceptual interpretation of the material presented. Thus, although a purely structure-directed strategy is possible for copying, it seems that in practice people cannot help but interpret line drawings conceptually, and are therefore lured into errors as when faced with the real object as a point of reference.

The influence of conceptual knowledge on copying in individuals with autism

We were interested to see how individuals with autism perform on the same task for several reasons. Firstly, if a child is asked to copy a line drawing, there should be little ambiguity over what is required. Another advantage in using a copying task is that it allows comparison between copies of pictures where conceptual knowledge might be involved (i.e. drawings of objects) and copies of pictures where there is no conceptual interpretation (i.e. an abstract design). If copies are poorer when the subject matter is the drawing of an object than when it is the drawing of an abstract design, the difficulty can be attributed to the conceptual difference between the two. In other words, it is possible to carry out much more tightly controlled experiments with copying tasks than with drawing tasks. Also, having discovered that meaningfulness of the subject matter seems to improve copying accuracy in typically developing children, we thought it might be worthwhile to investigate whether

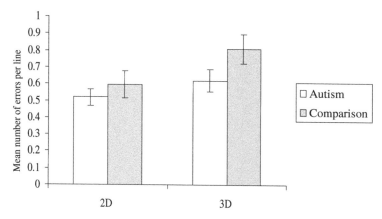

Figure 16.4 Mean number of errors per line on two-dimensional and three-dimensional line drawings.

people with autism could also benefit from the pictures being meaningful. We reasoned that if people with autism are less influenced by conceptual knowledge when copying, then the effects of meaningfulness and dimensionality that we observed for children of typical development would be attenuated or even absent altogether. We presented the stimuli from our previous study to a group of children and adolescents with autism, who had a mental age of around 8 years, and a comparison group with developmental delay and the same mental age (Sheppard, Ropar and Mitchell, 2007). We were surprised to discover that the participants with autism were influenced by meaningfulness to the same extent as the comparison participants of similar mental age. In other words, participants in both groups were more accurate on pictures that depicted meaningful objects than on those that were non-meaningful. However, the group with autism was less affected by dimensionality (Figure 16.4). Whilst participants without autism were much poorer at copying the three-dimensional than the two-dimensional stimuli, the difference was smaller for the group with autism (see Figure 16.5 for copies of meaningful and non-meaningful three-dimensional stimuli).

The results of this study suggest that whilst individuals with autism appear to use their conceptual knowledge to assist copying (deriving benefit from the meaningful items), they are better able to overcome or ignore conceptual information when it is detrimental to copying accuracy (were less influenced by dimensionality). A smaller effect of dimensionality when copying was also implicated in an earlier study carried out by Mottron, Belleville and Menard (1999). Adolescent and adult participants

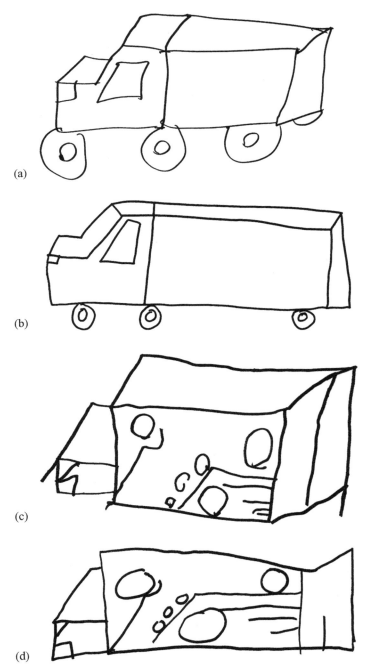

Figure 16.5 Copies of line drawings with three-dimensional interpretation by participants with autism (a, c) and participants without autism (b, d).

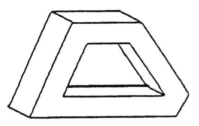 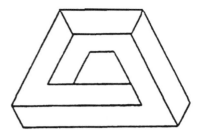

Figure 16.6 Possible and impossible figures used by Mottron *et al.* (1999).

with autism or Asperger's syndrome were asked to copy impossible geometric figures, such as the one depicted in Figure 16.6, along with closely matched possible versions of the same figures. Participants in both groups reproduced the figures with a high degree of accuracy, and both groups were faster at copying the possible figures than the impossible figures. However, although there was no difference between groups in the time taken to copy the possible versions of the figures, the participants with autism were faster at copying the impossible figures. As both types of figure were of similar complexity, it seems likely that difficulty arises when copying impossible figures precisely because they are perceived as being impossible. If one were able to focus simply on the lines without making a paradoxical three-dimensional interpretation, it should not be any more difficult to copy the impossible figures than the possible versions. Therefore, although Mottron *et al.* gave a slightly different explanation for their findings, they could be interpreted as reflecting a reduced dimensionality effect too.

Copying versus drawing

Studies in which participants were asked to draw real three-dimensional objects found no differences between the performance of individuals with and without autism. Studies where participants copied line drawings depicting three-dimensional objects reported a smaller effect of dimensionality for those with autism. Could it be that individuals with autism are less influenced by conceptual knowledge, even if this is only apparent when copying from line drawings? Light was shed on this suggestion in a study we carried out that investigated shape constancy mechanisms in autism. The experimental design was based on classic research carried out by Thouless (1931). Thouless placed a circular disc on a table, and then asked participants to view it from one end of the table and report how it looked from their particular vantage point. Participants were asked either to draw the disc or to select a matching ellipse from a number of alternatives. Rather than choosing an ellipse that matched the shape projected to their retinas, participants tended to select a shape that was a compromise between the projected shape and the 'true' shape of the disc, a circle. Similarly, their drawings of the ellipse were more circular than the projected shape.

We (Ropar and Mitchell, 2002) went on to carry out a similar experiment with a group of participants with autism. Participants with and without autism viewed a stimulus they knew was a slanted circle located inside a chamber that was either illuminated so perspective cues were present, or darkened, in which case only the stimulus itself was visible, without perspective cues. In a third condition the participant knew the shape really was an ellipse positioned upright within the darkened chamber. In this instance there was no discrepancy between the projected shape and the actual shape of the stimulus. Thus we were able to compare the relative contributions of conceptual knowledge and perspective cues to inaccuracy in depiction. Participants with autism and comparison participants of the same mental age exaggerated circularity to the same extent in the condition where the box was open and ambient perspective cues were present. However, the participants with autism were unique in exaggerating circularity to a far lesser degree in the condition where the box lid was closed, where only their prior knowledge of the true shape could influence performance.

Comparing copying and drawing in autism

Given the evidence, it seemed likely that differences in the three-dimensional drawing of individuals with and without autism are confined to copies of line drawings. However, it remained possible that individuals with autism can depict three dimensions in a superior manner, including when drawing from a real-world model, even if other studies had failed to uncover differences for methodological reasons. Charman and Baron-Cohen's (1993) and Eames and Cox's (1994) studies involved dichotomous ratings of drawing accuracy, which may have been unable to capture subtle differences between the artwork of participants. Also, they did not include a control condition (of drawings without a three-dimensional interpretation) to act as a measure of general drawing ability. This would necessarily have involved copying from a two-dimensional line drawing, as all real-world models are necessarily three-dimensional. Therefore, although their groups were matched on mental age, they may not have been matched on baseline drawing ability, and any adeptness

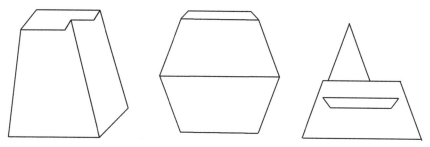

Figure 16.7 Line drawings with three-dimensional interpretation (left, middle) and with two-dimensional interpretation (right) used in a copying task by Sheppard *et al.*

at three-dimensional drawing could have been masked in the group with autism by generally poorer drawing skills.

We carried out a study (Sheppard, Ropar and Mitchell, in prep.) directly to compare copying and drawing accuracy in participants with and without autism. Participants were asked to copy two unfamiliar line drawings that had three-dimensional interpretations, and an unfamiliar line drawing that had a two-dimensional interpretation only (to act as a control measure), and also to draw a picture of a real and unfamiliar three-dimensional object. Figure 16.7 illustrates the three line drawings, the first two having a three-dimensional interpretation, while the third only allowed a two-dimensional interpretation. If participants with autism were encouraged to make three-dimensional interpretations of line drawings, would that be sufficient to eradicate any advantage for them? This would depend on the difference between groups being the result of those with autism not having perceived the line drawings as three-dimensional at all, rather than the result of being more able to set aside a three-dimensional interpretation when drawing.

Moore (1987) carried out an experiment with typically developing children that included such a manipulation. In her study, typically developing 7- and 9-year-olds were asked to copy line drawings that had three-dimensional interpretations. The children were then shown the real objects represented by each drawing (made from polystyrene), and the relationship between the picture and the object was explained. Moore found that, when asked to copy the pictures for a second time, children who had been exposed to the three-dimensional objects represented by the drawings produced poorer copies. Children in a control condition, who were asked to copy the drawings for a second time, without having seen the objects that they represented, produced drawings of the same standard as their first attempt. Moore (1987) argued that exposure to three-dimensional models made the three-dimensional properties in the line drawings more salient, and hence resulted in a decrement in performance. Here, exposure to the real three-dimensional object will be referred to as 'priming', as the aim is to prime participants to make a three-dimensional interpretation. Participants who were not shown the real three-dimensional object will be referred to as 'unprimed'.

In a partial replication of Moore's (1987) methodology, participants were asked to draw the unfamiliar three-dimensional line drawings twice, before and after exposure to the associated three-dimensional models. A crucial control test ensured participants could see and recall the relationship between the line drawings and the three-dimensional objects they represented. We reasoned that if participants with autism do not spontaneously interpret such drawings as representing three-dimensional objects, then when they were explicitly aprised through exposure to the real object, their performance might become equal to the control participants (or the difference would decrease, at least). Alternatively, if the participants with autism did perceive the drawings as three-dimensional but were more able to set aside this interpretation when drawing, then highlighting the three-dimensionality should have no effect for them, and the difference between the groups would increase after priming.

Figure 16.8 shows that for the line drawing with a two-dimensional interpretation, there was no difference between groups. But for line drawings that allowed a three-dimensional interpretation, participants with autism made fewer errors per line than comparison participants, and this difference between groups was apparent even after being primed to make a three-dimensional interpretation. For the drawings of the real three-dimensional object (not illustrated because a different measure was used), there was no difference between groups. As predicted, there was a difference between groups specifically when copying line drawings of three-dimensional objects. This finding assumes greater importance when considering that participants with autism were no better than comparison participants at drawing a real three-dimensional object.

The results suggest that any advantage in three-dimensional drawing in autism occurs exclusively when copying from a line drawing. The fact that the difference between groups was present even after participants had been encouraged to make a three-dimensional interpretation of the material implies that people with autism, unlike comparison participants, do not use this information when drawing. It seems rather ironic that individuals without autism are prone to error because they are unable to set aside information that leads to bias, while participants with autism fare much better in this respect.

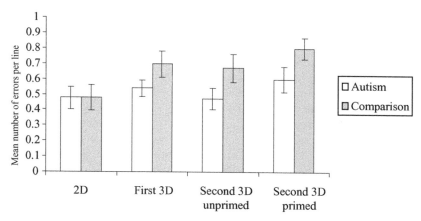

Figure 16.8 Mean number of errors per line produced when copying line drawings with two-dimensional interpretation, and with three-dimensional interpretation before and after priming.

Graphical and mental representations

The finding that typically developing children make the same kinds of errors whether drawing from a real three-dimensional object or copying from a line drawing of a three-dimensional object has been taken as evidence that a three-dimensional internal description is activated in both cases (Phillips *et al.*, 1978). This is thought to make it difficult to draw the object because a procedure for reproducing two-dimensionally must be generated from a description that is three-dimensional. The studies reported in this chapter on the unique performance of individuals with autism suggest crucial differences between what is involved in copying and drawing tasks.

More specifically, perhaps different kinds of representation are involved when drawing a real object and copying a line drawing. It has in fact previously been suggested that the type of representation produced when a line drawing is perceived is not the same as when a real object is perceived. Leslie (1987) makes a distinction between two kinds of representation: primary and secondary representations. When perceiving a real object in the environment, a primary representation is formed, which represents the true or real state of affairs in the world. In other words, as a real object does not represent something else, you see what is really there. However, a picture such as a line drawing does not necessarily represent the true state of affairs in the world. An object present in a picture is not present in the environment in the same sense as a real object. Therefore when perceiving a picture, the ensuing representation is marked as a secondary representation so that it cannot become confused with the true state of reality. In other words, when we look at a line drawing we produce a primary representation of the picture as a physical entity, and also a secondary, or meta-representation, which reflects our interpretation of the contents of that picture (a representation of a representation).

Following this line of reasoning, to copy a line drawing accurately, one needs to focus on one's primary representation of the drawing as it is (as lines on a piece of paper, without any three-dimensional properties) without interference from one's secondary representation of it (i.e. what it depicts, which has three-dimensional properties). It would seem that typically developing individuals cannot help but be influenced by their secondary representation of such line drawings. In contrast, in the case of drawing a real object, one can only draw from the primary representation of the object, which describes its three-dimensional properties. In terms of this framework, it is possible (but unlikely) that people with autism do not produce secondary representations at all when looking at line drawings. Alternatively, perhaps people with autism have a bias in (or increased ability to) focus on their primary representations rather than secondary representations, which would lead to more accurate copying. Such a bias would not improve drawings of a real three-dimensional object, as in this case the primary representation is three-dimensional. Instead one must find some way of translating the object's 'true' identity into a representation of it, albeit a representation that preserves some qualities of an advantage-point-specific view.

This suggestion of reduced focus on secondary representations in autism is supported by other pieces of research. It has been shown that primary representational abilities like object concepts appear to develop in line with mental age in autism (Baron-Cohen, Leslie and Frith, 1986). However, severe impairments in pretend play are a characteristic feature of autism (Baron-Cohen, 1987), and Leslie (1987) argues that secondary representations are crucial for pretend play, as they allow the individual to engage in pretence without interference from their knowledge of the true state of reality. It has also been shown that those with autism perform poorly on tests of the appearance–reality distinction (Baron-Cohen, 1989). On this test, participants are shown an object that looks like a rock but is in fact made out of sponge. When asked initially what the object is, participants usually state that it is a rock. They are then shown that the object is really a sponge and asked two questions: what does the object look like, and what is it really? Participants with autism in Baron-Cohen's study tended to continue to state that the object both looked like and really was a rock. Again, this might imply a tendency to focus on the primary representation (its appearance) in autism, rather than the interpretation (what is represented, its true identity). In addition, individuals with autism tend to respond according to the literal meaning of a verbal statement, rather than by considering the thoughts or ideas that are represented (Mitchell and Isaacs, 1994).

Therefore, perhaps the performance of those with autism on copying tasks can be conceptualized as reflecting a tendency to focus on primary representations, literal aspects of the environment, rather than to meta-represent. Such a tendency could even be problematic when drawing a real object, as an increased focus on the object's identity might make it harder to draw. To create a line drawing of an object, one must make a representation of a representation (i.e. meta-represent), which may explain the lack of superiority in the drawings of those with autism.

Summary

Research suggests that, for typically developing individuals, conceptual knowledge of an object and its properties influences its depiction, both when drawing and when copying, implying that the same internal representations are activated in both cases. Most often, this leads to visual inaccuracies, although some types of object knowledge appear to be beneficial to drawing. When copying line drawings, people with autism are less influenced by types of knowledge that are detrimental to task performance, whilst still using other aspects of object knowledge to assist with their reproductions. In contrast, people with autism do not produce more accurate drawings when a real three-dimensional object is the model. This implies that there may in fact be differences between the internal representations involved in drawing and copying tasks, which we have conceptualized here as reflecting the difference between primary and secondary representations.

REFERENCES

Baron-Cohen, S. (1987). Autism and symbolic play. *British Journal of Developmental Psychology*, 5, 139–48.
  (1989). Are autistic children behaviorists? An examination of their mental–physical and appearance–reality distinctions. *Journal of Autism and Developmental Disorders*, 19, 579–600.
Baron-Cohen, S., Leslie, A. M. and Frith, U. (1986). Mechanical, behavioral and intentional understanding of picture stories in autistic children. *British Journal of Developmental Psychology*, 4, 113–25.
Bremner, J. G. (1984). Errors towards the perpendicular in children's copies of angular figures: a test of the bisection interpretation. *Perception*, 13, 117–28.

Charman, T. and Baron-Cohen, S. (1993). Drawing development in autism: the intellectual to visual realism shift. *British Journal of Developmental Psychology*, 11, 171–85.

Chen, M. J. (1985). Young children's representational drawings of solid objects: a comparison of drawing and copying. In N. H. Freeman and M. V. Cox (eds.), *Visual order: the nature and development of pictorial representation* (pp. 157–75). Cambridge: Cambridge University Press.

Cohen, D. J. and Bennett, S. (1997). Why can't most people draw what they see? *Journal of Experimental Psychology: Human Perception and Performance*, 23, 609–21.

Eames, K. and Cox, M. V. (1994). Visual realism in the drawings of autistic, Down's syndrome and normal children. *British Journal of Developmental Psychology*, 12, 235–9.

Freeman, N. and Janikoun, R. (1972). Intellectual realism in children's drawings of a familiar object with distinctive features. *Child Development*, 43, 1116–21.

Frith, U. (2003). *Autism: explaining the enigma*. Second edition. Oxford: Blackwell.

Gombrich, E. H. (1984). *Art and illusion*. (Bollingen Series 35.) Princeton, NJ: Princeton University Press.

Hill, A. L. (1977). Idiot savants: rate of incidence. *Perceptual and Motor Skills*, 44, 161–2.

Kubovy, M. (1986). *The psychology of perspective and Renaissance art*. Cambridge: Cambridge University Press.

Lee, M. (1989). When is an object not an object? The effect of 'meaning' upon the copying of line drawings. *British Journal of Psychology*, 80, 15–37.

Leslie, A. M. (1987). Pretense and representation: the origins of 'Theory of Mind'. *Psychological Review*, 94, 412–26.

Luquet, G. H. (2001). *Children's drawings*. Trans. Alan Costall. London: Free Association Books.

Mitchell, P. and Isaacs, J. E. (1994). Understanding of verbal representation in children with autism: the case of referential opacity. *British Journal of Developmental Psychology*, 12, 439–54.

Mitchell, P., Ropar, D., Ackroyd, K. and Rajendran, G. (2005). How perception impacts on drawings. *Journal of Experimental Psychology: Human Perception and Performance*, 31, 996–1003.

Moore, V. (1987). The influence of experience on children's drawings of a familiar and unfamiliar object. *British Journal of Developmental Psychology*, 5, 221–9.

Mottron, L., Belleville, S. and Ménard, E. (1999). Local bias in autistic subjects as evidenced by graphic tasks: perceptual hierarchization or working memory deficit? *Journal of Child Psychology and Psychiatry*, 40, 743–55.

Phillips, W. A., Hobbs, S. B. and Pratt, F. R. (1978). Intellectual realism in children's drawings of cubes. *Cognition*, 6, 15–33.

Rimland, B. (1978). Savant capabilities of autistic children and their cognitive implications. In G. Serban (ed.), *Cognitive defects in the development of mental illness* (pp. 43–65). Oxford: Brunner/Mazel.

Ropar, D. and Mitchell, P. (2002). Shape constancy in autism: the role of prior knowledge and perspective cues. *Journal of Child Psychology and Psychiatry*, 43, 647–53.

Sheppard, E., Ropar, D. and Mitchell, P. (2005). The impact of meaning and dimensionality on the accuracy of children's copying. *British Journal of Developmental Psychology*, 23, 365–81.
  (2007). The impact of meaning and dimensionality on copying accuracy in individuals with autism. *Journal of Autism and Developmental Disorders* 37: 1913–24.
  (in prep.). Autism and dimensionality: differences between drawing and copying tasks.
Snyder, A. W. and Thomas, M. (1997). Autistic artists give clues to cognition. *Perception*, 26, 93–6.
Thouless, R. H. (1931). Phenomenal regression to the real object. II. *British Journal of Psychology*, 22, 1–30.

Index

accretion principle 142
action imitation 226
Adams, S. 46, 63
Adi-Japha, E. *et al.* 109–10
aging *see* Alzheimer's disease; graphic design expertise; semantic dementia
Akshoomoff, N. A. 144
Alzheimer's disease (AD) 282, 285
ambiguous figures 99, 132
Amsterdam, B. 23–4
anchoring 132, 134
apes 27, 28, 29, 33, 35
appearance–reality tasks 99, 101–2, 108–9, 340
Arber, A. 256
Arnheim, R. 67
Asendorpf, J. B. 26
Asonometric technique 229
attentional capacity *see* working memory
attentional focus 108–10
autism 16, 340–1; *see also* conceptual knowledge, influence of
autobiographical memory 6

Baltes, P. B. 265
Barlow, C. M. *et al.* 151
Baron-Cohen, S. *et al.* 327, 336, 340
Barrett, M. D. 223
Bartel, K. 246, 247*f*, 251
Barton, D. E. 69
Baschek, I.-L. *et al.* 265
Batten, A. 230
Baudonniere, P. M. 26
Beilin, H. 92, 97, 98
Bennett, S. 329
Biederman, I. 13
Binet, A. 251
biomechanical constraints 9, 124–30
  and cognitive constraints 133–5
  grip configurations 126–8
  stroke direction 128–30

variability 125, 126–8
see also motor aspects of drawing
blind adults 15–16, 305–22
  drawing experience 307
  drawings by Tracy T 305, 309–22, 310*f*, 311*f*, 312*f*, 313*f*, 314*f*, 315*f*, 317*f*, 318*f*
  Esref 308
  projection systems 15–16, 305–7
  Tracy 308
blind children 306, 308, 320
Bloom, P. 111, 112
Blöte, A. W. *et al.* 126
Bovet, D. 89
Bozeat, S. *et al.* 285, 286*f*, 293
Braswell, G. S. *et al.* 124, 125, 127, 134
Bremner, J. G. *et al.* 179–80, 225, 230
Brooks, V. 88, 89
Burns, N. M. 90

canonicity 223, 255
Case, R. *et al.* 178, 179, 180, 183, 189
Chaloupka, G. 250*f*
Charman T. 327, 336
Chen, M. J. 225, 229, 328
chimpanzees 26–7, 29, 30–2, 33–4, 35
cognition 1, 28, 261–2, 276; *see also* graphic design expertise
cognitive constraints 9, 130–1
  and biomechanical constraints 133–5
  representational redescription 130
  start position 131
  stroke direction 131
  variability 130
Cohen, D. J. 329
combines 64, 64*f*
communication 33–4
comparative research 29–30
conceptual knowledge, influence of 16, 325–41
  copying: adults 328–30, 329*f*
  copying: children 330–1, 330*f*, 332*f*

344

copying: individuals with autism 332–5, 333*f*, 334*f*, 335*f*
copying *vs.* drawing 335–7
copying *vs.* drawing in autism 336–8, 337*f*, 339*f*
drawing: adults and children 326
drawing: individuals with autism 326–8
graphical and mental representations 339–41
savant skills 326–7
see also semantic dementia
conservatism 2, 67, 68, 71*f*, 208
contingency 30–1, 33, 35
contour 13
 boundary contours 241, 241*f*
 camouflage 240–1, 240*f*
 contours drawn 244–54, 245*f*, 247*f*, 249*f*, 250*f*, 252*f*, 253*f*, 254*f*
 contours seen 239–44
 discrimination learning tasks 242–4, 242*f*, 244*f*
 eyes and eyespots 253–4, 254*f*, 255*f*
 texture gradients 239
 typical contours 241, 245–56, 245*f*, 246*f*, 248*f*, 249*f*, 250*f*
Cook, M. 225, 229
copying *see under* conceptual knowledge, influence of; semantic dementia
core-to-periphery progression principle 143
Courage, M. L. *et al.* 25
Cox, M. V. 43, 166, 167, 327, 336
cultural constraints 9, 124, 132–3

David, F. N. 69
Davis, A. M. 117
DeLoache, J. *et al.* 202
DeLoache, J. S. *et al.* 88, 89–90, 91–2, 96
Dennis, S. 177–8, 183
denotation systems 2, 221, 222
depiction strategy 64, 64*f*, 75*f*, 321–2
Deręgowski, J. B. *et al.* 198, 242–3, 246, 250–1, 256
development of drawing behaviour
 in blind people 305–7, 321–2
 conservatism 68, 71*f*
 forward-looking orientation 104
 intellectual to visual realism 51, 67, 223, 326
 research 1, 29, 42–3
 skills sequence 321–2
 variability 125
 see also graphic syntax
developmental research 1, 29–30, 42–3

Diamond, A. 105
Draw-A-Person Test 1, 3, 13
drawing implements 128
drawing ownership
 conceptual *vs.* physical aspects 54–5, 61
 and drawing quality 51, 54*f*, 57–8, 58*f*
 and level of self-involvement 4–5, 51–5, 55*f*, 56*f*, 57*f*
 recognition of others' drawings 4–5, 44–5, 51, 53
 recognition of own drawings 4–6, 44–5, 51, 53, 55*f*
 and self-awareness 46, 51–61
drawing production
 cognition of drawing topic 43, 45
 developmental accounts 43, 51, 67
 drawing skill 53, 54*f*, 57–8, 59*f*
 likeness 57–8, 59*f*
 and recognition of drawings 4–5, 51–5, 52*f*, 55*f*, 56*f*, 57*f*, 60
 see also biomechanical constraints; cognitive constraints; cultural constraints; human figure drawing; intention, action and interpretation; self-drawings; style; task constraints
drawing skill 53, 54*f*, 57–8, 59*f*
drawing syntax *see* graphic syntax
drawing systems *see* projection systems
Driver, J. *et al.* 199
dual nature of pictures: children's understanding 6–7, 86–100
 flexibility of thought 98–100
 independence of pictures from referents 91–4
 recognizing real exemplars from pictures 89–91
 recognizing referents from pictures 88–9, 107–8
 symbols 86–7
 understanding pictures as symbols and objects 94–8
 understanding the dual nature 87–8
Dukette, D. 144
Duval, T. S. 47–8, 49
dynamic tripod grasp 126
Dziurawiec, S. 198, 250–1

Eames, K. 327, 336
Ebeling, K. S. 110–11
Edelman, G. M. 199
Edelstein, W. *et al.* 203
Ekstrom, R. B. *et al.* 263, 266, 275, 276
Elkins, J. 126
empathy 34–5
Eng, H. 43

environmental constraints 124, 128
episodic memory 5, 262–4, 265, 276
Epstein, R. et al. 27, 32
executive function 7–8, 105, 108, 110
existence principle 92
expert knowledge *see* graphic design expertise

F-operators (field factors) 163, 173, 187
facture 64, 65, 75f, 76f, 80
failed symbolism 223
false perspective 179, 185
false picture tasks 92–7, 99–100, 101–1
Feldman, D. H. 218
figurative schemes 162, 217
figures and spatial fields 11–12, 195–212
  construction in actions 196–7
  figure and half-a-figure 198–9, 200f
  figure in spatial context 200–2
  habitual size and projective size 207–9
  object-driven/axes-driven size modification 203–7, 203f, 206f
  objects and displays 197–8
  spatial axes systems in other species 209–12
Flat technique 229
Flavell, J. et al. 84
Flavell, J. H. et al. 108
flexibility
  procedural and representational 2, 144, 148–53, 174–7, 224–5, 234
  of thought 98–100
fortuitous realism 64
Franklin, S. et al. 284
Freeman, N. H. et al. 1, 43, 45, 106, 111f, 112, 114–16, 118, 163, 165, 168, 326, 327
Frith, U. 16
Frontal technique 229, 230
functionalist view 2, 10

Gallo, F. et al. 185–7, 190–4
Gallup, G. G., Jr 4, 26–7, 31
Gardner, H. 110
Gellert, E. 4, 48
Gelman, S. A. 110–11
generic symbolism 223
geometric shapes 219–21
geometric solids 225–7
geometrical constraints 142
Gergely, G. 6

Gibson, J. J. 239
Glenn, S. M. et al. 129
Golomb, C. 110, 183
Gombrich, E. H. 218, 326
Goodenough, F. L. 1
Goodenough-Harris drawing scale 47, 48, 53
Goodnow, J. J. 8–9, 43, 130, 133, 140–1, 175, 177, 320
graphic design expertise 14, 261–77
  acquisition of mnemonic skill 271
  Card Rotation test 267, 269, 272f, 276
  cued recall: group differences 272–5, 273f, 274t
  episodic memory 262–4, 265, 276
  expertise research 262
  findings 275
  graphic fluency 267–9, 268t, 270–1f
  memory training study 262–3, 264–77
  Method of Loci 263, 266–7
  participants 265
  study limitations 264–5
  training programme 266–7
  two-component model of cognition 262, 276
graphic routines 224–5
graphic syntax 8, 10, 139–55
  accretion principle 142, 143
  core-to-periphery progression principle 143
  definition 139
  element-based strategies 146, 147, 149
  figure-based changes 149
  geometrical constraints 142
  global and local interaction 144–8, 145f
  global level of organization 142–3
  incidental modification 153–5
  inter-representational changes 149–51
  intra-representational changes 149–50, 151
  local level of organization 140–2
  part–whole-based strategies 146–8, 150, 152
  and prehension development 152
  procedural and representational flexibility 144, 148–53
  semantic constraints 143
  Start-Rotation Principle 153–4
  subsystem elaboration principle 143
  syntactical drawing behaviour 11
  unit-based strategies 146
graphical lexicon 14–15
Greer, T. 127

Index

grip configurations 126–8
Gross, J. 5, 44, 53, 71, 73, 78

Halligan, P. W. 199, 201*f*
handwriting 5, 126–7, 132–3
Harel, J. *et al.* 26
Hargreaves, D. J. *et al.* 183
Hargreaves, S. 125
Hayes, B. K. 65
Hayne, H. 5, 44, 53, 71, 73, 78
Hayworth, K. J. 13
Heller, M. A. 315–16
Hennessy, R. 65
Hesselberg, T. 210, 211*f*
hidden line elimination 163, 168
Hildebrand, D. K. *et al.* 171–2
Hochberg, J. 88, 89
Howard, D. 283, 284
human figure drawing 51, 52*f*, 53, 106–7, 116–18

iconography 67
implicit learning 10–11
information-processing mechanisms 163
Ingram, N. 143, 225
Inhelder, B. 1, 173
inhibition 105
inhibitory control tasks 98–9
Ino, T. *et al.* 10
intellectual realism 67, 161, 219, 223, 326
intention, action and interpretation 7–8, 104–18
  effort effect 109–10
  human figure drawing 106–7, 116–18
  from intention to interpretation 106, 107*f*, 110–13, 111*f*
  pictorial interpretation 107–10
  pre-representational intention and graphic action 113–16
  'reading off' 110
  'romancing' 110
intentional communication 34
intersubjectivity 33–4

Janikoun, R. 116, 118, 126, 326, 327
Jefferies, E. *et al.* 287
Johnson, B. 44
Jolley, R. P. 96, 98

Kagan, J. 44, 46, 63
Kao, H. S. R. 133
Karmiloff-Smith, A. 15, 30, 130, 148–9, 150–1, 296
Keller, H. *et al.* 33

Kellogg, R. 43, 64, 67
Kennedy, J. M. 229, 231, 315–16, 321
Kerschensteiner, D. G. 43, 67
kinaesthetic/proprioceptive memory 5
Kliegl, R. *et al.* 264, 271
Kuhn, D. 105

Lambon Ralph, M. A. 284
Lange-Küttner, C. *et al.* 16, 144, 180–1, 202, 203–5, 203*f*, 206*f*, 222
laterality 9
learning processes 10–11, 163, 218
Leavens, D. A. *et al.* 29, 34
Lederman, S. J. *et al.* 306
Lee, M. 179–80, 230, 331
Leroi-Gourhan, A. 247
Leslie, A. M. 105, 339–40
letter recognition in preschool children 5
Levine, R. A. 8–9, 130, 133, 140–1
Lewin, K. 195
Lewis, M. *et al.* 25
Light, P. H. 223
Lin, A. C. *et al.* 30–2
Lindenberger, U. *et al.* 262–3, 264–77
Lockman, J. J. 127
Longcamp, M. *et al.* 5
Lopes, D. 106
Lukens, H. T. 106
Luquet, G. H. 43, 64, 67, 106, 161, 165, 223, 326

M capacity 164, 167, 168–72, 171*t*, 174, 176–7, 179, 181–5, 187–9
M-operator 164
McGeorge, P. 243, 256
Marini, F. 161, 190–5
mark-and-mirror test 23
Markson, L. 111, 112
Marot, V. 141, 147, 148
Marr, D. 221
Marshall, J. C. 199, 201*f*
Marteniuk, R. G. *et al.* 143
Martlew, M. 126–7
Matsuzawa, T. 30
Matthews, J. 114
Mayer-Hillebrand, F. 198
meaning 2, 12
memory
  auditory-verbal short-term 287
  autobiographical 6
  episodic 5, 262–4, 265, 276
  kinaesthetic/proprioceptive 5
  for others' drawings 44–5
  for own drawings 44–5, 65

memory (*cont.*)
  perceptual 5
  working memory 2, 160, 161, 164, 179, 185–7
  see also graphic design expertise
Mental Rotation Test 13
metasubjective operators 163–4
Method of Loci 14, 263, 266–7
Meulenbroek, R. G. J. *et al.* 133
mirror images 3
mirror self-recognition (MSR) 3–4, 23–36
  chimpanzees 26–7, 29–30, 30–2, 33–4, 35
  comparative context 27
  comparative developmental study 30–2
  contingency 30–1, 33, 35
  development of self-awareness 24–5
  developmental comparative approach 29–30
  evolution of self-awareness 27–8, 32–3, 34
  human infants 23–6, 30–1, 31–2
  intersubjectivity 33–4
  mark-and-mirror test 23
  and praise/neutral feedback 48–9, 50*f*
  recent studies 25–6
  self-awareness 34–5
  social cognition 34–5
Mitchell, P. *et al.* 328, 336
Mixed techniques 230
monkeys 27–8, 29, 33, 35
Moore, V. 337
Morassi, L. 226, 227, 228, 229
Morra, S. *et al.* 166, 167, 170, 173–4, 176–7, 185
motor aspects of drawing 2, 5, 8–9, 53, 57, 124; *see also* biomechanical constraints
Mottron, L. *et al.* 333, 335, 335*f*
Mounoud, P. 148, 152
MSR *see* mirror self-recognition

naive perspective 179, 185, 230
Navon, D. 144
neurodegenerative disease *see* Alzheimer's disease; semantic dementia
neuropsychological aspects of drawing *see* biomechanical constraints; cognitive constraints; figures and spatial fields; graphic design expertise; semantic dementia
Nicholls, A. L. 229, 231

Nolan, E. 44, 46, 63
non-geometric figures 221–5

object drawings: 3–5-year-olds' style 45, 65–7, 65–72, 66*f*, 71*f*, 80; *see also* recognition of own drawings: object drawings
operative schemes 163, 217

Panofsky, E. 198
Papousek, H. 33
Papousek, M. 33
Parisi, M. 161, 190–5
Parker, S. T. 34
partial occlusion drawing 161, 165–73, 165*f*, 188
part–whole relationships 10, 146–8, 150, 152, 222
Pascual-Leone, J. 163–4, 173–4, 189
Patterson, K. 283
Pearlman, E. G. 92, 97, 98
Pease, M. 105
perceptual memory 5
perceptual organization 163, 218
perceptual reality 43
Perruchet, P. 153, 154
perspective 179, 185, 198, 230, 307, 321
Pew, R. W. 10
Phillips, W. A. *et al.* 219, 330–1, 330*f*
Piaget, J. 1, 3, 12, 16, 25, 106, 173, 198, 217–18
Picard, D. 141, 143, 149, 151–2
Pick's disease *see* semantic dementia (SD)
pictorial interpretation 107–10
Polizzi, P. 105
Povinelli, D. J. 6
praxic processes 226–7
prehension development 152
processing capacity *see* working memory
projection systems
  in blind people 15–16, 305–7
  in children's drawings 160, 179–80, 185, 221, 222, 229, 231
Prospective technique 230
prototypes 223
psychiatric patients 202
Pylyshyn, Z. 197

Quality of Three-Dimensional Representation Scale (Q3DS) 12–13, 228, 229–33

Index

Rakover, S. S. 233, 235–2
'reading off' 110
realism
  fortuitous realism 64
  intellectual realism 67, 161, 219, 223, 326
  visual realism 67, 223, 326
  see also appearance–reality tasks
recognition of others' drawings 5, 44–5
  and level of self-involvement 51–5, 56f, 57f
recognition of own drawings 4–6, 44–5, 55f, 60–1
  content 45, 64, 67
  depiction strategy 64, 64f, 75f
  and drawing quality 51, 54f, 57–8, 58f, 59f
  facture 64, 65, 75f, 76f, 80
  memory 44–5, 65
  object drawings 71–84
    after one-month delay 72–3, 74f, 75f, 76f
    matching and recognition 73–8, 77f, 78f, 79f
    and picture recognition memory 78–84, 81f, 82f, 83f
  and self-awareness 50f, 51, 53
  self-drawings 59–60, 59f
  style 45, 65–72, 66f, 71f, 80
Reith, E. 224
representational development 10
representational redescription 130, 149
Rey, A. 285
Rice, C. et al. 108, 117
Robinson, E. J. et al. 93–4
Rodet, L. 147
Rogers, T. T. et al. 293, 294f
'romancing' 110
Ropar, D. 336
Rose, D. H. 2
Rosengren, K. S. et al. 124, 125, 127, 134
Ross, B. M. 44, 63
Rothi, L. J. et al. 226–7
Rumiati, R. I. 227
Russell, C. L. et al. 34
Russo Pizzo, L. 161, 172

savant skills 16, 326–7
schema 326
Schier, F. 108
Schyns, P. G. 147
scribbling 113–14

SD see semantic dementia
Searle, J. R. 108
self-awareness 35–6
  developmental path 24–5
  and drawing ownership 46, 51–61
  evolution 27–9, 32–3, 34
  objective self-awareness (OSA) 47, 48
  and self-drawings 4, 47–50, 50f, 58, 59f
  subjective self-awareness 47
  see also mirror self-recognition
self-drawings 46
  children 3–7 years 51, 52f
  quality of drawings 47f, 48–9, 58, 59f
  and self-awareness 4, 47–50, 50f, 58–60, 59f
self-evaluation 47–8, 49–50
semantic code see symbolic (semantic) code
semantic constraints 143
semantic dementia (SD) 14–15, 281–302
  assessment tests 282–4
  auditory-verbal short-term memory 287
  delayed copy drawing 284–5, 286–93, 286f, 288–91f, 295–302, 297–301f
  deterioration of conceptual knowledge 282–4, 302
  object decision tests 294–5, 294f
  Rey figure test 285
  scoring procedures 293
  typicality of object features 293–7, 297–301f
  verbal/non-verbal comprehension 282–4
Serpell, R. 251
Servos, P. et al. 15, 293
Sheehan, K. 111f
Shepard illusion 328, 329f
Sheppard, E. et al. 220–1, 331, 332f, 337, 337f
Siegler, R. S. 125
Silk, A. M. J. 202
similarity effect 166, 172
Simon, B. B. 6
Skinner, B. F. 27, 32
Slater, A. M. et al. 91
Smedslund, J. 84
Smith, L. B. 125
Snodgrass, J. G. 78
Snyder, A. W. 327
social cognition 34–5
social referencing 34
spatial axes
  in children's drawings 180–5, 182f, 188
  in other species 209–12, 211f

spatial code 12, 217, 223, 224–8, 229*f*, 230*f*
spatial competence 178
spatial structures in children's drawings 11, 159–90
  'air gap' 159–60, 183
  dimensions of space 177–81
  drawing systems 160, 179–80, 181–5, 182*f*
  field dependence 163–4, 168, 169, 172, 174
  figurative schemes 162
  flexibility 174–7
  information-processing mechanisms 163
  M capacity 164, 167, 168–72, 171*t*, 174, 176–7, 179, 181–5, 187–9
  movement representation 174–7, 175*f*
  operative schemes 163
  partial occlusion drawing 161, 165–73, 165*f*, 188
  similarity effect 166, 172
  spatial axes 180–5, 182*f*, 188
  task demands 185–7
  theoretical background 162–5
  transparency drawing 161–2, 168–9, 170–3, 171*t*
  water level task 173–4
  working memory capacity 160, 161, 164, 179, 185–7
  see also figures and spatial fields
specific symbolism 224
Spencer, B. 250*f*
Spensley, F. 150
spiderwebs 209–12, 211*f*
Stacey, J. T. 44, 63
start position 131, 133, 141
Start-Rotation Principle (SRP) 153–4
Stiles, J. 144, 198
still life 179, 180
stroke direction 128–30, 131, 133
stroke patients
  half-a-figure drawings 199, 201*f*
  unilateral neglect 196–7, 199
style 5, 65
  3–5-year-old children 45, 65–7, 65–72, 66*f*, 71*f*, 80
  conservatism 2, 67, 68, 71*f*, 208
  iconography 67
  idiosyncrasy 65, 66*f*, 68
subsystem elaboration principle 143
Suddendorf, T. 90, 96
Sutton, P. J. 2
Swindler, M. H. 246, 249*f*

symbolic (semantic) code 12, 35–6, 86–7, 217–20, 223, 224–7, 231*t*, 232*f*, 233–4, 234*t*, 235–1
symbolism stage 223
syntax *see* graphic syntax

T-junctions 307, 308–9
Tada, W. L. 198
Tallandini, M. A. 224, 226, 227, 228, 229
TASC-based approach 124
task constraints 124, 127, 132, 141, 185–7
Taylor, J. 150
Tessari, A. 227
Teulings, H. H. M. 134
Thelen, E. 125
theory of mind 35, 108, 113
theory of self 6
Thomas, G. V. *et al.* 95, 98, 202
Thomas, M. 327
Thomassen, A. J. W. M. 134
Thouless, R. H. 335–6
threading 131, 133, 141
three-dimensional (3D) drawing 12–13, 218–19, 221–35
  geometric solids 225–7
  non-geometric figures 221–5
  Quality of Three-Dimensional Representation Scale (Q3DS) 12–13, 228, 229–33
  spatial code 225–8, 229*f*, 230*f*
  symbolic code 231*t*, 232*f*, 233–4, 234*t*
  see also geometric shapes
Torrance, E. P. 263, 266, 269, 276
transparency drawing 161–2, 168–9, 170–3, 171*t*

Valentini, P. 224
Van Sommers, P. 2, 5, 9, 46, 67, 129, 131, 132, 142–3, 144, 153, 208, 219–20, 224
Vanderwart, M. 78
Varesano, E. 224
Vauclair, J. 89
Vinter, A. 16, 141, 143, 144, 147, 148, 149, 151–2, 153, 154, 219–20, 234
visual field triage 196
visual-form agnosia 15, 292–3
visual neglect of left side 197
visual realism 67, 223, 326
visuo-manual tracking behaviour 10
Vollrath, F. 210, 211*f*

water level task 173–4
Wechsler, D. 266
White, R. 44
Wicklund, R. A. 47–8, 49
Willats, J. 2, 65, 68, 105, 179–80, 221–2, 229, 231
Wilson, B. 254
Wilson, M. 254
Wong, T. H. 133
working memory 2, 160, 161, 164, 179, 185–7
writing systems 9, 132–3

Zaitchik, D. 92–3, 94
Zhi, Z. *et al.* 151
Ziviani, J. 126

For EU product safety concerns, contact us at Calle de José Abascal, 56–1°,
28003 Madrid, Spain or eugpsr@cambridge.org.

www.ingramcontent.com/pod-product-compliance
Ingram Content Group UK Ltd.
Pitfield, Milton Keynes, MK11 3LW, UK
UKHW010858060825
461487UK00012B/1204